BIBLIOTHEK
DER KLASSISCHEN
ALTERTUMSWISSENSCHAFTEN

Herausgegeben von
JÜRGEN PAUL SCHWINDT

Neue Folge · 2. Reihe · Band 124

GLENN PATTEN

Pindar's Metaphors

A Study in Rhetoric and Meaning

Universitätsverlag
WINTER
Heidelberg

Bibliografische Information der Deutschen Nationalbibliothek
Die Deutsche Nationalbibliothek verzeichnet diese Publikation in der Deutschen Nationalbibliografie; detaillierte bibliografische Daten sind im Internet über *http://dnb.d-nb.de* abrufbar.

Gedruckt mit Hilfe der Geschwister Boehringer Ingelheim Stiftung für Geisteswissenschaften in Ingelheim am Rhein.

ISBN 978-3-8253-5590-6

Imprimé en Allemagne · Printed in Germany
Druck: Memminger MedienCentrum, 87700 Memmingen

Gedruckt auf umweltfreundlichem, chlorfrei gebleichtem und alterungsbeständigem Papier

Den Verlag erreichen Sie im Internet unter:
www.winter-verlag-hd.de

CONTENTS

PREFACE: UNFINISHED BUSINESS

> Ursprüngliche Wahrheiten [...] können nur festgehalten werden, indem sie ständig noch ursprünglicher zur Entfaltung kommen; nie aber durch bloße Anwendung ihrer und durch bloße Berufung auf sie. Ursprüngliches bleibt nur ursprünglich, wenn es die ständige Möglichkeit hat, das zu sein, was es ist: Ursprung als Entspringen.
> Heidegger, *Einführung in die Metaphysik*.

THIS BOOK IS SOMETHING OF AN ANACHRONISM. IT PRESENTS a reading of Pindar's epinician poetry from a theoretical perspective that had its day, such as it was and as far as Anglo-American criticism in general is concerned, in the 1980s and early 1990s, and then gave way to the more obviously political, historical and cultural-studies concerns which in many places have continued to dominate the landscape to the present. In Pindaric studies, this move towards interpretations more fully informed by questions of power and history and more aware of the ideological heterogeneity of Pindar's putative fifth-century audiences rapidly led to a highly productive rethinking of the odes as texts reflecting or negotiating tensions endemic to late archaic Greek society, and this is, for the most part, where attention has remained: the primary interest of the victory songs, one might be tempted to generalize, is currently seen by a large part of the research community to lie in their complex and varied relationships to their historical or societal contexts, and this interest in a certain kind of context has meant, in turn, that more 'formalist' readings, such as those associated with New Criticism or with early work in deconstruction, have come to appear curiously naïve, left behind by what appears most challenging and exciting in contemporary literary scholarship. What reason can we give, therefore, for what seems to be the return to a moment in theory which is itself already a matter of history?

If there is a suspicion which lies at the heart of the following 240-odd pages, it is that we have unfinished business with poststructuralism. Let us recall: the poststructuralist project—or rather, the ensemble of projects variously gathered under that name—was from the very beginning aimed at the conceptual foundations of understanding itself. (Amongst them, at notions like 'history', whose simplicity and authority has sometimes seemed oddly unexamined in the writings of those who have opposed it to such things as 'deconstructionism'). The work of Derrida and others raised complex questions about language and meaning, about reading and interpretation, and not least about scholarship and its distinctive institution, the university, and the implications of some of these questions, their range and theoretical force have, to date at least, been extremely difficult to judge. Perhaps it is for this reason that calls in the last decade or two to 'move on' from deconstruction or other forms of 'theory' have often rested less on genuine answers than on more or less obvious oversimplifications of the material (occasionally even with reference to the *ars longa, vita brevis*-topos). But if progress in literary studies is not to take the form of oblivion, or at best *naïveté*, it seems to me that the hard legacy of poststructuralism must be accepted, however unfashionable or untimely it may seem; what is required is not a less, but rather a more profound engagement with poststructuralist thought, not because the latter represents some kind of theoretical *ne plus ultra*, but because too many of the concerns raised by its readings and re-appropriations of the Western literary and philosophical tradition remain troublingly central to the entire enterprise of literary understanding within the academy.

Such questions have interrupted my studies of Pindar more than once in the last few years; they have challenged my interpretative certainties and caused me to rethink my ways of reading. To that extent, I have tried to give this book less the character of a description of results than that of the protocol of an exploration. I have been particularly concerned to avoid 'applying theory', given that doing so robs the theoretical project(ile) of all its destabilizing force; instead I have attempted to demonstrate how specific theoretical problems arise in the course of interpreting certain ancient texts and so, perhaps, to recreate the experience of seeing them unfold anew before one's eyes. 'Originary insights only remain originary', writes Heidegger, 'if they are constantly given the chance to be what they are: origin as event.'[1]

Pindar's Metaphors is the revised, English version of a doctoral thesis originally submitted to the University of Heidelberg in 2007 under the title *Pindars Metaphern: Rhetorik und Bedeutung in der*

[1] Heidegger [6]1998, p. 111, Engl. p. 155 (translation modified).

griechischen Lyrik des fünften Jahrhunderts v.Chr. I wish to thank my supervisor, Jürgen Paul Schwindt, who kindly proof-read the entire German manuscript and accepted the English translation for publication in his series *Bibliothek der Klassischen Altertumswissenschaften.* For helpful comments and suggestions during the writing- and revision-phases, I would like to thank Patrick Buchholz, Jost Eickmeyer, Jonas Grethlein, Gerrit Kloss, Eric Kuchle, Benjamin Mayer and Gerhard Poppenberg (Heidelberg); Matthias Erdbeer (Münster); Charles More (Yale); and Markus Asper (New York). Parts of earlier drafts were presented at different times to members of the research colloquium at the Department of Classical Philology in Heidelberg, to whom I owe a number of useful observations. Other kinds of support, no less important, were given by Rodney Harris, Meinrad Kreuzberger (*non modo veritatis causa, sed etiam amicitiae ergo*), Anette Krusholz, Ross and Margaret Piper, and the members of the Lutheran Jakobuskirche in Tübingen. Glenn Most (Pisa) was of assistance at an early stage of the project, Ernst A. Schmidt (Tübingen) very encouraging in the final throes. My first serious encounter with Pindar was in a *Hauptseminar* under the learned aegis of Richard Kannicht at the University of Tübingen; John Davidson of Victoria University of Wellington introduced me, many years ago, to reading Greek poetry in the original; to both of them also my thanks.

In the following pages, translations of ancient authors are my own unless otherwise indicated. (That being said, no one translates in a vacuum. My debt in particular to William Race's fine Loeb translation will be apparent each time I quote Pindar.) Where works originally in French or German are cited in the main text, I have endeavoured to be consistent in using the standard English translations; in cases of texts unavailable in English, I have given translations of my own. Pindar is cited from Snell and Maehler's Teubner edition unless otherwise noted, other editions used are listed at the beginning of the bibliography. The spelling and abbreviation of the names of ancient authors and works follows for the most part that of the *Oxford Classical Dictionary*. Further abbreviations can also be found at the beginning of the bibliography.

INTRODUCTION

Novem vero lyricorum longe Pindarus
princeps spiritu, magnificentia, sententiis,
figuris, beatissima rerum verborumque
copia et velut quodam eloquentiae flumine:
propter quae Horatius eum merito nemini
credit imitabilem.
Quintilian, *Institutio oratoria.*

Sors du tombeau, divin Pindare,
Toi qui célébras autrefois
Les chevaux de quelques bourgeois
Ou de Corinthe ou de Mégare;
Toi qui possédas le talent
De parler beaucoup sans rien dire,
Toi qui modulas savamment
Des vers que personne n'entend
Et qu'il faut toujours qu'on admire.
Voltaire, *Ode* XVII.

THE RELATIONSHIP BETWEEN RHETORIC AND MEANING HAS long been a matter of concern to literary studies. In 1921, Walter Benjamin (who, we are told, liked to read Pindar aloud to his friends in the original Greek[1]) wrote in 'Die Aufgabe des Übersetzers':

> Whereas all individual elements of foreign languages—words, sentences, associations—are mutually exclusive, these languages supplement one another in their intentions. This law is one of the fundamental principles in the philosophy of language, but to understand it precisely we must draw a distinction, in the concept of 'intention', between what is meant and the way of meaning it.[2]

[1] Scholem 1983, p. 162.

[2] 'Während nämlich alle einzelnen Elemente, die Wörter, Sätze, Zusammenhänge von fremden Sprachen sich ausschließen, ergänzen diese Sprachen sich in ihren Intentionen selbst. Dieses Gesetz, eines der grundlegenden der Sprachphilosophie, genau zu fassen, ist in der Intention vom Gemeinten die Art des Meinens zu unterscheiden.' Benjamin 1972–1986, vol. IV 1, p. 14, Engl. vol. 1, p. 257. For an interpretation of this passage in something like the sense I adopt here, see Paul de Man, 'Reading and history' (= de Man 1986, pp. 54–72), p. 61 f. and 'Conclusions: Walter Benjamin's "The task of the transla-

Benjamin argues here for the autonomy and theoretical interest of a level of utterances that has nothing directly to do with the predicative function of linguistic signs. In the context in which it stands, this distinction is intended to support a series of far-reaching claims: that translation does not serve the reader, that its true purpose is instead to reveal a suprahistorical kinship between languages, that this kinship is based on the fact (or at least the hypothesis) that they all, taken together, point to or 'intend' something which is both their source and their destiny, and that this something is an eschatological 'pure language', *die reine Sprache*, no longer burdened down by the alien weight of meaning it is forced to bear whilst history still endures. If there is to be evidence for this, even as a distant, theoretical possibility, it will only be found in a dimension of language that can *already* be seen to be different from the function of merely transmitting intended content. Benjamin locates this dimension by means of the heuristic of translation, a relationship not between the world of phenomena and a text but between one text and another. In what is and must be lost in translation, 'another side of language' is revealed whose defining characteristic the translator of the *Tableaux parisiens* had identified in an earlier study as *Sprachmagie*, 'language-magic', the 'immediacy of all mental communication' in language.[3] In 'Die Aufgabe des Übersetzers', Benjamin now speaks of 'something that cannot be communicated', precisely because it is itself a medium and not a potential content transmittable through a medium qualitatively distinct from itself.[4] The magic of language has to do, therefore, with the specificity of a constellation, with the arrangement and order of the signifier in its most spatial, most material sense. This incommunicable 'rest' would have, in the absence of the German philosopher's cabbalistic aesthetics of redemption, no legitimate name and no history, but rather the status of the inessential, of a detour or mere makeshift bridge from the semantic, ideal core of the one text to the other.[5] We will not hesitate, in a

tor"' (= *ibid.*, pp. 73–105), p. 86 f.

3 '[...] die *Unmittel*barkeit aller geistigen Mitteilung', in 'Über Sprache überhaupt und über die Sprache des Menschen' (= Benjamin 1972–1986, vol. II 1, pp. 140–157), p. 142 f. (his emphasis in the original), Engl. ('On language as such and on the language of man': vol. 1, pp. 62–74) p. 64.

4 'Ein Nicht-Mitteilbares'. Benjamin 1972–1986, vol. IV 1, p. 19, Engl. vol. 1, p. 261.

5 What seems most attractive about Benjamin's thought at this point is the radicality with which he attempts to think the remains of language—and that these turn out to be a rigorously non-essential essence of their own. One could compare the a-Hegelian 'history' (neither a sublimation nor an ascent) of the *Klang et al.* in Derrida's *Glas* (Paris, 1974).

moment, to identify it with the figurality of rhetoric. And as we will see in the course of this study, this is precisely the role it has traditionally been assigned.

In pointing to a divergence within the nature of language itself between meaning and the means of its creation, however, Benjamin also draws attention to the possibility that this detour may have effects of its own, 'magical' effects based on an irreducible materiality that cannot be sublimated or *aufgehoben* into translatable meaning.[6] These would be effects without necessary sense, with no obligatory connection to truth or meaning. They could, indeed, be placed in the service of meaning, but could just as easily be irrelevant to it, or even interfere with it. This potential for interference would, in fact, always be given; it would be *constitutive* of the distinction between meaning and the mode of its production in the first place. The force of Benjamin's argument here is that, inasmuch as it is *always* medium, always formed or shaped in a way irreducible to the simple ideality of its content, a text is not and can never be exhausted by its mere reference. As a consequence, however, the opposition between *die Art des Meinens* and *das Gemeinte* calls the heuristic categories of every conception of literary interpretation aimed solely at translating (explicating, interpreting) the ideality of what is *meant* into question. The eschatological potential of a division or split of this kind between meaning and saying means that λέξις and λόγος, the level of expression and the level of content, poetics and hermeneutics may always, in the final analysis, turn out to be incommensurable. It can come as no surprise, therefore, that literary scholarship has tended to draw back from the abyss this thesis would open before it. If it wishes to preserve the readability of its objects of investigation, it can scarcely do otherwise.

Amongst these objects and in the articulation of this potential, some texts, ancient and modern, have been found to speak less deniably, more radically and insightfully than others. The history of literary theory in the latter part of the twentieth century and the early part of

[6] Scholars have rightly stressed the origins of this notion of a *Sprachform* with a force of its own in Hamann and early German Romantic thought, and have seen Wilhelm von Humboldt, with whose work Benjamin had come into contact as a student in Berlin some seven years earlier, as a connecting figure (see Menninghaus 1980, pp. 9–50). The relationship to Humboldt is more complex, however, than the question of sources and conscious borrowings suggests: compare Hamacher's Benjamin-study 'The word *Wolke*—if it is one' (Hamacher 1988) with Frey's investigation of Humboldt's use of the word *Wolke* in Frey 1997. Benjamin himself did not believe that Humboldt had seen 'die magische Seite der Sprache': see 'Reflexionen zu Humboldt' (= Benjamin 1972–1986, vol. VI, p. 26 f., Engl. vol. 1, p. 424 f.).

the twenty-first has been, to a large extent, the history of the readings of such texts. The corpus of writings which have thus come to form the uncanonical 'canon' of theory in the last forty years is heterogeneous, its constituency in some cases surprising. The special aptness of a given work to cast light on a particular theoretical problem may indeed appear to us now, in retrospect, to be self-evident, but it is by no means clear that it could always have been predicted on the grounds of obvious thematic or historical relevance in advance. The converse is also true: there seems to be no cogent reason to exclude, in advance, the possibility that a text written centuries or even millennia ago might bring tensions inherent in the workings of language itself to light that have become central to literary theory, particularly poststructuralist literary theory, only in the wake and as the legacy of projects such as Benjamin's. We therefore find, among the writings which have been shown to be most salient to the questions which concern us here, the works not only of such authors as Rousseau, Hegel, Wordsworth, and Blanchot, but also of Sophocles, Plato and Aristotle. We do not, however, find Pindar.

Pindar's odes have suffered from a curious lack of interest from within poststructuralism.[7] His apparent political and social conservatism, the highly conventional nature of ancient epinician poetry so convincingly demonstrated by E.L. Bundy and others, and the efficacy of the songs as a form of literary communication between poet and public emphasized in the research of the last two decades has made him seem, perhaps, an unlikely candidate for a reading directed towards an allegedly troubled relationship between the rhetorical mediality of language and its meaning. It can nevertheless be shown—and this will be our task in the coming pages—that this neglect has been unjustified. Even a first, relatively superficial reading of the surviving corpus—some 45 odes for victors in the Pan-Hellenic games at Olympia, Delphi, Nemea and the Isthmus, written (as far as we know) between 498 and 446 B.C., and a not inconsiderable number of fragments from other genres of ancient lyric—reveals the intense interest in and exploitation of the potential of rhetorical figures and tropes commended by Quintilian; it also discovers an element of self-referential self-questioning that, throughout the history of Pindaric scholarship, has attracted much comment.[8] Indeed, few other poets of the Greek

[7] None of the contributions to Benjamin 1988, Hexter & Selden 1992 or de Jong & Sullivan 1994, for example, is devoted to Pindar. On the term 'poststructuralism', see below, p. 10 n. 17.

[8] See Quintilian, *Inst.* X 1. 61 (cited as motto above). The self-referentiality of the

archaic or classical period speak as much about their own texts and their rhetorical nature as Pindar, and none makes use of a comparable range of metaphorical and other forms of figurative speech in order to do so. In view of the discontinuity within language postulated by Benjamin and others between what is meant and the mode of meaning, we might on this basis alone ask what effects the rich figurality of the epinicians could have on what they intend to say. Are expression and intention, in these poems, always simply co-extensive? Or do the odes, read in the context of a series of specific theoretical concerns we have only begun to sketch here, reveal instead a level of reflection on the nature of literary language itself to which the assumption of such co-extension does not entirely do justice?

It is questions such as these that the following chapters set out to answer. We will be concerned, in different songs and on different levels, with tracing a tension between what the odes *must mean* if they are to be amenable to interpretation in its traditional, hermeneutical sense at all, and the disseminative, *rhetorical* effects of the tropes and figures they use to do so. This tension has been the often (and for good reason) unspoken obsession of Pindaric studies since the Alexandrians; it is no accident that numerous academic works on Pindar begin with reference to the obscurity of their subject.[9] Such references are not, or not only, *captationes benevolentiae*; rather, they can be read as the symptoms of a problem running through these treatises as their almost always implicit common thread. As though something in the nature of Pindaric language itself resisted being bound by interpretation to a meaning which no longer required the mediation of mere words. If we do not intend to subscribe to the hypothesis that the Boeotian poet did not wish to be understood—and Pindar's desire to communicate has been the consensus of scholarship now for at least two centuries—we will have to attribute such effects, should they be observed, to something in language beyond the control of any single author, something that resists and subverts the (by no means arbitrary or dispensable) literary canons of totality and closure in a way investigated more fully in the works of other, more theoretically prominent authors, and something, perhaps, related to the figurality that Quintilian and others saw as this poet's particular characteristic. To read Pindar in this way, therefore, is to attempt to draw the victory songs into a field of inquiry

Pindaric odes was already remarked on by Eustathius in the twelfth century (*Prooem.* 22); see Kambylis 1991, pp. 92–95. For more recent studies, see below, pp. 27 and 104 ff.

[9] On this *topos*, see Most 1985b, p. 11 ff. and Hamilton 2003.

defined by concerns with literary signification in general, in order to understand what links him, beyond all questions of chronology or reception, to other authors, both philosophers and poets, whose texts are structured or destabilised by the same rupture between rhetoric and meaning we will be examining here.

In the works of a number of theorists, a resistance to interpretation of precisely this kind—Benjamin's *Sprachmagie* in another guise—has served to define or redefine the relationship between literary studies and philosophy. One influential version of this line of thought takes Heidegger's *Destruktion* of European metaphysics as its point of departure. *Sein und Zeit* argued that the essential common feature of Western ontology from Parmenides through to Hegel and beyond consisted in the definition of being as 'presence', the pure *Vorhandenheit* ('presence-at-hand') or *Gegenwart* of the object.[10] This presence is the basis upon which both the rules of logic and, partly as a consequence, the concept of meaning are predicated: 'proper' or 'true' meaning, even in its minimal logical form as non-contradiction, and certainly as *adaequatio* or as coherence, is only thinkable on the basis of what presently exists or co-exists in the unity of the one 'now';[11] the ideal meaning signified by language or a text is 'present' in the sense that it is, in itself, neither spatially displaced nor temporally deferred by further signification.[12] The relationship between this present meaning and logic is given expression in grammar, which recapitulates logic's claim to universal ontological validity on the level of linguistic structure.[13] According to Heidegger, then, metaphysics has always been implicitly based on the thesis that logic, in describing the attributes of being as presence, in fact describes the properties of being as a whole. But if this has been the presupposition of Western philosophical thought

[10] See Heidegger [18]2001, pp. 25 and 95–101, Engl. pp. 47 and 128–134, and *cf. id.* [4]2000, p. 62. The notion of *Gegenwart* was taken up by Jacques Derrida as *présence*, not without misgivings: see Derrida 1967a, pp. 15–31, esp. 17 f. and 23, Engl. pp. 6–18, esp. 8 and 12, and—for the misgivings—*id.* 1972b, pp. 35–37 n. 2, Engl. p. 33 f. n. 6. Useful studies are Sallis 1984, pp. 597–601 and Bernet 1986.

[11] *Cf.* Derrida's analysis of this in 'Ousia et grammè' (= Derrida 1972b, pp. 31–78), esp. 58 f. and 62 f., Engl. pp. 51 f. and 54 f.

[12] It will thus be clear that, in our context, 'presence' signifies the exclusive self-reference of being: as the eschatological point at which the *signifiant* finally effaces itself completely and in so doing brings semiosis to a standstill, it is directed not against the (truth of) interpretation, as some critics have understood the term (*cf.* Egginton 2007), but is instead its only secure basis. See further below, p. 37 ff.

[13] See Heidegger [18]2001, p. 165, Engl. p. 208 f., and note the corresponding remarks of de Man 1986, p. 13 ff.

since Greek antiquity, it only becomes explicit in Hegel's collapsing of the distinction between logic and metaphysics altogether in the *Enzyklopädie*, a move which thus inaugurated what Heidegger was later to call the 'consummation of metaphysics'.[14]

Now the implication of metaphysics understood in this way for interpretation is that whatever in a text resists its incorporation or *Aufhebung* into logical or conceptual form will be unable to participate in the truth of meaning. As soon as there is something real behind or beyond the text, this implication is rigorously unavoidable and can be argued to be basic to the entire project of hermeneutics. But it is precisely here that the notion of the rhetorical figure in its broadest sense becomes a problem. A first, rather tentative definition of figurality might be that the figure or trope is a recognizable, formal feature of language which, despite a certain systematicity, is neither grammatically motivated nor required on logical grounds. The figure is not reducible to logical meaning, not because it is innately irrational or illogical, but because it *essentially constituted* by an element of non-logical form which has to be left behind in order to reach the conceptual truth of the text. Thus, the interpretation of a metaphor is itself no longer a metaphor; interpretation lays off, or must attempt to lay off, the metaphorical form in order to reach the semantic or logical core of the figure. Metaphor, so long as it remains—and this is precisely the scandal of catachresis, that it *always* remains—hinders or subverts

[14] Hegel, *Enzyklopädie*, §§ 19–25, esp. § 24: 'Die *Logik* fällt daher mit der *Metaphysik* zusammen, der Wissenschaft der *Dinge* in *Gedanken* gefaßt, welche dafür galten, die *Wesenheiten der Dinge* auszudrücken' (Hegel 1969–1971, vol. 8, p. 81, his emphasis). *Cf.* Heidegger [6]1998, pp. 93 and 143, Engl. pp. 128 f. and 200. On the 'consummation of metaphysics' see further Heidegger's 'Überwindung der Metaphysik' (= Heidegger 1954, pp. 67–95; English in *id.* 2003, pp. 84–110), in particular his remarks in section VI on Hegel (p. 72, Engl. p. 89), and his opening assertion that the 'dying' (*Verendung*) of metaphysics lasts longer than its history to date (p. 67, Engl. p. 85). This is of course the source of Derrida's frequently misunderstood distinction between the unforeseeable 'end' (*fin*) and the recognizable 'closure' (*clôture*) of metaphysics at the beginning of *De la grammatologie* (see Derrida 1967a, pp. 11–14, Engl. pp. 3–5). Heidegger's work from the 1930s onwards indeed announces an 'overcoming' of metaphysics *qua* philosophy, a 'post-metaphysics' achieved by or in 'thinking' (*Denken*); for Derrida, however, metaphysics is not a 'period' in any simple historical sense, its closure neither an event nor a task to be carried out, but rather a structural characteristic, akin to the closure of a circle or an algorithmic series: a specific endlessness entirely amenable to rigorous analysis. In *Positions* (Derrida 1972c, p. 23, Engl. p. 13) he comments: 'Ce qui est pris dans la clôture dé-limitée peut continuer indéfiniment.' On the complication this distinction effects (or at least implies) in the notion of 'history', see *ibid.*, p. 77, Engl. p. 57, and de Man [2]1983, p. 137 f.

metaphysics; the two are, in the final analysis, incompatible. And if a specific will to figure or to form is constitutive of literature itself, as many scholars have argued, then the difference between literature and metaphysics will be predicated on the basis of precisely this subversion, a subversion carried out by the signifier and affecting the logical properties of what can be meant. This will in fact be what is most 'literary' about literature: a non-dialectical essence on the outside of meaning.[15]

If this understanding of literature is correct, what possible implications could it have for the task of reading? There can be no question of giving up meaning in its authentically metaphysical sense: such a surrender would spell the end of understanding itself. But it is important to see that there is a price hermeneutics must pay for its insights. This price is the effacement or, at the very least, marginalisation of those elements in a text which do not readily become transparent for the historically intended, unified meaning it has traditionally been the exegete's task to (re-)construct. If metaphysics, or indeed philosophy in general, defines itself as the transparency of language for the true and present state of affairs—*alles, was der Fall ist*—it will be precisely in such elements that literature's specific resistance to hermeneutical or metaphysical strategies of recovering meaning will become apparent. A reading which treats them merely as detours on the way to meaning may thus be missing what is most distinctive about its object.

Are the victory odes really 'literature' in this 'post-' or, perhaps better, 'parametaphysical' sense? We should not foreclose the question on the basis of theoretical considerations alone. Pindar needs, therefore, to be read again. This study undertakes such a reading. It investigates the language of the songs as a complex of self-referential discussions of some of the most central, most metaphysically motivated categories in Pindaric studies to date: the specific epinician claim to veracity, the poetic unity of the individual odes, and the role and nature of the subject who speaks in them. These problems can be understood as

[15] *Cf.* Derrida 1984a, p. 112: '[...] when I speak of literature it is [...] an allusion to certain movements which have worked around the limits of our logical concepts, certain texts which make the limits of our language tremble, exposing them as divisible and questionable.' Lest we think that this is an element specific to deconstruction, the characterization of literaricity as resistance to reading is also to be found in philosophical hermeneutics: *cf.* Gadamer 1986/1993, p. 340, where hermeneutics is required 'wo etwas der Einordnung in die Erfahrung Widerstand leistet' (Engl. *id.* 1989, p. 31), and p. 351, where the eminent object of this hermeneutics, literature, is defined as 'Texte, die nicht verschwinden' (Engl. *ibid.* p. 41).

points of divergence in the relationship between rhetorical form and logical meaning, and are, we will argue, designated as such by the poems themselves.

The programme

The basic tension between rhetoric and meaning postulated by Benjamin, and the model of interpretation to which it has led in some forms of poststructuralist thought, is the topic of Chapter 1. Such a tension is implied by every concept of rhetoric which asserts the priority of persuasion over figurality. This assertion is, of course, the legacy of ancient rhetorical theory, but the inheritance for which it stands may not be as unambiguous as has usually been believed. A re-reading of Plato's investigation of the relationship between rhetoric and truth in the *Sophist* will demonstrate that, in the conversation between Theaetetus and the Stranger, something already interferes with the distinction, crucial to the Platonic philosophy of language, between the dissimulation of the rhetor and the true speech of the philosopher. This observation will lead us, in turn, to the rhetoric of indeterminacy in the work of Paul de Man, where we will find the first systematic treatment of this interference with a view to its consequences for the study of literature. In particular de Man's critique of 'readability' will suggest, in anticipation of Chapter 2, a characterization of the last two hundred years of Pindaric scholarship as a period in interpretation governed by the consummation of metaphysics announced in the philosophy of Hegel. The theory of meaning entailed by this philosophy is as inevitable as it is problematic; the rift it creates extends throughout the whole of the history of Western thought, from Plato and the Presocratics through to contemporary literary theory. Since we will be situating our reading of Pindar explicitly in the tension between this 'metaphysical' hermeneutics and the critique levelled at it by poststructuralism, representatives from both 'sides' of the discussion—Parmenides, Plato, Aristotle and Hegel himself on the one hand, Jacques Derrida, Gilles Deleuze and Paul de Man on the other—possess considerable heuristic value for the argumentation.[16] They will

[16] The model of two different 'sides' *opposed* to each other (one can still read, occasionally, that Derrida wrote *against* Plato and the like) is a fiction, as all such reassuring taxonomies are. It presupposes that metaphysics is sufficiently self-identical to be opposed to its 'other' in a simple, more or less binary fashion. The work of much deconstructive theory, however, has been to show that no such identity exists: the most rigorous texts of the metaphysical tradition, by virtue of their very rigour, are inhabited by an element they cannot contain and which makes the prospect of a simple border

therefore make more of an appearance than has been usual in traditional studies of the epinicians, also and precisely because it is just this tradition that, beyond all questions of exegetical detail, is at stake.[17]

In Chapter 2 we turn to the history of research. To what extent do the central works of Pindaric studies themselves support our hypothesis of a complicity between literary interpretation and the 'metaphysics of presence'? I begin here with an interrogation of the place and function of 'rhetoric' in Elroy L. Bundy's *Studia Pindarica*. This starting-point is not arbitrary: Bundy's commentary, published in 1962, was arguably the most important book on Pindar in the twentieth century; it remains one of the most rigorous, most attentive investigations of Pindaric language to date. If it can be shown that the interpretations offered by the *Studia*, despite their author's sober and empirical approach to reading, are nevertheless based on identifiably metaphysical assumptions about language—assumptions having to do with the relationship between the figurative, medial surface of the text and the true, literal meaning of the poems—then we may expect, *a fortiori*, that this will be the case for much of the rest of Pindaric scholarship. On this hypothesis, we leave Bundy's no-nonsense, down-to-earth study of parallels and generic features for the work of August Boeckh, the founder of Greek studies at the University of Berlin in 1811 and the

between them and what they (must) (claim to) exclude impossible. Which is not to say that there is *no* border, but merely to say that it does not exist in any undivided, unitary form. See further Derrida 1984a, p. 111 f. and below, p. 13 ff. I note at this juncture that, here and in what follows, the proper names of authors and their pronominal representatives refer exclusively to prosopopoeiae denoting particular sets of theoretical problems, and to authorial roles. Assertions about historical or contemporary persons, their states of knowledge or putative intentions, are nowhere the point at issue. This is also the case for the first person pronoun 'I'.

17 A word about the much-maligned term 'poststructuralism'. It is, as Nancy 1991, p. 2, remarks, 'a baroque designation, because there has never been one structuralism, and because what it deals with did not come "after," nor as a "posterity".' Certainly (and we recall, as we are doubtless meant to do, that for Deleuze the baroque was characterized by the self-reflexive, multiplying figure of the fold). Nevertheless, this 'post-' does seem to me to designate a move within theory, an indeed diverse response to a nonetheless shared disquiet in the work of a number of thinkers, many of them in Paris in the 1960s and 1970s, that without the models and figures, the questions and solicitations of the 'structuralists'—Deleuze names Jakobson and Lévi-Strauss, but also Althusser, Foucault, Lacan and Barthes on the first page of his 'À quoi reconnaît-on le structuralisme?' (= Deleuze 2002, pp. 238–269, Engl. pp. 170–192)—would surely have remained unthinkable (or at least unthought). On the definition of 'poststructuralism', compare also Culler's (1982, pp. 22–30) account with Weber 1986, the brief remarks of Bennington & Young 1987, pp. 1–9, and Derrida 1989, pp. 88–90.

colleague of Hegel, Schelling and Schleiermacher. Boeckh's interest in the theory of interpretation will provide us with an opportunity to study the interaction between metaphysics and reading in his groundbreaking four-volume edition of Pindar, *Pindari Opera*, and in his magisterial *Encyklopädie der philologischen Wissenschaften*. The importance of these texts lies not in their merely chronological priority—Boeckh is not the *originator* of the theory of meaning we will find in his commentaries and lectures, and he does not *bequeath* it to later scholars—but rather in their will to clarity, to the explicit formulation of their presuppositions. Many of these presuppositions and the aporias to which they inevitably lead serve to link, over two hundred years of classical scholarship, the works of interpreters as disparate as Ludolph Dissen, Ulrich von Wilamowitz-Moellendorff, Thomas Hubbard and Leslie Kurke. The troubled relationship in all of their texts between the hermeneutical postulate of true or literal meaning and the mediation of the figure serves to dismantle the series of conceptual oppositions—nature and culture, text and context, metaphor and literality itself—on which each of their readings of the epinicians depend.

We will find, in the commentaries and monographs of the nineteenth and twentieth centuries, different, specific articulations of this critical disassembly or deconstruction. If it is, as the theoretical considerations of the first chapter should already have made clear, no accident,[18] then one of the central premises on which it is based is the status accorded to *immanence* in interpretation, the traditional imperative to understand the text *on its own terms*. According to this imperative, the task of the commentary consists in revealing the text's identity with itself on a level of meaning beyond the mere epiphenomenality of the sign, a prevenient congruence between expression and intention within the work that is simultaneously hermeneutics' presupposition and its *telos*. It can indeed be argued that the entire plausibility of hermeneutics as a theory rests on the seductive power of this presupposition and on the possibility of carrying out the project for which it

[18] It is also not the result of a simple *reception* or a *history* of reception, both because it cannot be reduced to conscious borrowings (the question, for example, of whether Bundy had read Hegel or Heidegger is in our context misleading) and because the relationships between individual texts or bodies of texts which will interest us are not primarily generic or even chronologically ordered. Such relationships are 'structural' in the precise sense given that term by thinkers such as Jakobson or Lévi-Strauss: dependent neither on a genealogy nor a tradition, they form instead a transcendental topology which *creates* the effects of anticipation or reception to which, in traditional literary history, they are then attributed. See again Deleuze, 'À quoi reconnaît-on le structuralisme?' (above, n. 17), pp. 243–246 and 250–255, Engl. pp. 173–175 and 178–182.

stands. Problems arise, however, if it can be demonstrated that the text in question contradicts this thesis of identity, for of what value is immanence if it is only to be bought at the cost of disregarding the explicit poetological statements of the works it interprets? The reading of the *First Olympian* undertaken in Chapter 3 investigates this possibility. I will be concerned, here, to show that the discontinuity between rhetoric and meaning foregrounded in poststructuralist literary theory is already at work and addressed in this central Pindaric text; the rigorously catachrestic model of figurality it offers will inform our studies of other odes in Chapters 4 and 5.

Situated in the middle of the book, Chapter 3 thus acts as a kind of hinge between the first two and the last two chapters. In the latter, I attempt a rereading of two major themes in the interpretation of Pindaric poetry in such a way as to take account of the instability in the relationship between rhetoric and meaning argued on theoretical and research-historical grounds in the first sections of the book. The first of these themes, the obsession of scholarship on Pindar since Boeckh and Dissen's commentary in the first decades of the nineteenth century, is the *unity* of the literary text. Studies of unity have tended, on the whole, to address the problem of foundations, the question of the basis on which we might say that any given epinician or the genre to which they all belong is 'one'. I will argue in Chapter 4 that this question has metaphorical status; its figurality has to do with the nature of the concept of unity in literary studies, a concept not native to hermeneutics but rather derived or carried over from the discourse of metaphysics. The question of the 'one' in Aristotle's lectures on the πρώτη φιλοσοφία, therefore, and specifically the role and function of the 'boundary', τὸ πέρας, will serve as our point of departure here. In discussion with Jacques Derrida's notions of the *parergon* and the fold (*le pli*), we will then seek to circumscribe a specific double logic of the boundary in the victory odes. If it is, as our reading of Aristotle will have suggested, rigorously impossible to designate a concept of unity without the notion of the border, and if the research of the last two centuries has predicated Pindar's readability upon the basis of just this concept, then the equally rigorous subversion of unity in the texts and metaphors of the epinicians must lead to questions concerning the hermeneutical appropriation of the poems. If unity is one of the conditions of being readable, perhaps even the most important condition, then it is, on this theory, precisely the rhetoricity of the odes which undermines their readability.

Chapter 5 is concerned with the *subject* of language. It is not all too difficult to show that that the controversial discussions in research of recent decades about the Pindaric subject have to a large part been based on the desire to identify text with *voice*. Nothing else is meant by the insistence of many scholars on the occasionality of the odes and the imperative derived from this occasionality to refer the writtenness of the transmitted texts back to the orality of their first performances. This privileging of speech, however, can be motivated structurally only by its role as the guarantor of a meaning founded in the immediate presence of the speaker's intention for him- or herself. In this final chapter, therefore, I will try to trace the picture of subjective consciousness—not the identity of the subject, but the conditions on which something like subjectivity becomes possible—in the epinicians. There is an interesting tendency in Pindar to speak of the self or the speech of the self in metaphor or in a chain of metaphors whose coherence can be argued to be based on an interest in the mediality of language, of mediation as distance from the point of origin. The negation of any automatic co-extension of 'I' and song, the non-coincidence of *ego* and text is the implication of such distance; its proper place or name within language, I will argue here, is the figure of writing. The chapter therefore concludes with a study of Pindar's ode on writing and the self, the *Tenth Olympian*.

Interpreting (and) theory

The questions about readability raised by the theoretical and historical considerations of chapters one and two—is a tension between rhetoric and meaning intrinsic to the notion of literature as such? has it in fact always been implicitly at work in the history of research?—thus receive their philological grounding in chapters three to five. By the same token, the questions asked in the latter part of the book—what do Pindar's odes say about this tension?—only make sense in the context of the theory and narrative set out in the first. And since we are concerned with 'sense' here—as indeed we must be: scholarship does not profit from attempts to 'move on' from metaphysics by doing away with understanding altogether—it is worth looking a little more closely at this relationship between theory and practice. Are they really as mutually supportive as I have just suggested?

We can note, at the outset, that there is good reason to see literary theory and the interpretation of specific texts as genuinely distinct projects. In 'The resistance to theory', Paul de Man argues for a distinction between them on the basis of theory's concern with what he calls 'the modalities of the production of meaning':

> Literary theory can be said to come into being [...] when the object of discussion is no longer the meaning or the value but the modalities of production and of reception of meaning and of value prior to their establishment—the implication being that this establishment is problematic enough to require an autonomous discipline of critical investigation to consider its possibility and its status.[19]

This passage does two things: it sets theory resolutely apart from questions of literary value or aesthetics—'are the epinicians great

[19] De Man 1986, p. 7. This sentence is quoted by Hexter & Selden 1992, p. xvi in a discussion of the standards and agendas of literary criticism in classics in the early 1990s; they comment: 'If this formulation is correct, it suggests that literary theory and practical criticism are independent undertakings with differing points of departure, and it remains an open question whether the two will, in fact, ever really coincide.' Other scholars, however, have been less sanguine about the autonomy this analysis would grant to the theoretical enterprise. Galinsky 1992, p. 31 writes on theory in Latin studies: 'That [*sc.* the necessity for classicists to make a responsible and distinctive response to the questions theory raises] does not mean that theory should be embraced for the sake of theory and means converted into ends.' *Cf.* Taplin 1998, p. 157, in fact intended as a defence of the theoretical project against the polemical attacks of an unusually reactionary critic in the pages of *Arion*: 'It is not theory as such which is at fault, but the exaltation of theory over practice.' The problem with this plausible hierarchy of theory and practice or means and ends is that nothing guarantees that the results of theoretical work will serve to facilitate interpretation. What if theory makes practice more complex, more problematic, more paradoxical? Are we therefore to refrain from asking the questions and addressing the problems on the (theoretical) level on which they arise? Far from *demonstrating* the teleological priority of interpretation over theory, such arguments merely *assume* it. Harrison 2001, p. 3 ff., on the other hand, argues that a separation between literary studies and theory is impossible on the grounds that no interpretation of a literary text can be objective. (See also Fowler 2000, p. 3 f.) Objectivity, however, is as little the opposite of *theoria* as it is of methodology. Every interpreter and every group of interpreters has its own methodological axiomata, and these are obviously subjective in the sense that their validity is dependent on the extent of the group for which they claim to be binding; but the question of whether these principles themselves are made explicit, are put up for discussion, are modified in the course of reading—whether, in other words, they are at stake in the interpretative project alongside the exegesis of the text—is not *ipso facto* decided one way or the other. In an initially similar confusion of the mere possession of a methodology with the explicit work of theory, Goldhill 1994, p. 51 also suggests that a separation between classics and theory is not legitimate—'There's classics and *then* there's ... theory?'—but then recognizes that theoretical discussion does not serve to supply the study of classical literature with a methodology (since, to the extent that it is scholarship, it already possesses one), but rather to raise the meta-question of 'how explicit, how sophisticated and how self-aware a discussion of each and every critic's inevitable commitment to a methodology has to be.'

poetry?' may on this view be a literary question; it is not a theoretical one—and it defines its object as the 'possibility' and 'status' of the establishment of meaning.[20] It will be immediately clear that if de Man is correct about this second point, theory will be concerned with potentials or forces, a field of options and virtualities, whose effects will indeed only be visible in specific texts, but which will not themselves be irrevocably tied to any one particular text or corpus. And indeed, there is nothing innovative about this thesis: singularities have always been the special province of philology, as Friedrich Schlegel well knew; theory, on the other hand, has in most philosophical traditions always been concerned with the generality attributable only to ideal objects.[21] It would seem, therefore, that philology and theory, though distinct, could on this view be entirely complementary. But things are not quite so simple.

In fact, the status of literary theory within scholarship has been extremely controversial amongst precisely those scholars who accept de Man's definition and object neither to the critique of values nor to the concern with virtuality it implies. At issue has been the kind of knowledge to which literary theory, particularly poststructuralist literary theory, can legitimately lay claim.[22] The poststructuralism of the later twentieth century undertook in many of its forms a radical critique of the metaphysical foundations of the Western intellectual tradition, to which such notions as knowledge (*ἐπιστήμη*, *scientia*), truth (both *ἀλήθεια* and *veritas*) and reason (the λόγος or *ratio*, the *principium rationis*) belong. These, however, were and are precisely the concerns which define the language of scholarship and which serve to identify the community of reading associated with it. Whereas, therefore, it was no surprise that the questions raised by theory were in some quarters received as a *betrayal* of scholarship, others took poststructuralism, and specifically deconstruction, to be announcing a *liberation* from the constraints of the discourse of *Wissenschaft*.[23] The result was

[20] For two more recent 'resistances to theory' in classics on exactly these grounds, see Silk 2001 (the question of value in Pindaric studies) and Radke 2003, pp. 1–30 (the question of mere possibility or abstractness rather than specific actuality in the study of Attic tragedy).

[21] See Husserl, *Logische Untersuchungen*, Erster Band, § 64 (= Husserl 1992, vol. 2, pp. 235–238, Engl.: Husserl 1970, pp. 229–231) for a lucid discussion of the difference between the ideal objects of theory and those of the empirical disciplines. On Schlegel see Thouard 2002.

[22] Waugh 2006 provides a useful survey of some of the issues.

[23] See for example Rorty 1978, one of the most influential statements of this thesis with respect to Derrida (*cf.* Bennington's discussion in *id.* 1988, p. 73 f. with n. 2, and

a widening gap between the 'theory community' on the one hand and 'traditional scholarship' on the other, and in no discipline has this gap remained more noticeable and more intransigent than in classics. It is therefore of some importance to clarify the relationship between deconstruction and the tradition whose critique it embodies.

It is important to see that both of the responses described above are based on a misunderstanding of the work of Derrida and others no less plausible for being wrong. The problem begins with the etymological lineage of 'theory' itself and the metaphysical distinction it presupposes between subject and object (not to mention the priority it accords to the visible and present): Heidegger, who was under no illusions about the essentially metaphysical nature of scholarship, rejected the term θεωρία for his own version of post-metaphysical thinking for just this reason.[24] But even taken in the more common sense of the concern with concepts and principles, the ideal rather than the empirical suggested above, theory still gives rise to difficulties. Deconstructive thought has traditionally been concerned with questioning oppositions such as that between intelligibility and sensibility; a 'deconstructive *theory*', however, of literature or indeed of anything else would be compelled to make use of just this distinction in order to reach genuinely theoretical conclusions (with all the connotations of closure and logical force attached to a word like 'conclusion').[25] If this is a simple contradiction, it would seem that one must either abandon a theory vitiated by such an obvious logical failure, or argue that the criteria of logic themselves are somehow at fault. Intellectual honesty would require no less.[26]

Norris 1989; Rorty's reply to the latter is Rorty 1989); its consequences could be observed in numerous texts of alleged 'deconstructivists' in the 1980s and the early 1990s.

[24] See the 'Brief über den Humanismus' in Heidegger ³1996, p. 314, Engl. *id.* 1993, p. 218, and *cf. id.* ⁹2006, p. 48, Engl. p. 24 for his definition of the university as an intrinsically metaphysical institution founded on Leibniz's *principium reddendae rationis sufficientis*. On 'theoria' see also Godzich 1994, p. 164 ff.

[25] Culler 2007, pp. 83–85 notes de Man's awareness of this (*cf.* de Man 1986, p. 17) and compares it to the inevitable displacement of the unconscious in the interpretation of dreams in Freud.

[26] I suspect that the return to history, to the questions of historicity and historical meaning in the research of the last 15 years or so on Pindar is connected with this dilemma. This return can be read as a re-emphasising of the *local* nature of knowledge, of the specifically local validity of interpretative principles or results, and thus as an acknowledgement or at least assumption that models of explanation based on concerns 'with figures of language in abstraction, with deconstructing the principles of ordering and the "metaphysics of presence" that seem inescapably built into human language systems' (Rice & Waugh ²2001, p. 180 f.) are not inescapable at all. What Waugh in more recent

The most patient and sophisticated deconstructive readings of the literary and philosophical tradition presented thus far have nevertheless opted for a third response. There has been a broad consensus that if 'returning' to metaphysics (if indeed we were ever really there) by rescinding the critique levelled at it by deconstruction is not desirable, 'escaping' it by renouncing its inheritance altogether is not possible. An early statement of this is Derrida's discussion of the concept of the sign in his 1966 paper 'La structure, le signe et le jeu dans le discours des sciences humaines'.[27] The notion of the sign is subject to the hierarchical opposition between the sensible and the intelligible and can, in this sense, be deconstructed as being its product and its presupposition at the same time. But in order to undertake such an analysis, writes Derrida, we must make use of precisely that concept of the sign we are interested in disassembling:

> [W]e cannot do without the concept of the sign, for we cannot give up this metaphysical complicity *without also giving up the critique we are directing against this complicity*, or without the risk of erasing difference in the self-identity of a signified reducing its signifier into itself or, amounting to the same thing, simply expelling its signifier outside itself. [...] And what we are saying here about the sign can be extended to all the concepts and all the sentences of metaphysics [...].[28]

Deconstruction is thus not refutation: the 'complicity' of which Derrida speaks is a necessarily double allegiance to the language of metaphysics and to what remains unspoken in it, a doubling that cannot be reduced to a simplicity without erasing precisely the distinction it is meant to capture. This means that there can be no deconstruction of metaphysics from *outside* of metaphysics; there can be no question

work refers to as a turn on the part of theory to 'the problem of reconstruction, the question of how to rebuild legitimation' (Waugh 2006, p. 4) is also relevant here. Questioning this important move in Pindaric criticism, to which Kurke 1991, Hubbard 1992, Cole 1992, Dougherty 1993 and, more recently, Hornblower 2004 and Currie 2005 have been significant contributions, would require a careful study of the notion of 'history' it presupposes and implies. See further below, p. 115 ff.

[27] Derrida 1967c, pp. 409–428, Engl. pp. 278–293.

[28] '[N]ous ne pouvons nous défaire du concept de signe, nous ne pouvons renoncer à cette complicité métaphysique *sans renoncer du même coup au travail critique que nous dirigeons contre elle*, sans risquer d'effacer la différence dans l'identité à soi d'un signifié réduisant en soi son signifiant, ou, ce qui revient au même, l'expulsant simplement hors de soi. [...] Et ce que nous disons ici du signe peut se étendre à tous les concepts et à toutes les phrases de la métaphysique [...].' Derrida 1967c, p. 413, Engl. p. 281, my emphasis. *Cf.* also *id.* 1972c, p. 19, Engl. *id.* ²2002, p. 10 on Heidegger.

of simply leaving it behind.[29] Interestingly (if not altogether surprisingly), this position is anticipated by Nietzsche: a corresponding remark is already to be found in one of the late notebooks from early 1887 on the concept of the subject. Its author makes it clear that he would quite like to have done with this piece of metaphysical baggage, but—'Here there is a barrier: our thinking itself involves that belief (with its distinction between substance and accident, doing, doer, etc.), abandoning it means no longer being allowed to think.'[30] If it can be shown that the logic of the sign, the subject or metaphysics in general ultimately effaces itself or at least *can* efface itself, if this possibility of aporia is always given in principle and will therefore need to be made explicit (or at least taken account of) in the work of theory, then the mode and status of this recognition as knowledge (and not merely error) will depend crucially on just those epistemological truth-criteria whose aporetic nature it so rigorously describes.

There is, therefore, a twofold gesture entailed in deconstruction, both towards and away from, 'away from' in the mode of 'towards' metaphysics. How is one to take account of this movement which remains within the bounds of what it exceeds? We need a term which designates both recapitulation (or stability) and excession (or force).[31] I want to suggest here, taking up a figure central to the work of Paul de Man, that this double moment of theory is 'allegorical'.[32] Allegory, after all, designates a form of literature whose undoubted referential function—every allegory is an allegory *of* something, and has, within its own bounds, to satisfy the criteria of coherence and rationality metaphysics asserts—is nevertheless suspended. Benjamin, indeed,

[29] It is not without reason that when Derrida speaks, towards the end of the paper, of a 'passage au-delà de la philosophie' (Derrida 1967c, p. 421 f., Engl. p. 288), he is quick to point out that this does not consist of moving on from or abandoning philosophy altogether but rather of remaining within the text of philosophy, continuing to read it. *Cf.* Bennington 2000, p. 53 with n. 13, who observes that Derrida's consistent refusal to call for a 'break with' metaphysics in any simple sense is also informed by Hegel's demonstration in *Wissenschaft der Logik* I ii 1.2 (= Hegel 1969–1971, vol. 6, pp. 35–80) that absolute difference will always end up collapsing into absolute identity, and Culler 2007, p. 181 f.

[30] 'Hier ist eine Schranke: unser Denken selbst involvirt jenen Glauben (mit seiner Unterscheidung von Substanz-Akzidens, Thun, Thäter, usw.), ihn fahren zu lassen heißt nicht-mehr-denken-dürfen.' Nietzsche 1988, vol. 12, p. 317, 7 [63], Engl. *id.* 2003, p. 140, his emphasis.

[31] Derrida's own term for such a movement is *la jetée*: see Derrida 1989 and *cf.* Heidegger's *Sein und Zeit*, §§ 29–31 on the 'Entwurf' (Heidegger [18]2001, pp. 134–148, Engl. pp. 172–188).

[32] See below, p. 48 ff. for a discussion of de Man's theory of allegory.

defined it as the essentially negative knowledge of what we do not possess, of what cannot be subsumed under (a) presence.[33] Allegory, like catachresis, points to what is indefinitely deferred; the account it gives must be a *good* account—just as the readings theory offers must be good readings, characterised by the intellectual generosity and faithfulness to the primary text we rightly expect from careful and attentive scholarship—but it is nevertheless grounded in an irreducible distance from its signified that it does not cease to name. If deconstructive literary theory has, for the most part, taken place in the mode of commentary, this should give us pause for thought, for here we can again observe the double structure of repetition and innovation we noted above, of accepting a legacy but also of saying what has not been said before. Indeed, this is the specific 'truth' of the commentary: it asserts and denies its status as the *re-presentation* of its primary text at the same time.

It is thus always possible in reading to refrain from the work or discourse of theory, just as it is always possible to engage in allegory or allegoresis without making its figural nature explicit. Such restraint on the part of interpretation, however, runs the risk—and perhaps it is an unavoidable risk—of effacing the gap between itself and its referent, of being mistaken for *naïveté*. There can be no question that much of Pindaric scholarship in recent decades has declined to engage explicitly with theoretical issues, and the almost proverbial struggles faced by classics in contributing distinctively to the interdisciplinary project of literary theory have been made no easier by this abnegation.[34] Where such contributions have been made, however—and there have been some excellent studies of ancient authors from as different perspectives as the current theoretical landscape has to offer[35]—one can still fre-

[33] See Benjamin 1972–1986, vol. I 1, p. 406, Engl. *id.* 1977, p. 233, cited below, p. 50 n. 68.

[34] Silk 1995, p. 14 regrets that '[i]n our time, classical *littérateurs* seldom enter the lists of theoretical debate.' The role of literary theory for supporting classics' claim to making an independent contribution to the interdisciplinary debate amongst the literary disciplines is emphasized by Schmitz 2002, p. 15 f., Engl. 5 f.

[35] Almost nothing on Pindar from a structuralist or poststructuralist perspective, however: Hubbard 1985, p. 7 f. indeed expresses scepticism about the relevance of deconstructive literary theory to the victory odes, a surprising position in some respects; we will have occasion to discuss it below (see p. 110 ff.). The few studies which have claimed to deal directly with the implications of deconstruction for the interpretation of Pindar (see for example Farenga 1977a, 1977b) have not been such as to dispel the doubts of sceptics. Calame 2003, pp. 35–86, however, offers a not implausible reading of a number of the poems on the basis of the structuralist literary semiotics of Greimas.

quently observe a disturbingly untheoretical notion of theory as *useful*, as a methodological inventory to be *applied* to texts. Together with the opposing, no less common (if less often articulated) view that theory is *useless* and *inapplicable* to ancient literature, it is based on a reduction of theory to a *τέχνη* or *ars* which is thus drawn into all of the metaphysical oppositions between *φύσις* or *natura* and *νόμος* or *θέσις* it has been deconstruction's task to subvert. Here and in what follows, I have used the term in a different sense. Theory, its moment and its potential, springs from the reflection upon a *dimension* of literary studies neither contingent upon the choice of an interpreter nor the product of a merely historical fashion. It is a turning back upon the conditions of the possibility or impossibility of reading altogether, an attentiveness to questions raised by the fact and phenomenon of literature itself as ineluctable as they are troubling. If theory is 'uncanny' (a word applied more than once to the literary criticism of Paul de Man), the reason lies less in its alleged inapplicability to a given text, in the distraction from the serious work of interpretation it is held to represent, than in the fact that it places the hermeneutical project of recovering meaning from literature utterly at risk.

This is why the relationship between individual readings and the evolution of theory is predicated on the basis not only or even primarily of the logical priority of the *method* to the reading as the latter's 'condition of possibility' (Goldhill),[36] but also of the retrospective reflexivity of *language itself*, and thus the field of theory in general, described by Sartre: '[W]henever I form a sentence its meaning escapes from me, is stolen from me; meanings are changed *for everyone* by each speaker and each day; the meanings of the very words in my mouth are changed by others.'[37] Theory folds back upon reading, doubling and encompassing its possibility and its structure in a constant movement of overlapping. Martin McQuillan writes:

> Theory may challenge institutional traditions and [...] enable [readers] to question their approach to a reception of given *a prioris*. However, this does not mean that Theory should be applied universally and mechanistically as a set of techniques, procedures and operators to every book ever written, exposing them one by one as vile inscriptions of reactionary Western logomachy. [...] Nothing could be less 'radical' or more depoliticising than the closing-off of questioning in an endless repetition of predetermined

[36] Goldhill 1994, p. 51.

[37] '[...] chaque jour et chaque parleur altère *pour tous* les significations.' Sartre 1960, p. 180, Engl. *id.* 1976, p. 98, his emphasis

> textual exegesis. Theory should not be a stick to beat a canonical tradition on which it has always relied, in one form or another, but *an experience of critical reading which imbricates itself in the text it reads.* Ask not what Derrida can do for Jane Austen but what Jane Austen can do for Derrida.[38]

Reading-as-theory always implies (and implicates) itself; the point at which a new context of meaning is established changes by that very fact not only the conditions under which later readings of the same and of other texts must take place: it also casts a new light on readings already undertaken, which themselves must then be read anew. The autoreflective *theoria* of literary criticism, writes (not first, but suggestively) Derrida, offers the chance, by looking at the text, of seeing sight itself:

> The time for reflection is also the chance for turning back on the very conditions of reflection, in all the senses of that word, as if with the help of a new optical device one could finally see sight, could not only view the natural landscape, the city, the bridge and the abyss, but could 'view' viewing.[39]

Pindar's Metaphors therefore connects three levels of discourse with each other: the theory of literature, in particular that of literary-critical deconstruction; the history of research on Pindar; and the reading of the epinicians themselves. Each of these three levels will have implications for both of the others. We will be concerned to show that and how a reading of Pindar in the light of theoretical questions can be fruitful both for the inner-disciplinary discussion of the victory odes and for the interdisciplinary development of theory in literary studies. Since the theoretical tradition with which we will be engaging—the poststructuralist critique of metaphysics and the 'rhetorical' criticism of Paul de Man—has led, as we have noted, a rather marginal existence in Pindaric research to date, this study also intends to contribute to the discussion on the importance accorded by the discipline

[38] McQuillan *et al.* 1999, p. x, my italics. *Cf.* Derrida 1989, p. 65 f.: '[…] each jetty [*jetée*], far from being the part included in a whole, is only a theoretical jetty inasmuch as it claims to comprehend itself by comprehending all the others […].'

[39] 'Le temps de la réflexion, c'est aussi la chance d'un retour sur les conditions mêmes de la réflexion, à tous les sens de ce mot, comme si à l'aide d'un nouvel appareil optique on pouvait voir enfin la vue, non seulement le paysage naturel, la ville, le pont et l'abîme, mais aussi « télescoper » la vue.' Derrida, 'Les pupilles de l'Université. Le principe de raison et l'idée de l'Université' (= Derrida 1990, pp. 461–498), p. 497, Engl. 'The principle of reason: The university in the eyes of its pupils', in Derrida 2004, pp. 129–155, this passage p. 154.

to a series of problems that in this allegedly post-theoretical age have lost none of their disquieting potential.

CHAPTER 1: RHETORIC AS A THEORY OF LITERATURE

> Il y a donc deux interprétations de l'interprétation, de la structure, du signe et du jeu. L'une cherche à déchiffrer, rêve de déchiffrer une vérité ou une origine échappant au jeu et à l'ordre du signe, et vit comme un exil la nécessité de l'interprétation. L'autre, qui n'est pas plus tournée vers l'origine, affirme le jeu et tente de passer au-delà de l'homme et de l'humanisme, le nom de l'homme étant le nom de cet être qui, à travers l'histoire de la métaphysique ou de l'onto-théologie, c'est-à-dire du tout de son histoire, a rêvé la présence pleine, le fondement rassurant, l'origine et la fin du jeu. [...] Je ne crois pas pour ma part, bien que ces deux interprétations doivent accuser différence et aiguiser leur irréductibilité, qu'il y ait aujourd'hui à *choisir*.
>
> Derrida, *L'Écriture et la différence.*

THE EARLIEST SURVIVING MENTION OF THE WORD 'RHETORIC' in the interpretation of Pindar is a solitary remark on *Nem.* 10. 2 ff. preserved in two mediaeval collections of scholia. At this point, the beginning of a song for a wrestler from Argos, the poet has his singer speak of the endless number of Argive achievements (Ἄργος [...] φλέγεται δ' ἀρεταῖς μυρίαις, 2 f.) and maintain—this, at least, is how the commentator understands it—that it would take so long to do justice to even one of these stories (*μάκρα μὲν* [*sc.* ἂν εἴη λέγειν] τὰ Περσέος ἀμφὶ Μεδοίσας Γοργόνος, 4), not to speak of all of them, that he won't even make the attempt.

> καὶ ῥητορικῶς δὲ τοῦτο ποιεῖ· δοκῶν παραιτεῖσθαι τὸ λέγειν καθ' ἕκαστα <τὰ> τῶν Ἀργείων ἀνδραγαθήματα λεληθότως καταριθμεῖται αὐτά.

And he does this rhetorically: for since he creates the impression of refusing to relate the manly achievements of the Argives one after another, no one notices when he then enumerates them after all.[1]

The author of the scholium seems to be thinking of an ironic use of the *praeteritio* by means of which the singer's apparent refusal to recount Argos' achievements serves to misdirect his audience about what will follow.[2] Whether this is in fact what Pindar is doing here—some doubts may perhaps be entertained, both with respect to the poet and to his public—is, for the moment, of less importance. What interests us, rather, is the way the commentator formulates his interpretation. The 'rhetorical' language of this passage of the *Tenth Nemean* has, according to this ancient or Byzantine reader, the initial effect of concealing from the minds of his listeners what the poet intends to do: the *illusion* or *appearance* of intention (δοκῶν παραιτεῖσθαι τὸ λέγειν) masks or hides what is *really* intended, so that when it does in fact take place (καταριθμεῖται) it goes unnoticed (λεληθότως); the term ῥητορικῶς stands for this gap between language and desire. The rhetoricity of the passage in question, however, can itself only become apparent to the extent that its alleged 'surface' intent fails: the commentator himself has, as he sees it, not been taken in. Instead, the announcement in verse 4 has transmitted a *double* intention—to present a catalogue of Argive deeds and simultaneously to deflect attention away from doing so—all the more obvious (and thus ineffective) for being explicitly denied. Pindar does indeed enumerate the ἀνδραγαθήματα of the city in the subsequent fifteen verses; he has clearly intended to do so all along; the 'plain meaning' of the words in which he says he will not is thus mere appearance, a cover for the force or desire this negation 'really' communicates. In order to achieve this interpretative insight into the true intent of the text, however, the commentator must discard its 'literal' significance—which is at the same time, together with the catalogue that follows, his only evidence for what it really wants to say.

I cite this scholium here not merely because it is the first occurrence of the term 'rhetorical' with reference to a Pindaric ode, but also because it draws our attention to the problem with which we will be

[1] Σ *Nem.* 10. 6 Dr. 16–18, my translation. According to Arrighetti *et al.* 1991, this is the only case of the adverb in the Pindar scholia. In two further passages, the adjective ῥητορική is used to designate the τέχνη associated with Demosthenes (Σ *Olymp.* 6. 123 b and c Dr.). Eustathius discusses a series of rhetorical figures and styles in the poems and uses the word 'rhetoric' frequently (see in particular *Prooemium* 17 on metaphor [τροπή] and allegory, and Kambylis 1991, esp. pp. 64–66). On rhetorical terminology in the scholia in general, see Meijering 1987.

[2] *Cf.* Quint., *Inst* IX 2. 47. We return to this passage in *Nem.* 10 below, p. 71.

concerned in this book. The interpretation of literary texts aims, as a rule, to discover what they mean. 'Meaning', in this context, can be understood in a number of ways. It can refer to the conscious intent of an author to communicate or to other constructive factors guiding what is said (*e.g.* the unconscious, societal forces and structures, gender roles, *etc.*). It can also (and in fact always does) designate the significance of a text within a system of conventions or associations entirely beyond the author's control and of which he or she may not even be aware. And it can therefore also refer, in such fields as reception studies, to the meaning a text acquires on the basis of such a system for a specific group of readers who may by no means be identical with the audience the author originally 'had in mind'. In each of these cases, the 'meaning' to be discovered by interpretation underlies a series of constraints which serve to distinguish 'successful' readings from less successful ones and which become explicit whenever such criteria as historicity, poetic or conceptual unity, or even the systematicity of rhetoric itself are addressed. What gives the communicative intent of the text its coherence? How does it fit into its historical context, or make specific use of rhetorical forms? What factors have governed the construction or reception of the text in such a way as to produce this or that communicative result? If answers to questions such as these are not forthcoming, we may (and probably will) doubt whether the (or at least a) 'meaning of the text' has really been discovered.

Now if these various considerations comprise what we are accustomed to call the 'meaning' of the text and what we expect as the result of a successful interpretation, they also serve to ground interpretative practice in a level of the text, be it 'subjective', 'historical' or 'systematic', behind or beyond the mere words on the page. The crucial presupposition must always be that the latter are not placed at random with respect to the former—or if they are, that is precisely the extent to which they do not mean anything. This 'double' model of textuality can with some legitimacy be said to define the project of hermeneutics. Hans-Georg Gadamer, discussing the Greek ἑρμηνευτικὴ τέχνη, writes that it designates an art 'of proclamation, translation, explanation and interpretation, and includes of course the art of understanding on which it is based, an art necessary *wherever the meaning of something is not openly and unambiguously apparent.*'[3] It thus entails a hierarchical

[3] 'Hermeneutik meint in erste Linie eine kunstvolle Praxis [...] der Verkündung, des Dolmetschens, Erklärens und Auslegens und schließt natürlich die ihr zugrunde liegende Kunst des Verstehens ein, die überall dort erfordert ist, *wo der Sinn von etwas nicht offen und unzweideutig zutage liegt.*' Gadamer 1986/1993, p. 92, my italics and

relationship between the open materiality of the surface and the hidden ideality of what lies behind or below it: the 'words on the page' are a means to an end; their task is to efface themselves by becoming transparent for the meaning they are meant to convey. We could see this principle at work in the scholium cited above: the linguistic consistency of the text itself, the rhetorical 'surface' ('I will not narrate ...'), was a barrier to be overcome on the way to the 'real' meaning ('I have every intention of narrating, but I don't want anyone to notice'); interpretation consisted in penetrating through to this deeper level.

The quest for real meaning thus stands, it would seem, in a certain tension to something called 'rhetoric'; the success of the former depends on overcoming the latter. That is of course no problem as long as whatever is 'rhetorical' about a given text allows itself to be bound to a single, unambiguous, preferably intended meaning on the criteria we have listed above or others like them. This has indeed been the historical role of rhetoric in the philosophical tradition: Friedrich Schleiermacher's enormously influential lectures on *Hermeneutik und Kritik*, published posthumously in 1838, defined rhetoric as the exact counterpart to hermeneutics on the grounds that the latter was the task of decoding the 'thought' that the former had encoded.[4] Problems with this attractively symmetrical model of writing and reading would arise only if the linguistic-rhetorical surface of the text were to refuse its effacement in the interests of what lies behind it and were instead to remain involved in a dialectic between concealment and disclosure. Such 'rhetoric', if we could still call it that, would cast doubt not only upon the claim of hermeneutics to answer questions about the meaning of the text from the text itself, but also upon the basic conceptual categories it applies and must apply in order even to formulate such meaning. But it is important to see that a persistence of this kind would only be the extension of a moment of opacity which occurs in every interpretative process; the place or point of rhetoric is the point at which the text *does not yet mean* what it means or must mean, at which it does not yet (and the crucial question is: how long does this 'not yet' last?) fulfil the criteria of meaning on which hermeneutics is based.

The category of rhetoric—this is a first approximation, I will attempt a more precise definition in a moment—thus stands for an essentially negative potential of language: not to be (or to be something

translation.

4 See Schleiermacher 1977, p. 76, Engl. p. 7.

other than) the expression of an intention. It is not all too difficult to show—we will see a number of examples of this in Chapter 2—that the philological discourse on Pindar can be referred back to exactly this value of rhetoric. In the major works of Pindaric studies since the beginning of the nineteenth century, from Boeckh to New Historicism, the concept of rhetoric is constantly and consistently introduced at the point where, in the text, a certain persistence or resistance makes itself felt: a resistance to being dissolved into pure, intended, unified, historical meaning. As a category of language, it thus marks the limits of a reading which, despite this resistance, is based on the teleological presupposition that meaning and saying will always turn out to be coextensive.

Rhetoric of persuasion, rhetoric of figure

Now if this thesis proves to be true, we can already note two perhaps rather unexpected things about it. On the one hand, we find ourselves dealing with a notion of rhetoric which appears, at least at first glance, to be the exact opposite of rhetoric in its traditional sense. In the founding documents of Western rhetorical theory, the Platonic and Aristotelian discussions of the *τέχνη ῥητορική*, and in their wake, rhetoric has generally been grasped as a means or potential of effective communication, the transmission of a message or force from a speaker or writer to a public. The public should understand and believe or admire what is said; the content of the communication, its plausibility or specific aesthetic effect are to be conveyed across a distance between rhetor and audience in such a way that what arrives at the one end corresponds to what was intended at the other. The subordinate place of figurality in a model of this kind is clear: metaphor, metonymy, irony and other figures serve to further the communication, and therefore have to be transparent for the force or meaning intended.

This familiar concept of rhetoric is the basis upon which research in recent years has increasingly identified the epinicians as a kind of *rhétorique avant la lettre*: as texts designed to convince their immediate recipients of the praiseworthiness of a victorious athlete, they are obviously likely to be interested in the persuasive communication of the merits of the young men they celebrate.[5] Numerous studies in the

[5] See Slater 1976–1977, p. 195 with n. 12 ('I used to say that encomiastic poetry was basically rhetoric [...] and was astonished at the antagonism that this aroused [...] If this be considered too paradoxical, I suggest we look upon it as argumentation, structures of

last thirty years have thus devoted themselves to describing the argumentative strategies at work in the odes and to analysing the 'rhetorical situations' that determine them.[6] To the extent that Pindar's poetry is 'contingent, public, persuasive, and contextual', it fulfils all the essential conditions of rhetorical language in the tradition of classical rhetorical theory.[7] Read in this way, the victory songs clearly belong to the Aristotelian *γένος ἐπιδεικτικόν*: they consist of arguments that and why an athlete or other victor should be praised by a public gathered at a victory celebration; the role of the hearer is here that of a *θεωρός*: '*not to make rulings but to form opinions about and in response to the discourse presented.*'[8] To this end, the epinicians use a large number of identifiable *τόποι* which recur in different variations in more than one song and can be paralleled in later rhetorical texts, as well as argumentative structures that, a century later, Aristotle will call *ἐνθυμήματα*.[9]

It is no part of my intention here to question the incontrovertible legitimacy and importance of this work, or to depreciate its results. If, however, it were to turn out that precisely in that part of Pindaric research most directly concerned with rhetorical structures and communicative strategies, rhetoric still played the role of something to be

poetic argument for the end of glorifying the victor') and 1979a.

[6] Important studies of the communicative rhetoric of the victory odes are Miller 1982, 1982–1983, 1993a, 1993b and Race 1987, 1990, 2002; see also Walker 2000, pp. 185–207. Bundy's remarks on the conventionality of epinician poetry (see Bundy 1986, p. 3 and *passim*, and below, 61 ff.) were central for this branch of research in the latter part of the twentieth century. On the notion of the 'rhetorical situation', see Bitzer 1968 and Biesecker 1989.

[7] *Cf.* Lucaites & Condit 1999, p. 4. Studies on the ideology of the epinicians (and its subversion) such as Rose 1974 and 1992, pp. 141–184 or Kurke 1991 presuppose a 'rhetorical' understanding of the victory songs in this sense.

[8] Walker 2000, p. 9 (his italics) on the basis of Aristotle, *Rhet.* I 3, 1358 b2 ff.

[9] The most comprehensive study of encomiastic *topoi* in Pindar is still Dornseiff 1921 (see in particular p. 2 on *τόποι* and *γένος*). Notes on single *topoi* can be found in Schadewaldt 1966 (see p. 277 f. on the *χρέος*-motif), Steiner 1986 and Krummen 1990, p. 48 ff. (both on recurring metaphors) and Thummer 1968–69, vol. 1, pp. 138–158, who offers a survey. See also Race 1990, an analysis more closely tied to the argumentation of the epinicians than Dornseiff's (*cf.* Race 1990, p. 3). The most comprehensive analysis of the epinicians according to the terms and categories of the classical *partes orationis* is that of Erasmus Schmid (1616); see on this Most 1985b, p. 43 ff. (sceptical) and Heath 1986, p. 89 f. (essentially in agreement). On the *ἐνθύμημα*, see Aristotle, *Rhet.* I 2, 1357 a7–32; with respect to what is often described as Pindar's elliptic style of argumentation—'his general tendency towards implicitness', as Pfeijffer 1999b, p. 2 puts it—see in particular a17 ff.: *ἐὰν γὰρ ᾖ τι τούτων γνώριμον, οὐδὲ δεῖ λέγειν· αὐτὸς γὰρ τοῦτο προστίθησιν ὁ ἀκροατής* with an epinician example; see also Slater 1979a, p. 79.

removed, erased, overcome on the way to meaning—that would be a second unexpected aspect of the hypothesis advanced above. The investigation of this question in the history of scholarship will be the subject of Chapter 2. In this chapter, I want to attempt a definition of rhetoric that does justice to what we have observed to be problematic about its relationship to meaning, and to relate this definition to the traditional concept of rhetoric. My argument, simply put, is that the tension between rhetoric and meaning whose effects we will be investigating in Pindar's epinicians is already latent in the traditional understanding of rhetoric—that is, in the *classical*, Platonic-Aristotelian understanding which has remained authoritative for modern rhetorical theory and which, in its presuppositions and implicit teleology, is more closely bound to the philosophical context in which it was first formulated than has sometimes been realized.[10] Far from being 'untheoretical' or 'pragmatic', classical rhetoric is instead intimately connected with a series of hypotheses whose explication and demonstration have from the very beginning been among the most important tasks of philosophy as metaphysics. Among them are theories of the subject based on a relationship between intention and action; the notion of communication as the act of a subject conceived in just this way; an ontological theory of beings as made up of substances and accidents (this becomes, in semiotics, the model of a material vehicle and a cognitive content of language, which in turn provides the conceptual basis for what we might call the 'standard theory' of metaphor); a theory of cause and effect (Leibniz's 'principle of sufficient reason', which can also lead to a theory of perception as the effect of objects on a receptive subjectivity); and so on. It would be precipitate to call interrelationships such as these between classical rhetoric and the rest of metaphysics *complicities*; their partial catalogue here is merely intended to indicate that there is nothing about the traditional notion of rhetoric whose plausibility and canonicity is drawn from any source other than the familiarity of a particular philosophical programme. This programme formed the basis of the very first attempts to formalize rhetoric in the fourth century B.C.; if it is called into question, such an event cannot fail to affect rhetorical theory, least of all when this questioning is carried out by literature and the practice of literary interpretation.

But the connection between Plato's ῥητορικὴ τέχνη and Derrida's *l'époque de la métaphysique* also helps, conversely, to explain how a

[10] This is also true of the classical notion of the metaphor: see Derrida, 'La mythologie blanche' (= Derrida 1972b, pp. 247–324), p. 261 f., Engl. p. 219 f.

reinterpretation of rhetoric in the work of such theorists as Paul de Man could become a controversial topic in literary theory in the later twentieth century. What was being critiqued was less a specific branch of humanistic learning than its metaphysical foundations themselves. One of the central elements of de Man's critique was a re-ordering or reversal of the implicit teleology within rhetoric which subordinates figurality and its masking effects to the communication of persuasion and the disclosure of meaning, an opposition we have already seen to be at work in pre-modern commentary on Pindar.[11] Rhetorical theory, ancient and modern, has as a rule tended to marginalise the one side of the negativity postulated by Σ *Nem.* 10. 6—rhetoric as concealment or misdirection—by making the part of the theory concerned with the paradigmatic non-agreement between what a text explicitly says and what it in fact means—the theory of tropes as part of the theory of figures—to an explicitly subordinate part of a 'general' rhetoric of persuasion, and by viewing persuasion as the genuinely original moment of rhetoric. This strategy was indeed not always followed. Models of rhetoric from Ramus to structuralism attempted to respond to the epistemological difficulties caused by the classical grounding of rhetoric in factors necessarily external to speech—the hearer, the situation—by concentrating on the intertextual, essentially linguistic category of the figure. Ramus' polemical reduction of the system, inherited from the Middle Ages and in its essential contours still Aristotelian-Ciceronian, to the element of figurality in the mid-sixteenth century provided the basis for the complex theories of figurality developed by such rhetoricians as Du Marsais in the eighteenth century and Fontanier in the nineteenth. The systematic foundation of these taxonomies in the 'basic figures' of metaphor and metonymy was one result of the work of the Russian formalists (Èjchenbaum, Jakobson) and their successors and was taken over from them, in particular by Lacan, into psychoanalysis. But the consensus of rhetorical theory and historiography has in general been extremely sceptical of such models.[12]

[11] De Man attributes this move—incorrectly, I believe—to Nietzsche: see de Man 1979, p. 105 f. and *cf.* Nietzsche 1982–1995, vol. 4, p. 427.

[12] On Ramus, see Ong 1958 and Knape 1996, pp. 237–259 with further literature. On the theory of figures proposed by Du Marsais and Fontanier, see Todorov 1977, pp. 85–139, Engl. pp. 84–110—a chapter that fittingly enough bears the title 'Fin de la rhétorique'—the (mostly negative) discussion in Perelman 1979, p. 1 ff., and Eggs 2001, p. 1137 ff. See also Derrida 1972b, pp. 302–307, Engl. pp. 253–257, and Campe 1990, pp. 489–497. For a structuralist theory of figures, see for example Jakobson & Halle 1965,

Perhaps no modern literary theorist has protested against this 'restricted rhetoric' and called for a remarginalisation of the figure within a rhetoric of persuasion more emphatically (and influentially) than Gérard Genette, writing with reference to the structuralist *Rhétorique générale* of the *Groupe μ*:[13]

> Aristotle's *Rhetoric* made no claims to be 'general' [...]: yet in its range it was so, and so much so that a theory of figures did not yet merit any particular mention in it; just a few pages on comparison and metaphor, in one Book (out of three) devoted to style and composition, a tiny territory, an out-of-the-way region, lost in the immensity of an empire.[14]

The substitution and displacement carried out by tropes and figures formed the essential criterion of the notion of rhetoric propounded in the *Rhétorique générale*. Genette's opposition to this concentration on figurality presupposes that the operational centre of rhetorical theory—even if the French theorist rejects the notion of a 'centre' of rhetoric—lies somewhere else, in other parts of the Aristotelian work and the tradition which stems from it.[15] There, perhaps in the theory of evidence or the *genera causarum*, one would find a place, a *capitale*, which would be defined by rhetoric's persuasive effect and from whose perspective the theory of figures would build something like a periphery. And, of course, Genette is not wrong: classical rhetoric, as we find it first in Plato and Aristotle, does indeed intend a hierarchy in the rhetorical system in just this sense. Rhetoric wants to say what ought to be said; the communication of intent is at its very centre. The mere fact that, in order to achieve this, it has recourse to forms of language which give rise to a disjunction of meaning and saying is unimportant, a marginal phenomenon whose temporary historical reign in the realm of rhetorical theory was, in the eighteenth and

pp. 90–96. How much Lacan owes to Jakobson in this point becomes clear in 'L'instance de la lettre dans l'inconscient' (= Lacan 1999, vol. 1, pp. 490–526, Engl. pp. 412–441), originally published in 1957 (see in particular p. 503, n. 13, Engl. p. 440, n. 13).

[13] Dubois *et al.* 1970.

[14] 'La *Rhétorique* d'Aristote ne se voulait pas « générale » [...]: elle l'était, et l'était si bien, dans l'amplitude de sa visée, qu'une théorie des figures n'y méritait encore aucune mention particulière; quelque pages seulement sur la comparaison et la métaphore, dans un Livre (sur trois) consacré au style et à la composition, territoire exigu, canton détourné, perdu dans l'immensité d'un Empire.' Genette, 'La rhétorique restreinte' (= Genette 1972, 21–40), p. 21, Engl. Genette 1982, p. 103. On Genette's theory of rhetoric in general, see Harlos 1986.

[15] *Cf.* Genette 1972, p. 33, Engl. Genette 1982, p. 114.

nineteenth centuries, responsible for its death.[16]

Genette's thesis, put forward with explicit reference to Aristotle, that rhetoric should primarily be understood from the perspective of its occasionally conditioned work of communication has long since carried the field against the structuralist rhetoric of figurality and is authoritative in large parts of the contemporary discussion. Gert Ueding, whose 'Tübinger Rhetorik' belongs, together with Chaim Perelman und Lucie Olbrechts-Tyteca's *Nouvelle Rhétorique*,[17] to the most influential European approaches to rhetorical theory in recent decades, argues in his voluminous *Historisches Wörterbuch der Rhetorik* that as a result of its immense and diverse reception in different disciplines and media, the concept of rhetoric has been increasingly eroded. He identifies four (in his opinion insufficient) strategies which attempt to respond to this erosion: (1) the relegation of rhetoric to an area of merely antiquarian interest; (2) the oversimplified identification of rhetoric with whatever happens to have been called 'rhetoric' at a particular time in a particular place, and the concomitant surrender of its (trans-temporal) systematic character; (3) the normative recourse to an allegedly unified conception of rhetoric in the works of certain canonical ancient authors (Isocrates, Aristotle, Cicero, and Quintilian); and finally (4) the selective reception of single elements of the 'comprehensive, systematic and historically differentiated theoretical edifice' for specific lines of questioning in areas such as semiotics or textual theory.[18] Against these 'reductions', Ueding argues for an understanding of rhetoric as a comprehensive system articulated differently at different times, and for research on rhetoric that is concerned to demonstrate how a specific speech can be understood as the articulation of such a system. The condition of this articulation is the historically contingent hearer:

> Even if rhetoric can claim to be such a system, the point and content of rhetorical theory still remains the rhetorical practice which changes it. In

[16] Analyses of the 'death of rhetoric' as a result of its fixation on *elocutio* are offered, from different perspectives, by Curtius 1948, Perelman 1984, Barthes, 'L'ancienne rhétorique' (= Barthes 2002, vol. III, pp. 527–601 [first published in 1970]), pp. 555–559 (A. 7: 'Mort de la rhétorique'), Campe 1990 and Till 2004. On the 'resurrection' of the rhetoric of persuasion see in particular Bender & Wellbery 1990 and the contributions to Lucaites *et al.* 1999.

[17] Perelman & Olbrechts-Tyteca ^{2}1970.

[18] Ueding 2005, p. 1430, my translation. The fourth reduction presumably stands for Paul de Man's conception of rhetoric as a theory of literature; *cf.* Schmidt-Haberkamp 2005 and see below, p. 44 ff.

> the light of this principle, the order of the three instances of speaker, speech (or speech-object) and addressee which participate in every speech-act is determined [...]. Not the speaker, but rather the listener [is] in charge.[19]

Ueding's conception of a trans-historical, systematic rhetoric and the decipherability of the single speech as an articulation of such a system depends crucially on the notion of a hearer who shares a context with the speaker and thus constitutes it. He must therefore have recourse, like Plato, for the normative and epistemological foundations of this model to the presence of the addressee, which in turn is necessarily bound to the notion of the context of persuasion and thus to the occasionality of rhetoric. If, however, the addressee is decisive for rhetorical practice, then the communicative intention of the speaker no longer suffices to determine the specific form of rhetorical language. This is understood and intended both by Ueding's and by Plato's theory of rhetoric. The consequence, however, as paradoxical as it may seem, is this: as soon as the attempt is made on the basis of such a model to formulate the relationship between the content to be communicated on the part of the speaker and actual use of language in rhetorical practice, 'rhetoricity' reveals itself as that which, in the language of the speaker, *diverges* from the intention ascribed to him—in other words: it reveals itself as a figure. Ueding, and with him the tradition of classical rhetoric, has thus re-introduced the displacement of figurality as the criterion of persuasive rhetoricity whilst at the same time arguing in the most unambiguous terms for its teleological subordination to just that persuasion. A curious reversal, but one not without a tradition of its own.[20]

[19] 'Der Zweckinhalt rhetorischer Theorie bleibt auch unter solchem Systemanspruch die sie verändernde rednerische Praxis. Im Lichte dieses Prinzips gestaltet sich die Ordnung der drei an jeder Redehandlung grundlegend beteiligten Instanzen von Redner, Rede (-Gegenstand) und Adressat [...]. [N]icht der Redner, sondern der Zuhörer [ist] die richtunggebende Instanz.' Ueding 2005, p. 1431 (my translation). Slater 1979a, p. 79 cites Vico in this sense: 'The end sought by eloquence always depends on the speaker's audience, and he must govern his speech in accordance with their opinions' (from *De nostri temporis studiorum ratione*, ed. Ferrari, p. 10); *cf.* Perelmann & Olbrechts-Tyteca [2]1970, p. 31.

[20] On Ueding's Tübingen Rhetoric, see also the critical discussion in Till 2004, pp. 19–26. Disquieting from a deconstructive perspective is further the role played in these traditions of rhetoric by the presence or being-present of the speaker for him- or herself. Most theorists seem to assume that rhetoric can ultimately be referred to a solid core of present meanings, and that this presence is the *présence à soi* of the rhetor. What the speaker wants to say is present to him- or herself in such a way that it requires and indeed allows no rhetorical mediation. (*Cf.* however Perelman & Olbrechts-Tyteca

Renversement du platonisme

A close reading of Plato's dialogues on rhetoric can show that whereas contemporary rhetorical theory does not hesitate to invoke these texts to support an unambiguous definition of rhetoric as persuasive speech, they also contain elements which point towards a different notion of rhetoric altogether, and which indeed may do more justice to the relationship between concealment and disclosure observed within rhetoric (rightly, we have argued) by the author of Σ *Nem.* 10. 6 than the way they have usually been understood. Such a reading concentrates—in exactly the sense of that *renversement du platonisme* in which Gilles Deleuze saw the task of modern philosophy—on the most important dialogue on *διαίρεσις* or the 'division' of a genus into species, the *Sophist*.[21] In this conversation, the Eleatic Stranger attempts, at Socrates' request, to define the essence of the sophist. By dividing up the *genera*, the sophist's true mode of being is to be discovered in its specific difference to that of the statesman and the philosopher. The project is not new: as early as the *Gorgias*, Socrates proposes a division of activities in which sophistry and rhetoric form the two closely related species of that 'practice of toadying' (*κολακευτικὴ ἐμπειρία*) concerned with the state; in the terminology of the *Sophist*, they are 'false imitations' (*φαντάσματα*) of the 'art of law-giving' (*τέχνη νομοθετική*) or of 'justice' (*δικαιοσύνη*).[22] Neither in the *Sophist* nor in the *Gorgias* is the point at issue a complete or near-complete taxonomy of particular activities; the goal is rather—and this is what Deleuze discerns as the real concern of Platonic dialectics—to identify the legitimate candidate for the privileged representation of the quality in question.[23]

We recall: the *Gorgias* seeks to determine whose way of life represents the greatest good for himself and his city—the rhetor's or the philosopher's? The answer will depend on whose art or *τέχνη* can guarantee true knowledge of the good, that is, of justice and injustice. Gorgias points out that this is rhetoric's field (454 b7); if this is correct,

[2]1970, p. 8.) On the problems caused by this assumption, see Derrida 1967b (on an analogous thesis in Husserl's *Logische Untersuchungen*) and below, p. 217 ff. on the *Tenth Olympian.*

[21] See Deleuze 1968, p. 82, Engl. p. 71, alluding to Nietzsche's 'umgedrehter Platonismus' (*cf.* Nietzsche 1988, vol. 7, p. 199, 7 [156]). See further Foucault 1970 and Patton 1994, esp. 146 ff. (and *cf.* de Man 1979, p. 109).

[22] *Gorg.* 463 e5–466 a3; *cf. Soph.* 236 b4 ff.

[23] See Deleuze 1969, p. 292 ff., Engl. p. 253 ff.

and given the definition of a τέχνη in 465 a2–6, a *genuine* rhetor will necessarily possess the knowledge in question and thus—on the grounds of the principle in 460 b6 f. , ὁ τὰ δίκαια μεμαθηκὼς δίκαιος—himself be just;[24] in terms of the theory of Ideas, he will partake of the Idea of justice. But it quickly becomes clear that the rhetoric championed by Socrates' interlocutors, at least, knows nothing of justice in this sense; its practitioner merely imitates the just man, without any direct relationship to the Idea, in front of a carefully defined audience. This imitation is revealed as such in the conversation with Gorgias by means of division. After Socrates has characterized rhetoric as a 'manufacturer of conviction' (πειθοῦς δημιουργός, *Gorg.* 453 a1 f.),[25] he sets up 'conviction' itself (πειθώ) as a genre divided by διαίρεσις into subgenres whose specific difference from each other consists exclusively in their respective relationships to the truth. If πειθώ as rhetoric, practised by the ignorant in front of the ignorant, only produces 'belief' (πίστις) or 'opinions' (δόξαι), πειθώ as 'instruction' (πειθὼ διδασκαλική), like that imparted by teachers of medicine or mathematics and to which the 'genuine rhetoric' (ἡ ἀληθινὴ ῥητορική) of 517 c5 would necessarily belong, leads to true knowledge or ἐπιστήμη (*Gorg.* 454 c7–455 a5). This division of πειθώ and of rhetoric according to the criterion of truth serves to identify the simulacra as illegitimate or counterfeit members of the genres of true τέχνη; they have 'stolen into them' without permission (464 c–d). As a consequence, not only does dialectical philosophy turn out to be the best way of life; the philosopher also reveals himself to be the only possible 'true rhetor' (ὁ ὀρθῶς ῥητορικός, 508 c1), since only he who has seen the truth, about justice or anything else, can model it in speech; only his speech is true, is *rightfully* rhetoric.[26] The sophist-as-rhetor, whose speech is *by defini-*

[24] *Cf.* also *Prot.* 352 c1–d2, Aristotle, *Eth. Eud.* I 5, 1216 b6–8 and Xenophon, *Mem.* III 9. 5.

[25] This formulation captures a real element of Gorgias' theory of language (see Gorgias, *Hel.* 8), although it is most probably Plato's own (see Dodds 1959, p. 203 *ad Gorg.* 453 a2 and Hellwig 1973, pp. 26 and 32).

[26] The use and function of the ἀληθινὴ ῥητορική mentioned at 517 c5 are described at 480 b9 ff. and referred to again briefly at 508 b4; there can be no doubt that it is, to all intents and purposes, identical with the dialectics practised by Socrates. But Gorgias' rhetoric of mere opinion cannot hope to compete with a rhetoric that is in practice indistinguishable from philosophy—that discipline which makes claim to being a privileged representation of the truth. The *Phaedrus* confirms this result, as Rapp 2002, vol. 1, p. 223 remarks: 'Wenn die Wertschätzung der philosophischen Rhetorik im *Phaedrus* auf dem Anspruch beruht, daß die philosophische Methode eine uneingeschränkte Bedeutung auch in dem von den Rhetoren beanspruchten Bereich hat, dann nimmt der Dialog *Phaedrus* nichts von der für die Rhetorik-Kritik des *Gorgias* maßgeblichen Ver-

tion not an image of the truth, produces, in the eyes of the knowledgeable, only opinions.

It is striking that the characteristic structure of the δόξαι on which the rhetoric of simulation builds and which it evokes is the trope of *amplificatio* and its converse. The rhetor makes the small appear great and the great appear small.[27] These are exactly the terms in which the Eleatic Stranger—who designates the speech of the sophist as a certain 'art of persuasion' (*πιθανουργικὴ τέχνη*, *Soph.* 222 c9–d1)—describes the moment at which those who have been previously deceived suddenly realize the truth in *Sophist* 234 d7. The reversal of the situation and the equation of what is not identical but merely similar are the privileged effects of this rhetoric of appearance. How are they possible?

The possibility and necessity of rhetoric consists, in the *Gorgias*, in the absence of undeniable evidence of the truth. This grounding is achieved, as elsewhere in the Platonic corpus, by the myth.[28] In the closing myth of the Final Judgement (*Gorg.* 523 a–524 a), Zeus eliminates the conditions under which rhetoric functions as a *πειθοῦς δημιουργός* by taking from the dead the clothing of their bodies and uncovering their souls for the direct apperception and judgement of the judges.[29] Before this jury, no pleas or speeches are held, for no rhetoric can rely on the persuasive power of opinion when the evidence of the soul (non- and pre-linguistic, the pure vision of what is to be judged) is directly present to its arbiter. The myth creates a situation in which soul is directly perceived by soul (*τὸν κριτὴν* [...] *αὐτῇ τῇ ψυχῇ αὐτὴν τὴν ψυχὴν θεωροῦντα*, 523 e3 f.), and thus describes the theoretical model according to which the dialectical distinction between the rhetoric of mere persuasion without ontological foundation on the one hand and the rhetoric of instruction on the basis of having seen the truth on the other—as indeed between the two ways of life they

bindung der Rhetorik mit dem epistemischen Modus des Scheins und der Meinung und nichts von der Kennzeichnung dieses Modus als defizient zurück.'

[27] This description of rhetoric was obviously a *topos*; see, in Plato, *Apol.* 18b, 19b, 23d and *Phdr.* 267 a6–b2; *cf.* also Isocr., *Paneg.* 8 and Hermog., Περὶ ἰδεῶν II 7 on δεινότης. The variation that the rhetor makes the weaker argument the stronger, already exploited by Aristophanes (*Nub.* 889–1104), is ascribed by Aristotle (*Rhet.* II 24, 1402 a24) to Protagoras. On the philosophical characterization of rhetoric as a whole as *amplificatio*, see further Weische 1989 who quotes Quintilian, *Inst.* VIII 3. 89: *vis oratoris omnis in augendo minuendoque consistit.*

[28] On this function of myth in Plato, see Deleuze 1968, p. 85 ff., Engl. p. 73 ff., and *id.* 1969, pp. 293–295, Engl. pp. 254–256.

[29] *Cf.* Niehues-Pröbsting 1987, p. 108.

imply—can be carried out: the pure intuition of the characteristics of true being.

The conditions of merely plausible rhetoric in the *Gorgias* are analogous to the structural implications of writing in Plato's second 'rhetorical' dialogue, the *Phaedrus*. If the essence of counterfeit rhetoric demands that the intention and knowledge of the speaker are not evident, the absence of evident meaning is also part of the essence of writing, and this is why it replies so unsatisfactorily to questions that its father—the ground of its meaning—must rush to help it (*Phdr.* 275 d4–e5).[30] The complicity between rhetoric and writing in the *Phaedrus* can be seen not least in the fact that Lysias' speech is only present as writing and cannot defend itself when Socrates and Phaedrus begin to criticize it. Lysias himself is not 'present', as Socrates at the beginning of the dialogue ironically suggests (228 e1). Writing negates the presence of the father by substituting for him; it is as his representative a substitute that—as *simulacre*—usurps the place of what it represents.[31]

But this usurpation is fatal, for only the presence of the father—that is, the possibility of reaching a level of meaning or truth which is no longer merely the mediate representation of something beyond it, but rather the immediate present truth *itself*—allows for the distinction between the rightful and a false aspirant to the privileged representation of what is meant. In the *Gorgias*, the specific difference between the speech of the sophist and that of the philosopher was based not on

[30] The disturbing thing about this line of thought according to Derrida is that the lostness of writing is not merely a characteristic of letters, but instead of all language as soon as recourse is had to its systematicity and to the recoverability of its meaning in the absence of any particular speaker or addressee; see Derrida, 'Signature événement contexte' (= Derrida 1972b, pp. 365–393), pp. 369–381, Engl. pp. 311–321. It is the defining trait of a sign, including a linguistic sign, that it can, in principle, be repeated an unlimited number of times and still be recognisable as itself, and this in the radical absence of any particular speaker at all. This absence is demanded by the system of rhetoric, including the Platonic system, because it is essential to the Platonic-Aristotelian notion of τέχνη: the foundational λόγος must always contain within itself (a) the potential of its repetition in the absence of a specific speaker—a τέχνη is *teachable*—and (b) the possibility of its transference to individuals who, as specific individuals, were not intended by or even known to the τέχνη's teacher—a τέχνη is *applicable*. Rhetoric as a τέχνη thus presupposes the absence of any specific persons at all. It not only depends on the speaker being able to give reasons for the effects of his or her speech that are only verifiable in the presence of a hearer, but also on the principles of this effect being formulated in such a way that they can be applied to others—*i.e.*, absent persons—and can thus be taught.

[31] *Cf.* Deleuze 1969, p. 296 n. 2: 'L'écriture est un simulacre, un faux prétendant, pour autant qu'elle prétend s'emparer du logos par violence et par ruse, ou même le supplanter sans passer par le père' (Engl. p. 361 n. 2). Deleuze refers here to Derrida's 'La pharmacie de Platon' (= Derrida 1972a, pp. 77–213).

what they said, but rather on the different relationship between what they said on the one hand and the relationship of the speaker to the reality of his privileged topic, justice, on the other; a relationship which could be verified only at the scene of the Final Judgement, and which otherwise must and should remain unclear. In the *Phaedrus*, the difference between the writing of the logograph and the orality of the true philosopher consists in the fact that, whereas latter claims to preserve the immediacy of evidence, the former must do without it: the speechwriter does not speak in his own person, writing must displace the meaning (the living intention) of its father.[32] In the *Sophist*, the Stranger defines the sophist as a simulacrum of the philosopher: the *φάντασμα* looks like what it claims to be similar to, creates however this effect of similarity not by means of real (inward, ontological) similarity—similarity to the Idea of what it is meant to be similar to[33]—but only through (merely external) imitation of the object without the Idea (in which the true being of the image would have to partake) and by means of a real difference. As an example of this situation, the Stranger describes a building or a large picture whose proportions only create the impression of symmetry for an observer because they are, in reality, not symmetrical at all (*Soph.* 235 c9–236 a8).[34] The effect of similarity created by the simulacrum is based on an essential non-similarity; the simulacrum internalises the point of view of the observer that makes the imitation possible and necessary. We have already identified this internalised perspective as the essential presupposition of classical theories of rhetoric.[35] Here, Plato exposes the ontological implications of such a presupposition. Only someone with the privileged access of the philosopher to the Ideas, to the pres-

[32] *Cf.* Derrida 1972a, p. 84: 'Le logographe, au sens strict, rédigeait, à l'intention des plaideurs, des discours qu'il ne prononçait pas lui-même, qu'il n'assistait pas, si l'on peut dire, en personne, et qui produisaient leurs effets en son absence. Écrivant ce qu'il ne dit pas, ne dirait et sans doute ne penserait jamais en vérité, l'auteur du discours écrit est déjà campé dans la posture du sophiste: l'homme de la non-présence et de la non-vérité' (Engl. p. 68).

[33] According to *Prot.* 330 c–d and *Phd.* 100 c, the Ideas also predicate the qualities for whose presence in the *πράγματα* they are responsible of themselves; the 'Argument of the *τρίτος ἄνθρωπος*' in *Parm.* 132 a1–133 a7 depends crucially on this assumption (see Vlastos 1973, pp. 342–365). Thus, everything that possesses the quality *f* due to its participation in the Idea F also resembles the Idea F, since F also possesses the quality *f*. See however Fujisawa 1974 who denies that the self-predication of the Ideas is a genuinely Platonic doctrine, and Scaltsas 1992 who considers it to be necessarily false and the 'Third-Man-Argument' of the *Parmenides* untenable.

[34] *Cf.* Patton 1994, p. 150.

[35] See above, p. 32.

ence of truth, would be in a position to distinguish between the true similarity of the image (the philosopher) and the counterfeited similarity of the simulacrum (the sophist). Everything depends on who is speaking when, at the end of the *Sophist*, we find ourselves in a position in which—to all appearances—it is no longer easily possible to distinguish the sophist from Socrates—or even from the Stranger himself.

Deleuze describes the situation at *Soph.* 267 d4–268 b5 as follows:

> [I]t may be that the end of the *Sophist* contains the most extraordinary adventure of Platonism: as a consequence of searching in the direction of the simulacrum and of leaning over its abyss, Plato discovers, in the flash of an instant, that the simulacrum is not simply a false copy, but that it places in question the very notions of copy and model. The final definition of the Sophist leads us to the point where we can no longer distinguish him from Socrates himself—the ironist working in private by means of brief arguments.[36]

'... dans l'éclair d'un instant'? Hardly: this conclusion is foreshadowed long before the end of the dialogue, indeed after less than a third of its length, at the end of the last definition of the sophist before the central discussion of the being of non-being (the sophist as purifier of the soul: *Soph.* 226 a–231 c). Here it had already become very difficult to distinguish him from Socrates; according to Cornford—and a not inconsiderable part of the literature has followed him in this—Plato provides us in this passage with 'a description which [...] applies to Socrates and no one else'.[37] Did the British Hellenist allow himself to

[36] '[I]l se peut que la fin du *Sophiste* contienne l'aventure la plus extraordinaire du platonisme : à force de chercher du côté du simulacre et de se pencher sur son abîme, Platon dans l'éclair d'un instant découvre qu'il n'est pas simplement une fausse copie, mais qu'il met en question les notions mêmes de copie [...] et de modèle. La définition finale du sophiste nous mène au point où nous ne pouvons plus le distinguer de Socrate lui-même : l'ironiste opérant en privé par arguments brefs.' Deleuze 1969, p. 295, Engl. p. 256. See also Deleuze 1968, p. 168, Engl. p. 156.

[37] Cornford 1935, p. 177. In his lectures on the *Sophist* in the winter semester of 1924/25 in Marburg, Heidegger had already interpreted what the Stranger at 231 b7 calls *ἡ γένει γενναία σοφιστική* as 'die »*echtbürtige*«, die aus dem echten Stamm ihres eigentlichen Seins herkommende [*sc.* *σοφιστική*], die das eigentlich ist, als was der faktische Sophist sich lediglich ausgibt' (Heidegger 1992, p. 380, Engl. p. 263; his italics, my spacing). *Cf.* Trevaskis 1955–56, Bernadete 1960, p. 138 f., Sayre 1969, pp. 148–157, Starr 1973–74, Klein 1977, p. 26, de Rijk 1986, p. 80 n. 13, Cobb 1990, p. 16 and Vlastos 1991, p. 23. Dissent is expressed by Taylor ^{6}1949, p. 380 f. and Kerferd 1954. Friedländer ^{3}1964–1975, vol. 3, p. 237 relates the passage, like Cornford, to the philosopher, recognizes however at the same time the ironist's game with a similarity that can-

be misled by the similarity of description? As the Stranger says, the purifier of the soul works with questions and entangles his interlocutor (who, at the beginning, believes that he knows things which he, in reality, does not) in contradictions, so that at the end he only believes that he knows what he really does know (*Soph.* 230 b4–d4).[38] In the following lines, he warns Theaetetus not to take the 'purification' (*καθαρμός*) of the soul for the definitive task of the sophist, since mere 'similarity' (*ὁμοιότης*), does not, of itself, mean that two things are identical; he accepts the equivalence nevertheless (*Soph.* 231 a6–b1). The rhetorician (described at *Soph.* 235 a1 as an 'imitator' or *μιμητής*) convinces his young or inexperienced listener (*ἔτι πόρρω τῶν πραγμάτων τῆς ἀληθείας ἀφεστῶτας*, 234 c4) that things which are really only images of beings are themselves beings; in the *Phaedrus*, this confusion of similarity and identity was the specific effect created by rhetoric (*Phdr.* 261 e2–262 c3).[39] Now, at the end of the *Sophist*, we are presented with the following statement: the sophist is 'an imitator who belongs to that part of irony which produces contradictions;[40] irony itself belongs to the part of imitation based on 'opinion' (δόξα), opinion in turn belongs to the genre of simulacra-production, simulacra-production finally is a subdivision of the art of producing images and is not a divine, but rather a human part of the art of production

not be unambiguously distinguished from identity: '[E]in sehr ironischer Zufall [hat] mitten in das Verfahren eben des Sokrates hineingesteuert […]. Oder wenigstens in ein Verfahren, das dem des Sokrates zum Verwechseln ähnlich sieht. Ob wir hier nicht dem Sophisten zu viel Ehre antun, bezweifelt der Eleat selber. Daß wir vielleicht den Philosophen erfassen, wird durch den seltsamen Namen »hoch- und edelgeborene Wissenskunst« […] ebenso ausgesagt wie versteckt.' Notomi 1999, p. 277 folds the ontological relationship of the philosopher to his *φάντασμα*, the sophist, back onto itself and writes that 'the educational purifier, if properly understood, was *not* a sophist, though he appeared to be similar. [He was] an *apparition* of the sophist' (his italics).

[38] It is interesting that, in the fifth diaeresis, the Stranger defines the sophist as an eristic who earns money by conversing with his pupils (*Soph.* 224 e6–226 a4). The difference between him and Socrates consists here, it would seem, only in the biographical detail of whether the instruction he gives is also his means of livelihood, and some scholars have taken this to be in fact the most important distinction between sophistry and philosophy (so *e.g.* Hellwig 1973, p. 118). We are of course not informed about the Stranger's source of income.

[39] There we also find a description of the philosopher's technique of 'collection' (*συναγωγή*) which—as the counterpart of *διαίρεσις*—draws what is multitudinously dispersed back to an Idea (265 d3 f.). In the *Sophist*, it is the sophist who makes use of this method (*Soph.* 240 a4–6).

[40] The difference between *δημοσίᾳ τε καὶ μακροῖς λόγοις* and *ἰδίᾳ τε καὶ βραχέσι λόγοις*, which makes up the last step of the division in *Soph.* 268 b1–10, is declared in the *Phaedrus* to be irrelevant for the definition of rhetoric (*Phdr.* 261 a7 ff.).

(ποιητική) in general' (268 c8–d2). Is this *true*? The Stranger's last words in the dialogue are these: whoever defines the sophist in this way 'will, *it seems* (ὡς ἔοικεν), speak most truly' (d2–4). Once again, the point at which the definitions of the sophist and the philosopher part ways is the question of their respective knowledge of the truth (as already intimated at 253 e7–254 b1), and once again the εἴδωλον, the simulacrum that the sophist *is*, finds its way into the description of whomever it is who speaks just like Socrates. Who is ironically turning the tables here: the sophist—or the Stranger himself?[41]

As a result of this situation, two interpretations of rhetoric—perhaps even two interpretations of the interpretation of rhetoric—are open to us.

1. According to the first, successful interpretation depends crucially on identifying figurative or rhetorical language as such in order to translate it into literal meaning. In the terms of the *Sophist*, the question is therefore: are we to understand that the sophist, who is also a rhetorician, is *the same* as Socrates, or is he only *similar* to him? The distinction between these two options necessarily presupposes the possibility of distinguishing between identity and similarity. Similarity is not merely a lesser degree of identity, nor is identity merely a particularly high degree of similarity. Only what is different can be similar, only what is the same is identical: the terms can only be predicates of opposites.[42] The difference between the two assertions is therefore considerable, and everything depends on the epistemological authority of the person who determines the identity or difference of the philosopher and the sophist-rhetorician. Is the Eleatic Stranger a philosopher or a sophist? In the former case, the sophist will be *similar* to the philosopher; he is, as the Stranger openly asserts, merely an εἴδωλον of the philosopher; he does not partake of the Idea of philosophy, but instead only imitates Socrates. That is the proper, literal meaning of what is said, and if he is a philosopher, the Stranger will not be misleading us here. But the possibility also exists that the Stranger speaks just as ironically as the sophist. In this case, the definition of the sophist at the end of the dialogue that bears his name

[41] *Cf.* Rosen 1983, p. 313: 'One must be unusually obtuse not to see and wonder at the Stranger's own irony. The culmination of the hunt for the sophist is to identify Socrates as a practitioner of that art.' According to Derrida 1984a, p. 117, 'the 'Good beyond Being' (ἐπέκεινα τῆς οὐσίας) of Plato's *Republic* [509 b9] [...] or the confrontation with the 'Stranger' in the *Sophist* are already traces of an alterity [within the self-identity of the *Logos*] which refuses to be totally domesticated.'

[42] *Cf.* Deleuze 1969, p. 302, Engl. p. 261.

may be meant ironically, figuratively. The word σοφιστής will then denote the opposite of the sophist—and throughout the whole of the Platonic corpus, that has consistently been Socrates himself. To the extent that we decide to follow this branching path of interpretation, the sophist and his definition at the end of the dialogue are either meant *literally* (the Stranger speaks—in question-and-answer-form amongst friends—about the ironic *etc.* sophist and means him too: he is *not* the same as the philosopher) or *ironically* (the Stranger describes the sophist in such a way that he *appears* similar to the philosopher, but what he *really means* is that he and the philosopher are in fact identical). This first interpretation (of the interpretation) of rhetoric would see itself forced to decide between these two options: either the passage is meant literally/seriously/philosophically and what it says is what it means, or its meaning is figurative/ironic/rhetorical, and this layer of figurality must be set aside in order reach the true meaning. The 'either/or'-question forces us to decide between meaning and rhetoric; an interpretation of the text is only possible after we have made this decision.

2. The second approach to interpretation, however, would doubt the viability of this attractive plan, and that on the basis of Plato's own argumentation. We recall Deleuze's insight, quoted above, that the sophist-as-simulacrum 'is not simply a false copy, but [rather] places in question the very notions of copy and model.'[43] Binding the definition of the sophist to its own proper meaning is impossible because the *Sophist* itself invalidates the concepts on the basis of which one might decide about the identity or non-identity of the sophist and the philosopher—precisely the difference between the mere effect of similarity created by the simulacrum and the inward and spiritual similarity of the image. *When the Idea is absent*, there are only similarity-effects, and this absence affects the entire chain of Platonic notions of presence: the father and king of the *Phaedrus*, the sun of the *Republic*, the evidence of the soul in the *Gorgias*—the presence of the Idea. Let us not forget that the philosopher of the *Sophist* remains invisible only because he resides at the hidden, illuminating and blinding source of the Idea of being (*Soph.* 254 a8–10). But the non-presence of the truth, the lack of relationship to being is the constant and most basic presupposition of the speech of the rhetorician; indeed, it is—as the proliferation of the mere imitations of the simulacra—its defining trait. 'The sophist', says Deleuze, 'is not the being (or the non-

[43] Deleuze 1969, p. 295, Engl. p. 256 (cited above, p. 39).

being) of contradiction, but the one who raises everything to the level of simulacra and maintains them in that state.'[44]

To the extent that the λόγος of the Platonic sophist is rhetoric, its implications cannot be captured in the simple teleological scheme of the literal as goal and the figurative as detour. According to this model—attributed by traditional rhetorical theory to Plato with a legitimacy not entirely undone by what is being said here—the essence or truth of rhetorical language is literal or philosophical language, its destiny and end its sublimation or *Aufhebung* into meaning. But this, the properly metaphysical interpretation of language, is not the only tale the dialogues tell. A second line of argumentation in these texts, working against or within the first, suggests a troubling possibility: that rhetoric might *persist* beyond or beside meaning, a non-essential essence of rhetoric apart from or outside the truth that is meant. On this level, rhetoric would no longer be the situation in which we know that something is meant figuratively—subordinate to a literal meaning which lies behind the figurative one—but rather that in which we have no possibility of deciding between a literal and a figurative reading.[45] The *Sophist* indeed deprives us at this point of every possibility of deciding. Rhetoric would then be opposed to the literal meaning only at first glance, only as long as the possibility of unambiguous literality is held open. But if figurality were to refuse its effacement in the interests of meaning, then rhetoric would stand for the radical negation of the separation of literal and figurative by negating the criteria of this separation. If this is the last consequence of the *renversement du platonisme* in the theory of rhetoric, then a notion of rhetoric that would to do justice to this reversal must take the indeterminacy of rhetorical language as its point of departure. A theory of rhetoric of this sort, which could no longer be tied down to the value of communication, would be that of Paul de Man.

44 'Le sophiste n'est pas l'être (ou le non-être) de la contradiction, mais celui qui porte toutes choses à l'état de simulacre, et les porte toutes dans cet état.' Deleuze 1968, p. 93, Engl. p. 81. Deleuze draws his own conclusions from this situation for literary scholarship with reference to the notion of the 'œuvre non hiérarchisée': see Deleuze 1969, p. 300 ff., in particular p. 303, Engl. p. 260 ff., esp. p. 262, and *cf.* Eco [2]1967.

45 Rhetoric is thus present on both levels of the dialectical progression (which it might be better to characterize as a deconstruction or 'fall' rather than a sublimation or 'ascent'): it is both the language of figure in its initial opposition to literal meaning, and the encompassment of figure and meaning in a third term which in an authentically Hegelian *Aufhebung* would be meaning-as-result, but here—as in Paul de Man and, as I will argue, even Pindar—is again rhetoric, this time the rhetoric of indeterminacy.

The rhetoric of unreadability

If Deleuze points in his reading of Plato towards a conception of rhetoric which would take the insufficiency of presence as the basis of language into account, it is de Man who—at first independently of the French philosopher—develops just such a conception.[46] As early as the 1950s, de Man's work is concerned with the problem of the relationship of the self and its language to the world of phenomena. This question became a burning issue in post-war France in the wake of the interpretations of Hegel's *Phänomenologie des Geistes* carried out by Alexandre Kojève and Jean Hyppolite.[47] At the centre of these readings, alongside the relationship between *Herr* and *Knecht*, was the 'unhappy consciousness' of the fourth chapter, interpreted by both scholars as the incommensurability of self-knowledge (the knowledge of the displacement of the self in negation and desire) and the knowledge of the world (the inappropriable immutability and self-identity of nature). Hegel had said in the *Phänomenologie* that absolute knowledge was 'essentially a *result*'.[48] According to Kojève, this meant that it was only accessible to a total subject at the end of history; until then, the real consciousness of human beings is 'unhappy', since it knows itself to be separated from the world of identity and thus from the totality of being.[49] Kojève indeed argued that Hegel had believed such an 'end' to have been achieved, or at least initiated, in the Napoleonic empire, and that accepting one's own mortality was sufficient to reconcile self and world; other thinkers, however, saw in Hegel's description of the mind separated from itself an account of the conditions of consciousness *tout court*.[50] For Hyppolite, 'consciousness is, as such, *always* unhappy consciousness', for in being separated from the *telos* of knowledge towards which it strives, it is *constitutively* 'the consciousness of con-

[46] On de Man's work see most usefully Ray 1984, pp. 186–205, Waters 1989, Godzich & Waters 1989, Ellrich & Wegmann 1990, Cebulla 1992, Caruth & Esch 1995, Gasché 1998, Hamacher 1998, pp. 151–194, Cohen & *al.* 2001, Haverkamp 2002, Redfield 2005 and Culler 2007, pp. 73–96.

[47] Hyppolite 1946, Kojève 1947. See on this Waters 1989, xxx–xl. De Man was in regular contact from the 1940s onwards with Georges Bataille, the then editor of the journal *Critique* who like Jacques Lacan and Maurice Merleau-Ponty had attended Kojève's lectures on Hegel at the Parisian École Pratique des Hautes-Études between 1933 and 1939.

[48] Hegel, *Phänomenologie des Geistes* (= Hegel 1969–1971, vol. 3), p. 24, his italics; Engl. Hegel 1977, p. 11.

[49] See Kojève 1947, p. 162 ff., esp. p. 164 (Engl. p. 32 ff., esp. p. 35) and p. 528.

[50] On the 'end of history' in Kojève's reading of Hegel, see Riley 1981 and Roth 1985. For an account of the *unglückliches Bewußtsein* in the work of Jean Wahl and Alexandre Koyré, see Baugh 1993.

tradiction, that is, the consciousness of the I that is internally rent.'[51] This exile, far from the *présence à soi*—or from presence altogether—which in Deleuze's reading of Plato undercuts the epistemological status of rhetoric, is here the consequence of humankind's position in the unfinished historicity of its own existence, separated by time from the centre of being as from its own death.

Before we look at what de Man makes of this situation, and how it leads him from phenomenology to rhetoric, it is worth asking what implications such a philosophy might have for the study of literature. That the epistemological well-foundedness of interpretation depends on its claim to totality can easily be recognized from the privileged status enjoyed by interpretations of whole texts in traditional literary scholarship. The goal and *telos* of the practice of interpreting a text is the moment at which all the elements of the text come together to form a whole whose principle is gained from the text itself; the specific obsession of Pindaric research in the nineteenth and twentieth centuries with the unity of the epinicians is only a reflex of this basic hermeneutical structure which has constitutive meaning for the notion of the hermeneutical circle.[52] But if all knowledge, in order to be *real* knowledge, must be *total* knowledge—and this is of course the point of Hegel's insistence on totality as the defining characteristic of the true—then a conception of literary studies as an *in principle* endless striving to understand its object becomes extremely problematic with respect to its status as scholarship. The demand, basic to hermeneutics, for interpretative immanence, that is, for the non-contingent agreement between text and interpretation can—according to Hegel—only be fulfilled in the eschatological absolute. Kojève writes: 'The totality of what is real includes human reality, which only exists as creative *movement*. The complete and final assimilation of being (= substance) and speech (= the subject) can therefore only be achieved at the end of history, when the creative movement of humanity has reached its conclusion.'[53] Complete propriety in interpretation can therefore be

[51] 'En effet la conscience, en tant que telle, n'étant pas encore parvenue à l'identité concrète de la certitude et de la vérité, visant donc un au-delà d'elle-même, est *toujours* dans son principe conscience malheureuse [...], conscience de la contradiction—c'est-à-dire du moi scindé en lui-même.' Hyppolite 1946, pp. 184 and 187 f., Engl. pp. 190 and 194, my italics. (*Cf.* de Man [2]1983, p. 265, written in 1955: 'If there ever was a philosophy of necessary separation, it is Hegel's.') We will have reason to return to this problem in our discussion of subjectivity in Pindar (see below, p. 217 ff.).

[52] See above, p. 12 and below, p. 144 ff.

[53] 'Mais la totalité du Réel implique la réalité humaine, qui n'existe que comme un *mouvement* créateur. L'adéquation parfaite et définitive de l'Être (= Substance) et du Dis-

achieved only from the perspective of the Beyond; the absolute commentary can only be written after the death of the interpreter.[54]

But whilst the concept of scholarship, on these presuppositions, necessarily implies a claim to interpretative totality that can only be fulfilled in the *posthistoire*, from the perspective of death,[55] the reading of a text can nevertheless only be undertaken by the living. *Reading* is *not* a result, interpretation—unfinishable? At any rate (as long as reading is still going on) unfinished. And as unfinished, also (as far as its result is concerned) unknown.[56] Interpretative judgement results, first of all, from reading, and thus presupposes its end, its absence as the past. Philological reading, on the other hand—this is a formulation of de Man's—takes place as 'an examination of the structure of language prior to the meaning it produces'; '[it] is an epistemological event prior to being an ethical or aesthetic value.'[57] The epistemological event is, it would seem, irreconcilably opposed to the hermeneutical truth-as-result, the temporality of cognition to the timelessness of absolute knowledge and the absolutely known. But if there can (or indeed should) be such a thing as a scholarship of literature—which, as

cours (= Sujet) ne peut donc s'effectuer qu'à la fin des temps, lorsque s'achève le mouvement créateur de l'Homme.' Kojève 1947, p. 529, his italics, my translation.

[54] Must we then acknowledge, in the wake of Hegel and the death of the author, the death of the *interpreter*? Everything that is true in the commentary proceeds from this death that, in the final instance, also implies the mortality of the *work* considered (and rejected) by Benjamin (1972–1986, vol. IV 1, p. 13, Engl. vol. 1, p. 256). (*Cf.* de Man's—not unproblematic—interpretation of this moment in Benjamin's thought in 'Conclusions: Walter Benjamin's "The task of the translator"' [= de Man 1986, pp. 73–105], p. 85.)

[55] Cebulla 1992, p. 3 f. contrasts in this context de Man's position with that of Habermas: whereas Habermas reduces the poststructuralist critique of metaphysics to the demand for a fallibilistic consciousness that has long been an accepted part of philosophy (see Habermas ^{4}1988, p. 247 n. 74, Engl. p. 408 n. 28), de Man considers 'das Erreichen eines solchen Bewußtseins unmöglich. Die Kritik an den universalistischen Geltungsansprüchen der Tradition könne nicht als historisches Pensum ein für allemal geleistet werden, sondern sei auf den immer wiederholten Nachvollzug in der Zeitlichkeit der Subjektivität angewiesen. Aus diesem Blickwinkel erweist sich die Möglichkeit eines Bewußtseins, das erhobene Geltungsansprüche immer schon im Hinblick auf die triviale Möglichkeit künftiger Problematisierung relativiert, als Fiktion.'

[56] Nietzsche's description of the dissolution of the 'real world' in *Götzendämmerung* (Nietzsche 1988, vol. 6, 80 f., Engl. Nietzsche 2005, p. 171) is instructive in this respect. The dissolution of the truth of the text by means of interpretation does indeed lead to the abolition of its appearance: see below, p. 61 ff.

[57] De Man, 'The return to philology' (= de Man 1986, pp. 21–26), p. 24; *id.* 1989, p. 222.

Werner Hamacher has reminded us, is by no means certain[58]—then totality and temporality must be mediated. But how?

It is, as we have already noted, de Man who, from the late 1960s onward, makes this problem the central concern of his work in literary theory. His description of the dilemma can be found in an article published in 1966, 'La circularité de l'interprétation dans l'œuvre de Maurice Blanchot', on Blanchot's interpretations of Mallarmé.[59] Although in 'La solitude essentielle', Blanchot explicitly denies that any author is capable of reading his own work—'[F]or him, it is the unreadable, a secret, and he cannot remain face to face with it'[60]—it can, according to de Man, be shown that in *Le Livre à venir* the French critic does in fact read Mallarmé in order to read himself in the mirror of the poet's œuvre. The exodus and return of the self into and from the other gives rise to a possibility of authorial self-reading that would be impossible without the mediation of the earlier text, and this double gesture of displacement and reappropriation seems at first to be entirely analogous to the process within history by which self-consciousness arises and rises to ever-higher levels in the *Phänomenologie des Geistes*.[61] But whereas Mallarmé in his early works such as *Hérodiade* and *Igitur* does indeed seem to see time as an optimistic progression towards the Absolute, entirely in Hegel's sense,[62] Blanchot finds in his last texts, above all *Un Coup de Dés*, a view which now suggests the mere, closed circularity of the movement from the self to the world and back, with no prospect of ascending to the Absolute within temporality. This is the point, argues de Man, at which Mallarmé and Blanchot meet, for only if the possibility of a dialectical *Aufhebung* of self and other is abandoned can a position be reached from which the recognition of the absolute impossibility of

58 Hamacher 1998, p. 151, Engl. p. 181.

59 De Man 1966; the slightly revised English translation was published as 'Impersonality in the criticism of Maurice Blanchot' in de Man ²1983, pp. 60–78. See on this paper Marshall 1983, pp. 144–149, Cebulla 1992, pp. 100–107, Rosiek 1992, pp. 58–63, and *cf.* Waters 1989, xxvii.

60 '[L]'écrivain ne lit jamais son œuvre. Elle est, pour lui, l'illisible, un secret, en face de quoi il ne demeure pas.' Blanchot 1955, p. 17, Engl. Blanchot 1999, p. 403.

61 'A circular movement seems to take the writer, at first alienated in the work, back to himself, by means of an act of self-interpretation. In Blanchot, this process first takes the form of his critical reading of others as preparatory to the reading of himself' (de Man ²1983, p. 67).

62 De Man ²1983, p. 70 speaks of a 'dialectical movement of becoming'. On Mallarmé's 'Hegelianism', *cf.* Derrida, 'La double séance' (= Derrida 1972a, pp. 241–346), pp. 239 and 254 f., Engl. pp. 194 and 206 f.

reading oneself—in the sense of just such a sublimation—makes sense. According to Blanchot, writes de Man, '[t]he center *always* remains hidden and out of reach; we are separated from it by the very substance of time, and we never cease to know that this is the case.'[63] History, still taking place, thus separates the subject from absolute, unmediated knowledge, from the reading of him- or herself, since such a reading would presuppose an *Aufhebung* of the difference between subject and object which, this side of death, cannot take place. At the same time, however, history also prevents one subject from reading any other, since to the extent that the absolute truth of the text is to be grasped in the mode of temporality, this recognition must, precisely because it is temporal, misrepresent it. As the content of unhappy consciousness bound to time, history is thus the most important and most disturbing metaphysical condition under which interpretation must take place.

The problem of this discrepancy between truth and temporality—which corresponds to that between presence and its mediation in the sign we could observe in Plato's *Sophist*—leads de Man to rhetoric. It will already have become clear that a notion of rhetoric born of this dilemma will not be able to have recourse, in any axiomatic sense, to classical-rhetorical categories such as 'the speaker', since it will have been introduced precisely in order to take account of the problematic status of a subject who can only have very limited knowledge of him- or herself. The turn to rhetoric begins in his 'most openly metaphysical essay', 'The rhetoric of temporality'.[64] On the basis of observations made by Benjamin and Gadamer about the status of figurative language in the literature and aesthetics of the baroque and classical periods, de Man examines the relationship between the categories of the symbol and allegory in the aesthetics and poetry of German, English and French Romanticism. Contrary to the widespread opinion of literary scholarship in the twentieth century that Romantic poetry is best understood as a drama of the relationship between subject and object, de Man argues in interpretations of Wordsworth and Rousseau that this dialectic only grasps a transitory moment of another, deeper conflict. This profounder question of Romanticism is directed, rather, at the self's choice between the temptations of totality, whose synecdochal representation is the symbol, on the one hand, and the confession

[63] De Man ²1983, p. 76 f., my italics.

[64] De Man ²1983, pp. 187–228 (first published in 1969). The quotation is from Lentricchia 1980, p. 292.

of its principally temporal existence on the other: that historical and biographical temporality which, as inescapable historicity, forms the basis of the Hegelian unhappy consciousness and is—as Benjamin had already seen—constitutive of allegory.[65]

That the symbol implies a totality of knowledge can, writes de Man, be seen from its relationship to what it symbolizes. In his chapter on allegory in *Wahrheit und Methode*, Gadamer cites Schelling's *Philosophie der Kunst*:

> Mythology in general and any piece of mythological literature in particular is not to be understood schematically or allegorically, but symbolically. For the demand of absolute artistic representation is: representation with complete indifference, so that the universal is wholly the particular, and the particular *is* at the same time wholly the universal, *and does not simply mean it.*[66]

and comments:

> In fact, what distinguishes the symbol even as Goethe conceives it is that in it the idea itself gives itself existence. Only because the concept of symbol implies the inner unity of symbol and what is symbolized, was it possible for the symbol to become a basic concept universal to aesthetics.[67]

65 *Cf.* Benjamin, *Ursprung des deutschen Trauerspiels* (= Benjamin 1972–1986, vol. I 1, pp. 203–430), pp. 340–344, especially p. 342 f.: 'Unter der entscheidenden Kategorie der Zeit [...] läßt das Verhältnis von Symbol und Allegorie eindringlich und formelhaft sich festlegen. Während im Symbol mit der Verklärung des Unterganges das transfigurierte Antlitz der Natur im Lichte der Erlösung flüchtig sich offenbart, liegt in der Allegorie die facies hippocratica der Geschichte als erstarrte Urlandschaft dem Betrachter vor Augen. Die Geschichte in allem was sie Unzeitiges, Leidvolles, Verfehltes von Beginn an hat, prägt sich in einem Antlitz – nein in einem Totenkopfe aus. Und so wahr alle "symbolische" Freiheit des Ausdrucks, alle klassische Harmonie der Gestalt, alles Menschliche einem solchen fehlt – es spricht nicht nur die Natur des Menschendaseins schlechthin, sondern die biographische Geschichtlichkeit eines einzelnen in dieser seiner naturverfallensten Figur bedeutungsvoll als Rätselfrage sich aus.' Engl. Benjamin 1977, pp. 163–167, this passage p. 166.

66 '[D]ie Mythologie überhaupt und jede Dichtung derselben insbesondere ist weder schematisch noch allegorisch, sondern symbolisch zu begreifen. Denn die Forderung der absoluten Kunstdarstellung ist: Darstellung mit völliger Indifferenz, so nämlich, daß das Allgemeine ganz das Besondere, das Besondere zugleich ganz das Allgemeine *ist*, *nicht es bedeutet*.' Schelling 1856–1861, vol. 5, p. 411, Engl. in Gadamer ^{2}1989, p. 77 (Schelling's spacing, my [GP's] italics). Schelling continues: 'Diese Forderung ist poetisch gelöst in der Mythologie. [...] Die Bedeutung hier ist zugleich das Sein selbst, übergangen in den Gegenstand, mit ihm eins. Sobald wir diese Wesen [der Mythologie] etwas bedeuten lassen, sind sie selbst nichts mehr.'

67 'In der Tat liegt in der Auszeichnung des Symbolbegriffs schon bei Goethe der ent-

It is this assertion that de Man takes up and to which he now imparts a decisive Hegelian impetus:

> In the world of the symbol it would be possible for the image to coincide with the substance, since the substance and its representation do not differ in their being but only in their extension: they are part and whole of the same set of categories. Their relationship is one of simultaneity, which, in truth, is spatial in kind, and in which the intervention of time is merely a matter of contingency, whereas, in the world of allegory, time is the originary constitutive category [...]. Whereas the symbol postulates the possibility of an identity or identification, allegory designates primarily a distance in relation to its own origin, and, renouncing the nostalgia and the desire to coincide, it establishes its language in the void of this temporal difference.[68]

The 'void of temporal difference' is the abyss in which, according to de Man, interpretation must take place. For what kind of knowledge of a literary text does the gulf between origin and language, between the full presence of immediate meaning and its endless mediation in semiosis imply? If under the conditions of the Hegelian problematic 'the presence of allegory always corresponds to the unveiling of an authentically temporal destiny',[69] authentic interpretation can only take place in the mode of allegory. The alternative would be a symbolic knowledge that would postulate the possibility of the identity of *imago* and *substantia* as a synecdoche. In this case, the interpretation would differ from the work only in its extension, not in its essence; it would fall together with the totality of the work, would be a part of it. As it turns out, this identity is one pole of the tension on which interpretation as commentary is based: as Foucault remarks, the commentary has the task of saying at last—but also for the first time—what the primary

scheidende Ton darauf, daß die Idee selbst es ist, die sich darin Existenz gibt. Nur weil der Symbolbegriff die innere Einheit vom Symbol und Symbolisierten impliziert, konnte dieser Begriff zum universalen ästhetischen Grundbegriff aufsteigen.' Gadamer 1960/1990, p. 83, Engl. p. 77. *Cf.* also p. 79, Engl. p. 73 f.

[68] De Man ^{2}1983, p. 207. *Cf.* Hegel 1969–1971, vol. 13, p. 512, Engl. Hegel 1975a, vol. I, p. 399 on allegory as the representation of the 'separation between subject and predicate' and Benjamin 1972–1986, vol. I 1, p. 406 on allegory as a form of—negative—knowledge: 'Das schlechthin Böse, das als bleibende Tiefe [die Allegorie] hegte, existiert nur in ihr, ist einzig und allein Allegorie, *bedeutet etwas anderes, als es ist. Und zwar bedeutet es genau das Nichtsein dessen, was es vorstellt.* Die absoluten Laster, wie Tyrannen und Intriganten sie vertreten, sind Allegorien. Sie sind nicht wirklich und sie haben das, als was sie dastehn, nur vor dem subjektiven Blick der Melancholie; sind dieser Blick, den seine Ausgeburten vernichten, *weil sie nur seine Blindheit bedeuten*' (my italics; Engl. Benjamin 1977, p. 233).

[69] De Man ^{2}1983, p. 206.

text tacitly articulates.[70] The criterion of 'appropriateness' in interpretation means nothing else: the work should govern the interpretation, should incorporate it into the field of its influence. What must be avoided at all costs is an interpretation which introduces things into the text *from the outside*. *Homerum ex Homero*: poetry should read itself, should be the subject and the object of its interpretation at the same time. Where however this eschatological dream is not fulfilled, allegory, which indefatigably repeats the negativity of interpretation and the distance between the original and its repetition, at last comes into its own.

Herein lies for de Man the *specificum* of literature as a form of knowledge. '[T]he statement about language, that sign and meaning can never coincide', he writes in 1967 in 'Criticism and crisis', 'is what is precisely taken for granted in the kind of language we call literary. Literature [...] begins on the far side of this knowledge; it is the only form of language free from the fallacy of unmediated expression.'[71] Only a reading in the mode of the figurative, of that not-saying-the-same-thing which holds open the gap between totality and the temporality of reading will be an answer to literature's own knowledge of this gap.

It is therefore no accident that de Man's most important book bears the title *Allegories of Reading*. Here, a concept of rhetoric emerges which is based on the non-referentiality of rhetoric according to the model of allegory developed by Benjamin. When Yeats lets his poem 'Among School Children' end with the question, 'How can we know the dancer from the dance?', it is not, as de Man shows in the first chapter of *Allegories*, clear from the grammar of the passage alone whether the verse is to be understood figuratively, as a rhetorical question which would assert the metaphysical identity of the dancer with the dance, or whether in fact here rather the impossibility of a clear distinction between dancer and dance is being expressed in a question, this time literal:

> [...] *not* that sign and referent are so exquisitely fitted to each other that all difference between them is at times blotted out but, rather, since the two essentially different elements, sign and meaning, are so intricately intertwined in the imagined 'presence' that the poem addresses, how can we possibly make the distinctions that would shelter us from the error of identifying what cannot be identified?[72]

[70] Foucault 1971, pp. 23–28, Engl. pp. 56–58.
[71] De Man ^{2}1983, p. 17.
[72] De Man 1979, p. 11, his italics.

De Man's point here is not that one interpretation is correct and the other false, but rather that both allow for a coherent reading of the poem in retrospect.[73] The insistence of hermeneutics on unambiguous answers is at this point, initially at least, blocked. It is, however, more important to note that the two options mapped out here presuppose each other: whereas in the first, 'rhetorical' case the epistemological identity of *significans* (the dancer) and *significatum* (the dance) is asserted *as this identity*—that is, as the congruence, created by the interpretation, of form and content, the coincidence of the form with what is 'really' being said—in the second case precisely this hypothesis is revealed to be an aporia. The parallels with the situation at the end of the *Sophist* are striking: precisely the authority which is meant to decide once and for all about the interpretation of what is being said is what that interpretation will have to call into question. As long as the philosopher does not (or, at least, not as himself) emerge from the blinding light at the source of the Idea of Being to enlighten us without the dubiously sophistical means of similarities and analogies that he may, indeed, be similar to the rhetorician but is not, in fact, identical with him, so that instead (?) we are dependent on the answers of the Stranger; as long as the question of the independent status of what is expressed by the expression of the dancer cannot itself be read as the expression of an unambiguous, literal *or* figurative (but not both) *signifié*—then interpretation can rest on nothing other than the surface of the phenomena.

In such cases, rhetoric is not merely an option that one can choose to make use of or not in the interpretation of literature, as though in Yeats' case the one alternative could simply be ignored so that the text was not embarrassed by being made to contradict itself. On the contrary: the contextual indeterminacy of the question of whether we are dealing here with figurality or not and the concomitant loss of a final authority which out of the fullness of its own presence would govern interpretation is the centre of de Man's notion of rhetoric, and this is *constitutive* of literature: 'A literary text', we read in *Allegories of Reading*, 'simultaneously asserts and denies the authority of its own rhetorical mode.'[74] Where the text simultaneously asserts *and* denies the same, obviously and necessarily *either* negatively *or* positively meant statement, the very rhetoricity is at work which forces the

[73] The other, 'literal' Yeats-interpretation is undertaken in de Man's 'Image and emblem in Yeats' (= de Man 1984, pp. 145–238), pp. 197–203. De Man's conclusion: 'We are very far removed from a reconciliation between image and reality' (p. 203).

[74] De Man 1979, p. 17.

interpreter to read in that mode of allegory which takes account of the impossibility of total knowledge and of the unreadability of the text.

It is now easier to see how de Man's use of the term 'rhetoric' relates to the history of the rhetorical tradition. This use takes up the conflict between rhetoric and philosophy.[75] The accusation levelled against rhetoric by philosophers from Plato and Sextus Empiricus to Kant was the ambiguity it created in the relationship between what was said and what was meant. The *rhetorical* form—this was the philosophers' critique—allows no clear conclusions about the situation the speaker is describing, or indeed even about her intention to do so. Is she lying? Is she speaking the truth? Rhetoric arouses the suspicion of bad faith, and no protestations of innocence, however eloquent, can free it from this suspicion.[76] Alfons Weische has insightfully summarized this problem in the character of rhetoric as the problem of *αὔξησις*; as a figure which consists in making the small great and the great small, it fails *by definition* to correspond to what we might want to call the referential facts.[77] Traditional rhetoric thus reveals itself to be external to meaning or reference, and since we can speak of 'truth' only on the assumption of some kind of congruence between language and the world, the philosophical critique of rhetoric is directed from the very beginning against this art of *amplificatio*. Placed against the background of this history, de Man's understanding of rhetoric as indeterminacy, far from being innovative or reductive, reveals itself as an authentic re-appropriation of the tradition with which it is so frequently contrasted.

Rhetoric thus leads to the very centre of the problem of interpretative legitimacy. If there is no certain way back from the rhetorical surface of the text to the meaning whose carrier or vessel it is meant to be—which is only to say that the crucial epistemological precondition for subjecting figurality to meaning in literature is not given—then the claim of the means and instruments of philological understanding—

[75] It is striking that in de Man's controversial interpretation of the mediaeval *trivium*, logic and grammar appear exclusively in the epistemological light in which they were by seen by only some of the scholastics (Hugo of St. Victor, William of Conches, in particular Thomas of Erfurt and the tradition of the *grammatica speculativa*); *cf.* de Man, 'The resistance to theory' (= de Man 1986, pp. 3–20), p. 13. Gasché's critique (*cf.* Gasché 1998, p. 137 f. with n. 38) takes neither this focusing of the tradition in the interests of a specific philosophical accentuation, nor its roots in Heidegger's *Sein und Zeit* (*cf.* Heidegger [18]2001, p. 165, Engl. p. 209) into account.

[76] Wheeler 1989 offers an acute analysis of this situation from the perspective of analytic philosophy.

[77] Weische 1989.

methods, questions, goals—to appropriateness can no longer be legitimated by recourse to what a given text *has to* mean. It will be clear, before reading, neither that a text is the expression (in the sense of having-expressed-oneself) of a sovereign self, nor that it demonstrates the unity required by definition of a composition, nor indeed that its contextual relevance is in any sense determinable. Reading will not be able to rely on the alleged self-evidence of the unified, the subjective, or the thematic *a priori*.

The values of Pindar

It is nevertheless the case that a large body of scholarly opinion exists to the effect that Pindar's odes are or do indeed demonstrate all of the above. The concern of research for the last two hundred years has been to argue precisely this point: to show that the poet is in control of his material (against the Romantic view of the odes as essentially irrational products of poetic inspiration), that the songs are unified wholes (against the thesis, common at the end of the nineteenth century, that Pindar either was unable to fulfil the demands of compositional unity, or had no conception of them), and that they speak to their public in recognizable and reconstructable ways (a reaction to excessively recondite readings of imagery or structure produced by some scholars working in traditions such as New Criticism). Are we simply to dismiss this work as mistaken in the interests of projecting the concerns of a particular theoretical position onto the victory songs? Or is there a way to engage with previous and current interpretations of the epinicians as bearers of meaning without surrendering the questions about such interpretations raised by our reading of Plato and Paul de Man?

It would be foolish to deny that Pindar's poetry does indeed contain a strong element of what we have been calling 'metaphysics', and that it does demand, quite explicitly, to be read in terms of those categories of meaning to which rhetoric, understood in the way outlined above, seems to be opposed. The epinicians tell us frequently that they are telling us what the author (really, literally) wants to say; they refer to mythical and historical situations and persons—the distinction is of course entirely moot in the fifth century—and comment more than once on the appropriateness or necessity of these references within the generic aim of epinician literature to praise the victor and make him valuable in our eyes. Ignoring this 'will to meaning' would be perverse, especially since taking it into account is what crucially distinguishes the reading of Pindar proposed here from one that would fall back into a mystified evocation of 'poetic genius' far above the mundane claims of reason and interpretability (or, for that matter, a condemnation of the poet for failing to make any sense at all). The question is therefore not whether this evidence is to be given its due in the economics of interpretation, but rather of its precise relationship to those elements of the text that can be shown to resist their incorporation into the systems of value and exchange that make up the enterprise of hermeneutics and literary history. If what presents itself in the victory songs as their irreducible signified nevertheless turns out to be not a realm of immediate meaning or absolute value, but rather in its constituent structure inseparable from rhetoric, then its status with respect to what the odes (say that they) say about it and the kind of history of which it could be a part must be considered as a question re-opened by the work of reading rather than as a foregone conclusion on the grounds that what a text says about itself and its desires will always be a full and accurate account of what it does.[78]

The reading of Pindar that follows will therefore seek to be faithful to the double gesture of deconstruction described above.[79] I do not intend to ignore the generic programme of the epinicians or regard it as inconsequential, although I insist, for reasons which will now have become clear, that their author's obvious intention to fulfil the demands of this programme does not exhaust the texts and therefore cannot provide the final criterion or goal of interpretation. That the central, programmatic desire of the odes is to convince the reader or listener of the value of the man they praise, of his achievements, his virtue, has been a point of consensus in scholarship since antiquity, a desire so evident that it has seemed to many scholars to govern all else in the texts.[80] 'Pindar's poetry', wrote Hermann Fränkel in a classic characterisation of the victory songs in the 1940s, 'is concerned with the noble, the great, the good, the divine—in a single word: with value; and indeed so exclusively that everything without a positive or negative relationship to values is ignored'.[81] The question posed by this litera-

[78] *Cf.* Derrida 1967a, p. 299: 'S'il nous paraît impossible au principe de séparer, par interprétation ou commentaire, le signifié du signifiant […], nous croyons néanmoins que cette impossibilité s'articule historiquement. […] Même s'il n'y a jamais de signifié pur, il y a des rapports différents quant à ce qui du signifiant *se donne* comme strate irréductible de signifié' (his italics); Engl. p. 159 f.

[79] See above, p. 17 f.

[80] See above, p. 27 f.

[81] 'Pindars Dichtung ist auf das Edle, Große, Schöne, Gute und Göttliche ausgerichtet,

ture, on its own account and on that of its interpreters, is thus: what is a thing or a person worth? How is the value of an achievement, a song, a human being to be determined and how is it to be converted from one currency to another? By asking or presupposing this question, the epinicians direct our attention not only towards value, but also towards the *differentiality* of values, since, as Marx famously pointed out, there can only be values within a *system* of values which allows for the possibility of exchange, of the conversion or translation of value from one of its expressions to the next.[82] In doing so, however, the system always also admits the possibility of *false* translation, and this too is an issue of considerable concern in the epinicians. The theoretical possibility of a discrepancy between the value of a victory and the value of a song motivates not only a significant part of Pindaric self-reference—all of those places, for example, at which the singer appears to stop himself from singing something inappropriate—but also such striking and important figures as the so-called *χρέος*-motif: the victory *has earned* (= is equal in value to) a song, the latter is a *debt* that is owed to the victory by the singer and the city.[83]

This language of values, of debt and exchange needs to be taken seriously. The odes' concern is with establishing the specific worth of a specific object, with insisting that the respective incarnations or instantiations of this worth—for example, the reception of the victor and the praise that his fellow citizens bring him as the reward for his victory—remain the same. Within the system of values, the different signs of a given value must continue to designate the same, that is, the *right* value. Only in this way can the successful translation of the value, the equivalence of what is given and what is received, be guaranteed. But if this is true, then behind the single correspondences there must—this is what the logic of this argumentation necessarily implies, as Marx saw—be a value to which they must always simultaneously point as their *tertium* in order to remain translatable. Only with respect to a third, transcendent value which is no longer the sign of

mit éinem Wort: auf den Wert; und zwar so ausschließlich, daß alles ignoriert wird was keine positive oder negative Beziehung zu Werten hat.' Fränkel [4]1993, p. 554, my translation (und *cf.* p. 558). Kurke 1991, p. 8 speaks with reference to Bourdieu [2]2000 (first published in 1972) of 'symbolic capital'.

82 The classic analysis of this systematic, differential nature of value is the first chapter of *Das Kapital*; see Marx [7]1972, pp. 49–98, Engl. pp. 125–177.

83 On self-correction, see below, p. 208 ff. On the *χρέος*-motif, see Schadewaldt 1966, p. 277 f. for exposition and examples, Kurke 1991, pp. 97–103, and below, p. 72 for the crucial role this figure plays in Bundy's *Studia Pindarica*. It is notably not Bacchylidean.

some other, displaced value but absolutely present to and for itself, can the correctness of the value—the value of the value—be measured. The achievement of the athlete must therefore be made transparent for what it *means*, must be interpreted. So, at least, the programme, whose metaphysical nature will be entirely clear.[84]

As we have begun to suspect on theoretical grounds, there will be problems as soon as the logic of this necessity is brought together with the texts which assert it. I will attempt to demonstrate this in Chapter 3; there we will see that the threat of inconcinnity between transcendental (and thus always merely virtual) value and the given sign describes the situation of the songs in language. On the basis of this unavoidable folding back of the discourse of values onto the value of the discourse, the singer's self-correction in moments of potential error or referential failure finds its more than merely accidental reflection in the semiotic presuppositions of the epinician programme.

For de Man, as we have noted, this self-referential moment, the self-knowledge of the text, provides both the defining characteristic of literary language and the reason why it is always just out of reach of those discourses, such as literary studies or philosophy, which lay claim to a literality and truth not realizable from within the order of the signifier. 'We are entitled', writes de Man in his review of Derrida's *De la grammatologie*, 'to generalize [in] calling "literary", in the full sense of the term, any text that implicitly or explicitly signifies its own rhetorical mode and prefigures its own misunderstanding as the correlative of its rhetorical nature [...].'[85] On this theory, the demand for immanence of interpretation must result in an asymmetrical pursuit between the commentary which wants to and indeed must describe the text in the mode of literality, and the text which has, in

84 Let us note in passing that this is also the structure of the metaphor in Aristotle: *cf.* the fundamental role of analogy in the definitions of different kinds of metaphors in *Poet.* 21, 1457 b6–33 and above all *Rhet.* III 10, 1411 a1 ff. , where the metaphor *κατ' ἀναλογίαν* is described as the 'best form' of the metaphor.

85 De Man, 'The rhetoric of blindness' (= de Man ^{2}1983, pp. 102–141), p. 136. *Cf.* also 'Literary history and literary modernity' (*ibid.*, pp. 142–165), p. 164—'[A]pproaches to literature that take for granted the specificity of literature (what the French structuralists, echoing the Russian formalists, call literarity [*littérarité*] of literature) [are inadequate]. If literature rested at ease within its own self-definition, it could be studied according to methods that are scientific rather than historical. We are obliged to confine ourselves to history when [...] the entity steadily puts its own ontological status into question'—where what is denied of structuralism in its classical form is not literariness as such, but rather the possibility of conceptualizing it in the terms of a prestabilized totality. See further Culler 1982, p. 184, who notes the difference between this questioning of literature's ontological determinability and the traditional linking of literariness to *genres*.

reality, already withdrawn itself from the scope of this description.

In speaking of prefiguration, however, de Man alerts us to a phenomenon that deserves closer attention. The desire of the commentary to speak literally about the text recapitulates what we have said about the Pindaric or epinician will to value: both are versions of an essentially metaphysical hermeneutics and echo each other across the gap between primary and secondary texts. There is widespread agreement in the historiography of research that the interpretation of the victory songs underwent an important change with the co-operative commentary of August Boeckh and Ludolph Dissen completed in 1821. Boeckh and Dissen's innovation was to reject a reading of the texts as a *beau désordre* (Boileau) of striking conceits and rhetorical flourishes, and instead to argue that the poems were highly complex but nonetheless recognisable expressions of interpretable meaning.[86] It is crucial to realize that 'meaning', here, is anything but a philosophically neutral category: as we will see in the next chapter, Boeckh subjects it explicitly to a series of conditions amongst which unity, subjectivity and historicity are the most important. As a consequence, the task of the interpreter becomes helping the meaning of the songs to triumph over their rhetoric. And since this becomes, in subsequent work on the odes, the undisputed goal of interpretation, the texts can as a consequence only say what they can mean, where 'meaning' is unified, the expression of subjectivity, and historical.

There is no sense in which I want to declare the unquestionable successes of studies in this tradition for worthless or even obsolete; I wish merely to indicate the structure of the results made possible by this programme. They are, *as results*, only possible because the hermeneutical criteria for successful interpretation are themselves based on the philosophical criteria of the metaphysics of presence, in other words, because the kind of understanding that, in the wake of Boeckh and Dissen, became the unquestionable *telos* of research on Pindar subjects the epinicians to a reading which we must just as necessarily call 'transcendental' as the discourse of values in the victory songs themselves.[87]

[86] See below, p. 73 ff.

[87] *Cf.* Derrida 1967a, p. 229: 'À l'exception d'une pointe ou d'un point de résistance qui ne s'est reconnu comme tel que très tard, l'écriture littéraire s'est presque toujours et presque partout, selon des modes et à travers des âges très divers, prêtée d'elle-même à cette lecture *transcendante*, à cette recherche du signifié que nous mettons ici en question, non pour l'annuler mais pour la comprendre dans un système auquel elle est aveugle' (his italics), Engl. p. 160. See further 'La double séance' (= Derrida 1972a, pp. 215–

In tracing the outlines and limits of this reading, we will see that the specific impossibility of the programme upon which it is based—the impossibility of separating the *signifié* from the *signifiant*—is articulated differently in the history of research. Here—we anticipate a little—we will observe a dialectics which connects the moments of greatest insight in Pindaric studies with a specific blindness in the reading that leads to these insights. This ought not to surprise us: in a series of studies written in the mid- to late-1960s, de Man had already pointed to the curiously dialectical relationship between the literary-critical insights of authors such as Poulet and Blanchot on the one hand and what their various readings overlooked, but what remained subliminally present in their texts on the other.

> Their critical stance [...] is defeated by their own critical results. A penetrating but difficult insight into the nature of literary language ensues. It seems, however, that this insight could only be gained because the critics were in the grip of this peculiar blindness: their language could grope toward a certain degree of insight only because their method remained oblivious to the perception of this insight.[88]

It seems to me that precisely the most important insights in the interpretation of Pindar in the last two hundred years are in fact based on strategies of marginalisation and exclusion that cannot be addressed directly in the secondary texts which implement them without undermining the project of reading for meaning altogether. This, on the one hand. On the other, however, it can also be shown that what the commentaries of Boeckh and Bundy, Krummen and Kurke, Thummer and Theunissen pass over in silence in Pindar's texts, and what, in terms of their metaphysical premises, they *must* pass over in order to arrive at any conclusions at all, is still subterraneously present in their works. Tracing the contours of this silence, the limits and the system of exclusions which support and ground these interpretations is the task to which we now turn.

346), p. 299 f., Engl. p. 245 f.

[88] De Man ²1983, p. 106. Wlad Godzich speaks in this context of 'de Man's now familiar dialectic of blindness and insight [that] permits him to characterize various individuals' reading practices in terms of the necessary exclusions that their mode of reading implies, not simply as a form of neglect or ignorance, but as the very originating locus of such insight as they achieve or illumination as they provide' (Godzich 1994, p. 150). See also Culler 2007, p. 89 f.

CHAPTER 2: STUDIES

> Den ersten Anstoss, von meinen Hypothesen über den Ursprung der Moral Etwas zu verlautbaren, gab mir ein klares, sauberes und kluges, auch altkluges Büchlein. [...] Vielleicht habe ich niemals Etwas gelesen, zu dem ich dermaassen, Satz für Satz, Schluss für Schluss, bei mir Nein gesagt hätte wie zu diesem Buche: doch ganz ohne Verdruss und Ungeduld. In [*Menschliches, Allzumenschliches*] nahm ich gelegentlich und ungelegentlich auf die Sätze jenes Buchs Bezug, nicht indem ich sie widerlegte – was habe ich mit Widerlegungen zu schaffen! – sondern, wie es einem positiven Geiste zukommt, an Stelle des Unwahrscheinlichen das Wahrscheinliche setzend, unter Umständen an Stelle eines Irrthums einen anderen.
>
> Nietzsche, *Genealogie der Moral.*

IN THE LAST CHAPTER, I PROPOSED THE HYPOTHESIS THAT A close examination of what studies in Pindar have often meant by 'rhetoric' would lead to results which differed from the notion of rhetoric to which their authors have had explicit recourse. The task of this chapter is to pursue this hypothesis. Readings of work in classical studies with a view to its presuppositions about philosophy or language are rare, in Pindaric research no less than in other fields.[1] But the language of commentary is by no means theoretically neutral or innocent. Taking up Paul de Man's thesis that critical insight is always bought at the price of a specific blindness, I will argue here that only the consistent marginalisation or exclusion of those aspects of the texts we have been calling 'rhetorical' has allowed interpreters in the last two centuries to understand the odes as means of communication. It would be wrong to attribute this marginalisation to the conscious choice or

[1] One of the best examples remains Most's discussion of causal and teleological interpretations of the *principium rationis sufficientis* in Pindaric studies in the introduction to *The Measures of Praise*; see Most 1985b, pp. 25–41.

preference of particular authors, and equally wrong to criticize or depreciate their work on these grounds, as if the research of the last two hundred years were based on mere negligence, 'mistakes' which, with a little more care and attention to detail, could have been avoided without, at the same time, making the interpretations of which they are a part impossible. My goal here is instead to trace the contours of a particular tradition in the reading of Pindar, a metaphysical tradition whose end—I insist on this—is neither immanent nor indeed especially desirable, but whose closure has now become more than apparent. De Man's dialectic of blindness and insight can help us to understand the Pindaric criticism of modernity as a period in research shaped by a subterranean tension between the meaning of the epinicians and their rhetoric.

The rhetoric of the mask

There is scarcely a work in the twentieth century for which this dialectic is more relevant than Elroy L. Bundy's *Studia Pindarica.*[2] No other book in Pindaric studies since Boeckh has had a comparable influence on everything that followed, regardless of whether researchers in its wake adopted Bundy's project and continued it, or criticised what was felt to be its excessive formalism and limited scope and by means of this critique attempted to move beyond it. The *Studia Pindarica* can legitimately be considered a privileged example of that tradition in the interpretation of Pindar with which we are concerned and one, moreover, which explicitly addresses the topic of 'rhetoric' and places it at the very centre of the texts. Where else will we expect to find answers to the question of rhetoric, its nature and its function, if not here?

I want, therefore, to interrogate the significance of 'rhetoric' in Bundy. What role does it play in his interpretations of the poems, in what structures does it participate? When we look more closely at Bundy's use of this term, it becomes apparent that 'rhetoric' marks the point of a necessary convergence and at the same time the place of an unspoken tension.

Right at the beginning of the *Studia Pindarica*, Bundy calls programmatically and emphatically for a sensitivity to the 'high rhetoric' of the songs. Motives and forms which repeatedly occur in the epinicians should not be read as alleged obsessions ('personal preoccupations, tri-

[2] Bundy's role and importance in the history of Pindaric studies is summarized by Young 1970, pp. 85–88, Lee 1978 and Krummen 1990, pp. 19–20.

umphs, and embarrassments') of the historical Pindar of Thebes, but rather as conventions which, as Bundy puts it, guarantee the artistic integrity of a group of poets.[3] These conventions determine form and meaning in the poems and are constitutive of the genre of the epinician as a whole. Since the intention at the root of all texts belonging to this genre is exclusively the praise of a victor, there is therefore 'no passage in Pindar and Bakkhulides that is not in its primary intent enkomiastic—that is, designed to enhance the glory of a particular patron.'[4]

The first consequence of this definition of epinician poetry and its meaning is a specification of the task and the necessary qualifications of the interpreter. Whoever wants to read the poems aright must, according to the *Studia Pindarica*, first of all decode them, and that means that he or she must recognize, behind the diverse statements in the text, the already determined, generic and *uniform* intention of praise. A command of the generic conventions which govern the realization of 'primary intent' in linguistic form is therefore indispensable for the correct understanding of the texts. Where this knowledge is lacking, the texts' intentions cannot be understood: '[T]he enkomiast's rhetorical poses may take forms that speak to one *unschooled in the conventions* with something less than the precision intended.'[5]

In what sense, however, are the poses of the encomiast 'rhetorical'? The discussion of the Pindaric priamel at the beginning of the first *Studium* provides the first clues. Here, Bundy discovers a version of this figure in the so-called 'rhetorical pause' which creates an ἀπορία as a foil for the selection of a subject or a specific way of treating it.[6] The topics which are *not* to be discussed are denoted, in this variant, by expressions of totality or multiplicity (πᾶς, πολύς, μακρά *etc.*): the large number of possible topics is sometimes discussed for several verses; they form the backdrop for the selection of the one—the right—topic.[7] As examples of this strategy, Bundy chooses two passages from the *First* and the *Ninth Olympians*.

The mythological part of the *First Olympian* begins with a scene that cannot but evoke the traditional story of the dismemberment of Pelops by his father Tantalus and his partly being eaten by the gods. It is—Bundy implicitly presupposes this interpretation of the scene—the

[3] Bundy 1986, p. 2 f.
[4] Bundy 1986, p. 3.
[5] Bundy 1986, p. 10 (my italics).
[6] Bundy 1986, p. 8 f.
[7] See Dornseiff 1921, pp. 97–102, Race 1990, pp. 9–16; on Bundy's specific use of this category see Most 1985b, p. 32.

moment at which the reconstituted boy is taken from the cauldron, now with the ivory shoulder which—in this version of the myth—Hermes had to create in order to replace the shoulder which Demeter had inadvertently eaten (25–27).[8] But Pindar immediately rejects this version which he has just introduced into the narrative in a religiously motivated break-off (28, 35 f.):

> *ἦ θαύματα πολλὰ* [...].
> [...]
> *ἔστι δ᾽ ἀνδρὶ φάμεν ἐοικὸς ἀμφὶ δαιμόνων καλά· μείων γὰρ αἰτία.*
> *υἱὲ Ταντάλου, σὲ δ᾽ ἀντία προτέρων φθέγξομαι* [...].

> Indeed, there are many astonishing things [...].
> [...]
> It is, however, fitting for a man to say good things about the gods, for his guilt is then less.
> Tantalos' son, I will speak of you differently from those who have spoken of you before [...].

We will have occasion to concern ourselves with this passage in more detail later.[9] For the moment, we are interested only in the question that Bundy asks here: why does Pindar mention this story if he apparently thinks it is religiously questionable to tell it? In answering this question, Bundy begins by noting that Pelops is the *laudandus* of the following approximately 70 verses. He is meant to serve as a projection screen for the praise of the song's real addressee, Hieron of Syracuse: both have entered a horse-race in Olympia (Hieron in 476 B.C.), both have emerged as victors, and both owe their success to the special favour of a god, a 'son of Kronos' (verse 10).[10] In order to provide a motivation for the god's help in the myth, the poet needs to introduce the erotic relationship between Pelops and Poseidon, and in order to do this he uses the structure of the priamel. On the one hand,

[8] For the ancient sources of this story, see the scholia on this section and Frazer's notes on Apollodorus, *Epitome* 2. 3 (Frazer 1921, vol. II, p. 156 f., n. 2). The episode was apparently mentioned by Bacchylides (fr. 42 *apud* Σ Pindar, *Olymp.* 1. 40a Dr.), but the next-oldest text is Lucian, *De saltatione* 54 (which however only alludes to the dismemberment without actually telling the story). See also below, p. 137 ff.

[9] See below, p. 121 ff.

[10] The parallel between the hero and the tyrant is made all the more convincing by their both being presented in a symposial context: in verse 10 f. we are told of Hieron's hearth to which the 'wise' (*σοφοί*) have come in order to celebrate him as an Olympian victor, whilst Pelops now reclines (*κλιθείς*, 92) in Olympia and receives there (at the fire-altar) visitors from all over the world (vv. 90–93). See Slater 1989 and Burgess 1993.

there are *θαύματα πολλά*, *many astounding things* (28) about which one could, in principle, easily speak, and their paradigmatic example is the ivory shoulder of the boy (still in existence at Olympia[11]); on the other hand however, and set off against this backdrop of inexhaustible possibilities, the *laudator* will choose a single theme: the new *θαῦμα* of the abduction of Pelops by Poseidon. On this reading, the objection of verse 35 is not an outbreak of archaic piety, but instead an artificially produced aporia which motivates the shoulder-story and marks the transition from the foil to the topic which is *really* intended by abruptly ending the delay caused by the rejected version.

A passage from the *Ninth Olympian* is similar. Here the first two elements in the passage from the *First Olympian* are reversed: the gnomic statement that the Charites create all[12] that is pleasurable and that real virtue—not least in order to praise a people as excellent as the Opuntians—only comes from the gods (28 f.) is illustrated by the example of Herakles who, as son of Zeus, was able to take on Apollo, Poseidon and Hades (29–35). But this list of battles with gods, consisting entirely of *θαύματα*, is again only the back-drop; the story of the fighting must therefore be left behind in order to get to the Opuntians themselves, and once again it is religious doubts which end the delay and motivate the transition to the real topic of the encomium (35–39):

> *ἀπό μοι λόγον*
> *τοῦτον, στόμα, ῥῖψον·*
> *ἐπεὶ τό γε λοιδορῆσαι θεούς*
> *ἐχθρὰ σοφία καὶ τὸ καυχᾶσθαι παρὰ καιρόν*
> *μανίαισιν ὑποκρέκει.*

> Cast away from me this word,
> my tongue,
> since to speak ill of the gods
> is a hateful skill and boasting at the wrong moment
> the accompaniment to madness.

As in the *First Olympian*, the 'foil' contains a general statement illu-

[11] The shoulder is mentioned by Pausanias (V 13. 6) and Pliny (*Nat. hist.* 28. 34) ; neither had seen it themselves. Parke 1933, pp. 155 and 160 thinks it nevertheless likely that the shoulder was already on display in the first half of the fifth century (see also Howie 1984, p. 287). According to Pausanias, one could, in the second century A.D., also admire the knife in the treasury of the Sikyonians (Paus. VI 19. 6).

[12] Bundy 1986, p. 9: 'Although the passage omits the typical *πᾶς* or the like, it is nevertheless a summary priamel (*πάντα* might have been included before *τὰ τέρπν'* in line [27]).'

strated by examples; the sudden turn to the song's real concern is brought about by the aporetic statement that it would not be pious to dwell any longer on this first topic. Bundy's conclusion: 'It will be seen that such passages are entirely too sophisticated and rhetorical to be taken in a straightforward religious sense.'[13]

'[T]oo ... rhetorical': the assertion points to two characteristics of these two passages, and of epinician language in general. On the one hand, it denotes the self-referential force of the break-offs. The statements that one should only speak well of the gods and that blasphemy is a hateful skill are not meant as theological utterances, but refer rather to an economy of the text according to which the narrative voice constantly moves between the foil and the *laudandus*. Repeatedly approaching an interdicted topic and abruptly moving away from it again is a common means of topicalization in Pindar; in its apparently unmotivated introduction of irrelevant topics, it has often been felt to be highly problematic. But in the course of this movement, the precise choice of foil naturally plays only a subsidiary role, for its essential characteristic is only that it is a possible 'other' of what is intended. According to Bundy, therefore, it would be wrong to want to derive from passages such as *Olympian* 1. 35 f. or *Olympian* 9. 35–39 an epinician or Pindaric theology, a referential discourse on the part of the odes or the poet about the gods; in neither of these passages are the gods the point at issue, at least not in any 'straightforward ... sense' (and we will need to think about this notion of 'straightforwardness' more in a moment).[14] Instead, the songs speak at such places always only of themselves; the poetic function of self-reference is primary, the *denotative* meaning of the verses reveals itself as misdirection, as not really meant.

These passages are by no means unique in Bundy's reading of the epinicians. No different, for example, is the situation with respect to the problem with which he begins the *Studia Pindarica*: with the future κελαδήσω, *I will sing* (*Olymp.* 11. 14) and the relationship it allegedly expresses between *Olympian* 11 and the later *Olympian* 10, dedicated to the same victor and the same victory. Against those who believe they can discern here the promise of the second song in the first—this refers above all to the authors of the scholia—Bundy urges that 'certain rhetorical conventions make the true meaning of [κελαδήσω]

[13] Bundy 1986, p. 9.

[14] A comparatively recent example of the 'theological' reading is Mackie 2003, pp. 22–27 and 71 f., who interprets both of these passages solely in terms of the poet's 'anxiety about blurring the distinction between gods and mortals' (p. 25).

inconsistent with reference to anything beyond the compass of the ode [...] in which [it] appear[s]'.[15] The real meaning of the verses lies under their only apparently referential form as if hidden.

From a theoretical perspective, this self-referential moment of rhetoric in Bundy's work should not surprise us. Only two years before the publication of the *Studia Pindarica*, Roman Jakobson had argued in 'Linguistics and poetics' that a defining characteristic of literary texts is a basically self-referential orientation towards their own message.[16] The model of communication that Jakobson develops here takes account of six factors which, together, constitute a linguistic event: speaker, receiver, code, context, medium and message. Each element is assigned a specific speech function. The *poetic* function of language consists in a message being directed towards itself: 'The set (*Einstellung*) towards the message as such, focus on the message for its own sake, is the poetic function of language.'[17] 'Message', in this context, is not the referential content of speech, for Jakobson defines the referential function as an orientation not towards the message but rather towards the context. Instead, the poetic function emphasizes the form and structure of the speech-act. Jakobson's first examples are thus poetic techniques based on the sensory dimension of sound: rhyme, rhythm, paronomasia, *etc.* But it soon becomes clear that the poetic function—and therefore the 'message' towards which it is directed—cannot be limited exclusively to the 'sound level' of the linguistic event: this, as Jakobson points out in a sudden reversal of the usual burden of proof in the epistemologically positivist mid-twentieth century, would be a speculative reduction without empirical basis. Rather, its effects correspond to Valéry's description of poetry as an 'hésitation entre le son et le sens'.[18] In other words: the 'poetic function' consists not in directing the attention of the listener or reader towards the materiality of the text alone, but rather in pointing towards a *tension* between this materiality and its semiotic function. Jakobson sees that this tension threatens to dissolve the convergence of sign and object altogether: 'This function, by promoting the palpability of signs, deepens the fundamental dichotomy of signs and objects.'[19] When for Bundy the rhetoricity of the epinicians consists in the way they emphasize their own structure, and that at the cost of their apparent referentiality

[15] Bundy 1986, p. 1.
[16] Jakobson 1987, pp. 62–94.
[17] Jakobson 1987, p. 69.
[18] Jakobson 1987, p. 81.
[19] Jakobson 1987, p. 70.

towards what is outside or beyond the borders of the text, this orientation towards their own make-up is closely related to Jakobson's 'set towards the message as such'. And as we have seen, it has the same consequences.

The rhetoricity of epinician lexis now becomes, however—and this is the second implication of this term in Bundy—oddly ambivalent. Whereas its function, like the function of all language, theoretically consists in the revelation or communication of meaning, its role in the *Studia* has constantly to do with disguising or masking the intention of the epinician speaker. Bundy insists repeatedly on the crucial difference between the historical Pindar—'the personal Pindar of Thebes' (p. 3)—about whom we know next to nothing and the 'Pindar privileged to praise the worthiest of men' (*ibid.*), and it is in this context that the mask and the pose are most frequently mentioned.[20] But wherever this distinction is made, its only purpose is to motivate Bundy's thesis that the intention of the victory songs is rigorously invariant. The role of the *laudator*, to whose fundamental distinction from Pindar's historical persona Bundy returns again and again, reveals itself to be nothing other than a metonymy for the single intention of the *laus victoris*; its role in the individual interpretations of the odes consists exclusively in reducing the variety of lexis to the one desire to praise. Where on the surface of the texts this intention is not evident, where it is therefore necessary to interpret against the phenomena in order to achieve this uniformity, the appearance of difference—the *rhetorical* appearance—must be effaced to reveal the poems' naked meaning.

In this way, the true consequences of rhetoric as disguise for Bundy's exegetical practice extend further than the question of the Pindaric ἐγώ alone might lead us to suspect. Since all those expressions which do not, or at least not primarily, mean what they seem to say are 'rhetorical', Bundy must constantly de-rhetoricize them, relieve them of their rhetorical disguise, so that the reader of the odes can reach or recognize their real meaning. The rhetoricity of all such passages consists in the discrepancy between their denotation and their intention, between what they say and what they *mean* to say. The poses of the poet, the multiplicity of his masks and gestures, reveal his true intentions and disguise them at the same time.

[20] 'In all such contexts, Pindar himself is hidden behind the conventional mask of the laudator' (p. 32); the 'multitude of conventional masks and gestures that appear in the odes' are 'transformed into so many personal grotesqueries' (p. 35). *Cf.* also Schadewaldt 1966, p. 19.

It is obvious that Bundy's entire project is dependent on the recoverability of this identity of intention in the difference of expression.[21] The textual surface must be made transparent for the single meaning on which it rests, the 'less transparent forms'[22] of the rhetorical motives revealed as realizations of the one encomiastic intention. And it is here that the notion of convention becomes of crucial importance.

> In the determination of sense and effect as they subserve the harmony of the whole, convention rules. Language which admits, on the assumption of its uniqueness, a wide variety of interpretations, becomes, when the conventional elements have been isolated and identified, unambiguous or ambiguous only in a controlled sense. [...] [I]t seems apparent that in this genre the choice involved in composition is mainly a choice of formulae, motives, themes, topics and set sequences of these that have, by convention, meanings not always easily perceived from the surface denotations of the words themselves.[23]

It is the conventions which make the surface denotations of formulae and themes into disguises of their meanings. The identification of a motif or a series of motives as conventional simultaneously means asserting their rhetoricity and thus their masking function over against the intention that lies beneath them. Rhetoric as a contractual system of representation, as *θέσις* or *νόμος*, which—this too an essential presupposition of the project of the *Studia*—can be recognized in the repetition of its elements *as* a system, for the opposite of the determinable convention is indeed the hermeneutically uncontrollable singularity, 'the assumption of ... uniqueness'. Thus, repetition, the identification of the different as the same, is the most important category in which Bundy's reading of the epinicians takes place.

[21] This is the point at which, despite all the differences between them, Bundy is close to French structuralism; one can compare Lévi-Strauss' corresponding description of a structural(ist) anthropology: 'Que ce soit en linguistique et en anthropologie, la méthode structurale consiste a repérer des formes invariantes au sein de contenus différents' (Lévi-Strauss 1973, p. 322). Bundy's work is usually situated in the context of Anglo-American New Criticism (see, for example, Hubbard 1985, p. 3 n. 7 and Krummen 1990, p. 19 f.). But New Criticism was by no means closed to non-English-speaking influence, and received not inconsiderable impulses from the techniques of Russian formalism which were also of importance for the structuralists (key figures here are of course René Wellek and Roman Jakobson; see Culler 2007, p. 6 ff. on the essential similarity of the formalist and structuralist projects). *Cf.* further Kirkwood 1981, pp. 13 and 22 n. 4, Currie 2005, p. 12, and below, p. 117 n. 159.

[22] Bundy 1986, p. 12.

[23] Bundy 1986, p. 91 f.

It is therefore anything but surprising when Bundy, in order to designate the opposite of the disguising rhetoricity of the convention, turns to *natural* language: the artless, straightforward expression of what the speaker really wants to say. In Pindar, this opposite of artificial, encoded speech is connected to the notion of *φυά*, a connection that Bundy discusses in *Studia* I. One example, by no means the longest but certainly one of the most suggestive, is his reading of *Olympian* 9. 100–109:[24]

> *τὸ δὲ φυᾷ κράτιστον ἅπαν· πολλοὶ δὲ διδακταῖς*
> *ἀνθρώπων ἀρεταῖς κλέος*
> *ὤρουσαν ἀρέσθαι·*
> *ἄνευ δὲ θεοῦ σεσιγαμένον*
> *οὐ σκαιότερον χρῆμ᾽ ἕκαστον· ἐντὶ γὰρ ἄλλαι*
> *ὁδῶν ὁδοὶ περαίτεραι,*
> *μία δ᾽ οὐχ ἅπαντας ἄμμε θρέψει*
> *μελέτα· σοφίαι μέν*
> *αἰπειναί· τοῦτο δὲ προσφέρων ἄεθλον,*
> *ὄρθιον ὤρυσαι θαρσέων* [...].

> All that is natural is best; but many men strive by means of taught abilities
> to win fame;
> but without a god, a deed left in silence
> is no worse; for some
> roads are longer than others,
> and no one training will develop us all;
> wisdom is
> steep; but when you present this prize,
> boldly speak out straightforwardly [...].

This passage follows the description of the victory won by a certain Epharmastos in wrestling in the year 468 B.C., and the first verses can obviously refer to him. As Bundy notes, the language here is entirely conventional: we can find parallels for the gnomic statement with a term of totality (*ἅπαν*), for the following opposition (*πολλοὶ δέ*), for the return to the concept of *φυά* by way of its opposite *ἄνευ δὲ θεοῦ*, and for the priamel-like assertion in 104–106. As often in Pindar, however, the verses which introduce the transition to the call to praise (108 ff.) can also be taken to refer to the singer,[25] and this is how Bundy interprets them here. On this reading, the passage is expressing a question

[24] Bundy 1986, pp. 16 f., 30 and 37–38.
[25] See on this phenomenon Hubbard 1986b.

on the part of the singer: how should one praise the *laudandus*? Two options present themselves: either the encomium according to all the rules of acquired art, or a simple, direct affirmation of his self-evident qualities. The opposition between τὸ δὲ φυᾷ and διδακταῖς [...] ἀρεταῖς now reflects this opposition between artless speech and artificiality: whilst it is clear that a song that simply allows itself to be led by the nature of its subject is strongest, still some try nevertheless to achieve fame by means of learnt rules. As long, however, as a god is lacking, putting the achievement into speech in fact achieves nothing—this time not because the achievement is not qualitatively valuable, but because the song itself is not good enough to guarantee an increase of κλέος.[26] When in verse 107 ff. steep σοφίαι[27] are opposed to the call to speak out the praise of Epharmastos in a simple and courageous fashion, the contrast between φυᾷ and διδακταῖς is again the point at issue.[28]

Σοφίαι would, according to Bundy's interpretation, represent a detour neither necessary nor desirable; instead, the obvious virtues of the *laudandus* must now be enunciated clearly and without delay. Over against artistically formed language we find simple, natural speech. This is 'natural' in the sense that here the thoughts and desires of the singer are put into language 'without the devices of art'.[29] This agreement of thought and word is exactly what Bundy, following Pindar, opposes to rhetoric: simplicity, directness, straightforwardness. In the privileged region of being designated by god and nature, language no longer disguises; instead, it becomes transparent for pure meaning.

The assumption of this possibility of unmasked speech is of the utmost importance for Bundy's project. It motivates his interpretations

[26] On the connection between φυά and θεός, see Most 1985b, p. 158 f. and Miller 1993a, p. 114.

[27] Bundy (p. 16 f.) compares *Isthm.* 2. 34: There is *no* hill, and the way will *not* be steep (οὐ γὰρ πάγος οὐδὲ προσάντης ἁ κέλευθος γίνεται) when someone leads the honours of the Muses (τιμὰς Ἑλικονιάδων) to the houses of famous men (εὐδόξων ἐς ἀνδρῶν, *sc.* δώματα or the like). Here, the quality of the topic overcomes the difficulty of the task. In *Olymp.* 9, on the other hand, the concern is with finding a form of speech that corresponds to the self-evident nature of the victor—a nature, therefore, that does not call for sophisticated artifice to cover up its defects. *Cf.* Σ *Olymp.* 9. 161b (τουτέστιν ἐφ' ὑψηλοῦ καὶ προβάσεως κεῖνται αἱ σοφίαι, ὥστε εἶναι τὴν ἐπ' αὐτὰς ὁδὸν δυσχερῆ) and Gerber 2002, p. 86 *ad loc.* ('the roads leading to σοφίαι are steep'), both noting the return to the metaphor at verse 105.

[28] The alternative, that μέν has concessive force here—so that the δέ-clause does not form a contrast, but rather affirms that although art is steep, one will resort to it anyway—is maintained by Slater 1969 *s.v.* μέν and Gerber 2002, p. 68 *ad loc.* See however Race 1987, p. 145 and Miller 1993a, p. 145.

[29] Bundy 1986, p. 16.

not only with reference to his overall reading of Pindar, but also in detail. Thus, Bundy observes in his own discussion of the beginning of the *Tenth Nemean* for the Argive victor Theaios—we noted the passage briefly above—how the ode begins with a long catalogue of Argive achievements which is introduced by the assertion that there are ἀρεταὶ μυρίαι to be told (2 f.).[30] The obvious hyperbole of this word 'μυρίαι' gives, according to Bundy, the impression that the unlimited number of achievements demonstrates both the exceptional qualities of the Argives and at the same time the practical impossibility of ever narrating them to the end. The contrafactual *topos* serves not only as a 'rhetorical enlargement' of the theme, but also as a reason to leave it whenever opportune. This much is clear. In the list of ἀρεταί which now follows, however, 'rhetoric is abandoned': after the first two items, the 'long' (μακρά) story of Perseus and the Medusa (4) and the many (πολλά) cities founded by Argos in Egypt through Epaphos (5)—both terms pick up the enlargement motif again—the catalogue continues without recourse to obviously figurative language. In verse 19, however, the list is interrupted in order to emphasize, once again, the impossibility of ever completing it, and in view of this to effect the transition to the successes of Theaios (19–22). This new catalogue is then carried through 'without major rhetorical interruption' to verse 45 where the hyperbolic motif of the inexhaustible number of themes returns as the transition to the story of Castor and Pollux.

The possibility of abandoning rhetoric is here the possibility of a language which consists exclusively in the representation of the 'real' narrative intention of the speaker. In this one-to-one-relationship between meaning and form, no disguising rhetorical composition still stands between the surface denotations of the words and their real significance, the meaning meant by the *laudator*. In Bundy's overall interpretation of the epinicians, this possibility is signalled by the privileged category of those expressions which reveal Pindar's real desire, contained in such passages as *Nemean* 3. 29: 'ἐσλὸν αἰνεῖν', *'praise the noble!'* When at the beginning of his *Style and Rhetoric in Pindar's Odes*, published in 1990, William Race writes that he only intends to interpret those passages in Pindar in which 'meaning and style are in complete agreement',[31] he is faithful in this as in other respects to Bundy's project.

[30] Bundy 1986, p. 13 f. See above, p. 23 f.

[31] Race 1990, p. 5 f. The expression is borrowed by Race from Wilamowitz 1922, p. 459.

The order of φύσις—that inherent potential of an object for movement *by itself* which Aristotle analyses in the second book of the *Physics*—is what Bundy's commentary explicitly wants to recover. The odes are to 'speak for themselves', the songs to be treated 'as they deserve'.[32] It is no accident that this last formulation reminds us of the χρέος-motif, whose form and role in the epinicians Bundy at more than one place notes.[33] Like the victories for Pindar, so the texts for Bundy make claims by nature to which the interpreter must answer. By the force of the natural power of language, the disguise of materiality disappears; things find their own expressions without having to surrender themselves to the violence of interpretation. *Virtus se ipsa satis ostendit*.[34] The dream of the commentary to reveal, at last, the nature of the text without rhetorical disguise is the eschatological programme of the *Studia*.

Die Erkenntnis des Erkannten

This programme—interpretation as unveiling—is by no means Bundy's invention, although I believe that it finds its most rigorous and productive implementation in the *Studia Pindarica*. It is a version of that hermeneutics of presence which has been canonical for a large part of literary studies in general and for research on Pindar in particular since the first half of the nineteenth century.[35] In the history of Pindaric interpretation since Boeckh, interpretation presents itself as the *truth* of the text, truth understood here in the sense of the disclosedness (*Unverborgenheit*) of being which Heidegger argued was expressed in the word ἀλήθεια.[36] The revelation of this truth, the referential or literal φύσις hidden below the rhetorical surface of language, is the common goal of every form of scholarship based on a view of interpretation as translation, as the preservation of the intelligible, ideal meaning of a literary text in the new sensible form of the com-

[32] Bundy 1986, p. 35: 'I [have] tried to indicate what results we might achieve if we [...] let the odes *speak for themselves*'; p. 4: 'I shall treat it [*Olympia* 11] as it *deserves to be treated* [...]' (my italics).

[33] See above, p. 56 with n. 83.

[34] Bundy 1986, p. 16, to explain the sense of σὺν θεῷ in Bacchyl., fr. 20c. 20; the sentence is Sallust's: *De bello Iugurthino* 85. 31.

[35] Nietzsche, by no means unaware of the metaphysical underpinnings of the philology of his day, mocks 'theoretical man' for being obsessed with undressing the truth in Ch. 15 of *Die Geburt der Tragödie*; see Nietzsche 1988, vol. 1, p. 98.

[36] See Heidegger ^{18}2001, pp. 32–34, Engl. pp. 55–58, and *id.* ^{3}1996, pp. 177–202, esp. p. 188, Engl. pp. 136–154, esp. p. 145.

mentary. The enabling presupposition of such a procedure is not merely that both literary and scholarly language are essentially constituted by this relationship to a reality which is itself not merely another sign, but instead, as history or conscious desire, a presence or self-presence unmediated by further signification. The crucial assumption of this *philologie de la métaphysique* is in fact that the surface *can* be made transparent for what—no doubt—lies below it, that this transparency is in fact *the true nature* of the surface as the symptom of the real presence of the ground, and that the agreement of λέξις and λόγος, the ultimate convergence or *Aufhebung* of rhetoric and meaning in the absolute presence of what is meant is the teleological fulfilment of the text.

In the scholarly reception of Pindar's epinicians, the contours of this hermeneutics become apparent as a system for the first time in the final volume of *Pindari opera*, the edition with Latin translation and commentary published in 1821 by August Boeckh, professor of classics at the University of Berlin, and his Göttingen colleague Ludolph Dissen. In the commentary, to which Boeckh contributed the *prooemium* and the *explicationes* to the *Olympians* and *Pythians*, a theory of interpretation is at work that centres the songs around a point of meaning whose privileged role in stabilizing and unifying the text is based on its status as absolute presence. That this procedure was an innovation is emphasized by David Young:

> Boeckh's monumental edition not only signalled a new era in the establishment of the text but also marked a great advance over the previous literary criticism of Pindar, for Boeckh sought to show that the Pindaric ode *made sense as a whole*.[37]

Young characterizes the unstructured nature of the texts as seen by 'previous literary criticism' with Boileau's description of the odes as 'un beau désordre'.[38] Boeckh's own conception of the relationship between the text and its meaning is explained on the first pages of the commentary:

> This poet, who composes songs with reason and not with blind passion, and

[37] Young 1970, p. 3 (my italics). See also Krummen 1990, p. 11.

[38] Young 1970, p. 3 n. 3: Boileau, *L'art poétique* II 72 (= *id.* 1966, p. 164). Other scholars have argued that Boeckh's break with earlier practice was not as sharp as Young suggests: see in particular Heath 1986, pp. 90–95. On Pindaric studies in the modern period before Boeckh, see also Schmitz 1993, esp. pp. 71–146, Braswell 1996 and Vöhler 2005.

> who fits everything to the matters and persons, the circumstances and the purpose, is not to be accused of the crime of discordant or idle digressions.[39]

Boeckh's argument that the epinicians contain no digressions is generally read with a view to his specific theory of poetic unity. We should not, however, overlook the qualification of the *digressiones* of which Pindar must not be accused as *absonae et inanes*. For Boeckh, there is nothing in these poems that does not point beyond itself to a single, foundational meaning shared with the rest of the text. The basic structure of reading is thus the same as that we found in Bundy: whatever refuses to be bound back to the value of meaning is worthless, *inanis*—mere rhetoric.

This does not mean that there are no differences between Boeckh and Bundy. On the contrary, the two most important Pindarists of the last two hundred years are usually seen as exact opposites: on the one hand the authoritative forerunner of the historicism of such scholars as Wilamowitz, on the other the most important representative of formalist, 'rhetorical' Pindaric studies for whom there seems to be nothing 'outside the text'.[40] Such an opposition is to a certain extent superficial, based as it is only on the different historical articulations of the one hermeneutics that both interpreters presuppose. Nevertheless, the specific form of this hermeneutics in Boeckh is significantly more revealing than in Bundy; for whereas the American classicist only sketches the theoretical presuppositions of his interpretations briefly before moving on to the real work of reading, the German philologist goes to considerable lengths to formulate his own premises explicitly, most comprehensively in his lectures on the *Encyklopädie und Methodologie der philologischen Wissenschaften*. As a result—and this is what interests us about Boeckh—the limits of the period in the interpretation of Pindar which in effect begins with him appear all the more clearly. A reading of the commentary and the *Encyklopädie* will show this.

We begin with the commentary. In the last volume of *Pindari opera*, the Berlin Hellenist ties the understanding of those epinicians on which he himself comments to the reconstruction of the particular

39 '[...] *neque poeta ratione, non caeco impetu in carminibus pangendis versatus, rebusque et personis, temporibus, fini maxima quaeque accomodans absonarum et inanium digressionum crimine onerandus.*' Boeckh 1811–1821, vol. II ii, pp. 6–7. All translations from *Pindari opera* are my own.

40 *Cf.* the contrast between Boeckh's collaborator Dissen and Wilamowitz on the one hand and Bundy and his most important German follower Thummer on the other in Most 1985b, pp. 26–33.

historical circumstances in which they were composed as seen by the poet. Here, in the intuition of these circumstances, Boeckh finds the core of the victory songs as their proper meaning. The circumstances are originary; only they can ground the one natural meaning of the text as the poet's response to a situation which *hic et nunc* confronts him. Others may indeed, if they so desire, concern themselves with such things as the study of the 'inner meanings' of the myths, Boeckh writes in his *prooemium*;[41] he and his collaborator have restricted themselves to making only sporadic observations. 'But the most difficult and important duty of the interpreter is, we judge, to cast as much light as possible upon the poet's purpose and upon the situation in which those things and people who gave Pindar occasion to write as he did found themselves.'[42] The task of the interpreter is only fulfilled, the goal of reading only reached, when the immediate intuitions of the author have been so exactly identified that the text has become transparent for the facts—the identity and character of the victor, his family, the city, *etc.*—to which he consciously intends to refer.[43]

Boeckh's *explicationes* to the individual songs correspond exactly to this programme. A short song such as the *Sixth Pythian* is a good example.[44] The commentary begins with the identification of the main characters of the text (*hominum ... condicio*): Xenocrates, his brother Theron, his son Thrasybulus. The information provided by the scholia is assessed; other references in the epinicians are used to reconstruct the relationships between the characters. The family's victories are catalogued from the victory songs and the scholia; the problem of the real addressee—Xenocrates or Thrasybulus?—is decided in favour of the former. And he was *present* at the victory: 'That Xenocrates, however, really was present at this Pythian contest is clear from the words of *Isthm.* 2 [18], "In Krisa mighty Apollo beheld him (*i.e.* Xenocrates) and gave him splendour there too".'[45] The presence of the victor is

[41] Mythology had become a controversial undertaking in the wake of the four-volume *Symbolik und Mythologie der alten Völker, besonders der Griechen* (1810–1812) published by Boeckh's erstwhile Heidelberg colleague Friedrich Creuzer; *cf.* Boeckh ²1886, pp. 578 f. and 585, and Horstmann 1992, p. 122 n. 184.

[42] '*At illud et difficillimum et praecipuum interpretis munus iudicamus, ut poetae consilium rerumque et hominum, qui Pindaro talia scribendi occasionem praebuerat, condicio, quantum fieri potest, in luce ponatur.*' Boeckh 1811–1821, vol. II ii, p. 6.

[43] This understanding of classical literary studies is still authoritative for Krummen 1990 and Pfeijffer 1999b: see below, p. 152 with n. 19.

[44] Boeckh 1811–1821, vol. II ii, pp. 296–300.

[45] '*In Pythio vero hoc certamine* praesentem *fuisse Xenocratem, patet ex verbis Isthm. II* [18] Ἐν Κρίσᾳ δ' εὐρυσθενὴς εἶδ' Ἀπόλλων νιν (Ξενοκράτη) πόρε τ' αγλαΐαν καὶ τόθι.'

confirmed by the perception of the god, the anchor of the true meaning of the poem guaranteed in immediate intuition. (Boeckh is entirely prepared, at this point, to consider the possibility that Pindar himself had not seen the victory and did not himself attend the performance of the song, also in Delphi: 'I therefore do not doubt that the ode was written as a song for the Pythian victory celebration in Delphi itself, whether Pindar was present or whether he sent the song to Delphi from Thebes.' But that even in the latter case the report of an eye-witness could have reached him quickly, so as to allow for the composition of a song for the victory celebration in Delphi, is certain: 'From Delphi it is hardly ten German miles to Thebes, so that a messenger sent to Pindar could have brought back an ode to Delphi in a short space of time.'[46]) The poet also bears witness to the presence of Xenocrates' son Thrasybulus—*Etiam Thrasybulum victoriae affuisse poeta vs. 15 sqq. docet*—who steered the victorious chariot. Presence alone guarantees the intuition in which alone the meaning of the song is rooted.

In the commentary on the individual verses the concern is now to decode the information the text offers about place and time—*as* information about place and time and nothing more. Boeckh identifies the first word of the poem, ἀκούσατε, as an occasional allusion to the custom of the *praeco* to call for attention before announcing the name of the victor. For the commentator, the herald's voice, whose temporal and spatial existence is limited to the place and moment of its production, evokes once again an immediate perception whose permanence, created by its having been set down in writing, has to be revoked in order to arrive at its meaning. The question of whether the ὀμφαλός (verse 3) designates the stone of that name kept in the temple at Delphi or rather Delphi itself is decided, after careful consideration of the alternatives, in favour of the latter, since neither the stone nor the place where it was kept is a reconstructable part of the occasion: *quum praesertim nullum odae vestigium insit, ex quo supplicationem Apollini fieri in sacro loco colligeris.* Boeckh is well aware that the road of the song is a metaphor for the progression of its content; but this is only a secondary level of signification whose basis consists exclusively of stations which emerge from the performative occasion of the text. He

Boeckh 1811–1821, vol. II ii, p. 296 (my emphasis).

[46] *'Itaque non dubito Pythiae carmen victoriae ipsis Delphis celebrandae odam scriptam esse, sive praesente Pindaro sive carmen Thebis Delphos mittente, a quibus Thebae vix decem miliariis Germanicis aberant: ut hemerodromus ad Pindarum missus odam brevi tempore potuerit Delphos reportare.'* Boeckh 1811–1821, vol. II ii, p. 297.

notes approvingly that the scholia correctly interpret the *θησαυρός* as the hymn itself; the explanation of the metaphor is to be found in the treasure houses of the Apollonian *περίβολος*. When the song stands ready (*ἑτοῖμος*, verse 7) in the Apollonian valley, Pindar is informing us that it was performed there; this is the only comment Boeckh has to make on this verse. The German scholar argues that the metaphor of the treasure-house is continued in the verses about the storm and the seabed (this against Heyne, who in verses 10–14 seems to have seen a—necessarily *absent*—shipwreck[47]), and explains the function of the shining *πρόσωπον*, *facade* in verse 14 as the report of the victory, not to Xenocrates (who had seen it himself), but to the *λόγοι θνατῶν*, *the tales of mortals*, so that the news is passed on when the song, *sung* only in the immediate *here and now*, has fallen silent. The controversial verse 19—*σύ τοι σχεθών νιν ἐπιδέξια χειρὸς* [...] *ἄγεις*, as Boeckh prints it with the adverbial *ἐπιδέξια*—is paraphrased as *in dextero latere patris incedens manum manui eius iungis* and is thus an expression of the son's position of honour at the right hand of the father.[48] The following myth, whose sources and later versions Boeckh conscientiously lists, is pointless if Thrasybulus had made no contribution to his father's victory. Pindar's obvious comparison of the young Akragantine to Nestor's son and saviour Antilochus is intended to represent the praise Thrasybulus receives from his contemporaries, and this is the point of the whole passage: 'Thus is Thrasybulus now celebrated by his fellows as the first among them in piety towards his father', we are told in the comment on verses 40 ff., 'by the singing of this song: this is what the poet intends.'[49] The last verses do not express a general thought (*generalem sententiam*), as Heyne believed, but instead still relate to Thrasybulus; they have been added by the poet 'because the revel for which the song was intended has put him in mind of it' (*monente comissatione, cui carmen destinatum erat*)—not least as an allusion to the celebration at which the song is presently being sung: Thrasybulus' character, we are told, 'is also charming in the company of table-companions'—'and at a banquet', adds Boeckh, 'such as is now being held.'[50]

47 This seems, at least, to be the sense of his comment on verse 12 f., *ἐς μυχοὺς | ἁλὸς ἄξοισι κτλ.*: *respicit* [sc. *poeta*] *divitias navi transvectas* (Heyne 1807–1809, vol. i, p. 281 *ad* 10–14).

48 Exactly the opposite sense emerges from the text as currently printed by SM: *σύ τοι σχεθών νιν ἐπὶ δεξιὰ χειρός* [...], 'You have taken him/it in your right hand [...].'

49 *'Ita nunc Thrasybulus a sodalibus ut imprimis pius erga patrem celebratur hoc carmine canendo: hoc est, quod poeta voluit.'* Boeckh 1811–1821, vol. II ii, p. 300.

50 *'Eius mens autem etiam in convivarum societate* et convivio quale nunc habetur *tam*

There is little here that, in terms of its results, has to be seen after almost two centuries as fundamentally implausible.[51] The orientation of the interpretation towards the present, the actual, the immediate, however, is unmistakeable. Alongside individual remarks on the constitution of the text, and brief notes on grammatical constructions, what we find in the *explicationes* are above all explanations intended to give an account of what was present to Pindar as the occasion of the song. In this respect, Boeckh's discussion of the *Sixth Pythian* is typical for the commentary as a whole. The metaphor of the treasure house, for example, develops no logic of its own within the text; it is merely a vehicle for the tenor on which it is based, and only the correct identification of this tenor—the architecture of the Delphian sacred precinct—can be viewed as a satisfactory interpretative result. Everywhere, the important thing is to recover the intuition behind the words, for the simple reason that the present which centres the poem reveals itself exclusively in the immediate intuition of the poet. The intuition becomes in this way both the source and the referential goal—in other words, the meaning—of the song.

Intuition thus occupies the same position in Boeckh as the content of simple, non-rhetorical speech in Bundy: it is the centre which, because of its absolute presence in the mind of the poet, is eminently qualified for the status of the meaning of the texts. This view of things, ubiquitous if only implicitly assumed in the commentary, must have considerable implications for our understanding of the linguistic nature of the songs. For if interpretation is understood as the transfer of the objective presence of what the author has intuited to the self-presence of the reader, then the language of the text takes on the status of an *absence*, a *transition* or *bridge* between the originary presence of the poet and the secondary, reconstructed presence of the interpreter.[52] In fact, the figure of the double presence and the sign as bridge grounds not only the hermeneutical *modus operandi* of the commentary, but also Boeckh's entire conception of philology in the *Encyklopädie und Methodologie der philologischen Wissenschaften*, a conception that first provides the interpretations of the final volume of the *Pindari opera*

est dulcis […].' *Ibid.*, using Roman type in the Latin to distinguish his interposed commentary from the translation.

[51] *Cf.* Gentili *et al.* 1995, pp. 541–552, who offer a more or less similarly accentuated interpretation of the ode.

[52] Even Wilamowitz, no particular friend of hermeneutical theory, notices Boeckh's comparative lack of interest in the materiality of language: see Wilamowitz ^{3}1998, p. 54, Engl. p. 121 on Boeckh's *Antigone*.

with their theoretical plausibility and rigour. Here, the metaphysical premises of Boeckh's literary scholarship and that of his successors become clear.

The lectures which make up the *Encyklopädie*, published after Boeckh's death in 1867, were given some twenty-six times in repeatedly revised versions between 1809 and 1865.[53] They contain a comprehensive, formal and material theory of philology as hermeneutics and criticism—a division going back to the methodologies of Wolf and Ast and to Schleiermacher[54]—which takes as its point of departure Boeckh's famous dictum that the goal of philological study is 'the understanding of what is known' (*die Erkenntnis des Erkannten*).[55] With this definition, Boeckh sets up the notion of *Erkenntnis* as the theoretical and structural principle of his philology; his construction of the latter will be based upon his conception of the former. What, then, is 'understanding'?

Boeckh's answer to this question is given in the first chapter of the *Encyklopädie*, 'Die Idee der Philologie'. In the third section of this chapter, Boeckh discusses the relationship between classical scholarship and other disciplines. Classical philology, confronted with other forms of scholarly endeavour such as philosophy or history, can still make claim to its own specific knowledge, as indeed it must if it does not wish to be condemned merely to repeating the alien knowledge contained in the works it treats.[56] The acquisition of knowledge is

53 According to Bratuscheck (in Boeckh ^{2}1886, p. III), Boeckh held the lectures between 1809 and 1865 26 times in front of a total of 1696 enrolled students. On the constitution of the text, see Bratuscheck's description of his sources and method (*ibid.*, p. IV) and Horstmann's (positive) assessment of the edition after examining the (for the most part) still extant notebooks and notes (Horstmann 1992, p. 23 n. 2). Hackel 2006, pp. 21–73 provides a useful overview.

54 *Cf.* Pflug 1975, p. 139. Boeckh refers explicitly to all three (Wolf: Boeckh ^{2}1886, pp. 39–44; Ast: *ibid.*, pp. 38 and 44; Schleiermacher: *ibid.*, p. 75). On Schleiermacher's own readings of the encyclopaedias of Wolf and Ast, see the autobiographical fragment in Frank's introduction to Schleiermacher 1977, p. 8 f., and his speech to the *Akademie der Wissenschaften* in Berlin from 1829 on the concept of hermeneutics (*ibid.*, pp. 309–346).

55 Boeckh ^{2}1886, p. 11, Engl. p. 8. On Boeckh's definition, see Rodi 1990, p. 70–88 and Horstmann 1992, esp. pp. 76–87. Schleiermacher had already spoken of an 'Erkennen des Erkennens' in his *Brouillon zur Ethik* (Schleiermacher 1981, p. 93).

56 The danger of merely reiterating the content of its objects of study, of becoming merely the sign of a sign, is the result of philology's constitutive retrospectivity (*Nachträglichkeit*): see Boeckh ^{2}1886, 13: 'Es liegt in der That im Begriff der Philologie, daß jeder Philologe zwar in seinem Fache der Erste sein kann, aber in den einzelnen übrigen Wissenschaften der Zweite, gleichsam der Beta sein muss.' Boeckh's immediate reference to Eratosthenes' nickname 'Beta' (Suda ε 2898 = *FGrH* 241 T 1) here should not blind us to the essentially *temporal* dimension of philology's secondary nature as the under-

what is traditionally called 'cognition'. How does it take place?

> The requirement is [...] initially this: the reproduction of what is alien as something being assimilated to the self, so that it is no longer external; in this way, the status of philology as an aggregate is also overcome. At the same time, however, [the self] must take up a position over against this reproduced knowledge so as to view it again as something objective, despite its having been appropriated, and so as to possess an understanding of this understanding of what is known, now itself put together to form a whole. This will in turn lead [the self] to assign this understanding a place in its own thinking and to equate it with what is known itself, which is what happens in judgement.[57]

The accusation that philology was merely an aggregation of knowledge whose coherence or unity could not be derived from a single concept and thus was merely contingent or outward had been made most prominently by Hegel, from 1818 onwards Boeckh's colleague in Berlin, at the beginning of his own *Enzyklopädie*; Boeckh refers explicitly to this passage elsewhere (not without a brief jab at Wolf).[58]

standing of what has already been understood in the primary text.

[57] 'Es ist [...] zunächst die Forderung diese, das Fremde als Eigenwerdendes zu reproduciren, so dass es nichts Aeusserliches bleibe, wodurch eben auch der Aggregatzustand der Philologie aufgehoben wird; zugleich aber auch über diesem Reproducirten zu stehen, so dass man es, obgleich es ein Eigenes geworden, dennoch wieder als ein Objectives gegenüber und ein Erkennen von dieser zu einem Ganzen formirten Erkenntniss des Erkannten habe, was dann dahin führen wird demselben in dem eigenen Denken seinen Platz anzuweisen und es mit dem Erkannten selbst auf gleicher Stufe zu stellen, was durch die Beurtheilung überhaupt geschieht.' Boeckh ²1886, p. 20, my translation (*cf.* Engl. p. 18). Danz, who is one of the few scholars to take note of this passage, reads it (cited, significantly, without the reference to the *Aggregatzustand*) as a statement that all interpretation is historically mediated (Danz 1982, p. 140).

[58] Boeckh ²1886, p. 40: 'Wenn Hegel die Philologie für ein Aggregat erklärt, so scheint sich dieses Urtheil auf Wolfs Darstellung zu begründen.' See also Boeckh 1858–1874, vol. II, p. 192. The passage in question is Hegel, *Encyklopädie der philosophischen Wissenschaften im Grundrisse*, § 10 (= Hegel 1817, p. 11): '[D]ie philosophische Encyklopädie [schließt] 1) bloße *Aggregate* von Kenntnissen – wie z.B. die Philologie ist – aus [...].' Hegel changes this formulation, perhaps in response to the objections of his classicist colleague, in the second edition of 1827 to 'wie z.B. die Philologie *zunächst erscheint*' (now § 16; my italics); the passage remains unchanged in the third and last edition of 1830 (see Hegel 1969–1971, vol. 8, p. 61, Engl. Hegel 1975b, p. 21). The idea that philology is an aggregate is, however, neither exclusively Hegelian—see also Schleiermacher 1977, p. 75, Engl. p. 6—nor presumably originally, as some of Friedrich Schlegel's notes from 1797—*e.g.* 'Die Philologie ist kein *Aggregat* von Wissenschaft, sondern ein *Ganzes*: aber kein logisches sondern ein *technisches*' ('Zur Philologie' I, n. 60 in Schlegel 1958–, vol. XVI, p. 40, his italics)—suggest. It is still an element of Nietzsche's critique of philology in 1869 (see Nietzsche 1982–1995, vol. 1, p. 249).

The philologist now answers the philosopher's criticism by adopting the latter's model of theoretical cognition: after the transformation of what is foreign into what is one's own, a process that Boeckh represents as a process of reproductive internalisation ('so dass es nichts Aeusserliches bleibt'), the subject must objectivize this appropriated knowledge in himself anew, that is, he must posit what he has internalized in himself as something external, in order, finally, to reappropriate it again in the judgement of thinking.[59]

Cognition is, according to this description, a dialectical process of repeatedly internalizing and bringing forth (*producere*) what has been (re)cognized within one's own intelligence; the teleological moment of truth in this model, however, is that of internalization, not that of production. Boeckh now uses this figure of the inwardness of truth as the foundation of his conception both of the object of philological study and of this study itself:

> Something general must be found within which every characteristic part is contained. This is what philosophers call the *principle* of a people or an age, the inmost kernel of its total nature. This alone can be the principle; anything else would be alien, imported from outside. The particulars should not be *deduced* from this principle [...], but they should follow from a general intuition, and this must hold good in every particular. This intuition is the soul of the body and penetrates its earthly matter as its combining, ordering first cause, as the Greeks rightly define the soul. Through this ensouling, scholarship becomes *organic*. [...] For classical philology, this general intuition can only be the Idea of antiquity as such [...].[60]

[59] This is in its broad outline exactly the model of cognition described in the *Enzyklopädie der philosophischen Wissenschaften* III, §§ 451–464 (= Hegel 1969–1971, vol. 10, pp. 257–283; Engl. Hegel 2007, pp. 184–202). Here the three steps are: 1. The content of sensation or intuition is internalized in the inwardness of intelligence as *Er-innerung* or recollection (§ 452); 2. The recollected intuition is re-produced (*hervorgestellt*), that is, re-externalised by the agency of imagination (§ 455); 3. This representation of the imagination, a sign of what has been intuited, is then finally re-internalised as *Gedächtnis* or memory whose content, the names of things, provides the material of thought (§ 461). Hegel's influence on Boeckh's epistemology is noted by Irmscher 1987, p. 13. (*Cf.* however Rodi 1990, p. 86, who follows Steinthal in reading Boeckh's system as an essentially non-dialectical oscillation between conceptual poles without *Aufhebung*.)

[60] 'Es muss ein Gemeinsames gefunden werden, in welchem alles Besondere enthalten ist. Es ist dies dasjenige, was die Philosophen das Princip eines Volkes oder Zeitalters nennen, der innerste Kern seines Gesammtwesens; etwas Anderes kann es nicht sein; denn jedes Andere wäre fremdartig, von Aussen hereingenommen. Die Einzelheiten sollen nicht aus diesem Princip deducirt werden [...], aber sie sollen hervorgehen aus einer allgemeinen Anschauung, und diese muss sich wieder in jedem einzelnen Theile bewähren; sie ist die Seele des Leibes, durchdringt den irdischen Stoff als die zusammen-

As the ideal, inner principle of the material, outward body, the soul stands for the epistemological *telos* of philology, both in terms of its object—'the inmost core of its entire being'—and in terms of scholarship itself, which Boeckh here understands as the organic subject of cognition. The correspondence between the subject and object of cognition is a central concern of both Schelling's and Hegel's Idealism; Boeckh's construction of antiquity according to the model of the animate body of philology follows directly from his adoption of Idealist epistemology.[61]

By virtue of its spiritual inwardness, the Idea is eminently qualified to be the goal of interpretation. The material embodiment of antiquity, on the other hand, occupies the position of the external product. Its status is, as we might expect, characterised by a lack of truth and presence. At the beginning of the 'formal theory of the philological discipline', two realizations of this product are distinguished: the immediate object of philology is either

> a *sign* of the thing known, *i.e.*, different from it in form, like all linguistic communication, writing, musical notation, *etc.*; or it is an *image agreeing* in form with the object expressed in it, like works of art and technology, instutitions immediately accessible to intuition, and so on. But even the last-mentioned kinds of intellectual expression are to some extent *hieroglyphics* which must be decoded with the help of hermeneutics and criticism by proceeding from the right understanding of the forms to their significance in the works of human activity, or rather to the Ideas they represent, their content and meaning.[62]

haltende, ordnende Ursache, wie die Griechen die Seele mit Recht nennen: durch diese Beseelung wird die Wissenschaft eben organisch. [Eine solche allgemeine Anschauung] kann bei der Philologie des Alterthums nichts anderes sein als die Idee der Antike an sich [...].' Boeckh ²1886, p. 57, Engl. p. 39 f. modified (his emphasis in the original).

[61] Boeckh's relationship to Idealism has been variously assessed: see Pflug 1975, pp. 150–156, who concludes that Boeckh's 'deutliche Nachbarschaft zum deutschen Idealismus' (p. 156) was primarily mediated by his interest in Plato; Horstmann 1992, who notes the similarity of Boeckh's definition of scholarship to Schelling's (p. 33) and argues that his basic approach 'bleibt [...] vom Idealismus bestimmt' (p. 36; *cf.* also pp. 122 ff., esp. nn. 185 and 191); and Hackel 2006, pp. 67–69, who questions Horstmann's assessment of Boeckh's Idealist affinities on the grounds that his notion of the 'Idea' remains less clear than an authentically Idealist approach would lead one to expect.

[62] '[...] Zeichen des Erkannten, d. h. vom letzterem der Form nach verschieden, wie alle sprachliche Mittheilung, Schriftzeichen, musikalische Noten u. s. w., oder [er] ist ein Gebilde, welches mit dem darin Ausgedrückten der Form nach übereinstimmt, wie die Werke der Kunst und der Technik, die in unmittelbarer Anschauung gegebenen Lebenseinrichtungen u. s. w. Auch die letztere Art der geistigen Manifestation sind indess gewissermassen Hieroglyphen, welche durch Hermeneutik und Kritik ent-

The sign is distinguished from the image by the fact that its form does not reproduce the content it denotes: its relationship to its *signifié* is arbitrary. The image, on the other hand, stands in a non-arbitrary relationship of similarity to what it signifies. The non-arbitrariness of the relationship between the form of the signifier and the form of the signified in the image cannot, indeed, prevent the signified itself, as a new signifier, from requiring interpretation: it too must be 'decoded' so that it reveals its meaning. But the status of the first image's *signifié* as a 'hieroglyph'—the epitome of a non-arbitrary sign at the beginning of the nineteenth century—represents merely its structural repetition on the next higher level of interpretation.[63]

The sign, on the other hand, of which language is an example, is not repeated. Its structure is based rather on a fundamental foreignness which, *as such*, cannot lead by way of relationships of similarity to a signified, ideal content. In his own *Enzyklopädie*, Hegel describes the sign for this reason as a pyramid:

> The *sign* is some immediate intuition, which represents a wholly different content from the content that it has for itself;—the *pyramid* into which an alien soul is transferred and preserved. The sign is different from the symbol, from an intuition whose own determinacy is, in its essence and concept, more or less the content which it expresses as symbol; in the sign as such, by contrast, the intuition's own content and the content of which it is a sign have nothing to do with each other.[64]

ziffert werden müssen, indem man aus der richtigen Erkenntniss der Formen auf die Bedeutung derselben in den Werken der menschlichen Thätigkeit oder vielmehr auf die dadurch dargestellten Ideen, auf Inhalt oder Sinn der Werke schliesst.' Boeckh ²1886, p. 77 f., Engl. p. 46 modified (his emphasis in the original).

[63] It would be of interest to analyse the transformations, the value and the role of the hieroglyph in the discourse of semiotics in the eighteenth and nineteenth centuries. One would have to attend to the theoretical and systematic point at which it begins to stand for a possibility of writing that, like the Chinese graphemes, would lie *outside* the Western or Greek episteme. In Moritz, at least, the hieroglyph is still identical with a 'toten Buchstaben [...], der seinen ganzen Wert nur dadurch hat, weil er etwas außer sich bedeutet' (Moritz 1997, vol. 2, p. 1051), so precisely *not* a symbol in the Idealist or Romantic sense; *cf.* also Todorov 1977, p. 195, Engl. p. 162.

[64] 'Das *Zeichen* ist irgendeine unmittelbare Anschauung, die einen ganz anderen Inhalt vorstellt, als den sie für sich hat; – die *Pyramide*, in welche eine fremde Seele versetzt und aufbewahrt ist. Das Zeichen ist vom Symbol verschieden, einer Anschauung, deren eigene Bestimmtheit ihrem Wesen und Begriffe nach mehr oder weniger der Inhalt ist, den sie als Symbol ausdrückt; beim Zeichen als solchem hingegen geht der eigene Inhalt der Anschauung und der, dessen Zeichen sie ist, einander nichts an.' Hegel, *Enzyklopädie* III, § 458 (= Hegel 1969–1971, vol. 10, p. 270), Engl. Hegel 2007, p. 194 (his italics). On this aspect of Hegel's semiotics, see Derrida's 'Le puits et la pyramide' (= Derrida

The disjunction of form and content, the foreignness of the soul in the shroud of matter, recapitulates a tradition of thinking about the relationship between corporeality and disguise which goes back at least to Plato and which is constitutive of the notion of the sign as a pyramid.[65] In Boeckh's hermeneutics, the word thus rightly stands for an inferior level of cognition. It is true that in the process of interpretation the philologist must understand '1. the sign of the signifier, *writing*; 2. the signifier, *language*; 3. the thing signified, the *knowledge* contained in language'; but the mere palaeographer 'stops with the sign of the sign [...]; the mere grammarian confines himself to the sign of the signifier [...]; only when one presses on to the thing signified, to the thought, does genuine knowledge arise.'[66] With that, the implicit theory of the linguistic sign in the commentary to *Pindari opera* has now become explicit: language is distance from the absolute self-presence of thought, which itself is not essentially linguistic, but rather consists of intuitions whose object is immediately present to the mind of the subject. In order for this presence to be reappropriated in interpretation, the exodus of what is meant from the presence of consciousness in the production of the sign must only be that of a transition.

I hope my intention is clear: nothing is of less interest to me at this point than an attempt to *refute* this theory of philology or a model of Pindar-interpretation based on it, such as we were able to make out in Boeckh's commentary. Such an attempt would be self-contradictory in a very naïve sense, since it would have to except itself from the philological method it intended to criticise whilst at the same time, in order to reconstruct something like a 'theory' of interpretation from *Pindari opera* or the *Encyklopädie*, crucially relying on it. More generally: only by referring the material sign to something intelligible, a thought, as

1972b, pp. 79–127).

[65] The σῶμα-σῆμα-motif: *cf. Cratylus* 400 b–c, *Gorgias* 493 a, and *Phaedo* 66 e ff. It is invoked by Boeckh 1858–1874, vol. I, p. 38 as a description of *scientia* (*cf.* Horstmann 1992, pp. 29–31).

[66] '[Es] hat der Philologe bei der Erklärung 1. das Zeichen des Bezeichnenden, die Schrift, 2. das Bezeichnende, die Sprache, 3. das Bezeichnete, das in der Sprache enthaltene Wissen zu verstehen. Der Paläograph bleibt beim Zeichen des Zeichens stehen; es ist dies die Erkenntnisstufe, welche Platon in der Republik (VI, 509) εἰκασία nennt; der blosse Grammatiker beharrt beim Zeichen für das Bezeichnete, auf der Erkenntissstufe der δόξα; nur wenn man bis zum Bezeichneten selbst, bis zum Gedanken vordringt, entsteht ein wirkliches Wissen, ἐπιστήμη.' Boeckh ²1886, p. 81, Engl. p. 48 modified. Vogt 1979, p. 116 f. points out that the notorious polemic between Boeckh and Gottfried Hermann following the publication of the first volume of Boeckh's monumental *Corpus inscriptionum Graecarum* in 1825 centres less around their respective views of classics as a discipline than around their differing theories of language.

German Idealism intended, can the possibility of such a thing as meaning or ideal content be guaranteed at all which in its generality could become an object of theoretical discourse.[67] My interest is here rather in tracing a certain *outside* of this theory, an area that—in order to preserve the readability of its objects—literary scholarship has to exclude. This outside of philology makes itself felt at those places in Boeckh's theory of interpretation where the implications of his methodology turn against its explicit intention. The principle of these points marks the border between the hermeneutics of presence and its other, an other which would no longer be philology in any traditional sense but which is necessarily implied by it *ex negativo*.

The point at which this border becomes perceptible in Boeckh—and this is true, *mutatis mutandis*, for the entire tradition of Pindaric studies which looks back to him—is the question of the interpretability of the linguistic sign. If the relationship between a word and its content is not that of pictorial representation, how does the subject of cognition get from the word to the sense? Explaining this is, in the *Encyklopädie*, the task of hermeneutics. Boeckh's section on hermeneutics is divided into four parts: grammatical, historical, individual and generic interpretation. Grammatical interpretation, the philologist tells us, must

> start from the view that language did not arise through arbitrary statute (θέσει), but—as *Plato* has shown in his Cratylus—has proceeded from the laws of human nature (φύσει) […]. To the extent that it develops in accordance with nature, however, only *one* meaning lies at the base of every linguistic form, and from it all the different meanings are to be derived. But one cannot assert that every word and structural element has a fundamental *concept*, for a concept must permit definition, whereas the basic meaning of a linguistic form is in no way definable; it is an *intuition*.[68]

[67] This is the problem which vitiates conceptions of literary scholarship as the examination of (the production of) presence. 'Presence' tends in such models to be understood in a primarily spatial or physiological, almost Bergsonian sense (see for example Egginton 2007); it seems doubtful, however, whether argumentative structures based on apperceptive singularities—for example, the specific physical constitution or the mood of a single human being—are capable of intersubjectivity (no one has methodologically verifiable, or even falsifiable, access to the mood of another person). To extent that such intersubjectivity is constitutive of the discourse of scholarship—and this has of course been the consensus of the Western intellectual tradition since Plato, with which it would seem precipitate to break—it is difficult to understand how a form of literary studies based on 'presence' would differ, epistemologically, from mysticism. On the necessity of ideal objects in theory, see Derrida 1989, p. 91 f. (citing Husserl 1965).

[68] '[…] von der Ansicht ausgehen, dass die Sprache nicht durch willkürliche Satzung (θέσει) entstanden, sondern – wie schon Platon im Kratylos nachgewiesen hat – aus den

The concept of nature as the source of language stands here—as opposed to its role in Bundy or even Pindar—for the basic rationality and consistency of the linguistic, in this passage particularly the semantic system: only the assumption that language at its origin obeys a rule-governed necessity guarantees that interpretation can have recourse to regularities which connect, for example, the different, historically developed meanings of a polyvalent word with a single, originary and basic meaning.[69] The valence of the natural at this point has also, however, to do with the thesis that the basic meaning of a word is not definable, but is instead—like that of a poem—an intuition. This idea, the postulate of an originary phase of linguistic development in which a word stands exclusively and immediately for a—primarily visual—sensory perception, is not only a widespread *topos* of the rationalist philosophy of language in the eighteenth century.[70] It also plays a central role in Boeckh's theory of interpretation in the stricter sense and is taken up again at the beginning of the second part of the *Encyklopädie* on the 'material disciplines of the study of antiquity':

> Language originally expresses real, concrete intuitions, which are images of ideal ones. In antiquity, this natural meaning of the words is more vividly remembered; even in prose, therefore, language is more poetical. But in the final development of Greek scholarship, the universal intellectualization of language begins [...]. The words become immediate signs of ideal intuitions in such a way that the original, sensuous meaning is no longer recalled [...].

Gesetzen der menschlichen Natur hervorgegangen (φύσει) ist [...]. Naturgemäss liegt jeder Formation der Sprache nur ein Sinn zugrunde, woraus alle ihre verschiedenen Bedeutungen abzuleiten sind. Man kann jedoch nicht sagen, dass jedes Wort und jede Structur einen Grundbegriff haben; denn ein Begriff muss sich definiren lassen, die Grundbedeutung der Sprachformationen lässt sich aber keineswegs definiren: sie ist eine Anschauung.' Boeckh [2]1886, p. 94, Engl. 61 f. modified (his emphasis in the original).

[69] On Boeckh's interpretation of the Platonic *Cratylus* in this sense, compare his study from 1808, 'Von dem Uebergange der Buchstaben in einander' (now in Boeckh 1858–1874, vol. III, pp. 204–228, and *cf.* Pflug 1975, p. 153 and Horstmann 1992, p. 91); it returns at the end of the *Encyklopädie* in a slightly more sophisticated form (Boeckh [2]1886, p. 766 ff.). On the single, originary, basic meaning of words, *cf.* Schleiermacher 1977, p. 108, Engl. p. 36 ff. On Derrida's conception of a theory of the word and of language that would no longer allow any such return to an unified origin (Derrida 1972c, p. 120: 'Lapidairement : la dissémination figure ce qui *ne revient pas* au père' [his italics]), see Gasché 1986, pp. 237–239.

[70] See for example Leibniz's *Nouveaux essais sur l'entendement humain* (published in 1765) III, Ch. 1, § 5. Hegel's reception of this motif can be found in his lectures on aesthetics: see Hegel 2003, p. 146 f. and 2004a, p. 104, and Hotho's version in Hegel 1969–1971, vol. 13, p. 518 f., Engl. Hegel 1975a, vol. I, p. 404 f. *Cf.* also Derrida's 'La mythologie blanche' (= Derrida 1972b, pp. 247–324), pp. 267–269, Engl. pp. 224–226.

> But with the intellectualization of the words, the danger arises that their meaning evaporates into intuitionless, abstract concepts.[71]

Boeckh distinguishes here between two kinds of intuition, concrete and ideal. As frequently in the aesthetics of the early nineteenth century, the relevant background for the latter is Kant's analysis of the idea in the *Kritik der Urteilskraft*. There, the idea stands for a basic disjunction in the apperceptive system of consciousness: as the *transcendental* idea, it is a concept for which there is no adequate intuition; as the *aesthetic* idea, it is a 'representation' (*Vorstellung*) which cannot be represented in the form of a concept.[72] The aesthetic idea can, according to the third *Kritik*, only be grasped as an intuition of the imagination (*Einbildungskraft*);[73] Boeckh presupposes this correspondence between the non-conceptual and the perceptible when in his hermeneutics he rejects the possibility of defining the basic meaning of a word.

Now the image of the ideal intuition is the sensory-material intuition. Boeckh's description of the relationship between the idea and sensuousness as iconicity is by no means accidental. According to Kant, neither the transcendental nor the aesthetic idea can be an object of cognition:

> Ideas in the most general meaning of the word are representations related to an object in accordance with a certain (subjective or objective) principle, insofar as they can nevertheless *never become a cognition* of that object.[74]

[71] 'Die Sprache drückt ursprünglich reale, concrete Anschauungen aus, welche Bilder der idealen sind. Im Alterthum bleibt jene Naturbedeutung der Wörter noch lebendiger im Bewusstsein; die Sprache bleibt daher selbst in der Prosa poetischer. Durch die letzte Entwickelung der griechischen Wissenschaft aber beginnt die universelle Vergeistigung der Sprache [...]. Die Worte werden zu unmittelbaren Zeichen für ideelle Anschauungen, ohne dass die ursprüngliche sinnliche Bedeutung dabei ins Bewusstsein tritt [...]. Aber mit der Vergeistigung der Worte ist zugleich die Gefahr verbunden, dass sich ihre Bedeutung zu anschauungslosen, abstrakten Begriffen verflüchtigt.' Boeckh ^{2}1886, p. 277, my translation.

[72] See Kant, *Kritik der Urteilskraft*, § 49 (B 192 f.; = Kant 1956–1964, vol. X, p. 413 f.): '[U]nter einer ästhetischen Idee aber verstehe ich diejenige Vorstellung der Einbildungskraft, die viel zu denken veranlaßt, ohne daß ihr doch irgendein bestimmter Gedanke, d. i. Begriff, adäquat sein kann, die folglich keine Sprache völlig erreicht und verständlich machen kann. – Man sieht leicht, daß sie das Gegenstück (Pendant) von einer Vernunftidee sei, welche umgekehrt ein Begriff ist, dem keine Anschauung (Vorstellung der Einbildungskraft) adäquat sein kann' (his emphasis); Engl. Kant 2000, p. 192.

[73] *Cf.* Kant, *Kritik der Urteilskraft*, § 57 n. I (B 239–243; = Kant 1956–1964, vol. X, pp. 447–450, Engl. Kant 2000, p. 217–219).

[74] 'Ideen in der allgemeinsten Bedeutung sind, nach einem gewissen (subjektiven oder

It is evident that this situation must cause considerable difficulties for a theory in which philology is defined as 'die Erkenntnis des Erkannten'. Boeckh's response is therefore to anchor the aesthetic idea in sensory intuition as its non-arbitrary signified; only in this way can he guarantee its (re)cognizability despite its non-conceptual nature. The danger which threatens the words when they become 'spiritual' corresponds exactly to this necessity: it is the loss of their connection to the sensory world of the materially real. The concrete meaning of the words, their *natural* meaning—with all the connotations of originary force and regularity on which Boeckh has already insisted—could in principle become invisible, concealed behind the ideal, spiritual intuition as if behind a mask. In this case, the idea might become merely a concept and thus epistemologically uncertain, no longer necessarily accessible or present to the (re)cognition of the subject. One can profitably compare, at this point, Schelling's remarks in his *System des transzendentalen Idealismus*, published in 1800: 'The necessity of productive intuition, here systematically deduced from the entire mechanism of the self, must be derived, as a general condition of knowing as such, directly from the concept thereof; for if all knowing borrows its reality from an immediate cognition, this cognition is *only* to be met *within intuition*; whereas concepts, in fact, are merely shadows of reality [...].'[75]

Binding words to concrete intuitions is thus, according to the logic of the *Encyklopädie*, the only guarantee of their (the words') relationship to the inwardness and self-presence of the subject in the representation of intelligence. But if the iconic relationship between the material and the ideal is the only basis on which the representation of the idea can be a (re)cognition, the privileged place of this relationship is the language of poetry, in particular classical poetry. Here, the consciousness of the natural ground of linguistic signs—and thus their non-arbitrary connection to the ideas—remains in force, just as it is the tendency of (Greek) antiquity to emphasize 'the natural side of

objektiven) Prinzip, auf einen Gegenstand bezogene Vorstellungen, sofern sie doch *nie eine Erkenntnis* desselben werden können.' Kant, *Kritik der Urteilskraft*, § 57 n. I (B 239; = Kant 1956–1964, vol. X, p. 447, my italics). Engl. Kant 2000, p. 209 f.

75 'Die Notwendigkeit der produktiven Anschauung [...] ist als allgemeine Bedingung des Wissens überhaupt unmittelbar aus dessen Begriff abzuleiten; denn, wenn alles Wissen seine Realität von einer unmittelbaren Erkenntnis entlehnt, so ist diese *allein in der Anschauung* anzutreffen, anstatt daß Begriffe nur Schatten der Realität sind [...].' Schelling 2000, p. 96 (my italics), Engl. p. 73, translation modified. *Cf.* Schleiermacher 1981, p. 87 f. (= Schleiermacher 1977, p. 366).

intellectual life'.[76] But the connection of poetry to the sensory-material is not only a characteristic of *ancient* literature: inasmuch as the aesthetic idea is understood as an essentially non-conceptual, indefinable intuition of the imagination, art, as its objectification, can and must retain this naturalness. It is for this reason that Boeckh can say that prose approaches poetry when the one, sensory meaning of the words is still perceived.

We can now better assess the role of intuition in the commentary to *Pindari opera*. Only a teleology of interpretation that locates the meaning of the epinicians in intuition will be able to do justice to their character as poetry. This is the thesis which dominates Boeckh's exchange with Dissen some years after the conclusion of the last volume of their cooperative project. Dissen had contributed the commentary's *explicationes* to the *Nemeans* and *Isthmians*; in 1830, he published his own edition, *Pindari carmina*, together with interpretations of the *Olympians* and *Pythians* which had been treated by Boeckh nine years before. In a long introductory essay, *De ratione poetica carminum Pindaricorum et de interpretationis genere iis adhibendo*, the Göttingen scholar now set out his own hermeneutical approach.[77] There is, wrote Dissen, a *summa sententia*, a 'highest thought' for every song, whose function it is to hold all of the other parts of the song together. All of the individual parts of the specific text are related, in one way or another, to this *sententia*, which Dissen himself translates as the *Grundgedanke* or 'basic thought'.[78] In order to discover the *sententia*, which is expressible in language and thus has the character of a concept in the Kantian sense, the interpreter must compare increasingly large parts of the text with each other; whatever emerges as the common or connecting element of two such parts becomes the basis for the next comparison. As soon as it can be demonstrated that all of the parts of the text refer to a single thought, the integration of the disparate elements of the victory songs to coherent poetic texts has been achieved, which is in turn the only condition on which they can be viewed or recognized as products of an exceptional poetical intellect.

It is clear what is at stake here. If a thought *in the sense of a concept* were to be made the basis of poetry, this would be incompatible with

[76] Boeckh ²1886, p. 265, cited below p. 92 with n. 84. On the relationship between art and the Idea in general, see *ibid.*, p. 56 and 466 f., and *cf.* Schelling 2000, p. 296 ff., Engl. p. 229 ff.

[77] Dissen ²1843, pp. I–LXVI.

[78] See Dissen ²1843, p. II. The curious relationship of inversion between the Latin *summa* and the German *Grund* in this text will concern us in the next section.

the primacy of what is present to the poet as an object of perception—with extremely specific consequences for interpretation. Not only would the *rerum et hominum condicio* no longer necessarily be decisive for the *poetae consilium*, not only would the character of the epinicians as literary art no longer be guaranteed. The ability of the concept to instantiate itself entirely in a medium, and thus be exhaustively recoverable in language, would endanger the status of philology itself as 'Erkenntnis des Erkannten' in the sense of the idea. Boeckh writes the first review of *Pindari carmina*. The 'Kritik der Ausgabe des Pindar von Dissen' appears in October 1830; the reviewer is obviously trying hard to formulate his reservations about the *Grundgedanke* as gently as possible. For whereas Boeckh—in contrast to Gottfried Hermann, whose damning criticism of *Pindari carmina* will appear in the following year[79]—shares Dissen's position entirely that 'not blind enthusiasm, but rather conscious art rules in these poems, in which everything is fitted to the aim, the persons, times and circumstances',[80] the Berlin philologist cannot find it in his heart to agree with the thesis that the coherence of a literary work is achieved by a concept. It does not lie, writes Boeckh,

> in the nature of art to present concepts *as such*; Pheidias' Olympian Zeus, Praxiteles' Aphrodite are not concepts, and even if we admit that a living concept lies in the depths of the work, this is nevertheless not grasped as such by the artist; instead, its embodiment is immediately intuited by the artist in such a way that the concept is submerged and drowned in the intuition of imagination. If poetry uses concepts because its means of representation is language, then the concepts have to have been drowned in the object, and the intuitive unity of the poem cannot be grasped by means of a mere concept.[81]

79 See Hermann 1827–1877, vol. VI, pp. 1–69, and below, p. 95 n. 93.

80 Boeckh 1858–1874, vol. VII, p. 373. See above, p. 73.

81 '[...] im Wesen der Kunst [...], Begriffe als solche darzustellen; des Pheidias Olympischer Zeus, die Aphrodite des Praxiteles sind keine Begriffe, und geben wir zu, daß in der Tiefe des Werkes ein lebendiger Begriff liege, so ist er doch nicht als solcher vom Künstler gefasst, sondern seine Verkörperung ist unmittelbar im Geiste des Künstlers so angeschaut, dass der Begriff in der Anschauung der Phantasie versenkt und untergegangen ist. Bedient sich nun auch die Dichtung, weil ihr Darstellungsmittel die Sprache ist, der Begriffe, so müssen doch, wenn sie Dichtung bleiben soll, die Begriffe in dem Gebilde selbst untergegangen sein, und die anschauliche Einheit des Gedichtes kann nicht in einem bloßen Begriffe erfaßt werden.' Boeckh 1858–1874, vol. VII, p. 381 (his emphasis, my translation), and *cf.* the connection made between 'intuition' (*Anschauung*) and 'moment' (*Augenblick*), both of course terms for 'presence', at *ibid.*, p. 384: 'Dem Geiste des Dichters, indem er einen Bestimmten besingt, und zwar im Epinikos einen Sieger, steht vor dem innern Blicke klar vor [*sic*] die ganze Besonderheit des Sie-

The place of the *summa sententia* has been taken here by the immediate intuition of the poet, exactly as *Pindari opera*'s hermeneutics of presence has led us to expect: it is the ideal and simultaneously primary-sensory moment to which the text in its merely secondary materiality points. At the same time, Boeckh defines the relationship between the ideal content and the intuition which is its embodiment as one of internalisation: the idea is submerged and drowned in its own incarnation. This figure of submersion reappears in the *Encyklopädie*: it provides not only the paradigm for Boeckh's theory of art—'It is clear that *art* expresses ideas', he writes there, 'not indeed in conceptual form, but rather submerged in a sensory intuition'[82]—but also for the object of philology as a whole. When Boeckh buries both the idea and the concept in the materiality of the work of art, he covers everything about a text which does not consist in its immediate materiality itself and must therefore be the goal of its interpretation.[83]

The outside of reading is thus defined as the materiality of the non-arbitrary signifier. Boeckh makes the systematic connection between nature, bondage and non-arbitrariness on the one hand, and spirit, freedom and arbitrariness on the other explicit in the passage in the *Encyklopädie* in which he presents his idea of antiquity:

gers mit allen innig verbundenen Eigenthümlichkeiten, Lagen und Stimmungen, wie sie in diesem Augenblicke vorhanden sind; dadurch, dass in dieser Anschauung alles wurzelt [...] hat das Gedicht seine objektive Einheit [...].' On the notion of 'intuitive unity', see also Schleiermacher 1977, p. 174, Engl. p. 97. Although the rejection of the concept as the basis of a work of art stands in a very specific context in Boeckh's discussion of *Pindari carmina*, it is not unique to him, but rather related to the Romantic valorization of the symbol over against allegory; see for example Schopenhauer, *Die Welt als Wille und Vorstellung* III (published in 1819), § 50: '[W]enn [...] das Ausgehen vom Begriff in der Kunst verwerflich ist, so werden wir es nicht billigen können, wenn man ein Kunstwerk [...] zum Ausdruck eines Begriffes bestimmt: dieses ist der Fall in der Allegorie [...]', and above, p. 48 f.

[82] 'Dass die K u n s t Ideen ausdrücke, zwar nicht begriffsmässig, aber versenkt in eine sinnliche Anschauung, ist klar.' Boeckh ²1886, p. 56, Engl. p. 38 modified (his emphasis). *Cf.* also 'Ueber die Wissenschaft' (= Boeckh 1858–1874, vol. II, pp. 81–98), p. 87: '[D]ie machende Thätigkeit hat, inwiefern sie sich als schöne Kunst eben auf die Gestaltung des Schönen, das heißt der in dem Sinnlichen verkörperten und versenkten Idee bezieht, mit der Theorie die ideale innere Vision gemein, und ein Hauptzweig derselben, die vorzugsweise so genannte Poesie, stellt sogar in demselben Stoffe dar, dessen sich das Erkennen bedienen muß, in der Sprache; und die schönen Künste haben wieder keinen andern Zweck als die Darstellung jener innern Vision, die der Erkenntniß wo nicht gleich, doch als ihr Bild sehr ähnlich ist [...].' Hegel, too (2004b, p. 74 ff. and *cf.* 2003, p. 234), used the relationship between body and soul in his lectures on aesthetics to illustrate the relationship between the work of art and the Idea.

[83] *Cf.* Boeckh ²1886, p. 81, Engl. p. 49.

> The natural side of intellectual life still predominates amongst the Greeks, and only in the modern period has purely intellectual consciousness become predominant. The most general difference, therefore, between all ancient and modern education consists in the fact that in the former nature is relatively dominant and in the latter the intellect. Nature develops according to necessary laws; the intellect is indeed also subject to law, but is nevertheless free. Ancient culture therefore has more the character of necessity, modern culture that of freedom. In comparison to the Orient, however, the Greeks have achieved a higher level of freedom; their entire education is based on the development of the human intellect.[84]

The freedom of spirit as opposed to the bondage of nature: it is Hegel who draws out the implications for the production of intuition. 'In *signifying* therefore intelligence displays a freer wilfulness and mastery in the use of intuition than in symbolizing.'[85] The non-arbitrary symbol is not free, subjected to nature; Boeckh makes use of the same argument when he declares that the pictorial representation of thought in writing is imperfect: 'Writing as such has its origin in drawing. Its lowest level, the pictogram, is an imperfect, in part symbolic expression of the thoughts themselves.'[86] Pictographic writing is

84 '[Es] ueberwiegt bei den Griechen noch die Naturseite des geistigen Lebens, und erst in der modernen Zeit hat das rein geistige Bewusstsein das Uebergewicht erhalten. Daher besteht der allgemeinste Unterschied zwischen der gesammten antiken und der modernen Bildung darin, dass in jener die Natur, in dieser der Geist relativ vorherrscht. Die Natur entwickelt sich nach nothwendigen Gesetzen; der Geist steht zwar auch unter Gesetzen, ist aber frei. Daher trägt die antike Cultur mehr den Charakter der Nothwendigkeit, die moderne den der Freiheit. Im Verhältniss zum Orient haben die Griechen allerdings eine hohe Stufe der Freiheit erreicht; ihre ganze Bildung beruht auf der Entwickelung des freien Menschengeistes.' Boeckh [2]1886, p. 265, my translation. Boeckh's explanation of the decline of Greek culture (see *ibid.*, p, 285: '[D]ie hellenische Cultur [löste sich] auf, als sich der Geist der Griechen durch die Philosophie zur Anschauung des Uebersinnlichen erhob') must also be read in this context. If antiquity—which, for Boeckh, is essentially Greek antiquity—differs from modernity in the dominance of (fundamentally material) nature, then the end of this dominance must also mean its own. Antiquity is outward and sensuous, modernity inward and intellectual; the latter presents itself in the *Encyklopädie* as the sublimation or *Aufhebung* of antiquity in the inwardness of appropriation through interpretation. It is the abandonment of antiquity's sensuousness that allows for its sublimation to modernity.

85 'Als *bezeichnend* beweist daher die Intelligenz eine freiere Willkür und Herrschaft im Gebrauch der Anschauung denn als symbolisierend.' Hegel, *Enzyklopädie* III, § 458 (= Hegel 1969–1971, vol. 10, p. 270, his emphasis), Engl. Hegel 2007, p. 194.

86 'Die Schrift überhaupt hat ihren Ursprung in der Zeichnung. Ihre niedrigste Stufe, die Schriftmalerei, ist ein unvollkommener, z. Th. symbolischer Ausdruck der Gedanken selbst.' Boeckh [2]1886, p. 776, my translation. Boeckh's allusion to the inferiority of the Orient to the Greeks is connected to his assertion (*ibid.*) that the Chinese 'auf dem Standpunkte der Wortschrift stehen geblieben [sind]'.

inferior to alphabetic writing to the extent that it is symbolic, for the symbol, as an intuition, always also means *itself*; it therefore possesses something irreducibly material which resists its *Aufhebung* into the ideality of the idea. But as we have seen, it is precisely this irreducible something that is the necessary condition for its interpretability; interpretation thus reveals itself as an abstraction, as the removal of the self-referential material intuition of the symbol in the interests of its immaterial inwardness, the soul.

The sign, which contains a now explicitly *alien* soul, is thus already a sublimation, the *Aufhebung* of the symbol into the realm of meaning. But as a sublimation, it can never achieve the full inwardness of knowledge, if this knowledge, the product of *Erkenntnis*, is understood exclusively as the unveiling of the embodied soul, for interpretation presupposes the materiality of the produced intuition, *i.e.*, the signifier. It is precisely this materiality, however, which cannot be subjected to the reign of the spirit. As sensory nature, it is autonomous, independent of the (re)cognizing mind of the observer, who of course can only (re)cognize the image *as an image of the idea*. Art, technology—this latter no accidental example in Boeckh, as his repeated criticism of Leibniz's project of an *alphabetum cogitationum humanarum* shows[87]—the institutions of everyday life remain external to interpretation as long as they exist only as *matter* in which the ideal content is *submerged and sunk* and must now be raised and rescued.

The structure of the animate body grounds in this way the entire logic both of the *Encyklopädie der philologischen Wissenschaften* and of *Pindari opera*, although in both works the explicit *telos* of interpretation is not the body of the material, arbitrary sign, but rather the visible ideality of the soul. Far from reproducing the subjective inwardness of scholarship, the structure of philological *Erkenntnis* itself in fact recapitulates the outwardness of the work of art[88] in which the 'living concept' is buried like a soul, and of the material signifier which refuses to bow to the rule of the spirit. The truth of the philological object is thus not the immediate presence of the unveiled idea, but rather the endless mediation of the sign.

[87] Boeckh ^{2}1886, p. 764 and elsewhere. *Cf.* Heidegger 1957, p. 30 and Derrida, 'Le puits et la pyramide' (= Derrida 1972b, pp. 79–127), p. 127, Engl. p. 108.

[88] *Cf.* Boeckh ^{2}1886, p. 278: 'Die Kunst hat bei den Griechen das Uebergewicht über die Wissenschaft, während bei uns das umgekehrte Verhältniss stattfindet [...] Dies Verhältniss erklärt sich daraus, daß die Kunst gegenüber der Wissenschaft die *Objectivierung* des theoretischen Lebens ist' (my italics).

Species naturae

How have we arrived at this paradoxical result? A first hypothesis might be that Boeckh destabilizes his own theory of philology at a crucial point the moment he adopts Hegel's epistemology in the opening pages of the *Encyklopädie*. Such a hypothesis would imply that a hermeneutics based on different philosophical presuppositions might be in a position to avoid this fate. And a good candidate for a different hermeneutics of this kind might be that adopted by Boeckh's Göttingen colleague and, for a time, collaborator, Ludolph Dissen.

Traditionally, histories of the classical philology of the nineteenth century have given more attention to Boeckh's hermeneutics than Dissen's, not only because Boeckh has been seen as the more theoretically minded of the two,[89] but also because the Berlin scholar's obvious (and frequently mentioned) indebtedness to Schleiermacher, with whom he studied in Halle, allows him to be seen as part of the tradition which connects the Protestant theologian *via* Dilthey to Gadamer and the philosophical hermeneutics of the twentieth century. Dissen, whose philosophical teacher in Göttingen was the Realist and Hegel-opponent Johann Friedrich Herbart, has seemed un- or at least less likely to be entangled in the speculative metaphysics of German Idealism. But despite his very real differences from Boeckh, Dissen does not succeed in developing a rigorous theory of interpretation which avoids the aporias of the hermeneutics of presence that we have observed in the former classicist's work. This circumstance has not inconsiderable consequences for the most important thesis of *Pindari carmina*, the *Grundgedanke*, which, despite Boeckh's critique, played a similarly important role in the Pindaric philology of the nineteenth and early twentieth centuries to that played by the central theses of Bundy's *Studia Pindarica* (with which it has a number of things in common) in the latter part of the twentieth.[90]

The theory of interpretation on which *Pindari carmina*—published, as we have noted above, in 1830—is based is set out in the introductory

[89] See *e.g.* Wilamowitz ³1998, p. 54, Engl. p. 120, and Pfeiffer 1982, p. 222 f., Engl. p. 181 f.

[90] The academic reception of Dissen's *De ratione* has concentrated almost entirely on the aesthetics of content it proposes: see Young 1970, p. 5 and Newman & Newman 1984, p. 5, both stressing the importance of the essay. For Wilamowitz's quite different assessment of Dissen's work, see Wilamowitz 1922, p. 7 f. and ³1998, p. 58. See also Most 1985b, pp. 25–41 and Krummen 1990, p. 13. Even Theunissen 2000, V still declares allegiance to the *Grundgedanke*, although he is one of the very few who have no illusions about the essentially philosophical nature of the thesis.

essay in the first volume, *De ratione poetica*.[91] In contrast to the way Pindar was being read by contemporary Romanticism, Dissen insists that the epinicians are governed not by 'blind passion' but by *ratio*, the constitutive principle of classical Greek art—a hermeneutical presupposition that had formed the basis of the collaborative commentary nine years before and with which Boeckh had, naturally enough, agreed in his review.[92] In practice, Dissen proceeds, this means that even (!) Pindar's poetical spirit did not veil the acuity of his thought, but instead allowed it to achieve 'the clearest forms'.[93] Here, we can already see that the transparency of the form for the intention that lies beneath it will form the basis of Dissen's whole approach. It is therefore only consistent when the philologist goes on to tell us that an understanding of Pindaric art can only be achieved by identifying the highest thought (*summa sententia*) or *Grundgedanke* which binds the individual parts of the text together and makes them into a single work of art:

> For there is, in every classical work whatsoever, this principle, that the whole is present everywhere, so that every single passage, every single part pleases because of the unity (thus created), and another, greater bond is present which embraces all the parts.[94]

Dissen is convinced that the *Grundgedanke* is always moral: *Est*

91 Dissen ²1843, pp. I–LXVI.

92 See above, pp. 73 f. and 90.

93 '*Proprium fuit classicae Graecorum artis, ut ratione ageret, non caeco impetu, quum tantum haberet hic populus cum sensu acumen coniunctum, ut etiam poeticus spiritus non obscuraret mentis aciem, sed concentu mirabili virium quae invenirent ingeniosissime simul revocarent ad clarissimas formas.*' Dissen ²1843, p. I, the opening lines of the essay. The Göttingen scholar's *etiam* here is not the only trace in *De ratione* of an engagement with an aesthetics of Romantic sensibility. The contemporary relevance of the problem is impressively documented by Gottfried Hermann's review of the commentary: see Hermann 1827–1877, vol. VI, p. 4 f. ('Herr Dissen [scheint] durch seinen Scharfsinn verleitet worden zu seyn [...], auch das, was [...] durch bloßes Gefühl gefasst werden muss, mit dialektischer Subtilität zu analysiren [...]') and (at greater length) p. 21. *Cf.* almost a century after the first edition of *Pindari carmina* Wilamowitz 1922, p. 201 on the invocation of *Θεία* at the beginning of the *Fifth Pythian*: 'Was ist diese Theia? [...] Kein Wort verschwende ich an die antiken Torheiten und modernen Tüfteleien, daß *θεία* an *θεᾶσθαι* mahne [...] u. dgl. Gelehrsamkeit tuts nicht, Gefühl ist alles.'

94 '*Est enim omnis omnino classici operis ratio haec, ut totum ponatur ubique, ut et singulus quisque locus, singula quaeque pars unitate placeat, et aliud maius vinculum adsit omnes partes complectens.*' Dissen ²1843, p. LXIII, probably the most quoted sentence in the entire essay (*cf.* Young 1970, p. 5 with n. 13). All translations from *De ratione* are my own.

igitur satis clarum, opinor, quales sint sententiae Epiniciis subiectae. Sunt omnes ethicae [...].[95] What hermeneutical consequences does a notion of art of this sort have? In order to describe the relationship of the *Grundgedanke* to the text, *De ratione*, like the *Studia Pindarica* more than a century later and on the grounds of the same exigency, splits the text into two levels. The *sententiae* the interpreter seeks are always to be found at the base of the whole (*toti subiecta*): they build a foundation (*fundamentum*) into which the interpreter must constantly penetrate more deeply (*penitius*).[96] If they often agree with the paraphrase of a part of the text in practice, such agreement is not necessarily implied by the theory of the *Grundgedanke*.[97] Rather, Dissen assumes

[95] Dissen ²1843, p. XI. He shares this emphasis on the ethical in poetry with Herbart, who accused Hegel and Schelling's Idealism of illegitimately mixing aesthetics with metaphysics, and attempted to develop in its place a theory of aesthetics and moral judgement independent of speculative philosophy. The most important part of the philosophy of art thus became for Herbart practical philosophy, to which the second chapter ('Aufzeigung der sittlichen Elemente') in his *Lehrbuch zur Einleitung in die Philosophie* (first published in 1813) was devoted (see Herbart 1993, pp. 143–153). Apart from the *Aphorismen* (Herbart 1897–1912, vol. IV, esp. 398 ff.), this third section of the *Lehrbuch* is the only substantial treatment of aesthetics in the Göttingen philosopher's *œuvre*. Here, following Kant (*cf.* Kant, *Kritik der Urteilskraft*, § 52 [B 214 f.; = Kant 1956–1964, vol. X, p. 429, Engl. Kant 2000, p. 203]), 'moral content' is defined as the central component of the beautiful, since this 'nicht bloß als eine Sache von Wert besessen wird, sondern den unbedingten Wert der Personen selbst bestimmt' (Herbart 1993, p. 134). Since aesthetic judgements are further only possible on the basis of relations—'das völlig Einfache ist gleichgültig, d.h. weder gefallend noch mißfallend' (*ibid.*, p. 143)—moral relations are the primary possible objects of a philosophical aesthetics. In Herbart's opinion, there are five such relations: the ideas of inner freedom, perfection, benevolence, law, and legitimacy (*Billigkeit*). Herbart believes that these 'practical ideas' are already to be found completely developed in Plato and Cicero, and considers them therefore to be aesthetic universals (*ibid.*, pp. 144–145; the formulation 'praktische Ideen' p. 154). On the putative ahistoricity of this series, see Henckmann's remarks in Herbart 1993, pp. XXXVI–XXXIX with the literature cited there. Dissen was a student in Göttingen from 1804 to 1808 and belonged to Herbart's inner circle; the latter wrote a preface to his *Kurze Anweisung für Erzieher, die Odyssee mit Knaben zu lesen* published in 1809; during his one-year term in Marburg in 1812, the Hellenist is reported (by K.O. Müller in Dissen 1839, pp. XLII and LXVII) to have been working on a defence of Herbart's pedagogical theories, which however was never published and apparently not found in his papers after his death in 1837. If Dissen believes in *De ratione* that the *summae sententiae* of the epinicians are always ethical ideas—the idea of *virtus*, the concept of *felicitas*, the praise of *pietas et moderatio*—then the formal agreement between his approach and Herbart's postulate that art deals above all with clearly definable, universally valid ethical relationships is more than striking.

[96] Dissen ²1843, pp. II–III.

[97] *Pace* Most 1985b, who sees in Dissen's *Grundgedanke* a form of restrictive privileging on an element within the text: 'With one exception, all parts are merely parts, and

that the interpreter must wrest the one, unifying *summa sententia* from the disparate wording of the poem, specifically by methodically resolving apparent contradictions or tensions on the surface of the text through the comparison of single sections, one after another, which, on their own, would not be interpretable.[98] But in this way, the singularity of the given becomes oddly problematic: the individuality of the single passages of a Pindaric epinician, the fact that they do not all say the same thing, and thus the differential form of the poem itself becomes—despite Dissen's initial express statement that the *formae* are *clarissimae*—the most important hindrance for the (re)cognition of the foundation, since the task of the true interpreter consists precisely in not becoming enamoured of this differentiality, but rather in breaking through it to the unified meaning that lies beyond: 'However, in general many [interpreters] allow themselves to be captivated by the attractions of single passages', writes Dissen critically, 'and see no need to penetrate further into the interior of the compositions.'[99]

are passively determined as such; but one part is also the whole, and faces both outwards towards the *ratio* for the whole to which it alone has access and inwards as the active determiner of all the parts' (p. 40). This description is a good critique of an aesthetics of the Moritzian type: *cf.* Moritz 1997, vol. 2, p. 1021 on the necessity 'in dem Werke selbst den *Gesichtspunkt* aufzufinden, wodurch alles Einzelne sich erst in seiner notwendigen Beziehung auf das Ganze darstellt' (his italics). But whereas Dissen's *Grundgedanken* are often paraphrases of a passage in the text (as Most rightly points out: 1985b, p. 40), this is by no means a necessary corollary of his hermeneutics. The Göttingen Hellenist seems, rather, to have been thinking of the relationship between the body and the soul which, being immaterial, is not strictly a *part* of the body at all: the beauty created by the *summa sententia* in the epinicians is '*in ipsis fundamentis carminum posita atque inde tanquam anima per corpus diffusa in omnes partes* [...]' (Dissen ²1843, p. XI). We have identified this thought at the theoretical centre of Boeckh's notion of philology; in Dissen, it plays a much more marginal role. The explicit formulation of the 'basic thought' of an ode in a specific passage is then, however, a contingent occurrence which, in any individual given case, is neither predicted nor demanded by the theory.

98 Dissen ²1843, p. LXII ff., *e.g.* p. LXIV: '*Patet ex his exemplis, quomodo comparatione partium eliciatur et definiatur summa sententia, nec nisi omnibus satis bene conciliatis dici posse perspectam poetae mentem*'—this, too, a Herbartian element, for in contrast to the procedure of Hegel's speculative dialectics which makes the contradictory nature of concepts into the principle of their immanent development or sublimation, Herbart calls for a metaphysics whose only task would be to remove such contradictions altogether by reformulation of the concepts involved. See Herbart 1993, p. 269 and esp. n. 1 on the necessity of overcoming contradictions in order to make experience 'thinkable', and 1897–1912, vol. II, p. 218 ff. on the 'Methode der Beziehungen' by which this is to be achieved.

99 '*Quanquam vulgo multi* (sc. *interpretes*) *singulorum locorum luminibus capiuntur*,

Now Dissen asserts explicitly, as we have seen, that Pindar's epinicians possess the reconciliatory character ascribed to classical art in the aesthetics of the nineteenth century, where the absolute unity of form and content *qua ratio* governs the reciprocal semiotic relationship between inside and outside. Strategically, however, Herbart's former student has already made the step to romanticism that Hegel's aesthetics called for and described, since the all-encompassing role of the *Grundgedanke* leads in *Pindari carmina* as in Hegel to the exile of language from what is essential, indeed valuable in poetry.

Let us take a moment to recapitulate the necessity and systematic consequences of this progression in Hegel. As early as 1800, the Swabian philosopher had argued that art, religion and philosophy all had the same goal.[100] In 1816, in the second volume of the *Wissenschaft der Logik*, he refined this thesis to assert that, with a view to their respective ability to grasp the absolute Idea, art and religion were innately inferior to philosophy:

> Nature and spirit are completely distinct modes of presenting its (*sc.* the absolute Idea's) existence, and art and religion are its different modes of understanding itself and giving itself an appropriate existence; philosophy shares with art and religion the same content and the same purpose; but it is the highest mode of grasping the absolute Idea, because its mode is the highest mode, namely the concept.[101]

The inferiority of art to philosophy is a consequence of the former's inadequate capacity for the *conceptual*; in what follows, Hegel makes the changing relationship between this conceptual inside that is realized only in the course of history and its variously contingent outward veil into the driving force behind the development of art as a whole. The differences between symbolic, classical and post-classical or romantic art find their systematic exposition in the *Enzyklopädie* and their phenomenological description in the lectures on aesthetics; in both works they are predicated exclusively on the basis of the relationship between the outside of the work of art and the hidden centre it expresses.[102]

altius penetrare in intimo compositionum non opus habent.' Dissen ²1843, p. XII (his emphasis; *cf.* p. I: '*quo penitius in intima compositionum penetres* [...] *eo magis quam clare sint omnia cogitata sentis et quanta perfectione artis expressa*'). Boeckh quotes this sentence approvingly in his review (*id.* 1858–1874, vol. VII, p. 381).

[100] In the *Systemfragment von 1800*: see Hegel 1969–1971, vol. 1, p. 422 f.

[101] 'Die Natur und der Geist sind überhaupt unterschiedene Weisen, *ihr* [*sc.* der absoluten Idee] *Dasein* darzustellen, Kunst und Religion ihre verschiedenen Weisen, sich zu erfassen und ein sich angemessenes Dasein zu geben; die Philosophie hat mit Kunst und Religion denselben Inhalt und denselben Zweck; aber sie ist die höchste Weise, die absolute Idee zu erfassen, weil ihre Weise, die höchste, der Begriff ist.' Hegel, *Wissenschaft der Logik* II (= Hegel 1969–1971, vol. 6), p. 549 (his italics), my translation.

[102] The decisive passages are *Enzyklopädie* III, §§ 556–563 (= Hegel 1969–1971, vol.

In symbolic art, whose example, in the lectures on aesthetics, Hegel finds in above all in Egypt, there is a surplus of form in relation to the content, so that the outside is not able to express the inward thought clearly.[103] In the *Vorlesungen über die Philosophie der Religion*, this specific inability is interpreted as a lack of transparency:

> The form [*sc.* of Egyptian works of art] is not yet spiritualized to the free and beautiful form, not yet to clarity; what is sensory and natural is not yet completely transfigured into the spiritual, so that it is only the expression of the spiritual; this organisation and the characteristics of this organisation are only signs, only the indication of the spiritual. The Egyptian principle lacks this transparency of the natural, exterior aspect of the form [...].[104]

In the 'not yet' of this passage, a teleology of art announces itself whose essential criterion will be the increasing transparency of the outside for the inside. Over against the still inadequate stage of the 'Egyptian principle' in the (self-) representation of the inward idea, Hegel posits—as the explicit centre of his aesthetics[105]—the classical art of Greco-Roman antiquity, represented in the lectures on aesthetics above all by the Greek sculpture of the fifth and fourth centuries B.C. Here, the complete unity of appearance and concept rules:

> Classical art [...] is the free, adequate working of the form into the concept; a content that has the form appropriate to it, which as true content does not lack the true form. This is where the ideal of art comes from.[106]

10, pp. 367–372, Engl. Hegel 2007, pp. 259–262) and (for the third series of aesthetics-lectures in 1826) Hegel 2004b, pp. 66–68. On the reasons for preferring the lecture notes taken by Hegel's students to H.G. Hotho's posthumous reconstruction of what he took to have been Hegel's aesthetics (= Hegel 1969–1971, vols. 13–15), see Gethmann-Siefert's remarks in Hegel 2003, pp. XXI–XXXIII, and Hegel 2004b, pp. 9–24.

103 Here, 'die der Idee angemessene Gestaltung [ist] noch nicht gefunden [...], vielmehr [wird] der Gedanke als hinausgehend und ringend mit der Gestalt als ein negatives Verhalten zu derselben, der er zugleich sich einzubilden bemüht ist, dargestellt [...]. Die Bedeutung, der Inhalt zeigt eben damit, die unendliche Form noch nicht erreicht zu haben, noch nicht als freier Geist gewußt und sich bewußt zu sein' (*Enzyklopädie* III, § 561; = Hegel 1969–1971, vol. 10, p. 369 f., Engl. Hegel 2007, p. 260 f.).

104 'Die Gestalt [*sc.* der ägyptischen Kunstwerke] ist noch nicht zur freien, schönen erhoben, noch nicht zur Klarheit vergeistigt, das Sinnliche, Natürliche noch nicht zum Geistigen vollkommen verklärt, so daß es nur Ausdruck des Geistigen, diese Organisation und die Züge dieser Organisation nur Zeichen wären, nur Bedeutung des Geistigen. Es fehlt dem ägyptischen Prinzip diese Durchsichtigkeit des Natürlichen, des Äußerlichen der Gestaltung [...].' Hegel, *Philosophie der Religion* I (= Hegel 1969–1971, vol. 16), p. 442, my translation; *cf. Phänomenologie des Geistes* (= Hegel 1969–1971, vol. 3), p. 511, Engl. Hegel 1977, p. 423.

105 *Cf.* Hegel 2003, p. 159.

106 'Die klassische Kunst [...] ist die freie adäquate Einbildung der Gestaltung in den Begriff; ein Inhalt, der die ihm angemessene Gestalt hat, der als wahrhafter Inhalt der wahrhaften Form nicht entbehrt. Hier fällt das Ideal der Kunst her.' Hegel 2003, p. 36,

If the opaque materiality of symbolic art was the decisive hindrance on the way to knowledge of the spiritual content enclosed within it, the perfect concinnity of inside and outside in classical art requires the dematerialisation of the form as its essential prerequisite. The transition from the enigmatic nature of the symbolic to the clear beauty of classical art takes place, at the same time, as the externalisation of the semantic surplus created by the materiality of the symbol. But even this reconciled substantiality of the classical image is provisional. The progression towards the immateriality of the essential announced in the lectures on the philosophy of religion gives rise, in a final step, to the definition of Romanticism, in which there can be no more classical unity because the content of post-pagan, Christian art is no longer capable of an adequate material expression. For this third phase of history, Hegel's paradigm is poetry: its material is not, however, the word as such—for prose, too, is made up of words—but rather the imaginative representation transported by the word. This *Vorstellung*, writes Hegel, takes up a middle position between language and thought; the bipartite constitution of art in symbolic architecture and classical sculpture, the simple relationship between form and content, is extended to encompass a third term. The consequence of this extension is that whereas language as a whole now becomes the expression of the expression—a position that in the *Enzyklopädie* was reserved for alphabetic writing as the mere image of the voice[107]—the essential 'matter' of literature takes place on the far side of language:

> The matter of poetry is no longer directly exterior, but lies rather in imaginative representation; for a work of poetry can be read, it can also be translated into other languages, brought into other relationships to sound. Whether we hear or see a poet is of no consequence. The imaginative representation is the real element through which the matter becomes objective for us.[108]

The transfer of the immediate expression into the inwardness of the *Vorstellung* leads to a radical expulsion of the materiality of language from literature: language is not a part of poetry in any essential sense. This exclusion is the most important prerequisite for the postulate of the last part of the *Wissenschaft der Logik* that art is historically transcended by philosophy.[109] From the perspective

my translation.

[107] Hegel, *Enzyklopädie* III, § 459 (= Hegel 1969–1971, vol. 10, p. 271). This definition of alphabetic writing is already to be found in Aristotle's *De interpretatione* I, 16 a5–8; we have also observed it in Boeckh (^{2}1886, p. 81; see above, p. 91). On some of its further implications, see Derrida 1967a, 15 ff.

[108] 'Die Sache der Poesie ist nicht mehr unmittelbar äußerlich, sondern in Vorstellungen; denn ein Dichtwerk kann gelesen werden, auch ist es in andere Sprachen zu übersetzen, in andere Verhältnisses des Tönens zu bringen. Ob wir einen Dichter hören oder sehen ist gleichgültig. Die Vorstellung ist das eigentliche Element, durch welches die Sache uns objektiv wird.' Hegel 2003, p. 272, my translation; *cf.* p. 275 ff.

[109] This is the so-called 'theory of the end of art' (*cf.* also Hegel 1969–1971, vol. 13, p. 25 f and 2003, p. 5 f.). Although Hegel locates this moment of transcendence in history

of the nineteenth century, it thus forms an imperative to think of art as *ideal*, a requirement which holds retrospectively for the works of every historical epoch. Transcending art by interpreting literature, breaking through what is merely material or individual on the way to the intellectual-conceptual absolute is however only possible because the problem of poetry has been completely reduced to the level of content, of the signified.[110] As the expression of the expression, language is the specifically material element of a given text and belongs essentially to the *outside* of the work of art, an outside that has to become completely transparent for the inwardness of the *Vorstellung* and for the idea contained within it. We have already seen how Boeckh's theory of philology is overtaken by this logic; in Dissen, who believes himself to be far from all Hegelianism, it is no less virulent.

In the metaphors which structure Dissen's theory of hermeneutics, only the inside has value: it is always the *fundamentum*, the *subiectum* that must be sought; the imperative *altius penetrare in intimo* must always be obeyed. The commentary on the individual odes is correspondingly laid out in steps that proceed from outside (primarily the historical context of the songs) to the inside, to *ratio* and *summa sententia*. In the *introductio* to the *Second Olympian*, Dissen describes first the dates and biographical circumstances of the victor, in this case Theron of Akragas; we then move to the *carminis ratio*, the 'plan of the song', which is worked out on the basis of the single discursive steps of the poem (*expositis singulis*), before we arrive at the climax, the 'internal connection of them all' (*nexus interior horum omnium*) consisting of a general thought.[111] Most rightly observes that this *nexus*—'thus, the basic thought is that the miraculous fate of the family of Cadmus and the Emmenidae is divinely ordained by means of an eternal marked alternation of contrary and beneficial circumstances, whereby earlier ills repeatedly become painful again and the same are always also counterbalanced by following happy fortune'—is a 'loose translation of O. 2.19–24';[112] more important for our purposes, however, is the fact

and thus gives it the appearance of historical contingency, it is in fact necessarily required by his understanding of the inner dynamics of art in the lectures on aesthetics; there, the potential of transcendence is from the very beginning already implied by the epistemological superiority of philosophy, a superiority predicated on the grounds of the latter's structure and operation in terms of *concepts*. *Cf.* de Man, 'Sign and symbol in Hegel's *Aesthetics*' (= de Man 1996, pp. 91–104), who locates the reason for the 'end of art' in Hegel's theory of subjectivity.

110 Rightly noted by Zima ^{2}1995, p. 29.

111 Dissen ^{2}1847, p. 27 f.

112 Most 1985b, 40 on Dissen ^{2}1847, p. 28: '*scilicet fundamentum est Cadmidarum et Emmenidarum divinitus constitutum mirabile fatum, aeterna vicissitudine adversarum*

that with the identification of this thought Dissen believes that he has finally arrived at the *centre* of the song. His procedure in the commentaries on the other odes is no different. Everywhere we find the metaphors of penetration, entering, leaving the surface and going deeper; they stand in odd contrast to what Dissen himself sees as the essence of his hermeneutics, namely the postulate of the absolute harmony of successful form and rational content.

It can be shown that this curious tension in the conceptual system of *De ratione* is a consequence of the attempt to declare the linguistic surface of the text to be the outside of literature. If the separation into outside and inside governs Dissen's entire aesthetics of the epinicians, we find that this Göttingen philologist, who wants so desperately to speak of the inside of the poem, is constantly forced to do so in the language of the outside. This is nowhere more fateful than in those passages in which Dissen attempts to describe the effect of the *Grundgedanke* in terms of his aesthetic postulates. At the end of the first section of *De ratione*, entitled *De sententiarum ratione, quae epiniciis subiectae*, the author sees himself confronted with the fact that some songs apparently possess *two* 'basic thoughts'. But this does not lead to a lack of unity:

> These compositions are [...] of such a kind that the two parts which have been combined are not held together by force, like those which (only) agree in appearance, on the inside however contradict each other; instead, they agree and go together by their very nature, joining in one as though they had to, and at the same time they effect everywhere in their genre a perfect whole lacking in nothing.[113]

The thought on which the song is based is meant to guarantee that the unity of its single parts is not forced upon them from outside, *non vi*, but rather follows from the nature of the parts themselves.[114] Dissen locates this potential for violence in the relationship between

et secundarum rerum insigne, malis pristinis iterum iterumque recrudescentibus iisdemque semper etiam compensatis laetiore succedente fortuna.' Cf. *Olymp.* 2. 19 f.: ἐσλῶν γὰρ ὑπὸ χαρμάτων πῆμα θνᾴσκει | παλίγκοτον δαμασθέν [...].

113 *'Sunt* [...] *hae compositiones tales, ut non vi contineantur duo quae composita membra, quemadmodum quae specie conspirant, intus vero dissident, sed suapte natura congruunt et coeunt, in unum quasi debeant coniungi, simulque totum ubique efficiunt in suo genere absolutum, cui nihil desit.'* Dissen ²1843, p. XI.

114 On the notion of 'organic' unity suggested by Dissen's descriptions of the songs, see Most 1985a. On the eminent unity of what is 'one' by virtue of φύσις and not βία, see Aristotle, *Met.* I 1, 1052 a23 and below, p. 156.

the external appearance and the inside of the text: the *composita membra* do not merely agree *specie*, 'in appearance', whilst *intus* striving in different directions; instead, their congruence takes place *suapte natura*, as if it were necessary: *in unum quasi debeant coniungi.* The author almost seems at this point to be setting up an uncharacteristically Hegelian tripartite figure: the opposition between the outward appearance of art and the inward reality of nature that we have been able to observe both in Bundy and in Pindar is now to be dialectically *aufgehoben* into nature.[115] But the very moment this sublimation is postulated, it suddenly collapses, for the language of the 'as if' carries the dissonance between *species* and inwardness immediately back to the level of appearance: the connection of the parts is only *apparently* a result of their nature. If the polarity between true nature and mere appearance structures Dissen's description of the unity of the songs at this point, it becomes clear that the postulate of unity, inasmuch as it is based on the separation of inside and outside, can only be made in the language of appearance, of the *quasi* which in Plato's *Sophist* undermines the difference between being and non-being.[116]

Given these difficulties, the third important work in German Pindaric studies in the nineteenth century, Mezger's *Pindars Siegeslieder* from 1880, can be seen as an attempt to break down the form-content-dichotomy. The Augsburg *Gymnasialprofessor*'s edition with commentary declares allegiance to the principle of Dissen's *Grundgedanke*, although Mezger is not persuaded by the Göttingen philologist's concentration on morality.[117] In contrast to Dissen, however, Mezger ascribes a constitutive role in the construction of the *Grundgedanke* to the level of expression of the text: especially tautometrical repetitions are seen as the key to understanding the individual songs. Nevertheless, even this Pindarist cannot escape from the attraction exerted by the difference between thought and language, for as soon as a status for these repetitions is claimed that subordinates them to a centre of meaning, a tension arises between the wording and the thought, the surface and the ground. This is because Mezger's thesis that the repetitions are indicators of the *Grundgedanke* and intended as such by the poet—this is what his critics attacked most vociferously—is, in a strict sense and for reasons which can be analysed, unverifiable; Race, for example, observes that Mezger can provide no criterion by which the

[115] I am indebted to Jost Eickmeyer for this observation.

[116] On the *Sophist*, see above, p. 34 ff.

[117] Mezger 1880, p. 33; on Mezger see Young 1970, pp. 25–28; Most 1985b, pp. 43–47; Krummen 1990, p. 14.

real significance of his responsions could be proved, and asks: 'Are they simply a feature of Pindar's exuberant use of language or are they *serious indicators of meaning*?'[118] Between the exuberant play of the signifier and the serious realm of meaning, the same gap widens in Mezger's book that Boeckh had already attempted to overcome, and that many of works on Pindar that follow him will, one way or another, themselves attempt to close.

The praise of genre

Boeckh, Dissen and Mezger differ from Bundy in their reluctance to use the tern 'rhetoric', which stands in the nineteenth century for a dead science seen as the epitome of artificiality, mannerism and insincerity.[119] They nevertheless share with the author of the *Studia Pindarica* the problem of a textual surface that does not readily allow itself to be dissolved into literal meaning and must therefore in its figurality be overcome or effaced. The greater part of Pindaric studies in the twentieth century tries to deal with this problem with one of three strategies.

A first, highly influential approach aims at determining the persuasive semantics of the 'rhetorical' language of the songs on the basis of a generic intention which must admittedly first be reconstructed, but then is binding for all of the parts of a given ode. The awareness that assigning the texts to the rhetorical genre 'encomium' would have consequences for the way they would need to be read was, in the first half of the twentieth century, not new. Scholars in Alexandria and Byzantium had already realized that the epinicians could be read according to the categories of the rhetoric of persuasion; accordingly, ancient and Byzantine Pindaric studies made extensive use of the system and terminology of classical rhetorical theory, as the indices to Drachmann's edition of the scholia and the relevant entries in Arrighetti *et al.* show.[120] In the course of the Renaissance, this system becomes authoritative, its relevance for the interpretation of Pindar unques-

[118] Race 1990, p. 2 (my italics). *Cf.* Most 1985b, p. 55 ('what matters [...] is the paralleling and contrasting of elements of thought'). See Derrida, 'La double séance' (= Derrida 1972a, pp. 215–346), p. 299 ff., Engl. p. 245 ff. for a critique of the possibility, constitutive of the kind of thematic criticism for which the *Grundgedanke* stands, of deciding whether a given element or configuration in a text is a thought or a meaning.

[119] On the 'death of rhetoric', see above, p. 32 with n. 16.

[120] See esp. the indices xvi *Figurae* and xx *Sermones technici* in Drachmann's edition of the scholia and the lemmata of the relevant terms in Arrighetti *et al.* 1991. *Cf.* also above, p. 23 f.

tioned, so that at the beginning of the seventeenth century, the German humanist Erasmus Schmid can publish a study of Pindar in which the poems are rigorously analysed according to the *partes orationis*.[121] But in the later seventeenth century and in the eighteenth and nineteenth, the repute and scientific status of rhetoric is on the wane and such approaches—apart from Westphal's theory of the Terpandrian *nomos* which enjoyed a certain popularity in the second half of the nineteenth century[122]—receive little attention; the possibility of devoting serious scholarly attention to a subgenre of encomium entitled 'epinician' is out of the question.[123]

Instead, Pindaric scholarship at the end of the nineteenth century is preoccupied with attacking the notion, defended by Boeckh and Dissen, that the odes are unified wholes. Drachmann's rejection of Boeckh's ideas (or at least of those ideas he attributed to Boeckh) leads him to abandon any attempt to discover a binding form for the epinicians on the level of *dispositio*.[124] The victory songs possess no unitary meaning because it is impossible to reduce or refer their linguistic form to a single proposition. In the work of Wilamowitz, who believes himself to have adopted Drachmann's position, the function of structural unity is taken over by the songs' historical-biographical context, this time however without the idealist metaphysics that had motivated Boeckh's referral of the poems to just this context.[125] In comparison to Boeckh's more complex hermeneutics with its many and diverse connections to philosophical theorems of the early nineteenth century, Wilamowitz's archaeologically based historicism appears insufficiently theorized, especially since the Prussian scholar seems not to recognize that in privileging the unquestioned category of the historical—which must always be unitary, consistent and meant—he has in fact revoked Drachmann's critique of unity in all essential respects.

Almost the last, certainly the most important work on the linguistic

121 Schmid 1616 (and see Heath 1986, p. 89 for an overview of Schmid's analysis of the *Second Pythian*).

122 See Mezger 1880, p. 23 ff.

123 An exception is Dissen's discussion of the genre 'epinician' in Dissen ²1843, II ff., where the poetics of the genre is based on content. *Cf.* however Hermann's critique (1827–1877, vol. VI, p. 22 f.) who questions the relevance for these considerations, since they are 'bloss *a priori* aus dem Begriff des Epinikion geschlossen' and serve only as the basis for the content, not the form.

124 Drachmann 1891, p. 280 f. Newman & Newman 1984, p. 31 n. 58 note Drachmann's frequent confusion of Dissen's views with those of Boeckh. See also *ibid.*, pp. 246–266.

125 Wilamowitz 1922, p. 9.

form of the epinicians written in this theoretical context is Dornseiff's *Pindars Stil*, which appears a year before Wilamowitz's *Pindaros* and provides the older Pindarist with an obviously welcome opportunity to dispense almost entirely with a treatment of the lexis of the poems.[126] Here, one can observe a rediscovery of the textual surface of the songs as an object of scholarly interest, although the implications of this shift in accent do not immediately become apparent. The author possesses historicism's clear consciousness of the historical contingency of the forms of Pindaric poetry and distances himself from the Romantic call for individuality as the sign of the truly poetic: it never occurred to any poet to break out of a genre merely because he was 'a different kind of "personality"'.[127] Whereas Dornseiff owes his conception of language to the nineteenth century and the vitalistic hermeneutics of Dilthey, student of both Boeckh and Schleiermacher,[128] his understanding of the communal character of choral lyric, based both upon the obvious conventionality of the *topoi* and upon comparison with other forms of poetry, is an important sign of things to come.

> Choral lyric is pre-personal, religious, the voice of a group [...]. Only for an early society ordered and divided into houses, estates or on some other principle is the chorus an appropriate means of expression.[129]

Although, in what follows, *Pindars Stil* argues vehemently for a rhetoric of pure *elocutio*,[130] Dornseiff's reflections on the function of the victory songs open, surprisingly enough, the way for studies of the structural rhetoric of *dispositio* as a characteristic of the genre and in so doing for a concept of the rhetoric of the epinicians that is once again

[126] Dornseiff 1921; *cf.* Wilamowitz 1922, p. 9 ('Ich habe vieles in dem Buch gefunden, was ich sagen wollte; nun kann ich mich kürzer fassen'). On Dornseiff, see also Young 1970, pp. 48–52 (critical, perhaps unduly so).

[127] Dornseiff 1921, p. 2 (my translation).

[128] Dornseiff 1921, p. 11 emphasizes the sensuous origins of language in the experience of previous generations; language is 'der ererbte Niederschlag von vergangenem Leben'. On Dilthey's theory of language in the wider context of his hermeneutics, see the essay 'Die Entstehung der Hermeneutik', first published in 1900, now in Dilthey 1959–, vol. V, pp. 317–338.

[129] 'Chorlyrik ist vorpersönlich, religiös, Stimme einer Gruppe [...]. Nur für eine frühe Gesellschaft, die in Geschlechtern, Ständen oder sonstwie gebunden und abgesondert ist, ist der Chor ein angemessenes Ausdrucksmittel.' Dornseiff 1921, p. 4, my translation.

[130] And thus follows the tendency of the time: see Curtius 1948, 71–88 (esp. 80) and Barthes, 'L'ancienne rhétorique' (= Barthes 2002, vol. III, pp. 527–601), p. 541 (A.4.9) and pp. 555–559, and above, p. 30.

based on the Aristotelian rhetoric of persuasion.

The decisive step towards a renewed notion of genre in Pindaric philology is taken by Schadewaldt seven years after the publication of *Pindars Stil*. In *Der Aufbau des Pindarischen Epinikion*, we read that

> [...] the epinician belongs to a specific genre which determines its outward, formal unity, not only in terms of language and style (in the popular sense of the word), but also in terms of certain ideas and a certain outward behaviour on the part of the poet.[131]

Schadwaldt's theory of the programme, the series of items of information that a victory song had to mention in order to be a satisfactory example of the genre epinician, is probably the most important anticipation of the generic hermeneutics of Bundy.[132]

Formally, the central point of Schadewaldt and Bundy's studies is not far from Boeckh's occasional 'purpose' (as Schadewaldt indeed admits). The most important difference between Boeckh and the interpreters of the century which came after him lies in the fact that

[131] 'Auf der anderen Seite gehört das Epinikion einem bestimmten Genos an, das die äußere formale Einheit und zwar nicht nur Sprache und Stil (im landläufigen Sinne) sondern auch gewisse Vorstellungen und ein gewisses äußeres Gebaren des Dichters bestimmt.' Schadewaldt 1966, p. 3 f., my translation. On Schadewaldt see Young 1970, pp. 60–64; Most 1985b, p. 46; Krummen 1990, p. 17 f.

[132] The recurrence of the programme (already recognized in its basic features by Dissen ²1843, XII ff.) is genetically a consequence of the probable historical development of the genre 'epinician'. In terms of its programme, the victory ode is the choral-lyric form of the victory epigram (*cf. e.g.* the Olympian inscription of Kleisthenes of Epidamnos at Pausanias VI 10. 6, dated to 516 B.C.: Κλεοσθένης μ' ἀνέθηκεν ὁ Πόντιος ἐξ Ἐπιδάμνου | νικήσας ἵπποις καλὸν ἀγῶνα Διός), the epigram in turn the poetic formulation of the *kerygma* of the herald who announced the victor (*cf.* Timotheus fr. 802 *PMG* which describes a fictitious *kerygma* with some of the same elements: the name of the victor, his home city and discipline). The elements of the programme are thus generic traits: they show the text to be an epinician. It would, in principle, be possible to construct the coherence of the text on the basis of the relationship between the parts of the ode and the elements of the programme. Schadewaldt, however, is hindered from doing this by the fact that he views Boeckh's concept of subjective unity in complete isolation from his notion of objective unity: the genre is, so Schadewaldt, 'nicht so bestimmt, daß der Dichter nur den Sieger zu verherrlichen hätte [...]' (p. 261), a statement that in consequence makes it possible to attribute anything that seems not to fit to the unknowable inner recesses of the poetic psyche. That with this move the way to a plausible theory of epinician unity is blocked is seen by Drachmann 1929, p. 1096 ff., Young 1970, p. 61 ff. and Most 1985b, p. 46. That may also be the reason why Bundy refers to Schadewaldt only once (1986, p. 6 n. 22 on *Isthm.* 7. 1 ff.) and nowhere notes the theoretical proximity of his genre-based hermeneutics to Schadewaldt's emphasis of precisely this aspect of the epinicians in *Aufbau*.

whereas for the former the purpose of a song involves every possible performative link between the text and the situation which makes up its context—thus also whatever the poet in this situation feels and thinks[133]—the philology of the twentieth century concentrates much more on the systematic implications of the trans-situational genre of the epinician. Not only the notion of rhetoric authoritative for this approach, but also the concept of 'epinician' as a persuasive genre related to context is strongly influenced by the Platonic-Aristotelian model of rhetoric discussed in the first chapter.[134] Where on the surface of the text forms are present which, in their figurality, must be read 'rhetorically'—in practice, this means above all the figures of the classical *elocutio*—they serve, *ipso facto*, the persuasive force of the text. This force must support the thesis that, and why, the victor is to be praised. That follows, as we saw with Bundy, necessarily from the definition of the epinician as such which is determined in advance. Given this generic expectation, an interpretation of rhetorical language is thus only successful if it can demonstrate an encomiastically relevant statement for the specific linguistic form. Race's definition of the rhetoric of the songs as 'the poet's [...] use of language to fulfil his generic purpose'[135] can only be understood on the basis of this tradition; only the definition of this purpose, laid down at the outset, allows him to identify those passages in which 'meaning and style are in complete agreement.'[136]

It is not difficult to see that in all of these works the generic identity of the songs takes over the centring function fulfilled, in Dissen, by the *Grundgedanke* and, in Boeckh, by the immediate intuition of the poet. The genre is the basis of meaning that stabilizes the readings of

[133] See for example Boeckh 1854–1877, vol. VII, p. 385.

[134] On epinician as a genre based on argument, see Slater 1976–77, esp. p. 195, and above, p. 27 f.

[135] Race 1990, p. 5 f.

[136] Is a synthesis of this generic model with structuralist theories of figuration such as Roman Jakobson's possible? An attempt to think in this direction is Stoneman 1981. Stoneman's initial thesis is that 'Pindar's images can be better understood if regarded as metonymies' (p. 128) whose rhetorical force does not lie in that creative, new description of phenomena in which Jakobson (and, in his wake, Jacques Lacan [1999, vol. 1, p. 504, Engl. p. 422]) had seen the essence of the metaphor; the American Pindarist draws the conclusion that 'Pindar's language does not stimulate new understandings; on the contrary, it reflects assumptions familiar to the hearer in the same way as rhetoricians do. In so far as his images fall into consistent patterns [...], they reproduce or reflect a vision of the world which gives epinician poetry its raison d'être [...]. They are a means of persuasion (always best effected on those who already believe what they are about to be told) not of imagination' (p. 137). See also Schmid 1998a, p. 62 f.

Schadewaldt, Bundy and Race, for only it can guarantee that the interpretation of every new poem can have recourse to a criterion which is not itself first constructed by means of this interpretation. The intention of an epinician as an epinician—*ἐσλὸν αἰνεῖν* and so forth—does not, after it has been discovered, itself have to be interpreted once again; here, the text is finally identical with itself in the absolute self-presence of its generic meaning.

We have already seen at the beginning of this chapter to what kind of interpretative practice this hermeneutics leads. It is not to be criticised because it attempts to carry the texts back to the basis of their generic meaning; every theory of meaning as presence must presuppose such a basis. The alternative, if there is one, would not be to substitute some other meaning for that of the genre, but to disrupt the hierarchy between the centre and the periphery by refusing to subscribe to a logic of interpretation as the unveiling of the (single, literal, true) meaning of the songs altogether. Some first steps towards a reading of the epinicians of this kind—'disseminative' in the sense that its results would no longer return to a centre—are undertaken in the latter chapters of this book. Here, we are merely concerned with demonstrating the structural analogy between the generic approach to reading Pindar and that which preceded it historically. Despite their real and obvious differences, both Boeckh and Bundy believe in the one foundational basis of the meaning of the texts. Both *Pindari opera* and the *Studia Pindarica* belong in this sense to the *philologie de la métaphysique*.

This conclusion should nevertheless not blind us to the fact that there are already reasons within the implicit logic of the generic theory to doubt its theoretical coherence within the metaphysics of presence that it implies. Derrida has pointed out that although generic traits must always be part of the texts they identify as members of a given genre, they nevertheless cannot belong to these genres themselves in any simple sense.[137] This is because the function of signalling that a specific text is an exemplar of a certain genre (or of several genres) is not itself included in the definition of the genre that it identifies. A generic trait is like a border: its ontological status cannot coalesce with

[137] See Derrida, 'La loi du genre' (= Derrida ²2003, pp. 231–266, Engl. *id.* 1980). The observation that sets containing themselves as one of their elements lead to paradoxes led to the development of the theory of types in Russell and Whitehead's *Principia Mathematica* (1910–1913) and to the axiomatic set theory of Zermelo and Fränkel. Derrida's thesis is that literary genres always create exactly such sets; see on this Culler 1982, p. 201 f. and Bennington 2000, p. 51.

that of the object it defines without leading to an infinite regression.[138] Derrida himself speaks of a 'genre-clause, a clause stating at once the juridical utterance, the precedent-making designation and the law-text, but also the closure, the closing that excludes itself from what it includes'.[139] In our case, this means that the passages of non-rhetorical language in Bundy, such as *Nem.* 3. 29 quoted above, to the extent that they are interpreted as meta-statements about the generic identity of the texts in which they occur, do not belong to this genre: they are not epinician, for the simple reason that according to a functional definition of epinician such as *ἐσλὸν αἰνεῖν*, it is precisely *not* epinician to *point to the fact that* a text that praises a noble man is an epinician; it is precisely this signalling function that is not covered by the definition of the genre that it itself provides. From this perspective, Bundy's assertion, quoted at the beginning of this chapter, that there is 'no passage in Pindar [...] that is not in its primary intent enkomiastic'[140] is not binding for his own hermeneutics; he must assume that the *primary* function of certain privileged passages—the function on which all of the other functions of these texts depend and which alone allows them to be seen in their proper light—is precisely *not* encomiastic, but rather that of the identification of a genre.

Deep structures

In the context of structuralist and poststructuralist developments in literary theory, the convergence, raised by Bundy and his predecessors to a methodological axiom, of rhetoric and intention appears, at the very least, questionable. The centring of the texts around intuitions, *Grundgedanken* or generic purposes are merely different strategies for dealing with a discrepancy between language and an Other which is the presupposition for the interpretability of literature. Nothing, however, guarantees that the intuition of the poet or the generic purpose of the epinician is always realized both completely (*everything* that the poet or the genre wants to say is said) but also exclusively (*only* what the poet or the genre wants to say is said) on the surface of the text. The obedience of language to the desire of the subject or to the generic

[138] See further pp. 157 ff. below.

[139] '[...] que j'appellerai la *clause de genre*, clause disant à la fois l'énoncé juridique, la mention faisant droit et texte de lois, mais aussi la fermeture, la clôture qui s'exclut de ce qu'elle inclut [...].' Derrida ^{2}2003, p. 246 (his italics), Engl. *id.* 1980, p. 212. On this double structure of openness and closure see also below, p. 180 ff.

[140] Bundy 1986, p. 3 (already cited above, p. 62).

will to form is itself not capable of demonstration; it always presupposes—and this is the point at which the second approach governing studies on Pindar in the twentieth century intervenes—a mechanism that ensures this agreement between a text and something behind it.

The reading of Plato undertaken in the first chapter made this assumption seem questionable from a theoretical perspective; Paul de Man's work in literary theory offered a model of interpretation that tried to take account of the aporias of a presence-based hermeneutics. But although a form of reading based on absence and rhetoric would seem, in principle, to present a cogent alternative to traditional theories of reading, its influence on the interpretation of Pindar has to date been minimal.

One of the very few substantial works to distance itself explicitly from what its author calls 'critical strategies for centring the text and thus reducing its structural elaboration into a more tractable comprehensibility' is Thomas Hubbard's *The Pindaric Mind*, published in 1985.[141] Hubbard criticizes studies like the *Studia Pindarica* for privileging the metonymic dimension of the epinicians (Bundy's insistence on the strictly linear progression of thought from an ode's beginning through to its end) at the cost of the metaphorical dimension (the constantly possible substitution of a given conventional building-block in one text for the corresponding building-block in another) on the grounds that the teleological notion of meaning such a model implies is entirely foreign to the kind of literature the epinicians represent.

> All these approaches subordinate the text to a unitary *telos*, whether this end is viewed as the poem's ultimate "meaning" or its ultimate function. But there is considerable question to what extent *telos* as "intention" was even a contemporary concept. [...] Since Pindar himself probably had no consciously formed concept of literary "intention" [...], it is arguable that the whole notion of programmatic intention or unitary *telos* is best bracketed from our critical vocabulary, at least when we are dealing with texts of this period.[142]

[141] See Hubbard 1985, p. 1 and *cf.* Hubbard 1987, p. 3: 'Pindaric criticism of the last twenty years has maintained an unmistakable functionalist bias, privileging the epinician "praise of the victor" as the intentional center of each ode and interpreting all the poem's constituent elements as rhetorical devices subordinate to this controlling program.' Glenn Most's *The Measures of Praise*, published in the same year as *The Pindaric Mind*, contains a similarly accented critique of the traditional interpretation of Pindar: see Most 1985, p. 36 ff.

[142] Hubbard 1985, p. 4.

Let us postpone questioning this notion of the 'contemporary' for a moment, and the concept and value of history as the history of consciousness it entails. Hubbard's proposed alternative is a broadly structuralist interpretation of the odes which will direct attention towards the ateleological structures of the Pindaric unconscious:

> What we must ultimately probe is the cognitive structure of Pindar's mind [...]; this depth-analysis must therefore drive beneath the superficial intentionality of the ego into the more revealing [...] associative patterns of the unconscious.[143]

Given the role that metaphor and metonymy have played in psychoanalytic theory, it is no accident that Hubbard seeks to interpret above all the metaphors contained in the songs as signs of the generative deep structures of Pindar's unconscious mind. Here, the single text is to be seen as a nexus or field of interaction of a series of quasi-subterranean systems, the hidden lines of an archaic form of thought which in principle is at work in all the songs, but which by no means necessarily agrees with the consciousness or the intention of the poet. In this way, the subject of epinician speech is to disappear; language itself will speak as the unconscious.[144]

> Structural analysis [...] implies the poet's *absence* from a seemingly autonomous text which does not execute any *a priori* intention, but crystallizes an array of unconscious perceptions and ingrained semantic relations. On this level of meaning, contradiction and ambiguity may be rampant [...].[145]

Hubbard accordingly develops a concept of meaning which consists in the logical relationships between the abstract categories implied by the binarily organised unconscious perceptions and deeply rooted semantic relationships he discovers in the texts. Interpretation proceeds (a) by categorizing the sequences of antitheses on the surface (such as near/far, early/late, *βραχύς/μακρός et al.*); (b) by examining the semantic and associative range of these polarities (so that, *e.g.*, the

[143] Hubbard 1985, p. 5.

[144] The connection of language with the unconscious was of course the project of Jacques Lacan, in accordance with his programmatic assertion: '[L]'inconscient est structuré comme un langage' (Lacan 1973, p. 28; see also p. 167 ff. and p. 227 ff.). Hubbard 1985 makes almost no use of theoretical work in psychoanalysis in developing a concept of the unconscious (see Hubbard 1985, p. 4 f.; the brief reference at p. 5 leads to no substantial engagement with the theory).

[145] Hubbard 1985, 6 f. (his italics).

antithesis near/far can be associated with oppositions such as domestic/foreign, present/absent, possible/impossible and so on); (c) by identifying analogous connections between the polarities. The network of opposing concepts that emerges from this last step in a given song is its 'meaning'.

But here, two dangers threaten. On the one hand, Hubbard stresses that he does not believe in a 'key polarity' that would form the basis or the structure of all the others. If such a polarity existed, the structuralist reading would of course become yet another one of the centring strategies that the author has just rejected.[146] Nor can the reading of the text in terms of its unconscious polarities make a claim to totality, since the chain of oppositions 'may encompass increasingly minute linguistic antitheses in and behind the text, and can as a result be extended to a potentially infinite degree of associative elaboration.'[147]

On the other hand, the text's oscillation between the two poles of an opposition realized in it must not be read as self-destruction:

> Criticism of an explicitly 'deconstructive' bent has produced much challenging and provocative work on texts which put their own rhetorical identity into question. [...] The notion of a 'self-destructive' text has great potential in the analysis of those dramatic, narrative, or even lyric texts which bracket their elements ironically, but seems out of place in a fundamentally pre-ironic text such as Pindar's. [...] The relational network of a Pindaric ode does not 'break down' or 'fail,' but becomes more elaborate as successive levels of difference are taken into account. What is called for here is not deconstruction, but a mode of critical reconstruction which in addition to charting the interstitial ambiguities of the poetic text, is also cognizant of its own provisionality and necessary incompleteness.[148]

Instead of experiencing deconstruction, Hubbard argues that the epinicians are in dialogue with themselves: they can modify or correct themselves in the course of their discourse, but do not cancel themselves out. That means: although the poles of the single oppositions are in tension with each other, they are nevertheless all present in a com-

[146] It is nevertheless interesting that the polarity of inside *versus* outside is not explicitly discussed in *The Pindaric Mind*. See Jean Hyppolite's commentary on Freud's 'Verneinung' (in Lacan 1999, vol. 1, pp. 527–537, esp. 533; Engl. p. 750 f.) and Derrida 1972c, p. 45, Engl. p. 32 f. on the special status of this opposition.

[147] Hubbard 1985, p. 6.

[148] Hubbard 1985, p. 7. On Hubbard's domestication of reading as 'provisional', *cf.* Cebulla's remarks on a similar move in Habermas cited above, p. 46 n. 55.

mon field that is constituted by the individual text itself, its coherence or limitability.

In Chapter 4, we will discover reasons to doubt this comforting assumption. But Hubbard's reference to the 'fundamentally pre-ironic' nature of the Pindaric *œuvre* must already raise our suspicions that something here is awry. Leaving the question of genre ('dramatic, narrative, or even lyric texts') aside: the historicization of irony at this strategic point in his argument refers us back to Hubbard's invocation of the 'contemporary' in his critique of teleological models of meaning. There, the project of *The Pindaric Mind* was based on a specific absence in Pindaric consciousness, the lack of a concept of literary intention. Here, the odes are prevented from 'breaking down' by another lack, this time the lack of a discrepancy between what is said and what is meant, and this harmonious epinician agreement between λέξις and λόγος, safely dated to the years before 446 B.C., entails that history, here, is once again the history of consciousness, conscious intention realized (seriously, literally) in language.[149] It is in the value accorded to what Pindar *meant*—in the integrity and closure of that meaning—that Hubbard's insistence on the unity of the victory odes is founded. If this is questioned, the barrier between the texts and their deconstruction will fall.

The stated necessity of preserving the coherence of the epinicians is indeed a sign that Hubbard does not, ultimately, escape from the attractions of centring. For even in *The Pindaric Mind* we can observe the separation of the text we could already discern in Bundy and Boeckh, this time so to speak in its theoretical 'purity' as the essential assumption of structuralism as a whole. The structure itself is not a part of the text; its existence is not essentially textual at all, but rather (to use Deleuze's term) *virtual*.[150] But at the same time, the structure itself is by definition *coherent*; an incoherent structure is not thinkable.[151] For this reason, Hubbard must believe in the coherence and unity of the victory songs as realizations of the closed structure underlying them. The latter may bear the possibility of its endless

149 In fact, we can go further: the model of primitive language (the 'pre-' in 'pre-ironic') implied here is that of complete congruence between intent and utterance. *Cf.* Lacan's position, for whom irony is the language of the constitutive alterity of the subject (Lacan 1999, vol. 1, p. 518, Engl. p. 433 and elsewhere).

150 See Deleuze 2002, p. 250, Engl. p. 178 f.

151 *Cf.* Derrida's remarks in 'La structure, le signe et le jeu dans le discours des sciences humaines« (= Derrida 1967c, pp. 409–428), p. 409, Engl. p. 278 f. on the constitutive coherence of structure in the context of his critique of centring strategies.

refinement within itself, but this refinement must be seen as the refinement *of the same structure*; abandoning this unity of the same would call the structurality of the structure itself into question.

The structure thus takes on the unity accruing to the historical subject of consciousness as a figure of the metaphysical one. It is not at all clear that Hubbard could have avoided this entanglement in the hermeneutics of presence, since it is entailed by the structuralist model to which he owes many of his most insightful interpretations of single passages. But if the transcendental point of unity and truth is to be removed from its traditional position as the final authority in the interpretation of the texts, then the unified field of the structure will also need to be interrogated. In what follows, we will not hesitate to call the coherence of the victory songs as structures of meaning, and thus the successful closure of the structure itself, principally into question—although we will in fact be much more interested in the way in which the epinicians themselves subvert the conditions of such success.

New histories

Readings of the epinicians based on an explicitly structuralist or poststructuralist model of literary language were felt as early as the 1980s to be problematic, primarily on account of their frequently unclarified relationship to history and to the entire complex of problems connected with historicity and the contingent conditions under which the odes were heard and understood. For many interpreters, it seemed and seems at least doubtful whether the language of a genre as public as that of the victory ode can be understood entirely without referential links to a context which one could call 'historical' in the broadest possible sense. A third approach in Pindaric studies attempts for this reason to read the rhetoric of the odes—here, too, understood as the language of persuasion—on the basis of specific, identifiable sociological and historical developments in the first half of the fifth century B.C. The results of this research have led both to an increased interest in the conditions under which individual songs were performed[152] and, particularly in Anglo-American work, to a heightened sensitivity to the ideological dimension of Pindaric rhetoric.[153]

Among the earliest and most comprehensive interpretations of the

[152] See *e.g.* Krummen 1990, whose hermeneutical approach is closely related both to Bundy's monofunctionalism and to the *Konstanzer Schule* of Hans Robert Jauß.

[153] An early example is Rose 1992, pp. 141–184 (first published in 1982), who undertakes a broadly Marxist reading of the *Tenth Pythian*.

epinicians from this perspective, Leslie Kurke's *The Traffic in Praise* deserves particular attention.[154] Kurke situates the odes in a complex social context consisting of three concentric circles. At the centre of this context is the house, the *οἶκος* of the victor, which commissions the song and pays the singer(s). The house itself is only one of a number of noble and/or wealthy houses which compete with each other for prestige and influence, but which also share a common ideology. The major houses are also, finally, a part of the growing *πόλεις* of the fifth century, and thus stand in a sometimes tense relationship to the group of citizens who provide the chorus for the performance of the epinician.[155] It is clear that the interests of these three groups can contradict each other; as opposed to tragedy, however, whose function Kurke sees as the questioning of the ideology of the polis, the victory ode must achieve the harmonious reintegration of the victor into his different social contexts and thus mediate the tensions implied by the plurality of these contexts.[156]

The consequence of this political hermeneutics is an understanding of the language of the epinicians that views the metaphors of the texts as moments of different systems of values and convictions held by Pindar's ideologically heterogeneous public.[157] By dividing the public up into different groups with differing value-systems, Kurke can interpret the ambiguity of the poet's rhetorical figures by reference to their different receptive contexts: Pindar's metaphors are ambiguous because they have to be able to function within different symbolic systems simultaneously. The poet uses the figures in the texts in this sense as political tools; their persuasive force enables him to intervene directly in the social constellations of the families and *πόλεις* that commission him.[158] The observation that the values of the audience are *sys-*

[154] Kurke 1991. A (highly critical) appraisal of Kurke's project in comparison to more traditional studies (Lefkowitz 1991 and Race 1990) is Lidov 1993.

[155] See Kurke 1991, p. 5 f.

[156] On the subversive social role of Attic tragedy, see in particular Goldhill 1990. The reintegrative function of epinician had already been emphasized by Crotty 1982. *Cf.* also Mackie 2003.

[157] Kurke 1991, p. 10 f.

[158] Other historical, *e.g.* political contexts have stood at the centre of some of the most interesting readings of the last fifteen years. *Cf.* Hubbard 1992, Cole 1992 (who takes the tensions between Aegina and Athens in the fifth century as the frame of his interpretation), Dougherty 1993 (a post-colonial reading of a number of the odes), Dougherty and Kurke 1993, Carnes 1995, Hornblower 2004 (on Thucydides' reception of Pindar) and Currie 2006 (a reading focused on what one might call the politics of religion).

tematic is a connection between Kurke's New Historicism and the structuralist readings of Hubbard: like Hubbard, Kurke is working towards an implicit grammar of the songs, a grammar, however, that would not be located in the poet's unconscious, but rather in the social structures in which even the epinician is a form of social practice.[159]

One would fail to do justice to this kind of interpretation if one were to accuse it of describing a simplistic model of the relationship between 'life' or history and literature.[160] Kurke is by no means asserting that the victory odes are 'products' of the circumstances under which they were produced or heard in any mechanical or automatic sense; rather, her thesis suggests that Pindar's dealings with his heterogeneous public can be seen as a conversation about their common socio-political context, a context, furthermore, that includes not only the epinicians themselves, but also other literary and non-literary texts, as well as monuments, coins and rituals. The goal of *The Traffic in Praise* is to map the ways in which the songs take up and intervene in this conversation.[161]

It is here that the concept of communication becomes of decisive importance. For the only hermeneutics on the basis of which Kurke can carry out her project must place the subject and the communica-

159 Currie 2006, p. 14 f. describes the relationship between Bundy's (quasi-) structuralism and New Historicism, which he understands as its heir, in terms of continuity: 'The objection to Bundy's approach is the arbitrariness of where it draws its boundaries. Whereas Bundy and Thummer tended to treat the victory ode as if it were a closed system, structuralist social anthropologists have applied the linguistic model to whole cultures.' On the notion of 'social practice' see Bourdieu ²2000.

160 This accusation is made, *e.g.*, by Abrams 1989, p. 365 against the representatives of what he calls 'political criticism'. See on this the observations of Liu 1989, p. 770 n. 92 and—with respect to Pindaric criticism—Nicholson 2007.

161 A rather different critique of emphatically political readings of literary texts is offered by Bennington 1999. For him, the thesis put forward by critics such as Terry Eagleton and Fredric Jameson that *all* interpretations are politically motivated (and thus ought to make this motivation explicit) is not easily reconcilable with the fact that the meaning of a text is essentially extrinsic or indeterminable, since a politically motivated interpretation will also be a text whose meaning will again be extrinsic (*cf. ibid.*, p. 105). This is clearly correct; applied to Kurke's project, however, it leads to an infinite regression, since the plural reception of the epinicians in the light of the differing political interests reconstructed by *The Traffic in Praise* entails, in principle, an unlimited number of individual readings, every one of which would have to demonstrate the same characteristics of indeterminability that Bennington argues are the characteristics of every politically engaged interpretation of literature. In this case, Kurke would have carried out the deconstruction of the victory odes in the mode of the deconstruction of their audience. On the discursive basis of an explicitly political hermeneutics of classical texts, see Rose 1992, pp. 1–42.

tion between poet and public at the centre:

> [...] I wish to suggest that as a participant in the culture speaking to other participants, the poet incorporated various cultural symbols and thereby transmitted a coherent message to his audience through his imagery. [...] [P]recisely because the poet's imagery was culturally grounded and meaningful to his audience, it was systematically employed in the service of the poetic program.[162]

The metaphors of the odes serve the generic programme, the common framework of expectations shared by the poet and his heterogeneous audience. Kurke can, therefore, and must return the subject and his communicative intention to the central role in interpretation from which Hubbard's structuralist reading had intended to remove them. And whereas Hubbard had attempted to protect the odes from self-destruction by the thesis of their essentially pre-ironic nature, Kurke achieves the same end by recourse to the *success* of the communication between poet and public. If no communication were to take place, then the songs would not succeed in mediating the different interests of the family, the nobility and the πόλεις. Since, however, Pindar's epinicians obviously did succeed in this respect (the poet's career and the survival of his work allow no other conclusion), there can be no question that the songs did indeed accurately transmit his intention in accordance with the expectations of his hearers by means of the performance of the song in their presence.

Intention, expectation (or desire), performance (or event) and presence: the metaphysical presuppositions of this model of communication are those of the rhetoric of *persuasio*; we analysed them in Chapter 1. They are not examined in *The Traffic in Praise*, nor can they be, without making the narrative of the book impossible. The shifting of interest from the figurative structures of language, whose complicity with the unconscious had been argued by Hubbard, to the description of successful, persuasive communication on the basis of principally describable value-systems represents a desire to postpone the collapse of the structures of meaning. *The Pindaric Mind* had tried to avoid this collapse by historicizing irony; Kurke in turn must stop her argument before the final act, in which the mediation of the values by means of communication is found to be without secure basis. In one of the most perceptive assessments of the New Historicism of the 1980s, Joseph Litvak writes:

[162] Kurke 1991, p. 11.

> By concentrating on the institutional interests served by local undecidabilities, and by emphasizing the power of conceptually imperfect differentiations, [the new historicism] does not so much escape from deconstruction as linger in—and dilate—the anxious intervals *before* deconstruction. [...] [A]nxiety itself has a narrative (i.e., implicitly history-making) structure. As a 'mode of expectation, closely resembling desire,' it both anticipates and defers the deconstructive cancellation of its sustaining techniques.[163]

Kurke's interpretations thus recapitulate the moment before the aporia into which a deconstructive reading of the rhetorical, metaphysically unfoundable structures of the odes would necessarily lead. This is less the naïve presupposition of the readability of the texts than the conscious decision to remain within their readability in order to be able to tell the story of how they function on the basis of the ideology—'the *confusion* of linguistic with natural reality, of reference with phenomenalism' (de Man)—they create and to which they answer.[164]

The decision to pause at the brink of the abyss in the name of the hermeneutics of history is thus revealed as the postponement or the exclusion of an end whose indefinite postponement is a necessary prerequisite of the notion of interpretation as the unveiling of meaning. As long as the epinicians are to be interpreted in this sense—and this will

[163] Litvak 1988, p. 126 f. (his italics). The quotation—'By showing us that anxiety is a mode of expectation, closely resembling desire, Freud allows us to understand why poetry, which loves love, also seems to love anxiety. Literary and human romance both are exposed as being anxious quests that could not bear to be cured of their anxieties, even if such cures were possible'—is from Harold Bloom (Bloom 1981, p. 225).

[164] De Man, 'The resistance to theory' (= de Man 1986, pp. 3–20), p. 11 (my italics). *Cf.* Koschorke 1997, p. 57, who describes this decision, and with it the agenda of much contemporary Pindaric criticism, as a movement *beyond* deconstruction: 'Wenn man müde wird, sich von der Tatsache absorbieren zu lassen, daß alle Wahrheitsdiskurse immer schon ein Dementi mitführen, wenn man also der Dekonstruktion auf eine unaufgeregte Weise beipflichtet, dann wird man zu der Frage geleitet, warum die Selbstdementierung dem Funktionieren solcher Diskurse in ihren unterschiedlichen materiellen und historischen Ausprägungen gewissermaßen nichts anhaben konnte. Statt immer zu der gleichen Pointe zu gelangen: "Jede Präsenz ist von ihren Implikationen her dekonstruierbar", wird man fragen: "Wie wird sie, und zwar gerade unter den beschriebenen Bedingungen ihrer (metaphysischen) Grundlosigkeit, kulturell generiert?"' Noteworthy here, alongside conventional elements that in the last few decades have taken on the status of classical *topoi* in the polemics against deconstruction—the accusation of monotony, the insinuation that deconstructive criticism is intellectually indiscriminate and slightly hysterical, *etc.*—is the very real question of how exactly the 'conditions of [presence's] (metaphysical) unfoundedness' are to be taken into account in the epistemology of reading, since without such an account it will of course be difficult to distinguish these 'post-deconstructive' readings from their romantically mystified, pre-deconstructive predecessors.

continue to be the business of scholarship within the closure of metaphysics—such an end will be unwritable. In this respect, the historicism of researchers like Kurke is a further strategy of exclusion, a moment of necessary blindness for the sake of the insights of reading.

Blindness and insight: it seems—looking back at this chapter—that de Man's dialectic well describes the structure and principle of a long tradition of Pindaric studies, extending from Boeckh's *Pindari opera*, where meaning is anchored in the absolute inwardness of intuition, through Bundy's *Studia Pindarica* and the dream of a language without rhetoric, through to Kurke's *Traffic in Praise*, where the success of communication depends crucially on a subjectivity not (or not yet) threatened by the aporias of deconstruction. The exclusion of rhetoric, the autonomy of a figure not yet subordinated to unified, conscious, intended meaning, is the price at which the insights of these studies are bought—and if this price is necessary, as we have argued, so it is also willingly paid, for is this not—as Bundy asserts—what *the songs themselves require*? The hermeneutics of presence, the common premise of modern Pindaric studies, is thus anchored in the odes, and it is this claim to interpretative immanence, to repeating only what the texts themselves have said, that provides these approaches with a large part of their plausibility. It is here, therefore, that a rereading of Pindar must begin. What do 'the texts themselves' say? And to what conclusions might a reading of the epinicians come which refused from the very beginning to subject them to the metaphysics of presence?

CHAPTER 3: THE RHETORIC OF MEANING

> To understand primarily means to determine the referential mode of a text and we tend to take for granted that this can be done. We assume that a referential discourse can be understood by whoever is competent to handle the lexicological and grammatical code of a language. Neither are we helpless when confronted with figures of speech; as long as we can distinguish between literal and figural meaning, we can translate the figure back to its proper referent. [...] [T]he necessity of making such a distinction cannot be avoided [...]. It would be quite foolish to assume that one can lightheartedly move away from the constraint of referential meaning.
>
> Paul de Man, *Allegories of Reading*.

IT SEEMS THAT THE SEPARATION OF THE TEXT WE OBSERVED IN more than one interpretation of Pindar in the last chapter is explicitly affirmed at a prominent place in the epinicians themselves: the *First Olympian*. The problem with which research on this ode has to date been most concerned—the so-called 'revision of myth' in the first mythological section—is directly connected with a reflection on the relationship between truth and fiction, meaning and embellishment which provided the strategic terms for strategies of exclusion from Boeckh to the present. In the traditional interpretation of the song going back to the scholia, the verses 26–53 are read in the sense that Pindar first introduces the old version of the myth of Pelops and then immediately rejects it and replaces it with his own, new version.[1] Bundy's interpretation of the passage proceeds, as we saw in Chapter 2, on the basis of this understanding of the cauldron-scene in 26b–27 and its relationship to the following verses.[2] And not without reason:

[1] See Σ *Olymp.* 1. 40a–e Dr.

[2] See above, p. 62.

not a few statements in the poem appear to suggest precisely this reading of the verses in question. Thus, in verse 35 the speaker rejects explicitly what his 'predecessors' have said in favour of a new and different narrative, and this substitutionary gesture is supported by the considerable energy he invests in distancing himself from the old story: not only is the new version introduced with the emphatic *ἀντία προτέρων φθέγξομαι* (36), but after the secret genesis of the tradition of the gods' cannibalistic feast has been found in the envy of the anonymous neighbour (*ἔννεπε κρυφᾷ τις* [...] *φθονερῶν γειτόνων*, 47),[3] the narrator places himself a second time unmistakeably outside the dubious group of those who invent such stories or pass them on: *ἐμοὶ δ' ἄπορα γαστρίμαργον μακάρων τιν' εἰπεῖν· ἀφίσταμαι* (52).

Now of central importance for this interpretation is the passage which comes between the cauldron-scene and Pindar's new version (28–35):

ἦ θαύματα πολλά, καί πού τι καὶ βροτῶν
φάτις ὑπὲρ τὸν ἀλαθῆ λόγον
δεδαιδαλμένοι ψεύδεσι ποικίλοις ἐξαπατῶντι μῦθοι·
Χάρις δ', ἅπερ ἅπαντα τεύχει τὰ μείλιχα θνατοῖς,
ἐπιφέροισα τιμὰν καὶ ἄπιστον ἐμήσατο πιστόν
ἔμμεναι τὸ πολλάκις·
ἁμέραι δ' ἐπίλοιποι
μάρτυρες σοφώτατοι.
ἔστι δ' ἀνδρὶ φάμεν ἐοικὸς ἀμφὶ δαιμόνων καλά· μείων γὰρ αἰτία.

Indeed, there are many astonishing things, and yet, I imagine, in men's
talk stories are also embellished beyond the true account
and deceive by means of elaborate fictions.
For Charis, who makes all things pleasant to mortals,
transfers honour to them and devises that even what is implausible
is often plausible.
But later days
are the best-informed witnesses.
It is, however, fitting for a man to say good things about the gods, for
his guilt is then less.

Scholars have long agreed about the strategic role this passage plays in the context of the whole poem, for it seems to provide a model for understanding the relationship between the two versions of the myth

[3] The form of the narrative, as the neighbour tells it, is not quite identical with the traditional myth: see Kakridis 1970, p. 187 n. 44 and Howie 1984, pp. 295–297.

of Pelops that Pindar tells in the first mythological section of the ode.[4] The transmitted text identifies the βροτῶν φάτις appositively with the μῦθοι.[5] Neither of the two words forming the double subject here has a truth-value of and for itself. Instead, from the class of all possible μῦθοι, it is only those that are embellished with ψεύδεα that deceive, and that these are summarily described as the 'talk of mortals', whose access to truth and reality is limited, cannot surprise us.

The ethical and epistemological neutrality of φάτις is uncontroversial: at the three other places where Pindar uses the word, its content is basis once for the (presumably correct) decision of the gods to marry Thetis to Peleus (*Isthm.* 8. 40), and twice for a reflection on the power of poetry to grant permanence to the deeds of a human being, whether these are good (Nestor, Sarpedon: *Pyth.* 3. 112) or bad (Phalaris: *Pyth.* 1. 96), and thus to lead to (presumably merited) praise or blame.[6] As far as μῦθος is concerned, the situation seems at first glance less certain. In epic, the term seems primarily to refer to any coherent statement, from which the meaning 'intention' or 'plan' results.[7] In Homer, the μῦθος—as opposed, for example, to ἔπος—is always related to the authority of the person speaking; there is no connotation that what is said is always or even in general untrue.[8] With respect to Pindar, however, the claim is often made that both in the *First Olympian* and at the other two places where the word occurs—*Nem.* 7. 23 and *Nem.* 8. 33—μῦθος has a pejorative connotation.[9] In fact, not a few commentators have seen here a change in the semantics of the word taking place at the beginning of the fifth century for which Pindar offers us the first example.[10] A closer consideration of the two passages in the *Nemeans*, however, shows that the hypothesis that the word here has taken on a new, negative sense over against its use in Homer is by no means necessary in order to interpret the verses coherently. In *Nem.* 8. 33, the

4 That is already seen, at least in principle, in the scholia: *cf.* Σ 43a Dr., where the reference of the statement to the myth of Pelops is assumed.

5 This is also the text that the scholiasts had before them: *cf.* Σ 44b and c Dr. The variant reported in Σ 44b, φάτιν (as object to ἐξαπατῶντι and with the same meaning as φρένας) was adopted by Boeckh and Bowra; see Gerber 1982, 61 f. who rightly prefers the *lectio difficilior* of the apposition of the singular φάτις and the plural μῦθοι.

6 So also Gerber 1982, p. 61 f. *ad loc.*

7 *LfgrE* III, col. 272.

8 See Martin 1989, p. 12, p. 13 n. 42, pp. 22–26 and *passim*, and de Jong 1992, p. 392 f.

9 See for example Köhnken 1971, p. 49 n. 62; Gerber 1982, p. 64; Richardson 1986, p. 386; Verdenius 1988, p. 20.

10 And is this not, in fact, just what we expect: the victory of the λόγος through the power of reason over the primitiveness and obscurity of the mere μῦθος? The earlier the history of this triumph is introduced into the history of Western literature, the more enlightened the authors in whose works its harbingers can already be discovered appear. *Cf.* Heidegger [5]1997, p. 7, who describes this alleged victory with reference to Parmenides DK 28 B 8 as 'ein auf dem Grunde des Platonismus vom neuzeitlichen Rationalismus übernommenes Vorurteil der Historie und der Philologie'.

fact that the μῦθοι in question are instrumentalized by an ἐχθρὰ πάρφασις and modified by the adjective αἱμύλοι (already unambiguously negative in epic[11]) are by themselves enough to specify them as negative; the same connotation results from their function as a means of seduction by σοφία in *Nem.* 7. 23.[12] In neither of the two cases do we need to make a distinction between the meaning of the word in Pindar and its sense in epic as mere coherent speech; the Homeric meaning of μῦθος can also explain its use in the Pindaric texts where the specific nature of particular μῦθοι and the use made of them is the point at issue.

If the μῦθοι in our passage become problematic because they are embellished with ψεύδεα and thus—by definition—the subject of the verb ἐξαπατῶντι, then it is on this reading only the ψεύδεα that constitute the specific difference between the φάτις as μῦθοι and the ἀληθὴς λόγος. But how is their relationship to the two other categories to be understood?

It is initially striking that the *First Olympian* describes the relationship between the λόγος and the ψεύδεα in spatial terms: the μῦθοι are 'embellished *beyond* the true λόγος with elaborate ψεύδεα'.[13] The arrangement of the two categories of speech denoted by the preposition ὑπέρ places the one, the λόγος, within or beneath the other.[14] It thus structures the relationship between the two narratives—the 'traditional' one, initially evoked in the cauldron-scene, and the second one, Pindar's own—not as a simple opposition between two entirely different stories of which the one can be substituted for the other in its entirety, but instead as a bipartite structure in which the false myth is dependent on the true one as its carrier or 'kernel' (Verdenius). The true λόγος is a foundation, a ὑποκείμενον, the ψεύδεα its accidents, parasites of their carrier, the λόγος.[15] And as the further progression of

[11] See for example Hes., *Op.* 374: μὴ δέ γυνή σε νόον πυγοστόλος ἐξαπατάτω αἱμύλα κωτίλλουσα.

[12] Nothing speaks in this passage against the possibility that σοφία could also make other use of the μῦθοι.

[13] The syntax of ὑπὲρ τὸν ἀληθῆ λόγον—does it belong to δεδαιδαλμένοι or to ἐξαπατῶντι?—is not entirely clear. Neither of the two resulting collocations can be paralleled elsewhere in Greek literature. The scholia introduce an extra verb into the construction in order to make it clearer (Σ 44d οἱ μῦθοι ὑπὲρ τὸν ἀληθῆ λόγον ἰσχύουσι καὶ ἐξαπατῶσι [...]; similarly Σ 51b with φάτις as subject). Gerber 1982, p. 63, whom I follow here, constructs the prepositional phrase with δαιδάλλω; he is also followed by Fisker 1990, p. 35 f.

[14] Rightly here Verdenius 1988, p. 19 and Fisker 1990, p. 36. See also Nagy 1990, p. 66 with n. 75. For ὑπέρ in this figurative sense, see KG I § 435, esp. *Iliad* 17. 321 ὑπὲρ Διὸς αἶσαν and 327 ὑπὲρ θεόν.

[15] Heidegger 1954, p. 203 connects the λόγος as that which is 'laid down' or 'laid out' in speech with the ὑποκείμενον as the *presence* of what is brought out into the truth as

the ode shows, this is indeed the structure of the narrative as Pindar constructs it: the lies of the neighbour only arise on the basis of real events (the feast of the gods, the disappearance of the boy), and can only be 'correctly' understood on this factual basis. The possibility of removing the added untruths and revealing the truth about Pelops concealed by them thus seems already to be laid down in this concentric model.[16]

But before we get to the truth, it is the puzzling plausibility of untruth that interests Pindar first. How are we to explain the reception of stories that can make no legitimate claim to credibility but are nevertheless believed? The double character of the category thus introduced is described in the following three verses: narratives that are really *ἄπιστοι* become, in an uncertain number of cases, *πιστοί*.[17] The discrepancy which arises in this way between the real ontological status of what is averred in such *μῦθοι* and the status accorded to it by the *βροτοί* is ascribed by Pindar to the effects of *χάρις*, a primarily aesthetic force which is already signalled in the participle *δεδαιδαλμένοι* and in the description of the *ψεύδεα* as *ποικίλα*.[18]

disclosure (ἀ-λήθεια: 'das *Anwesen* des Vorliegenden in die Unverborgenheit', his italics). See also *id.* [18]2001, p. 34, Engl. p. 58.

[16] *Cf.* Nagy 1990, p. 59 on a model of truth and forgetting (λήθη) arranged like concentric circles.

[17] The impossibility of knowing whether what poetry says is true or not is already an issue in Hesiod: the Muses can tell both truth and untruth, but *εὖτ' ἐθέλωμεν* in *Th.* 28 indicates that in any single given case 'there is no way of knowing whether the song with which the Muses inspire [the poet] is authentic truth or falsehood that simulates it' (Thalmann 1984, p. 148). See further Stroh 1976, Rösler 1980, Kannicht 1988 and Pratt 1993.

[18] Pratt 1993, p. 124 notes that these terms—δεδαιδαλμένος and ποικίλος—are used at other places for the effect of Pindar's own poetry: *cf.* *Nem.* 11. 18 *μελιγδούποισι δαιδαλθέντα μελιζέμεν ἀοιδαῖς sc.* Ἀρισταγόραν with proleptic participle and *Olymp.* 1. 105. An interesting passage in this context is *Parth.* 2 (= fr. 94b SM). 31 f., where a similar opposition between what has gone before, adorned by the singer with verses (*δαιδάλλοισ' ἔπεσιν*, 32), and other things that only Zeus knows (= the truth?) leads to the statement, also reminiscent of *Olymp.* 1. 35, that she should think and say with her mouth things befitting a girl (*ἐμὲ δὲ πρέπει παρθενήια μὲν φρονεῖν* | *γλώσσᾳ τε λέγεσθαι*, 34 f.). On *ποικίλος*, *cf.* *Olymp.* 6. 87, *Pyth.* 9. 77 f. *ποικίλλειν*, *Nem.* 5. 42, fr. 179 and fr. 194, 2–3 *εἶα τειχίζωμεν ἤδη ποικίλον* | *κόσμον αὐδάεντα λόγων* and Detienne & Vernant 1978, pp. 18–20 (who note the connection between the adjective and the concept of *μῆτις*; it is presumably not an accident that the activity of Charis in *Olymp.* 1. 31 is designated by the verb *μήδομαι*). Pratt's conclusion: 'The rhetorical structure of the passage seems to confirm what Pindar's subtle comments only suggest: that in composing mythical narratives, even the truthful poet of praise fictionalizes' (p. 125). As we will see, the situation is slightly more complicated.

Now the range of this reflection in the text is by no means restricted to the story of Pelops. Precisely because there is no indication that the passage refers only to its immediate context, it must be taken not merely as a contingent commentary on a poetic intention valid only for this single poem, but rather as an attempt to offer a paradigm for understanding the relationship between truth and untruth altogether. The spatiality of the model, the separation into core and surface (or 'within' and 'beyond') seems to be anything but accidental; in fact, the structure of inside and outside can be found everywhere a separation between the truth of the λόγος and its alternative—lying, appearance, seduction—is carried out. Let us consider an example of this with by no means purely illustrative character.

In the first fragment of Parmenides (DK 28 B 1), the narrator is brought by the Heliadae in a chariot to 'the doors of the paths of the night and the day' (11).[19] On the other side of the doors—that is, beyond the place where day and night come into being and vanish again—he is met by a goddess unnamed in the extant fragments who welcomes him and promises instruction about the truth and about the opinions of mortals (B 1. 28–32):

χρεὼ δέ σε πάντα πυθέσθαι
ἠμὲν ἀληθείης εὐπειθέος[20] *ἀτρεμὲς ἦτορ*
ἠδὲ βροτῶν δόξας, ταῖς οὐκ ἔνι πίστις ἀληθής.
ἀλλ' ἔμπης καὶ ταῦτα μαθήσεαι, ὡς τὰ δοκοῦντα
χρῆν δοκίμως εἶναι διὰ παντὸς πάντα περῶντα.

But you must be informed of everything,
both of the unmoved heart of persuasive reality
and of the beliefs of mortals, which comprise no genuine conviction;
nevertheless you shall learn these also, how it was necessary that the things that are believed
should have their being in general acceptance, ranging through all things from end to end.[21]

One can scarcely speak, here, of an argumentative, literary or pragmatic context similar to Pindar's. Between the victory ode for the

[19] On the journey beyond the gates of day and night, see Burkert 1969. The gates do not stand *between* day and night (as *e.g.* Coxon 1986, p. 14 and p. 162 assumes), but are their common point of departure.

[20] With Plutarch, *Adv. Colot.* 1114d–e, Sextus Emp., *Adv. math.* vii 111, Clement, *Strom.* v 59 and Diog. Laert., ix 22 (followed by Coxon), against Proclus, *In Ti.* i 345 *εὐφεγγέος* and Simplicius, *De caelo* 557 *εὐκυκλέος* (followed by DK).

[21] Translation Coxon 1986, pp. 48 and 50.

Sicilian tyrant and the Eleatic philosopher's didactic poem lies a world of difference. All the more conspicuous, therefore, is the latter's conceptual proximity to Pindar at this point. Like the epinician poet, the philosopher too is concerned with the relationship between truth and a category that contains, not the truth, but instead what is merely believed by mortals.[22] Parmenides' goddess calls the members of this second category δόξαι; they may lack all πίστις—an attribute that legitimately belongs only to the truth—but at the same time they 'explain' the world of phenomena δοκιμῶς, and this characteristic is obviously meant to account for the reception of the δόξαι as if they were ἀληθείη.[23] This description is repeated shortly after the beginning of the δόξα-section in B 8. 60: the order of things, as humans have incorrectly (πεπλανημένοι, 54) explained it to themselves, is nevertheless in all respects ἐοικώς, 'plausible'.[24] The Pindaric transformation of ἄπιστον into πιστόν by χάρις finds here only a partial philosophical parallel, for Parmenides attributes the persuasive power of the δόξαι not to the beauty of their expression in language, but rather to the blindness of their recipients, humankind.[25]

The Eleatic configuration of the relationship between truth and untruth now exhibits a further, curious similarity to our passage in the *First Olympian*. Parmenides speaks in verse 29 of what his narrator is to learn first as the ἀληθείης [...] ἀτρεμὲς ἦτορ. The formulation is initially unexpected: elsewhere in Greek literature, ἦτορ is used exclusively, it seems, for the heart or the inner self of a human being or a god. Its use here with respect to reality as an object of knowledge or cognition must therefore be metaphorical, but in what sense? Coxon finds here a reference to the *vitality* of the real: 'P[armenides'] phrase [...] characterises [reality] as living; the sense is 'the unchanging and persuasive living reality.'[26] But ἦτορ also means, of course, that the

[22] On Parmenides' concept of truth, see Wiesner 1996, pp. 170–177; on its relationship to ἀλάθεια in Pindar, see Cole 1983, esp. pp. 9 and 25.

[23] Already observed by Reinhardt ^{3}1977, p. 9 f.

[24] In this sense Coxon 1986, p. 225 *ad loc.* (against Verdenius 1942, p. 51, Bormann 1971, p. 128 *et al.*). He points out the lines of the tradition that connect this passage with Xenophanes, fr. 35 ταῦτα δεδοξάσθω μὲν ἐοικότα τοῖς ἐτύμοισι (already noted by Cornford 1939, p. 46 n. 2) and with Hesiod's Muses.

[25] See B 6. 7 and 7. 4.

[26] Coxon 1986, p. 168 *ad loc.* In the eleventh chapter of *Philosophie im tragischen Zeitalter der Griechen* on Parmenides, Nietzsche argues that the transfer of vitality—more specifically, breath—to being is the originary metaphor (*Urmetapher*) of metaphysics, curiously without observing this transfer in the fragments of the Eleatic philosopher himself: see Nietzsche 1988, vol. 1, p. 847. On the systematic ascription of

place of experiential reality is clearly located on the inside; the ἀληθείη with which we are concerned is the middle-point, the transcendental centre of what can be communicated, whilst the δόξαι, described in the following verse as 'misleading' because they stand in no relationship to this core, are explicitly exiled to the outside: τῆλε μαλ' ἐπλάχθησαν (B 8. 28). Here, outside or beyond the region of being (πάρεξ τοῦ ἐόντος, B 8. 37), nothing *is*.

Now it is not all too difficult to show that the role of the centre consists in being the singular point around which the plural, merely apparent realities of becoming and ceasing to exist, of day and night are structured. But the unchanging centre itself, ἀτρεμὲς ἦτορ, is only perceptible or knowable beyond the transformations of the phenomenal world that it governs: this is what the narrator's journey to the πύλαι Νυκτός τε καὶ Ἤματος [...] κελεύθων (B 1. 11) signifies, since only behind them can he gain knowledge of this centre. And not only of it: the knowledge of the centre also determines all knowledge of the periphery, for the δόξαι can only be revealed as δόξαι because they—unlike reality (see *e.g.* B 8. 26–30)—are subjected to alteration. What is *really* real is one and does not change.[27]

On the basis of this Parmenidean ontology of the real and the unreal, the metaphysical ramifications of Pindar's description of the relationship between truth and untruth now become somewhat clearer. The constellation of the inner, foundational ἀληθὴς λόγος buried under the outward, parasitic ψεύδεα recapitulates the gesture of a metaphysical exclusion that, as Parmenides shows, is basic to the possibility of contraphenomenal knowledge. It is therefore neither surprising nor accidental when both Pindar, in order to criticise the mythical tradition about Pelops, and Bundy, in order to interpret the epinicians, must revert to the figure of the inward truth identical to itself. In the history of the myth of Pelops, the true core of the story has vanished behind the embellishments of the added fictions; in the *Studia Pindarica*, the true meaning of the odes lies hidden behind a veil of rhetorical disguises. If Bundy can only discover the real meaning of the epinicians by penetrating beneath their rhetorical surface in order

vitality or life to the agency of meaning, see Derrida 'La pharmacie de Platon' (= Derrida 1972a, pp. 77–213), p. 98 f., Engl. p. 79 f., and 'La mythologie blanche' (= Derrida 1972b, pp. 247–324), p. 321, Engl. p. 269 on the 'end of metaphor' in the determination of its meaning as 'une anamnèse intériorisante (*Erinnerung*), une recollection du sens, une relève de la métaphoricité vivante dans une propriété vivante.'

[27] On a similar privileging of the inside over against the outside in Plato, see Derrida 1972a, pp. 123–129, Engl. pp. 99–104.

to rescue the truth of the text from its submerged ground, Pindar can only reach the true λόγος about Pelops by removing the mask of fictional disguise that has been placed over it. Here as there, a necessary exclusion takes place that in Parmenides is constitutive of the category of the δόξαι, in Pindar of the category of the ψεύδεα, in Bundy of the category of rhetoric.

The place of this externalisation, the position in the system from which it is carried out, is clearly delineated by Parmenides: only from a point beyond the δόξαι can the difference between truth and mere opinion be recognized. The truth is thus also the authoritative basis for the distinction between truth and its alternative; the structure of the difference must have recourse to itself, must itself be true and not δόξα. We will come back to this.

As we have seen, Bundy's location of the truth of the text in the hidden substrate of its surface appearances was correlated with the postulate that the relationship between the deep structure and this surface consisted of different, conventional realizations of the one basic meaning. In practice, this led to an interpretative procedure that searched the epinicians for elements that could be identified as repetitions of this one thing. If it seems that the textual model of the *First Olympian* agrees with that of the *Studia Pindarica* for reasons relating to the conditions under which we can speak of something such as truth, Pindar's method of getting through the surface of ψεύδεα to this truth also seems to presage the commentary's hermeneutics of repetition. The truth of history, the poet tells us, is revealed when an event that, if it were only to have occurred once, would remain uncertain, takes place again; its repetition is the guarantee and sign of its really having happened.[28]

33 ἁμέραι δ' ἐπίλοιποι
μάρτυρες σοφώτατοι.
...
ἔνθα δευτέρῳ χρόνῳ
ἦλθε καὶ Γανυμήδης
45 Ζηνὶ τωὔτ' ἐπὶ χρέος.

33 But later days
are the best-informed witnesses.

[28] This in contrast to the usual interpretation of the 'later days' which sees in them only the general, rather banal statement that 'time will reveal the truth' (Gerber 1982, p. 67) or that 'only further experience of an individual can help us evaluate his worth' (Pratt 1993, p. 124 f., who admits that she finds the passage 'somewhat mysterious').

...
That is where, in a later time,
Ganymedes too came
to Zeus for the same service.

The reference to Ganymede has been interpreted in various ways in the research.[29] Should one not, however, consider its relationship to the 'later days' in verse 33 f.? Witnesses in Pindar are always *eyewitnesses*;[30] the later days can thus only make inferences about earlier events from contemporary ones, events that are immediately present to them. The (in Pindar's version) later abduction of Ganymede[31] is just such an event; it allows inferences about the historicity of an alleged abduction of Pelops by virtue of the fact that it can be identified as the repetition of the same. Pindar thus binds historical veracity to the iteration of events; the one truth, according to the *First Olympian*, reveals itself in repeating itself.

The model of verses 28 ff. presents the task of the interpreter as a journey into the inmost part of the text, where the real, the natural, the true is to be found. What makes this procedure difficult and epistemologically complicated both in the *First Olympian* and in the *Studia Pindarica* is one of the primary effects of language as *δεδαιδαλμένοι ψεύδεσι μῦθοι*: *deception*. This arises, we are now told, because of *χάρις*,[32] a circumstance that ought to make one think twice before

[29] According to Gerber, the myth of Ganymede is intended not merely to praise Hieron, but also to make the abduction of Pelops more plausible (1982, p. 79): 'The reasoning is that if one myth is true, so must the other be.' Gerber, who assumes a very simple reasoning on Pindar's part here indeed, leaves the question of *why* this must be the case unanswered. Theunissen 2000, p. 627, on the other hand, believes that he can see in this passage an aesthetics of production that he describes as bearing all the marks of the poetics of genius: although it is 'odd' (*befremdlich*) that Charis is placed in opposition to the truth here, this can be explained by the fact that composing poetry, for Pindar, was limited to the moment (*Augenblick*), whereas the truth remains forever. '[U]nd die Zeitweiligkeit der durch die Produktion von Schein erzielten Wirkung führt er [*sc.* Pindar] auf die Augenblicksverhaftetheit des Produktionsaktes zurück.' This is allegedly a 'Wesenszug des Überschwangs' and the 'Kehrseite der Plötzlichkeit, mit welcher der dichterische Schaffensprozeß nach langer Zeit hervorbricht.' On the 'sudden eruption' of creativity as a mark of poetic genius in the eighteenth century, see Schmidt 1985, vol. 1, p. 116 f. on Hamann and p. 182 ff. on Pindar. Horace, *Carm.* IV 2 is not entirely innocent with respect to this *topos*.

[30] Most 1985b, pp. 176–177; *cf.* further Krisher 1965.

[31] On the sources and the problems raised by the mythical date of the abduction, see Kakridis 1970.

[32] δ' in verse 30 is, as frequently in Pindar, *ἀντὶ τοῦ γάρ*; the effect of *χάρις* is not a *contrast* to the phenomenon of deception (*pace* Slater 1969, *s.v.* δέ 1a), but rather *explains* it.

translating *ψεύδεα* with 'lies'. *Χάρις* is of course not an attribute belonging exclusively or even primarily to the blasphemous myth of the dismemberment, but rather an aesthetic term; in the epinicians, it designates that quality of an object that enables its beholder to experience it aesthetically—*ἅπερ ἅπαντα τεύχει τὰ μείλιχα θνατοῖς*—and it is used by Pindar at several other places for his own works.[33] *Χάρις* is what pleases us and is meant to please in the objects we perceive, in this case in linguistic objects.

In Pindar, however, pleasure is not neutral with respect to cognition or to the knowledge of truth: it *seduces*. This is intimated in the *First Olympian* when, in the first part of the poem, the *χάρις* of Olympia and the racehorse Pherenikos influence the mind (*νόος*) of their beholder: *εἴ τί τοι Πίσας τε καὶ Φερενίκου χάρις | νόον ὑπὸ γλυκυτάταις ἔθηκε φροντίσιν* (18 f.). But seduction is also the crucial characteristic of the reception of what is *μείλιχον* or 'pleasant' in Pindar's version of the story of Kyrana in the *Ninth Pythian*, and here it is of course Apollo whose inborn access to truth and reality—an access that Pindar explicitly identifies with his *νόος* in the *Third Pythian* (29)—is confused by his astonished and admiring response (*θαύμασον*, 31) to watching the woman wrestling with a lion. Chiron, asked by Apollo who this woman might be and whether he is allowed to abduct her, now finds himself in the role of the seer or *μάντις* usually played by his divine questioner, and answers not without irony (42–49):[34]

καὶ γὰρ σέ, τὸν οὐ θεμιτὸν ψεύδει θιγεῖν,
ἔτραπε μείλιχος ὀργὰ παρφάμεν τοῦτον λόγον. κούρας δ' ὁπόθεν γενεάν
ἐξερωτᾷς, ὦ ἄνα; κύριον ὃς πάντων τέλος
οἶσθα καὶ πάσας κελεύθους·
ὅσσα τε χθὼν ἠρινὰ φύλλ' ἀναπέμπει, χὠπόσαι
ἐν θαλάσσᾳ καὶ ποταμοῖς ψάμαθοι
κύμασιν ῥιπαῖς τ' ἀνέμων κλονέονται, χὤ τι μέλλει, χὠπόθεν
ἔσσεται, εὖ καθορᾷς.

For even you, for whom it is not lawful to touch untruth,

See Denniston 1950, p. 169 f. and Slater 1969 *s.v.* *δέ* 3h.

[33] See Gundert 1935, pp. 30–75, Gianotti 1975, p. 75 ff. and Scott 1984. *Cf.* above, p. 125 n. 18 on *δεδαιδαλμένος* and *ποικίλος*.

[34] The exchange of roles between Apollo and Chiron is noted by Dougherty 1993, pp. 147–149; see also Gildersleeve ²1890, p. 342, who sees Chiron rather in the role of educator, Farnell 1932, p. 204, Köhnken 1985, p. 77, and Calame 2003, p. 68. Woodbury 1972, p. 564 ff. finds no irony in this passage, takes account, however, as Köhnken notes (1985, p. 84), only of the last part of Apollo's question (*ὁσία κτλ.*, 36 f.) and the corresponding answer of the centaur on the legitimacy of the abduction.

have been led by sweet urgings to speak this word awry; you ask
whence the girl's lineage
comes, lord? You who know the appointed end of all things
and all paths;
and how many leaves the earth puts forth in spring, and how many
grains of sand in the sea and in rivers
are driven hither and thither by the waves and blasts of wind, and what
will come to pass, and whence
it will come—all this you know full well.

The essential totality of Apollonian knowledge is emphasized in this passage very strongly.[35] All the more dramatic, therefore, is the contrast between the god's privileged access to truth and the effect of the aesthetic experience caused by watching Kyrana fight. It is as if the aesthetic moment of admiration and astonishment suddenly overcomes Apollo's epistemological competence as knower and speaker of absolute truth; the mere appearance of the girl and the *μείλιχος ὀργά* it triggers (mis)lead him—*παρφάμεν*—to deny his divine omniscience.[36] But this denial is effectively identical with its repeal, for the narrator of this remarkable encounter between the god and the centaur gives us no grounds for believing that Apollo, here, is lying.[37]

[35] Compare the similar description in *Pythian* 3. 27–30, there in emphatic contrast to Hesiod, for whom Apollo found out about Koronis' unfaithfulness not by means of his omniscient mind (*πάντα ἰσάντι νόῳ*, 29) but instead from a raven (fr. 60 *apud* Σ *Pyth.* 3. 52 Dr.).

[36] So also Köhnken 1985, p. 90 f. *παρφάμεν*, the centaur's word for the god's question, denotes in Pindar not merely speech, but rather a speech that misses the truth. *Cf. Olymp.* 7. 66, *Nem.* 5. 32 (here, the *παρφαμένα* are the cause of an *ὀργά* instead of its effect; Köhnken 1985, p. 90 n. 50 notes that here too this word could be translated as 'desire') and *πάρφασις* in *Nem.* 8. 32; *cf.* also *Od.* 16. 287 = 19. 6, the only passage in Homer where this connotation of untruth is clearly present. Köhnken 1985, p. 90 points out that *μείλιχος* also occurs in erotic contexts (*cf. Hymn. Hom. Ven.* 2; Mimnermos 1. 3 West); but the connection of the word with *πειθώ* (*cf.* alongside the beginning of Chiron's speech Hes., *Theog.* 84 and Semon. 7. 18; this is the most common context of the related form *μειλίχιος* in Homer) is also anything but accidental. In Xenophanes, wine too is *μείλιχος* (1. 6).

[37] Gentili *et al.* 1995, p. 600 *ad loc.* understand the verb here in the sense of a deceptive intention on the part of the god (*cf.* Hesychius *s.v.*: *παρφάμεν· [...] ἀπατᾶν*) and translate (p. 251) 'un dolcissimo impulso spinse a dire parole non sincere' without making any attempt to explain the *sense* of trying to deceive the centaur at this point. Pratt 1993, p. 61 reads the passage similarly: '[I]n an amorous mood, even the unerring prophet may turn to indirection.' This is implausible: if Apollo had wanted to kidnap Kyrana without Chiron noticing, he should surely not have called him out of his cave in the first place. The correct interpretation seems more likely to be that argued by Köhnken 1985, p. 90: 'Bewunderung gepaart mit Liebesverlangen täuscht [Apollons] unfehlbaren Sinn

The transformation which takes place in the moment of the encounter with Kyrana entails an explicitly temporal element: at the moment of seduction, the god, it seems, no longer has that knowledge of the end of all things (πάντων τέλος, 44) at his disposal that we are entitled to call 'absolute'.[38] His condition, rather, suddenly consists in a separation from the *telos* (at least, from this one) that is constitutive of the structure of desire, and in a new (if only momentary) submission to time: Apollo desires Kyrana, but does not yet possess her (and is not allowed to take her immediately and in public, as Chiron remarks in 39–41).[39] It is notable that when the centaur stops speaking, the text reports immediately on the rapidity with which the 'marriage' is effected (ὠκεῖα δ' ἐπειγομένων ἤδη θεῶν | πρᾶξις ὁδοί τε βραχεῖαι, 67 f.). The immediacy of the relationship between desire and its fulfilment is reconstituted, and indeed just in that moment in which Apollo, after Chiron's instruction, knows the goal of his longings.[40]

The time of Apollonian desire is thus also the time of the aesthetic experience; it is incompatible with the knowledge of the truth as a whole. This is also the import of a passage in the *Seven Nemean* con-

und veranlaßt ihn zu seiner falschen Rede [...]. Apoll [verführt] sein Verlangen nach Kyrene zu Äusserungen, die mit seiner göttlichen Kompetenz unvereinbar sind.' Köhnken points further to the parallels between this passage and *Iliad* 14. 292 ff., where the effect of Hera's magic girdle on Zeus also puts his omniscience temporarily out of action. Miller 1997, p. 156–161 however follows Σ *Pyth.* 9. 75a Dr. in suggesting that μείλιχος ὀργά refers not to Apollo's desire for Kyrana, but rather to his friendly condescension towards the centaur in pretending for the moment not to be omniscient. This seems to take no account of γάρ in verse 42, which must surely indicate that Chiron interprets Apollo's questions as evidence for his statements about love and αἰδῶς in verses 39–41, not as proof of the god's friendly attitude towards himself.

38 On the role of this category in Hegel and de Man, see above, p. 44 ff. It is interesting that Fränkel [4]1993, p. 508 describes the shyness of Apollo's desire as an essentially *human* characteristic. *Cf.* also Theunissen 2000, p. 871 f.

39 So Köhnken 1985, p. 84, who in verses 36 f. sees an expression not of shame but rather of desire. *Cf.* also Wilamowitz 1922, p. 268, who speaks of the god's 'aufwallende Begierde', and Burton 1962, p. 40. Note that Chiron is not rebuking Apollo at this point for wanting to sleep with Kyrana immediately, but rather interpreting his speech as a sign that the god too is aware that he must hold off (*cf.* καὶ γὰρ σέ, 42). Carson 1982, pp. 125–128 emphasizes the interest of this ode in temporality, and comments that '[t]he dilemma of time in which human chances are set presents one face to men (a demand to act) and another to women (a requirement to wait)' (p. 126). But the initial deferral of Apollo's desire in his conversation with Chiron indicates that for men too there can be a time to wait.

40 *Cf.* Dickson 1986, p. 122: '[F]or the god there is a virtual equivalence of *dunamis* to desire: no distance intervenes between the inner movements that are his desire and will and their perfect accomplishment in and as reality' with reference to *Pyth.* 9. 67. Woodbury 1972, p. 566 lists further examples of this motif.

cerned with the effects of beauty in language (20–30). Here, the poem is speaking of Homer (or perhaps Odysseus, or perhaps both):[41]

> [...] ἐγὼ δὲ πλέον' ἔλπομαι
> λόγον Ὀδυσσέος ἢ πάθαν διὰ τὸν ἁδυεπῆ γενέσθ' Ὅμηρον·
> ἐπεὶ ψεύδεσί οἱ ποτανᾷ <τε> μαχανᾷ
> σεμνὸν ἔπεστί τι· σοφία δὲ κλέπτει παράγοισα μύθοις. τυφλὸν δ' ἔχει
> ἦτορ ὅμιλος ἀνδρῶν ὁ πλεῖστος. εἰ γὰρ ἦν
> ἓ τὰν ἀλάθειαν ἰδέμεν, οὔ κεν ὅπλων χολωθείς
> ὁ καρτερὸς Αἴας ἔπαξε διὰ φρενῶν
> λευρὸν ξίφος· ὃν κράτιστον Ἀχιλέος ἄτερ μάχᾳ
> ξανθῷ Μενέλᾳ δάμαρτα κομίσαι θοαῖς
> ἃν ναυσὶ πόρευσαν εὐθυπνόου Ζεφύροιο πομπαί
> πρὸς Ἴλου πόλιν.

> [...] But I suspect
> that Odysseus' tale has become greater than what he really suffered through Homer's sweet verse;
> for upon his fictions and winged craft
> there lies something sublime; and his skill deceives, misleading its hearers with tales. For the great majority
> of men have a blind heart. Since, if they could have
> seen the truth, strong Aias, in anger about the weapons, would not have planted in his chest
> the polished sword; the strongest in battle apart from Achilles,
> the accompanying winds of straight-blowing Zephyros brought him in swift
> ships to Ilos' city to bring back to fair-haired Menelaos
> his wife.

The similarities between these verses and our passage in the *First Olympian* have often been noticed. Here as there, we are dealing with seductive power of a language that achieves its results by virtue of its beauty alone. Not *what* is said is crucial for belief or disbelief—it is made up of ψεύδεα and deserves no belief—but rather *how* Odysseus' invented πάθα are presented in language. The undefined 'sublime'[42] that lies on Homer's stories corresponds in its consequences to the χάρις spoken of in the *First Olympian*. The inability of human beings to escape the seductions of language is connected with their inability to

[41] On the question of whether οἱ (22) means Homer (so Lloyd-Jones 1973, p. 130 and most of the rest of the secondary literature) or Odysseus (so Fränkel ^{2}1960, p. 360 and Köhnken 1971, pp. 47–60)—or indeed whether this question is meant to be answerable at this point at all—see Most 1985b, p. 150.

[42] *Cf.* Köhnken 1971, p. 51 and Most 1985b, p. 148.

see the truth (ἰδέμεν, 25) without mediating and therefore also potentially misrepresenting linguistic signs.[43]

The effect of the Homeric presentation of Odysseus' πάθα is naturally that of a well-known rhetorical trope, hyperbole or αὔξησις. The contrafactual element of this trope, defined by Quintilian as *decens viri superiectio*,[44] forms not only the basis for how the emerging discipline of rhetoric saw itself in the fifth century, but also how the entire philosophical tradition opposed to it since Plato has seen it. Is it not, asks Socrates in Plato's *Phaedrus* (267 a–b), the characteristic claim of the rhetors that they can make the great small and the small great?[45] In turning away from representing the real dimensions of things, in their transformation by means of tropes, it is not only Homer's poetry which seduces (παράγοισα, *Nem.* 7. 23) its audience into believing what is said by granting it alien honours. The effects of χάρις in the *First Olympian* also result from the application of a tropological procedure, the metaphorical transferral of a name—πιστόν—to a story that has no legitimate or natural claim to it. The effect of rhetoric as trope veils the φύσις of the thing, for there is no epistemologically certain way to get from the aesthetically well-formed language of the figure to the truth about the world, to pass from the merely beautiful to the real. As an artefact, rhetoric belongs to the realm of νόμος or of τέχνη; its proper place is on the outside of language, in exile from the natural core of meaning, for only the externality of rhetoric can guarantee the integrity of truth at its centre and the possibility of a critique of mere appearances from the privileged, Parmenidean vantage point of this centre. The heart of truth must lie beyond the region of aesthetics and the tropological operations belonging to it; only in this way can the substitution of truth and meaning for the lie, the fiction and the misrepresentation be well-founded.

It is therefore clear that the distinction made in verses 28–29 between the nature of truth and the fictions of beautiful language must be presented as true—real, literal, *propre*. This is indeed the sense in which it has always been understood: the categories of fiction and truth are kept neatly separate; Pindar rejects the lie and intends to tell us the truth, purified from the tropical embellishments it has suffered at the hands of the tradition.[46]

43 On this motif in Plato's *Gorgias*, see above, p. 36.

44 Quint., *Inst.* VIII 6. 67 f.

45 *Cf.* Quint., *Inst.* VIII 3. 89: *vis oratoris omnis in augendo minuendoque consistit*, and above, p. 53.

46 So for example Krummen 1990, p. 169.

But it soon turns out that Pindar's text does not stick to this separation. The metafigural theory of the escapability of rhetorical language is undermined by the practice of the ode; the plausible assertion of the possibility of the naked λόγος owes all its suggestive power at this point to exactly those metaphorical transferrals of meaning that it intends to exile from the centre of language. This begins with the figure of the ἀληθὴς λόγος itself: its concealment by the *ψεύδεα ποικίλα* presupposes the synaesthetic *translatio* both of visibility and its opposite to the λόγος that accrued, in the *Seventh Nemean*, not to speech but rather to its attribute, *ἀλάθεια*. The displacement of the roles of substance and accident, the metonymic complication of the border between *ὑποκείμενον* and *συμβεβηκός* is only the first consequence of this procedure. For the argumentative basis of the mythical revision in the name of the truth is itself a tropological effect of *χάρις* as a figure in producing an analogy, based on similarity, between the two abductions of Ganymede and Pelops (since the *ἁμέραι ἐπίλοιποι* are witnesses of the *later* abduction, not the earlier). But even Pindar's construction of the relation between the truth of history and its alternative can be seen, on closer inspection, to be the operation of a rhetorical figure, and this is not without consequences for the figure of the truth.

We recall that the narrator of the *First Olympian* distances himself emphatically from the first story about the death of Pelops. In the first version, as in the model of 28 ff., the true events (confirmed by repetition) are covered over by embellished myths (*fabulae artificiose exornatae*, writes Boeckh).[47] The first version of the Pelops-story is thus in reality a synecdoche of the truth: *totum* (the *μῦθοι*) *pro parte* (ἀληθὴς λόγος), and we can read the extensive research on Pindar's revision of it in this song as the investigation of this synecdochal relationship. It seems to have been Dissen who first noticed that the substitutionary gesture of the first section suggested by the narrator does justice neither to the grammatical structure of verses 25–27 nor to the narrative coherence of the section as a whole.[48] The cauldron-scene at the beginning of the account is by no means presented as a fiction or a rumour, and certainly not as one of the *ψεύδεα* mentioned in verse 29. Instead, it is appended in the form of an adverbial clause to a relative clause which itself is clearly meant to be taken as a description of fact:

λάμπει δέ οἱ κλέος

47 Boeckh 1811–1821, vol. II ii, p. 106 f.
48 Dissen ²1847, p. 14 f.

ἐν εὐάνορι Λυδοῦ Πέλοπος ἀποικίᾳ·
τοῦ μεγασθενὴς ἐράσσατο Γαιάοχος
Ποσειδάν, ἐπεί νιν καθαροῦ λέβητος ἔξελε Κλωθώ
ἐλέφαντι φαίδιμον ὦμον κεκαδμένον.

But fame shines on him
in the well-manned colony of Lydian Pelops;
with whom the strong Earthshaker fell in love,
Poseidon, when Clotho took him out of the pure cauldron,
distinguished by a shoulder gleaming with ivory.

Now if the episode described in verses 26b–27, after the factual main and relative clauses, is suddenly meant to be contrafactual, then Pindar's continued use of the indicative here is striking to say the least. But on the level of the narrative logic, too, there is a serious problem. Verses 25–27 tell us that Poseidon fell in love with Pelops either *after* he had been taken out of the cauldron with his ivory shoulder, or *because* he was taken out with an ivory shoulder, according to whether one reads ἐπεί as temporal or causal.[49] In both interpretations, this scene is a central part of the new version, since the latter is based crucially on Poseidon's love for Pelops.[50] Dissen describes the paradox that arises from the traditional understanding of the verses as follows:

> Interpreters assert that the poet here first places a popular myth that he then rejects as untrue. But consider what Pindar says on this account: 'Hieron has won in the most noble colony of Pelops who was loved by Neptune on account of an ivory shoulder that he in fact did not possess.'[51]

Propter humerum eburneum quem tamen non habebat: however we decide to understand the relationship between the cauldron scene and the love-story, Pelops' re-appearance with ivory shoulder has to be rescued, whether as point of time or as reason, from the traditional version so that it can play its appointed role in the new one. The

[49] See below, n. 55. Hermann 1827–1877, vol. VI, p. 52 disputes that the shoulder had anything to do with Poseidon's falling in love with Pelops at all.

[50] It is unclear whether the relationship between Poseidon and Pelops also belongs to Pindar's revision of the myth or whether it was in fact already a part of the tradition known to the audience and merely given a new motivation. See Köhnken 1983 and Howie 1984.

[51] '*Statuunt interpretes poetam hic primum vulgarem fabulam ponere, quam deinde neget. Sed vide quid dicat Pindarus ex hac ratione: »Hiero vicit in nobilissima Pelopis colonia, qui amatus est a Neptuno, propter humerum eburneum, quem tamen non habebat«.*' Dissen ^{2}1847, p. 15, my translation.

cauldron scene must not be completely rejected if the new version is still to function—and nevertheless: the narrator's rejection of the dismemberment-story leaves little room for doubt.[52]

To solve this problem, Dissen now argued that the scene in fact had nothing to do with the dismemberment: it was instead nothing other than the description of the first washing of the new-born child, such as is recounted in the Homeric Hymn to Apollo (*Hymn. Hom. Ap.* 21).[53] The ivory shoulder that Pelops possesses when he is lifted out of the cauldron is, on this reading, not a substitute for an early shoulder inadvertently eaten by Demeter, but rather a kind of birthmark; Pelops had it from the very beginning.[54] The overwhelming beauty of the child, symbolized (*pars pro toto*) by his gleaming shoulder, leads Poseidon to fall in love with him.[55]

[52] Two further problems with the traditional interpretation may be mentioned here: 1. Some interpreters see a difficulty in the attribute καθαρός, 'pure', which seems not to fit the cauldron in the dismemberment version (so especially Howie 1984, p. 285 and Krummen 1990, p. 174). It is not entirely clear, however, that the cauldron used for Pelops' reconstitution could not be designated in this way in order to distinguish it from the cauldron into which he was cut up in verse 48. 2. A further problem lies in the fact that there are other cases in which Pindar seems to change traditional versions of myths without drawing all too much attention to the revision, not to speak of telling the rejected version of the story. Hubbard 1987, p. 16 n. 3 points to the *Thirteenth Olympian* (and see Hubbard 1986a); further examples can be found in Dornseiff 1921, p. 126 f. and Gerber 1982, p. 69 f. *ad* 35. Here the traditional interpretation must fall back on the notion of what Pindar, allegedly, could not afford *not* to mention: the dismemberment story was so well-known and believed that the poet *had to* mention it in this case. The recourse to unverifiable extra-textual circumstances of this sort in order to explain singularities in the odes is analysed by Most 1985b, 28 ff.

[53] This reading of verses 25–27 as the unambiguous description of Pelops' birth is taken up by Wilamowitz 1922, p. 234, Kakridis 1970 (first published in 1930), pp. 188–190, Lloyd-Jones 1973, n. 25 and Köhnken 1974, p. 200 n. 3.

[54] Howie 1984, p. 287 considers the possibility that ἐλέφαντι was meant to be understood as a figurative description for the white skin of the child.

[55] Dissen offers two different versions of his interpretation. In the first, quoted above, he obviously understands ἐπεί in verse 26 in a causal sense: *propter humerum eburneum*. In the second, however, ἐπεί is (additionally?) given a temporal meaning: '*ego ita intelligo locum: Vicit Hiero in nobilissima Pelopis colonia, qui a Neptuno amatus est inde a prima infantia, quum Clotho recens natum sustulisset e lebete eburneo humero splendentem.*' When Gerber 1982, p. 55 *ad* 26 remarks that 'Poseidon could obviously not have fallen in love with a new-born babe, as Dissen grotesquely represents him', he is only taking this second passage into account. His own interpretation presupposes the identity of the verses 25–27 with the dismemberment-scene—Pelops is thus at this point already a teenager—and reads ἐπεί (in contrast to the scholars cited above, n. 53, all of whom prefer the causal interpretation; see further Scodel 1985, p. 267) in a temporal sense. Boeckh had already preferred the temporal interpretation of the passage in *Pindari opera* (1811–1821, II ii, p. 29: *postquam eum [...] exemerat Clotho*, and *cf.* p. 106). He is also

Now this interpretation has the advantage of seeming to integrate the cauldron-scene into the abduction-story in verses 36 ff. It is, however, at least in the simple form in which Dissen suggested it, not without problems of its own. First, the cauldron-scene, on this assumption, seems extremely misleading. Gerber, for example, objects that '[t]he audience, familiar with the traditional account, would automatically assume that the ivory shoulder was a replacement for what had been eaten at the cannibalistic feast.'[56] Second, Dissen's interpretation appears to require that Poseidon fall in love with a newborn child, which seems rather unlikely, even in the case of the obscure psychology of a god.[57] But even if the cauldron-scene does not describe the point of time, but merely the reason for Poseidon's attachment to Pelops, namely his innate beauty, the verses 25 and 26b–27 still describe two different events at quite different times, and a number of interpreters have argued that some indication of this in the text is surely necessary: we need a signal that verse 25, ἐράσσατο relates to the feast in Sipylos to which verse 41, δαμέντα φρένας ἱμέρῳ also refers, whilst verses 26b–27 describe the washing of the child many years before.[58] Finally, this version makes the immediately following verses appear completely unmotivated: why does Pindar follow this passage with a critique of untrue and blasphemous stories if the scene he has just described is in fact entirely innocuous?

In the course of the discussion in the last couple of decades, it has become clear that Dissen's interpretation can be modified or extended to reply to the objections of its critics. Whilst some interpreters read the attribute καθαρός and in the role of Clotho as unambiguous if subtle indications that we are dealing with the washing of a child that the first audience would have known to understand in this sense,[59]

followed by Slater 1979, p. 65, Verdenius 1988, p. 17, and Hummel 1993, p. 343, § 427.

[56] Gerber 1982, p. 55 *ad* 26.

[57] Verdenius 1988, p. 16 believes that Poseidon could fall in love with a child because 'as a god he was able to foresee into what a beautiful boy the baby would develop'.

[58] Gerber 1982, p. 55: 'This is harsh and the harshness is not overcome by Kakridis' statement that Pindar sometimes omits ποτέ.'

[59] There are three arguments. First, the adjective καθαρός is placed prominently before its noun and in this way attracts attention to itself. The audience is thus made to understand that this is a specific cauldron which is not or does not need to be identical with the cauldron expected at this point. Second, the quality of purity is also traditionally connected with birth: the Homeric *Hymn to Apollo* describes how the new-born god is washed ἁγνῶς καὶ καθαρῶς (21). Third, Clotho is otherwise unmentioned in the tradition: the scholia to Pindar name Hermes and Rhea as the gods who preside over the reconstitution of the child (Σ 40a Dr.). For this reason, argues Howie, the audience would have understood '26b–27 as a revision, not as a straight account, of the myth of

others have suggested that the natural misunderstanding of the cauldron-scene as Pelops' reconstitution is to be seen as a part of the interpretation of the whole and to be included in it. As Krummen, for example, has argued, the traditional interpretation can be initially intended, although not as the final truth of the passage.[60] The single elements of the cauldron-scene can all, by themselves, be integrated into the dismemberment-myth and are meant to be associated with it by contemporary hearers. According to this reading, Clotho presides over the reconstitution in order to signal that the hero's resurrection is determined by fate, and the cauldron is 'pure' in the sense that it contrasts with the impurity of the dismemberment. From this perspective, it is easy to understand how the poetological statements in verses 28 ff. connect with the cauldron-scene, for the break-off is directed not at what has 'really' been said, but rather at what has been going through the minds of the audience during the immediately preceding verses. In the course of the narrative, however, the audience is led to revise its original, 'traditional' interpretation of the cauldron-scene: at the end, the identification of the scene with the washing appears cogent. At the same time, the hearers are shown by means of their own example how the misunderstanding of the dismemberment-version could arise from the misinterpretation of a few elements that were really present in the true story by simply adding extra items to them which served to make the recognition the real context impossible.

The result of these arguments is the following: as soon as the first version of the story has been revealed as a fiction invented by Tantalus' neighbours which has come to conceal the truth, a new totality of the story emerges which retains the true core of the *μῦθοι* and locates the fictions in a larger context by identifying them *as* fictions (so that they are no longer able to disguise the true story). The synecdoche (*figura cryptica*) is revealed to be a figure, but not simply by being opposed to the truth. Rather, the new version has adopted the tropological form of the relationship between truth and fiction in verses 28–32 and reversed it: with the embedding of the dismemberment-story in the revised version, it is now the truth which contains the fiction. The synecdoche is retained, but the roles of the true λόγος and the colourful ψεύδεα are exchanged. Now the deception is seen in retrospect, as

the revival and slaughter of Pelops' (Howie 1984, p. 288). Verdenius 1988, 17 f. argues similarly, esp. with respect to Clotho: she is 'introduced to show that this was Pelops' natural birth, not a rebirth'.

[60] See Krummen 1990, p. 176: Pindar 'lenkt den Zuhörer so, daß ihm dieser Schluß [*sc.* that the verses 25–27 really must have described the birth-scene] zwingend erscheint.'

it were, to have consisted in taking a part for the whole: the *totum pro parte* has become a *pars pro toto*.

Not only has the structure of the revision of myth been strangely inverted at this point, and the most important epistemological category of the ode, historical truth, revealed to be a *rhetorical* category, supported by mechanisms of the text just as rhetorical as the seductive ψεύδεα it is meant to replace. The observation that the supplementation of the false story by the correct one has taken place by means of the chiastic reversal of the synecdoche rather suggests that the logocentric structure of literal truth and rhetorical figurality cannot itself be governed by the transcendental agency of the truth. On the contrary: in order to achieve the mythical revision in the *First Olympian*, the structure of the difference between the truth and its alternative must itself be a trope. The true, the literal, the *proprium* thus turns out to be its own metaphor.

It is therefore almost superfluous to note that the agency of this transformation—χάρις—is a further figure. Who or what, literally, is χάρις? The self-referential personification of an attribute of poetry—or a goddess, whose influence on his work Pindar, in other odes, is only too ready to admit? If this question is decidable—and the overwhelming majority of scholars have decided in favour of self-referentiality[61]—then only on the basis of an iterable convention whose argumentative force is itself crucially dependent on an analogical-metaphorical transfer.

That literary scholarship, in order to describe the effects of rhetoric phenomenologically—or even to *name* them—is dependent on this metaphorical transfer, was remarked as early as 1971 by Derrida in 'La mythologie blanche':

> If one wished to conceive and to class all the metaphorical possibilities of philosophy, one metaphor, at least, would always remain excluded, outside the system: the metaphor, at the very least, without which the the concept of metaphor could not be constructed, or, to syncopate an entire chain of reasoning, the metaphor of metaphor.[62]

Pindar's description of the difference between truth and fiction in

[61] See Gianotti 1975, pp. 75–80 and *cf.* Gerber 1982, p. 64 f. *ad loc.*

[62] 'Si l'on voulait concevoir et classer toutes les possibilités métaphoriques de la philosophie, une métaphore, au moins, resterait toujours exclue, hors du système: celle, au moins, sans laquelle ne se serait pas construit le concept de métaphore ou, pour syncoper toute une chaîne, la métaphore de métaphore.' Derrida 1972b, p. 261, Engl. 219 f.

the mode of the metaphor thus corresponds exactly to the impossibility of controlling metaphoricity as such from a standpoint that would, itself, not be metaphorical. It inscribes itself in this way in the tradition of the critique of metaphysics that we connected in Chapter 1 with the name of Paul de Man. Like de Man, Pindar demonstrates in this poem the aporias that result from the assumption that one could arrive, in the interpretation of literature, at some absolutely present point from which the meaning of a text could be determined. Boeckh and Bundy both proceed, as we saw, from just such assumptions. The philosophical dream of a point, a privileged place of nature or of pure intuition from which one could distinguish (ultimately, finally, literally) rhetoric from non-rhetoric, referentiality from self-referentiality or even simply a deep structure from its surface is what the *First Olympian* is concerned to dispel. Pindar will not cease pointing to the necessity of these distinctions; at the same time, however, his text robs us of any means of making them.

What results from this situation for the reading of the victory odes that follows? We recall de Man's insight from Chapter 1: if literality is not reachable under the conditions of the temporality of knowledge, separated from the eschatological absolute, then interpretation must take place in the form of a figure that, above all, speaks of the absence of what, in the hermeneutics of presence, would be its meaning.[63] Here, Benjamin's remark that allegory, as opposed to the symbol, is a figure of ontological negation develops its real potential in literary studies: since there is no criterion by which we could distinguish the interpretative status of the rhetorical surface from the literal content really meant by the poem, reading must do without the category of the inside of the poem, together with everything that belongs to it; it must oppose itself to what is literal, true and present.[64] The language of the odes, their tropes and figures, are pure surface; there is—to vary Derrida's *dictum* about Rousseau—nothing behind the text.[65]

In the final two chapters of this book we will turn to the conse-

[63] *Cf.* above, p. 44 ff.

[64] See above, p. 50 n. 68. Menke ^{2}2001, p. 12 speaks in this context of a 'negative Semiotik [...], eine Figuralität, die zugleich den internen Zusammenhang der Figuralität zersetzt, den von Trope und Bedeutung.'

[65] On the notion of the 'pure surface', see Deleuze 1969, pp. 13–21, Engl. pp. 4–11 and *cf.* Benjamin 1972–1986, vol. IV 1, p. 19, Engl. vol. 1, p. 261 on the 'reine Sprache, die nichts mehr meint und nichts mehr ausdrückt' (see also above, p. 2). Derrida's *Il n'y a pas de hors-texte*—probably the most notorious and least understood sentence in his entire *œuvre*—is in Derrida 1967a, p. 227, Engl. p. 158.

quences of this disconcerting view of things for two questions that have determined Pindaric studies in the last two hundred years more than all others: the question of the unity of the Pindaric epinician and the question of the subject who claims to speak in Pindar's name.

CHAPTER 4: UNITY

Mais quand [Nietzsche] dit: « *Il me semble important qu'on se débarrasse du* Tout, *de l'Unité, … il faut émietter l'univers, perdre le* respect *du Tout* », alors il entre dans l'espace du fragmentaire, il prend le risque d'une pensée que ne garantit plus l'unité.
Blanchot, *L'Entretien infini.*

THE UNITY OF THE EPINICIAN ODE BELONGS, IT SEEMS, TO THE insoluble and nevertheless indispensable problems of modern classical studies. The discussion can now look back on a history of over two hundred years that reaches from even before Boeckh and Dissen's *Pindari opera* into the early twenty-first century. Leonard Pfeijffer's *Three Aeginitan Odes of Pindar*, published in 1999, begins with a section about unity, and here the author describes this history as 'a chain of religious wars about method, each new school of interpretation claiming to have found the hidden universal master key to Pindar's odes, making obsolete what has been said about them before and branding any method different from their own as heresy.'[1] It is indeed

[1] Pfeijffer 1999b, p. 1. According to Most, poetic unity 'bezeichnet […] einen Imperativ, der jedem Leser aufgegeben ist: die Einheit des Textes durch seine deutende Lektüre zu konstruieren. Dies soll er, und er darf nicht anders: denn auf die Wechselbeziehungen der Teile und die daraus sich ergebende Einheit des Ganzen zu verzichten hieße, seine eigene Kontinuität durch die Zeit des Lesens hindurch und letztendlich die Integrität seiner eigenen Identität aufs Spiel zu setzen. […] [D]ie Vereinheitlichung des Textes dient als Figur für die Selbstvereinheitlichung seines Lesers' (Most 1985a, p. 2). The motif of self-constitution grounds the imperative of unity existentially in the reading subject. This recourse to the psyche gives the impression that we have arrived at a basic reality behind which we cannot go, but this is only true as long as one can prevent the figurative relationship between the text and the subject from reversing itself and making Most's reader into a metaphor for his text. Indeed, Most seems to imagine just such a dialectic—obviously without any hope of *Aufhebung*: '[D]ie Frage, wie weit die Wechselbeziehungen der Teile zu verfolgen sind, […] kann niemals vom Text selbst beantwortet werden – in dieser Hinsicht läßt ein Text fast alles mit sich machen –, sondern nur vom Urteilsvermögen des Lesers. […] Daher ist die poetische Einheit zumindest zum Teil unbeweisbar' (*ibid.*, p. 2 f.). Here, an abyss opens before us, for what ontological status can such a capacity for judgement claim if it must first constitute its own subject?

striking that since Boeckh, new developments in research have almost always been presented as new theses about the unity of the texts, and this has had the result that progress in Pindaric studies has been understood as an 'ascent to the one' in the odes. The question about unity is the obligatory frame—the *passe-partout*, which is of course also a master key—for every new reading of the epinicians; it identifies such readings as serious, legitimate contributions to the discussion, marking both continuity and difference within the one discourse.[2]

There can, of course, be no question that the work of interpretation is dependent on the unity of its object, and this is where we expect to find the primary interest of literary studies in unity. We expect from a text that, inasmuch as it is a text, it will be a whole with a beginning and an end, and it is first this totality which legitimates the concrete project of interpretation and criticism within specific limits and by means of proximate and less proximate relationships between different parts of the text. To the extent that the weave of words is a *textus*, the search for elements of unity—that unity which constitutes the text *as a text*—is justified from the outset. It is questionable whether there can be such a thing as the meaning of a text at all without a notion such as unity.

In Pindaric studies, in any case, 'unity' has indeed been understood as the essential precondition of meaning altogether. No one has expressed this more concisely and quotably than David C. Young, who noted that '"Unity", when applied to a poem, is a critical term simply meaning that the poem makes sense as a whole.'[3] The self-evident nature of this remark, the simple meaning that Young ascribes to it, is indicated not least by the fact that the author appends it in a footnote, on the edge of his text, as if the meaning of the critical term 'unity' itself was a subordinate point, something that did not belong to the thematic concern of the main text to the same extent or in the same way as the presentation of the history of scholarship. But almost every word in this definition deserves our attention. For example, we could note that 'unity' is not limited to poems, but is merely applied to them, that is, is taken from a discourse or a meta-discourse that does not only, or perhaps even primarily, have to do with poetry ('*when* applied to a poem'). The name of this discourse that supplies Young's critical

[2] The criticism levelled at books such as Kurke 1991 consists for the most part in the assertion that '[t]hese books do less to advance *our understanding of the odes as unified wholes*, than to demonstrate the validity of their models by applying them to Pindar's odes' (Pfeijffer 1999b, p. 12, my italics; *cf.* also Carey 1994).

[3] Young 1970, p. 2 f., n. 3. *Cf.* Krummen 1990, pp. 8 and 10 and Poiss 1993, p. 126.

terminology—from above or without, in any case from beyond the border of what the author believes he ought to be speaking about—is not given at this point. Instead, the relationship between meaning and unity is made very clear: under the condition of unity, the meaning results from the *whole* text. Unity and totality are thus interdependent: if unity is not given, then meaning could, at best, be attributed to parts of the text, but not the whole text, whereas if wholeness is not given, the text is a fragment, dependent on something outside of itself if meaning is to result at all. In either of these cases, it would, strictly speaking, have no meaning, for 'as *a* whole' (and we should not overlook the singular in this formulation) it would be unable to demonstrate a coherent, meaningful structure that was co-extensive with the text. The borders of the meaningful and the borders of the text would, in this case, be identical. But would the 'rest' of a text, a part that did not belong to what was genuinely, really meaningful, be a part of the text at all?

Perhaps. It would be a part that was not of the same importance for the meaning of the text as the main part. A part that, if necessary, could be omitted altogether. Like a footnote. Or an example. Or what was called, in the aesthetics of the eighteenth and nineteenth centuries, the 'accessory'. In any case nothing that ought to be seen as the main concern.

'The accessory' is a term, for example, in Schleiermacher's aesthetics:

> *The accessory* is everything that can be different or lacking entirely without the essential elements being changed. For one essential element cannot be added or changed without all being changed. Nor does the accessory participate in the significance of the main parts to the same degree.[4]

'Beiwerk' only participates in meaning to a reduced extent. It is not constitutive of unity, does not take (its) place in the region of the things that contribute to the unity of the work of art for the simple reason that it can be absent without the rest of the work being adversely affected. This is of course an Aristotelian criterion; it will

[4] '*Beiwerk* ist alles das, was anders sein kann oder fehlen, ohne daß die wesentlichen Elemente dürfen geändert werden. Denn ein wesentliches Element darf nicht hinzukommen oder abgeändert werden, ohne daß alle geändert werden. In demselben Maaß nimmt auch das Beiwerk nicht Theil an der Bedeutsamkeit der Haupttheile.' Schleiermacher 1984, p. 39 (his emphasis), my translation.

not be the last.[5]

One needs to know, therefore, what a main part is and what is only an 'accessory' so that one does not ascribe meaning to what is merely *Beiwerk, ornamentum, parergon.* For literary criticism and interpretation, this is a requirement of the greatest significance. For the real carrier of meaning is, for Schleiermacher as indeed for the entire theory of art in the early nineteenth century in the wake of Moritz, the *work*: that product of purposeful activity, designed to last, whose perfection is to be found in itself and which is characterized by the attributes of closure, independence and consistency.[6] Since the ornament does not own these attributes to the same extent as the work itself, it is not to the same extent the bearer of meaning. But because this meaning at the same time limits and defines the work that carries it, the accessory tends towards meaninglessness and becomes, as a consequence, a highly problematic category in the theory of art.

The quest for unity in Pindaric studies tends, in any case, to be opposed to *Beiwerk*, and this as early as Boeckh's *Pindari opera.*[7]

[5] *Cf.* Aristotle, *Poetics* 8, 1451 a32–35. The same motif of the unchangeability of the parts is used in the Italian Renaissance in order to define beauty: *cf.* for example Leone Battista Alberti's *De re aedificatoria* (Alberti 1975 [first published in 1485]) VI ii, fol. 93v.: '[...] *ut sit pulchritudo quidem certa cum ratione concinnitas universarum partium in eo cuius sint: ista ut addi aut diminui aut immutari possit nihil quin improbabilius reddat.*' Here too, the difference between the *pulchritudo* that accrues to the work from the beginning and the *ornamentum* added to it later plays a central role, if indeed with a different assessment of the latter.

[6] On the work of art as a 'ganz nach Zwecken eingerichtete[s] Produkt', see Kant, 'Über den Gebrauch teleologischer Prinzipien in der Philosophie' (= Kant 1956–1964, vol. IX, 137–170, first published in 1788), p. 166; on the perfection that is to be found in the work of art itself as the defining characteristic of the latter, see Moritz's essay from 1785, 'Versuch einer Vereinigung aller schönen Künste und Wissenschaften unter dem Begriff *des in sich selbst Vollendeten*' (= Moritz 1997, vol. 2, pp. 943–949, his italics in the title); on the attributes of closure and consistency, see Thierse 1990, p. 410. *Cf.* Hegel 1969–1971, vol. 15, pp. 266–270, Engl. Hegel 1975a, vol. II, pp. 993–996. The role of the work as the ontological carrier of meaning is stressed by Cassirer 2001, p. 25 ff. See further Pudelek 2005.

[7] Boeckh's theory of unity is complex; we sketch it here only in broad outline. The commentary itself contains only a few programmatic sentences; Boeckh first makes the individual elements of the theory explicit in his discussion of Dissen's *Pindari carmina* (Boeckh 1858–1874, vol. VII, pp. 369–403 on which see above, p. 90 ff.). According to Boeckh, the reference of the ode to a clearly definable historical situation is the first condition of unity. Boeckh understands this *condicio*, as we have seen in Chapter 2, as the presence of the historical object, whose immediate intuition on the part of the poet leads to the unity of the text. (*Cf.* also Schadewaldt 1966, esp. p. 263.) The embedding of the song in the historically real situation can serve as evidence for its unity because unity is an attribute of historical reality *per se* (as *e.g.* Deleuze 2002, p. 241, Engl. p. 172 points

Boeckh directs his hermeneutic project, inasmuch as it concerns Pindar, explicitly against those who, for lack of understanding, have wanted to view parts of the poem as mere decoration.

> For as long as those concerned to understand and interpret [*sc.* Pindar] were happy to view everything that did not seem to belong to the topic as a digression or an ornament, it appeared to be a law of Greek, or at least Pindaric, lyric poetry that the song is held up by this kind of ornamentation; but a different understanding leads to the recognition of a different law, and if the latter has indeed been grasped, then an explanation [...] on the basis of that less stringent law is no longer satisfactory.[8]

If the odes are aesthetically valuable, then that is because they contain no ornamentation that does not participate in their beauty, which

out). Boeckh calls this situative unity 'objective', in order to distinguish it from a second, 'subjective' unity whose guarantee is allegedly to be found in the coherence of the intention of the poet (Boeckh 1858–1874, vol. VII, p. 384 ff.; *cf.* above, p. 90 with n. 81 and Schleiermacher 1984, p. 133, who will have been one of the immediate sources of this distinction for Boeckh). This intention is formally close to Dissen's *summa sententia*: despite the difference of object that Boeckh emphasizes in his review—in Dissen a concept, in Boeckh an intuition—subjective unity implies, like the *Grundgedanke*, an aesthetics of content which creates unity on the basis of the ascription of unity to what the poet wants to say. For this reason, Boeckh can also call it a 'unity of thought' (*Gedankeneinheit*) (Boeckh 1858–1874, vol. VII, p. 386). That Dissen is very much more explicit than Boeckh about the precise nature of this aesthetics is certainly one reason for the fact that the realization of the (always given and repeatedly implemented) logical possibility of a unity of content in the epinicians has usually been associated with Dissen's *Grundgedanken* rather than with Boeckh's first two unities. (Fränkel [4]1993, pp. 557–567 sees the unity of the individual odes, in the sense of just such an aesthetics of content, in the fact that they offer exemplary realizations of a unified *Wertewelt* [p. 566].) Boeckh also mentions a *material* unity—'Indem die objective von [der subjectiven Einheit] beherrscht wird und jene nur die Grundlage dieser bildet, einige sie sich völlig wie Subjectives und Objectives zu einer ungetrennten materialen Einheit [...]' (Boeckh 1858–1874, vol. VII, p. 386; *cf.* Newman & Newman 1984, p. 7)—and a *formal* unity; Boeckh offers no detailed description of the latter, however, and refers his readers instead to the third part of Dissen's *De ratione* ('De dispositione partium': Dissen [2]1843, pp. XLV–LXII; *cf.* above, p. 107 n. 132). On Boeckh's theory of unity, see further Young 1970, p. 8–11 (critical) and Newman & Newman 1984, pp. 6–18.

8 'Denn so lange man sich bei dessen [*sc.* Pindars] Verständniss und Auslegung damit befriedigte, was nicht zur Sache zu gehören schien, als Abschweifung oder Schmuck anzusehen, schien es Gesetz der Hellenischen, oder wenigstens Pindarischen Lyrik, mit solchem Schmucke das Lied aufzustutzen; anderes Verständniss dagegen führt zur Erkenntniss eines anderen Gesetzes, und ist letzteres zum Bewusstsein gekommen, so genügt [...] eine Erklärung nicht mehr, die jenem loseren Gesetz angepasst wäre.' Boeckh 1858–1874, vol. VII, p. 374, my translation. *Cf.* Hermann 1827–1877, vol. VII, p. 111 and Heath 1986, p. 87.

is here co-extensive with their meaning.

Ornamentation does not belong to the topic, to *what is meant*; it is external to it. Boeckh's rejection of the accessory is an motif found frequently in the reaction of the late eighteenth century to the aesthetics of the Baroque, for example in the *Kritik der Urteilskraft*. In a section of the analytic of the beautiful, Kant explains that pure judgements of taste are independent of 'charm and emotion' (*Reiz und Rührung*).[9] A merely empirical, sensuous pleasure, the Königsberg philosopher argues, cannot lay claim to the generality constitutive of pure aesthetic judgements for the simple reason that it is always based on the interest of the beholder: something hurts, something pleases. The pure judgement of taste, however, has 'only the purposefulness of form as its determining ground' (*bloß die Zweckmäßigkeit der Form zum Bestimmungsgrunde*). What now follows are examples (§ 14). Material, colour in art, timbre in music are, as objects of perception, a supplement to the form and therefore are not possible objects of pure aesthetic judgement. Kant then continues:

> Even what one calls ornamentation (*parerga*), i.e., that which is not internal to the entire representation of the object as a constituent, but only belongs to it externally as an addendum and augments the satisfaction of taste, still does this only through its form: like the borders of paintings, draperies on statues, or colonnades around magnificent buildings. But if the ornament itself does not consist in beautiful form, if it is, like a gilt frame, attached merely in order to recommend approval for the painting through its charm—then it is called decoration, and detracts from genuine beauty.[10]

We can observe, here, the complicity between the inside of the work's genuine object of representation and its beauty. The external, the *parergon*, constantly threatens to become too substantial and thus detract from the beauty of the work. In Boeckh, this danger to the

[9] Kant, *Kritik der Urteilskraft*, § 13 (B p. 37 f.; = Kant 1956–1964, vol. X, p. 302 f., Engl. Kant 2000, p. 107 f.).

[10] 'Selbst was man Zieraten (*parerga*) nennt, d. i. dasjenige, was nicht in die ganze Vorstellung des Gegenstandes als Bestandstück innerlich, sondern nur äußerlich als Zutat gehört und das Wohlgefallen des Geschmacks vergrößert, tut dieses doch auch nur durch seine Form: wie Einfassungen der Gemälde, oder Gewänder an Statuen, oder Säulengänge um Prachtgebäude. Besteht aber der Zierat nicht selbst in der schönen Form, ist er, wie der goldene Rahmen, bloß um durch seinen Reiz das Gemälde dem Beifall zu empfehlen angebracht: so heißt der alsdann Schmuck, und tut der echten Schönheit Abbruch.' Kant, *Kritik der Urteilskraft*, § 14 (B p. 43; = Kant 1956–1964, vol. X, p. 306, his emphasis; Engl. Kant 2000, p. 110).

meaning and beauty of Pindar's epinicians is excluded from the outset, for in these texts, everything is fitted to their topic. 'The basic thesis', as Boeckh explains in the description of the commentary cited above, 'was thus as follows: that not blind enthusiasm, but rather conscious art rules in these poems, in which everything is fitted to the aim, the persons, times and circumstances'.[11] That with this formulation, the necessary condition of genuine lyrical beauty has been given, is shown by the definition of beauty in the *Encyklopädie und Methodologie der philologischen Wissenschaften.* There, we read:

> Aesthetics has for its subject the consideration of the beautiful; beauty consists in the fusion of matter and form in harmony with the inner end, whether in works of art or scholarship.[12]

The total participation in meaning is thus also the necessary condition for the beauty of the songs. If they are beautiful, then that is because they are unified with respect to their 'inner purpose'. Mere finery, on the other hand, would have little or nothing to do with the purpose; it would therefore play a role, as we saw above, neither in the interpretation nor in the aesthetic evaluation of the work, for the *parergon* would undermine the connection of the work as a whole with the purpose. What is beautiful about the work results, on the contrary, from the specific connection between form and material—for Boeckh, the intuition of the poet and its linguistic realization—and that is, once again, an Aristotelian element.

The purpose of the odes prescribes their content. Boeckh says elsewhere explicitly that unity only arises when the form exclusively serves the content.[13] The opposition 'content/matter' and 'form' is thus placed in a hierarchy. Now this content is not arbitrary. In Pindar, as we have read, everything is fitted to 'the persons, times and circum-

[11] See above, p. 90.

[12] 'Die Aesthetik hat die Betrachtung des Schönen zum Gegenstande; das Schöne aber besteht in der dem innern Zweck entsprechenden Verschmelzung des Stoffes mit der Form, gleichviel ob bei Werken der Kunst oder der Wissenschaft.' Boeckh ²1886, p. 156, Engl. p. 120 modified.

[13] *Cf.* Boeckh ²1886, p. 132: 'Subjectives und Objectives [einigen sich völlig] zu einer ungetrennten materialen Einheit. Hieraus ergiebt sich dann zugleich die formale Einheit, d.h. die Art, wie dieser Stoff auch äusserlich zu einem Ganzen gestaltet ist; sie liegt darin, dass die verschiedenen Glieder des Werkes in ihrer Aufeinanderfolge *im Dienste jener materialen Einheit* logisch und rhetorisch verbunden sind. Selbstverständlich müssen die materiale und formale Einheit, wie Form und Materie überhaupt, ein unzertrennliches Ganzes bilden [...]' (my italics) and p. 470: 'Die Schönheit des Kunstwerks besteht darin, dass der Ideenstoff in die Form dem Zweck gemäss eingeführt wird.'

stances'. Purpose and content are thus closely tied to the occasion of the individual poem. Times and circumstances are the presupposition and the purpose of this poetry at the same time. We can only understand Pindar's epinicians, Boeckh's argument implies here, if we constantly and consistently contextualize them, and this context is the specific present of the individual commission and the individual performance.[14]

The situative present as the originary unifying moment and thus as the authoritative criterion of interpretation: the return of this paradigm in work on Pindar in the last decades can be observed in numerous studies, particularly perhaps in those of the influential Urbino school around Bruno Gentili.[15] Let us cite, instead, two other scholars. Eveline Krummen writes in *Pyrsos hymnon*, a reading of the odes published in the early 1990s:

> [T]his study takes as its point of departure Boeckh's thesis that the 'external' (he called it the 'objective') is to be interpreted with the help of historical facts as a coherent context of meaning and that the effects of this context must be constitutive of the poem. Our only advantage over Boeckh is that we have a few instruments and facts more than he did, which may perhaps allow us to reach better conclusions.[16]

Krummen accordingly presents her results primarily as a demonstration that the different elements of the odes are held together by virtue of their common reference to a historically identifiable situation: 'If one looks back on the poem from the perspective of the actual circumstances (*der aktuellen Rahmenbedingungen*) [*sc.* under which the performance took place]', she writes at the end of her reading of the

[14] I do not want to suggest that Boeckh and the interpreters who follow him are not being faithful to a certain element in the texts when they privilege presence in their readings of the poems: see Mackie 2003, p. 39 ff. on the epinicians' very real concern with the present. My interest here is rather in the structural or theoretical implications of this concern, both in Pindar and in his interpreters.

[15] See Krummen's brief remarks at Krummen 1990, pp. 5 and 26 and the literature cited there.

[16] '[D]ie vorliegende Arbeit setzt bei einem Gedanken Boeckhs an, nämlich, daß das 'Äußere' (er nannte es 'Objektives') mit Hilfe von historischen Fakten als ein Sinnzusammenhang zu interpretieren sei und in seiner Wirkung für das Gedicht konstituierend sein müsse. Es sind also nur einige Mittel und Fakten, die wir Boeckh heute voraushaben, um vielleicht zu schlüssigeren Ergebnissen zu kommen.' Krummen 1990, p. 13, my translation. For Most's rather different assessment of Boeckh's exemplarity, see Most 1985b, p. 40 ff. (and *cf.* 26 ff. on the approach adopted in the co-operative commentary with Dissen).

Fourth Isthmian, 'one moves [...] increasingly into the centre, to the celebratory present occasion (*die festliche Gegenwart*) and the victory feast [...]. What the audience will have been able to experience in reality (*das in der Wirklichkeit Erfahrbare*) is never ignored; rather, all statements are interpretations of precisely this reality.'[17]

Leonard Pfeijffer, in turn, explains his concept of unity in his commentary from 1999 as follows:

> The unity of a Pindaric ode cannot be severed from the ode's occasional nature. [...] '[S]ystematic unity' resides in the encomiastic purpose of the ode. [...] [T]he ideal at which the interpreter must aim is a situation in which he can explain how every single detail in a specific ode makes sense as part of a unified whole that contributes to enhancing the glory of the specific victor [...] celebrated for the specifically defined audience at the specific moment in time.[18]

The projects that Krummen and Pfeijffer programmatically lay out here have led to significant insights. They are based, however—and this emerges very clearly from both of these passages—on rigorous strategies of delimitation. In question are always '*aktuelle* Rahmenbedingungen', the '*specifically defined* public', the *specific present* of the performance. What lies outside of this frame, what is not present or relates to what is not present, is, as far as the unity of the ode is concerned, of little or no account. And presence—we must not forget this—is oral, relying on the simultaneity of voice and song.[19] The singer performs the epinician in front of the present audience, an audience that is defined by being present at the performance; the presence in question here is constituted by this situation of oral communication.[20] The value that, for example, Krummen lays on orality ('a funda-

[17] Krummen 1990, p. 93, my translation (and *cf.* p. 79).

[18] Pfeijffer 1999b, p. 18.

[19] *Cf.* Krummen 1990, p. 4: 'Die Gedichte selbst richten sich an ein *unmittelbar anwesendes*, dem Dichter bekanntes Publikum [...] Die primäre Vermittlung erfolgt *mündlich* [...] Pindar [kann] eine unmittelbare Anschauung [...] als bekannt voraussetzen. Es handelt sich also um *eine Form der Gesprächssituation*, und wie in jedem Gespräch können Informationen unterbleiben; der Sprechende macht sich eine bestimmte Vorstellung vom Wissen des Gesprächspartners, auf dessen Hintergrund er argumentiert. Es ist dieses »Wissen«, das der Leser Pindars teilen muß, um die Gedichte zu verstehen' (my italics).

[20] Heath 1986 is no exception in this regard. The author criticises the search for unity in post-Boeckhian Pindaric studies and argues that, whereas 'few critics even today would willingly burden Pindar with the *crimen digressionum* against which Boeckh sought to defend him', one must ask why this ought to be the case. 'Do we know that

mental given [*Grundgegebenheit*] of Pindaric poetry [...] that it is today no longer legitimate to ignore'[21]) serves to construct the concept of this specific present. The inmost centre of the song, the moment of its unity, only takes place in its spoken presence, and the limits of this presence are identical with the moments in which the singer begins to sing and ceases to do so. What precedes is anticipation, perhaps expectation or desire, but not presence; what follows is remembrance and scholarly reconstruction, but not presence. The notion of presence in these authors is governed just as securely by the opposition between inside and outside as that of the space that functions as its metaphor.[22]

But let us return to the accessory. If the project of unity relies on setting up clear boundaries between the inside of the song, the logical subject of unity, and its outside, then the text ought, according to the

Pindar and Pindar's audiences would have shared our distaste? Has that been established by literary-historical arguments, backed by sounder evidence than the mutable preferences of modern criticism? For digression was no crime until Pindar's licence to digress was revoked, and that [...] was a relatively recent development', specifically in the later eighteenth century (p. 98). The theoretical basis of this recourse to Pindar and his public as the final authority in the question of what is to be seen as unified, is provided in Heath 1989, and here it becomes clear that this theory of a rhetorically multifunctional unity is also based on the specific presence of the voice: 'When someone speaks to us, we will generally try to make sense of what has been said. If the utterance consists of two apparently unrelated sentences, we are likely to infer that it is in some way pregnant; we will then find ourselves looking for a latent or unobvious connection between the two sentences, which might explain why they were uttered together' (p. 1). This attempt, writes Heath, offers a simple illustration of the problem with which one sees oneself confronted in the interpretation of ancient literature. Here, the difference between writing and speech which so troubled Plato is all too easily collapsed into the immediacy of face-to-face conversation.

[21] Krummen 1990, p. 8, my translation.

[22] Most divides research into two groups based on whether the agency of unity is sought inside or outside the text (see Most 1985b, p. 25 ff.), and distinguishes on this basis between 'applied' and 'immanent' unity (*ibid.*, p. 42 ff.); the task of *The Measures of Praise* will be to demonstrate the latter. As we saw in the *First Olympian*, however, this distinction between the inside and outside of language is, for Pindar, not entirely unproblematic; the border between rhetoric and its other which is meant to provide the foundation for the opposition between the inner region of truth and the outside of mere figurative appearance (and is at the same time based on it) is sublimated asymmetrically not on the side of the truth, but on the side of the figure. This asymmetry does not remain without consequences for the question of unity. Is there such a thing as the 'outside' of a text that would stand up to critical examination? How certain is the border that separates the outside from the inside, the text from its context? If in the course of reading we come to the conclusion that this border is constantly being subverted by Pindar's metaphors, we will have to admit that Most's arrangement of research on Pindar on the basis of such plausible categories as outside and inside is itself not immanent, but applied.

aesthetic and hermeneutical criteria we have been discussing, to constitute a strictly definable space within which form and content are co-extensive. This co-extension of form and content leaves no place, at least on the assumption of unity, for accessories. For Pfeijffer, this was the condition for the successful interpretation of the odes ('every single detail'), for Boeckh, in addition, the criterion of their beauty.

In all of these cases, we are dealing with the question of the unity of a poem in the Aristotelian sense. This unity depends on the clear distinction between the essence of a work and what is non-essential: what belongs to the inside and what to the outside. The place of the accessory would be between these two categories, if there were to be a 'between'. Which there must not be.

And if there were one nevertheless? This time not merely as an aesthetic accident or the lapse of an interpreter, but rather as something that cannot be governed by this division into inside and outside, something that instead precedes it and enables it? And could it be that, with this question, literary studies recapitulates a problem that it had already inherited in antiquity from metaphysics—perhaps even from *the* metaphysics, namely the *Metaphysics* of Aristotle?

Philology and metaphysics

At a well-known place in the *Poetics*, Aristotle defines tragedy according to the criteria of closure, wholeness and the size or scale of the action it represents (*Poet.* 7, 1450 b23–25): 'We have laid it down that a tragedy is an imitation of an action that is complete in itself, as a whole of some magnitude.'[23] The explanations that follow this sentence—the seventh chapter on the completeness and scale of the *μῦθος*, the eighth on unity—analyse the form of the plot according to categories whose development and definition Aristotle undertakes in different books of the *Metaphysics*.[24] There, the two first terms in the definition—*τὸ τέλειον* and *τὸ ὅλον*—are the subject of parts of the fifth book, where the notion of the 'one' (*τὸ ἕν*) is discussed; this last is also a

[23] *κεῖται δὴ ἡμῖν τὴν τραγῳδίαν τελείας καὶ ὅλης πράξεως εἶναι μίμησιν ἐχούσης τι μέγεθος*, tr. Bywater in Barnes 1984, p. 2321.

[24] The specific relevance of Aristotle's definitions in the *Physics* and *Metaphysics* to the terms used in the *Poetics* has been variously evaluated: see *e.g.* Halliwell ²1998, p. 96 ff. (cautious) and Kyriakou 1993 (emphatic). The relative dating of the texts is complex, since different books of the *Metaphysics* appear to have been written at different times, and many scholars suppose at least two periods of work on the *Poetics* as well. A survey of the individual texts can be found in Düring ²2005, p. 46 ff. On the dating of *Metaphysics* Δ, on which we shall be concentrating, see Jaeger 1912, p. 118 ff.

topic in the tenth book and in the fifth book of the *Physics*.[25] This overlapping of themes and theorems between ontology and poetics is presumably not accidental, for it is otherwise difficult to explain the persistence with which the tradition of Western philosophical aesthetics has returned again and again to exactly this interface in asking how and to what extent metaphysics can help us to understand art.[26] If the quest for epinician unity since Boeckh has been governed by the categories of Aristotelian ontology—and this seems to have been the case—then this merely indicates something of Pindaric criticism's continuing indebtedness to this tradition.[27]

What criteria of unity does Aristotle offer us in the *Metaphysics* that might be relevant for defining the specific unity of a work of art, such as we have seen scholars attempting to define it in Pindaric studies? We will concentrate here on the discussion in *Metaphysics* Δ 6. In 1016

[25] τὸ τέλειον: *Met.* Δ 16, 1021 b12–1022 a3; τὸ ὅλον: *Met.* Δ 26, 1023 b26–1024 a10; τὸ ἕν: *Met.* Δ 6, 1015 b16–1017 a6, *Met.* I 1–6, 1052 a15–1057 a17 and *Phys.* V 3, 227 a10–17.

[26] *Cf.* for example the—in a certain sense paradigmatic—relationship between Baumgarten's *Aesthetica* and the metaphysical epistemology of Leibniz's *Nouveaux Essais*, or Kant's adoption of the logical functions of the *Kritik der reinen Vernunft* in the analytics of the beautiful in the first book of the third *Kritik* (see Kant, *Kritik der Urteilskraft*, § 1 n., B 3 f.; = Kant 1956–1964, vol. X, p. 279 f., Engl. Kant 2000, p. 89 n.). It is not clear that more recent critiques of this gesture do not in fact, with lesser or greater necessity, simply repeat it. Bubner 1989, for example, argues that the recourse of aesthetics to epistemology represents the 'Majorisierung der Kunst durch philosophische Begrifflichkeit' (p. 34): by binding art to the metaphysical question of truth, philosophical aesthetics has illegitimately subjected it to a heteronomous model of explanation dependent on the obsolete concept of the 'work of art' as truth's ontological carrier. But Bubner's appeal to the privileged notion of autonomy is, certainly historically and, it could be shown, systematically, just as bound up with the concept of the 'work' as the approaches he opposes: *cf.* Moritz's 'In wie fern Kunstwerke beschrieben werden können?' (= Moritz 1997, vol. 2, pp. 992–1003, written in 1788), p. 994 on the requirement that the work of art is to be interpreted exclusively 'aus sich selbst heraus'. The philosopher's critique, for which parallels could readily be found in other German and in Anglo-American criticism, thus rests on a circular argument: a certain conception of art, crucially dependent on the postulate of an autonomy which accrues first and foremost to the work, is used to criticize other notions of art for this very dependence. On the function of autonomy and heteronomy in philosophical aesthetics, see further Derrida 1978, esp. p. 53 ff.

[27] Aristotelian categories are also still at work if the construction of unity is no longer, as in Aristotle, mediated by the mimetic relationship of the text to a represented action, but is based instead on an order which emphasizes immanent relationships, as *e.g.* in the Renaissance in Alberti and his successors. In Pindaric studies, we can think of theories of immanent unity in the wake of New Criticism such as Most 1985b (*cf.* esp. p. 43). Here, too, the categories of totality, closure, form and material as constitutive attributes of the work form the foundation on which the possibility of unity is first of all based.

b6–11, Aristotle summarizes the results of his argumentation up to this point on the basis of his initial division of unity into two categories: *accidental* unity (κατὰ συμβεβηκός) in which sense most things are 'one' because they behave as one with respect to something else, and unity *as such* (καθ' αὑτό) which is the first and proper meaning of the word. According to Aristotle, unity in this second sense can be predicated of a being inasmuch as it possesses either a continuous body (this has been the topic of 1015 b36–1016 a17) or a form based on an indivisible substrate (1016 a17–24) or a definition relating to a single object (1016 a32–b6).[28]

Let us begin with continuity. In a study of poetic unity in Greek antiquity using Pindar's *Eleventh Pythian* as an example, Glenn Most has called this unity 'the Aristotelian minimal condition' that every intact surviving poem fulfils simply by proceeding in 'an uninterrupted sequence of words'.[29] A closer look at the development of this criterion in the Aristotelian corpus shows however to what problems it can lead. Aristotle illustrates the concept of continuity in the *Metaphysics* with two examples: a wooden torch is called 'continuous', συνεχής, because it is held together by a piece of string or cord (δεσμός); wooden planks are 'continuous' if they are joined together with glue (κόλλα). After a discussion of the specific continuity of straight and broken lines, of the eminent unity of what is one by φύσις (and not, for example, by βία[30]), and of the heuristic value of necessarily simultaneous movement for determining whether an object is continuous (if a thing is continuous, all of its parts must necessarily move at once), the philosopher returns to the planks. It is not enough, writes Aristotle, for things merely to touch each other in order to be 'continuous as such': 'for if you put planks in contact with each other, you will not assert that these are one plank or body or anything else continuous'

[28] On the conflation of the four unities in three in the summary, see Ross 1924, vol. I, p. 302. The same list is found in a different context in *Phys.* I 2, 185 b7–9.

[29] Most 1985a, p. 1 (my translation) with reference to this passage and *Met.* I 1, 1052 a19–20. Kyriakou 1993, p. 345 f. argues that the unity of which the *Poetics* speaks with respect to tragedy is the unity of continuity, since Aristotle uses terminology from the discussion of primarily mathematical unity in *Met.* Δ 13, 1020 a7 ff. (μέγεθος and τέλειον) in the definition of *Poet.* 6, 1449 b24–28. This is correct inasmuch as the action to be imitated and the text which imitates always consist of more than one element whose unity must be created in the process of composition (*cf. Poet.* 10, 1452 a14–16 on the definition of a 'simple action', ὥσπερ ὥρισται, as συνεχὴς καὶ μία).

[30] *Met.* I 1, 1052 a23. On Dissen's use of this criterion in his commentary on Pindar, see above, p. 102.

(1016 a7–9).[31] What is missing is obviously the glue that creates continuity between the planks and thus constitutes the unity of the object consisting of them. The unity constituted by the continuity of the planks is thus the function of something 'between' them.[32]

Now, what is this 'between'? What is its status? Does the glue possess the same status as the string that in 1016 a1 holds the torch together and thus provides it with its continuity? Are glue and string part of the continuous object that they themselves constitute? Aristotle's argumentation in *Metaphysics* Δ 6 gives us no clear reason to answer this question in the affirmative, for no string binds the string to the torch and the glue is not itself glued to the planks: in the text, the planks are the logical subject of what is 'one', not the glue. But if, on the basis of this uncertainty and in order to escape the infinite regression, the search for the glue of the glue (of the glue ...) such an answer would imply, we respond to the question with 'no', the consequence would be that between or around the components of what is 'one' there would be something that makes their unity possible but which does not itself—at least not on the basis of Aristotle's discussion in this chapter—belong to it in any proper sense.[33]

We could therefore be tempted, in order to understand the status of this 'between', to have recourse to *Physics* V 3, where 'the continuous is better defined'.[34] But here, further difficulties arise, if with the same result. In a discussion of the unity of processes, Aristotle offers a definition of continuity that seems to leave no place for a 'between' (227 a10–13):

31 *εἰ γὰρ θείης ἁπτόμενα ἀλλήλων ξύλα, οὐ φήσεις ταῦτα εἶναι ἓν οὔτε ξύλον οὔτε σῶμα οὔτ' ἄλλο συνεχὲς οὐδέν*, tr. Kirwan ^{2}1993, p. 36.

32 The connecting link occurs also in the definition of unity in the *Poetics*, in the later, often overlooked chapters on *λέξις* (19–22) which close off the discussion of tragedy and border on the discussion of epic. In *Poet.* 20, 1457 a28–30, Aristotle describes two conditions under which a *λόγος* can be unified: it can either be 'one' by means of a 'link'—*συνδέσμῳ*, and the philosopher's example is the *Iliad*—or by means of reference, just as the definition of a human being is 'one' definition because it defines a unified object. The unity of the human being is the unity of the genre which remains the same genre in all its species and single exemplars; the unity of the definition is thus a derived unity and so falls under the *ἑνότης κατὰ συμβεβηκός* in *Met.* Δ 6, 1015 b16–34. The *σύνδεσμος*, however, apparently fulfils the same function in the *Iliad* as the *κόλλα* between the planks in *Met.* Δ 6, 1016 a1.

33 The problem of the infinite regression in attempting to anchor the unity of the epinicians in a (necessarily composite, because predicatively constituted) thought is one of Boeckh's objections to Dissen's *Pindari carmina*: Boeckh 1858–1874, vol. VII, p. 382 f.

34 Ross 1924, vol. I, p. 302 *ad loc.*

τὸ δὲ συνεχὲς ἔστι μὲν ὅπερ ἐχόμενόν τι, λέγω δ' εἶναι συνεχὲς ὅταν ταὐτὸ γένηται καὶ ἓν τὸ ἑκατέρου πέρας οἷς ἅπτονται καὶ ὥσπερ σημαίνει τοὔνομα συνέχηται. τοῦτο δ' οὐχ οἷόν τε δυοῖν ὄντοιν εἶναι τοῖν ἐσχάτοιν.

The continuous is a subdivision of the contiguous: things are called continuous when the touching limits of each become one and the same and are, as the word implies, contained in each other.[35]

The two parts of the unity that is to be created must possess a single common boundary, not merely one on either side towards the other. The identity of these two borders must be absolute: the specific unity of the continuous is not possible as long as one can speak of two edges that are distinguishable on the basis of even the smallest ontic difference. But in what follows, this *ταὐτὸ καὶ ἕν* is revealed to be the product of a 'between' as well (13–17):

τούτου δὲ διωρισμένου φανερὸν ὅτι ἐν τούτοις ἐστὶ τὸ συνεχές, ἐξ ὧν ἕν τι πέφυκε γίγνεσθαι κατὰ τὴν σύναψιν. καὶ ὥς ποτε γίγνεται τὸ συνέχον ἕν, οὕτω καὶ τὸ ὅλον ἔσται ἕν, οἷον ἢ γόμφῳ ἢ κόλλῃ ἢ ἁφῇ ἢ προσφύσει.

This definition makes it plain that continuity belongs to things that naturally in virtue of their mutual contact form a unity. And in whatever way that which holds them together is one, so too will the whole be one, *e.g.* by a rivet or glue or contact or organic union.

The principle on which a composite becomes a whole turns out to be something for which, in the constitution of this whole, there can by definition be no place. It must efface itself.[36] The position of the agency of unity as continuity is thus ambiguous. Although it is implicated in the central structures of this unity, it is at the same time outside the field of its own operations. None of these operations is self-reflexive enough to grasp its own origin; the source of the continuous, the centre of the structure, is essentially beyond its range. Derrida has called this phenomenon, which seems to be a general feature of the notion of structure, the logic of the supplement: the agency that centres, orders, governs a structure must be both at the centre of the structure and at the same time beyond the borders of the structurality

35 Tr. R.P. Hardie and R.K. Gaye in Barnes 1984, p. 384, as also in the following quotation.

36 In this respect, the continuity of space in Aristotle is structurally identical with the continuity of time (as also in Hegel: see Heidegger [18]2001, p. 432 n. 1, Engl. p. 500 n. xxx): see *Physics* IV 1 and Derrida's 'Ousia et grammè' (= Derrida 1972b, pp. 31–78, Engl. pp. 29–67).

it produces.[37] Is poetics affected by this logic? And could that offer a first explanation for the curious fact that precisely those passages in Pindar which function as transitions and bind the parts of his odes together have always been felt to be particularly problematic for the unity of the epinicians?[38]

For our purposes, however, the second criterion that Aristotle discusses here, the unity of the undifferentiated form of the substrate (*τῷ τὸ ὑποκείμενον τῷ εἴδει εἶναι ἀδιάφορον*, *Met.* Δ 6, 1016 a17 f.), is more important. Inasmuch as every *εἶδος* is the *εἶδος* of a *ὑποκείμενον*, this unity can be referred to merely as the unity of form; it is introduced in this sense in *Metaphysics* I as that unity which accrues to any object which possesses *τινὰ μορφὴν καὶ εἶδος* (*Met.* I 1, 1052 a22). Aristotle's first examples in *Met.* Δ are water and wine: since, as liquids, they do not consist of discrete parts, one cannot divide their form into separate components. But the *εἶδος* as the criterion of unity reappears in this chapter in the summary of secondary and primary unities in 1016 b6–11. Instead, this time, of concluding the discussion of the different meanings of being 'one' and moving on to the next topic, the definition of 'one' as the principle of number and measure, the philosopher interposes a further section on the unity by virtue of the *εἶδος* (b11–17):

> *ἔτι δ' ἔστι μὲν ὡς ὁτιοῦν ἕν φαμεν εἶναι ἂν ᾖ ποσὸν καὶ συνεχές, ἔστι δ' ὡς οὔ, ἂν μή τι ὅλον ᾖ, τοῦτο δὲ ἂν μὴ τὸ εἶδος ἔχῃ ἕν· οἷον οὐκ ἂν φαῖμεν ὁμοίως ἓν ἰδόντες ὁπωσοῦν τὰ μέρη συγκείμενα τοῦ ὑποδήματος, ἐὰν μὴ διὰ τὴν συνέχειαν, ἀλλ' ἐὰν οὕτως ὥστε ὑπόδημα εἶναι καὶ εἶδός τι ἔχειν ἤδη ἕν· διὸ καὶ ἡ τοῦ κύκλου μάλιστα μία τῶν γραμμῶν, ὅτι ὅλη καὶ τέλειός ἐστιν.*[39]

> Again, although in a way we assert that anything whatever is one which is a quantity and continuous, in a way we do not if it is not some kind of whole, that is, if it does not possess one form; as for instance if we observed the parts of a shoe put together anyhow we should not so readily assert that they were one (unless on account of their continuity), but only if they were put together in such a way as to be a shoe and thereby possess some one form. That is why a circular line is of all lines most one, because it is whole and complete.[40]

37 See Derrida 1967a, pp. 203–234, Engl. pp. 141–164 *et passim* and 1967c, p. 410 f., Engl. p. 279 (and *cf.* Most 1985b, p. 85).

38 Numerous studies discuss this difficulty, and the priority of what is one by virtue of *φύσις* is frequently mentioned. See for example Carey 1989, which sets out to demonstrate that the transitions in *Olymp.* 8. 52–55 and *Nem.* 5. 37–42 are 'natural' (p. 287).

39 *Cf.* also *Met.* I 1, 1052 a22–28 and *Phys.* VIII 9.

40 Tr. Kirwan ^{2}1993, p. 38.

This passage introduces—so much is clear—a hierarchy of unities into the discussion. Whereas everything that possesses extension and continuity is 'one' in a certain sense—this has already been said in 1015 b36 ff.—there is also a respect in which such an object does not yet have to be 'one', namely when it does not make a whole; and this condition, making a whole, is not fulfilled if it does not have its own εἶδος. In Aristotle's example, the unity of the shoe is only given for the observer when the εἶδος of the shoe is also present. Here, 'being a shoe' and 'having the εἶδος of a shoe' are co-extensive conditions: *ὥστε ὑπόδημα εἶναι καὶ εἶδός τι ἔχειν ἤδη ἕν*. With this assertion, Aristotle binds his discussion of unity at this point to the centre of his ontology, for to the extent that the εἶδος of an object is identical with its *οὐσία*—as *Metaphysics* Δ 8, 1017 b24 f. lays down—the unity constituted by the εἶδος is at the same time a necessary condition for its (the object's) existence as something specific.[41]

Now: what *is* an εἶδος? The question gives rise to a certain embarrassment. To ask for the definition, the essence or the *τί ἦν εἶναι* of the εἶδος is, according to what has just been said, obviously the same thing as to ask for the εἶδος of the εἶδος. Such an undertaking accordingly presupposes the unity of the εἶδος as a concept, but this says no more than that we have to assume that the εἶδος *has* an εἶδος. The infinite regression that we observed as a constant threat in the Aristotelian discussion of the unity of continuity appears to return here, a troubling circumstance when we consider the rich sedimentation of the term under discussion in the history of metaphysics, from its foundational role in the ontology of Plato's academy all the way through to its still powerful complicity in the truth of being as disclosure in Heidegger.[42] The tendency to endlessness is also not neutralised if we recall that the word (ϝ)εἶδος comes from the indo-European root **vid-* for 'see', and that, in Homer, it means the visible form of an object or a person; it is the opposite of what one does not or cannot see, for example a person's thoughts.[43] The εἶδος is the outline that one sees—it is certainly no accident that Aristotle in the case of the shoe adopts the perspec-

[41] On the connection between τὸ ὄν and τὸ ἕν, see also *Met.* Γ 2 and Gloy 1985.

[42] See for example § 7 of *Sein und Zeit* (Heidegger [18]2001, pp. 27–39, Engl. pp. 49–63) where Heidegger develops his approach to ontology on the basis of the notions of 'appearance' (*Schein*), the 'manifest' (*das, was sich zeigt, das Sichzeigende, das Offenbare*) with its explicit connection to light and visibility, and truth as 'disclosure' (*Unverborgenheit*).

[43] *Cf.* Dickson 1988 for Pindar's deconstruction of this etymologically plausible opposition in the *Eighth Olympian*.

tive of the spectator, ἰδόντες (1016 b14); Heidegger translates the word at more than one place as 'appearance' (*Aussehen*); Derrida speaks of a *figure de la visibilité intelligible*.[44] But what counts, here, is not the etymological wealth of this one lexeme, as if the word 'εἶδος' had the character of an indispensable signifier. We are concerned, rather, with marking a specific position within the Aristotelian system that enables it to function, without being grasped by or within this system itself.

We recapitulate the simplest definition the *Metaphysics* offers us. When the εἶδος becomes the criterion of the definition of individual things, it enters, in the logic of Aristotelian ontology, into an opposition with matter, ὕλη, which is as matter indeterminable because entirely undifferentiated. Only when the εἶδος is added can mere bronze become a bronze sphere; and whereas the moment the εἶδος vanishes, the sphere vanishes with it, this is not the case with the disappearance of the bronze, for a sphere can also consist of wood or stone. All the characteristics of things, all their determinability, definability and knowability are the result and product of their εἶδος. Aristotle himself makes a connection between the notion of the εἶδος and two other definitions of essence in *Met.* Z 7, 1032 b1: εἶδος δὲ λέγω τὸ τί ἦν εἶναι ἑκάστου καὶ τὴν πρώτην οὐσίαν.

Nevertheless: the mode of being of the εἶδος itself remains unclarified in these definitions as well. The εἶδος is here each time the πρώτη οὐσία of something else; as Wieland has pointed out, the problem of its own 'first essence' is not really solved in the *Metaphysics* at all.[45] The solution to the problem is nevertheless available. The εἶδος, according to *Metaphysics* Δ 17, is a kind of border (1022 a4–9):

> πέρας λέγεται τό τε ἔσχατον ἑκάστου καὶ οὗ ἔξω μηδὲν ἔστι λαβεῖν πρώτου καὶ οὗ ἔσω πάντα πρώτου, καὶ ὃ ἂν ᾖ εἶδος μεγέθους ἢ ἔχοντος μέγεθος, καὶ τὸ τέλος ἑκάστου [...] καὶ τὸ οὗ ἕνεκα καὶ ἡ οὐσία ἡ ἑκάστου καὶ τὸ τί ἦν εἶναι ἑκάστῳ.

> We call a 'limit': the terminus of each thing, i.e. the first thing outside which there is nothing to be found and the first thing inside which everything is to

44 Heidegger ^{8}2003 (first 1950), p. 19, and *cf.* 1954, p. 48; Derrida, 'La double séance' (= Derrida 1972a, pp. 215–346), p. 232, Engl. p. 189. On Derrida's notion of an 'intelligible visibility'—that is, a (or rather, the) notion of intelligibility in the sense of the presence of being, which therefore lays claim the structural attribute of visibility, the primary attribute of what is 'before our eyes' (*prae sensu*) and thus is itself 'there'—*cf.* Plato, *Resp.* 508 d ff. It is this ontological premise that leads to metaphors of the truth as *light* and its immediate apperception as *evidence*.

45 See Wieland ^{3}1992, p. 137.

> be found; and anything that is the form of a magnitude or of [something] possessing magnitude, and the fulfilment of each thing [...] i.e., that for which [change and action take place], and the substance of each thing, i.e. what it is to be each thing.[46]

As a border, the εἶδος possesses the status of a 'between': it enables an object to come into being by drawing a line between it and whatever does not belong to it but instead to its outside.[47] At the same time, the εἶδος is also responsible for the emergence of this outside, for there can only be an *outside*, the specific non-existence of an individual thing, if there is an *inside* whose border defines the area within which the non-existence of the thing does not hold. The border between the two is thus constitutive of both areas, both of what is and of what, in each specific case, is not.[48]

But is the kind of border that, according to Aristotle, the εἶδος is, a being? On the basis of the preceding remarks, that can scarcely be the case. The εἶδος cannot possess its own being for the simple reason that in this case it would have to become the inside or the outside of something else, and this something else would have to be separated from it by virtue of the function of an εἶδος. Wherever being is predicated of something, the εἶδος must always already ~~be~~ between it and its

[46] Tr. Kirwan ^{2}1993, p. 54.

[47] *Cf.* Kojève 1947, p. 491 n. 1: 'Parménide avait raison de dire que l'Être *est* et que le Néant *n'est pas* : mais il a oublié d'ajouter qu'*il y a* une « différence » entre le Néant et l'Être, qui *est* dans une certaine mesure au même titre que l'Être, puisque sans elle, s'il n'y avait pas de *différence* entre l'Être et le Néant, l'Être lui-même ne serait pas' (his italics; Engl. p. 221 n. 20). Kojève describes the situation here too simply (as we will soon see), but he already indicates the problematic status of the 'between' with respect to being and its ontological implications. The conceptual proximity of this observation to Derrida's later theory of *différance* (see in particular 'La différance' [= Derrida 1972b, pp. 1–29] p. 24 ff., Engl. p. 23 ff.) is unmistakeable.

[48] A connection between the problem of being and the border may already have been a principle of pre-Socratic thinking. Almost the only fragment of Anaximander that survives (DK 12 B 1) asserts that the originary principle of being is 'the infinite', *τὸ ἄπειρον*. Buchheim 1994, pp. 56–74 suggests that this hypothesis is not to be understood as just another position in the Presocratic discussion of substantialistic *ἀρχαί*—on a level with Thales' thesis that the first principle is water—but rather as the recognition that the phenomenal world can only emerge as the differentiation or mutual bordering of things against the background of a theoretically possible condition of absolute undifferentiation. On this argument, Anaximander's insight is that beings only emerge by means of their delimitation from a logically prior state of non-existence as limitlessness. Hegel recapitulates this problem and the progression from undifferentiation to definition and quality in his discussion of time and space in the second part of the *Enzyklopädie*, § 254 ff.: see Hegel 1969–1971, vol. 9, p. 41 ff. and Derrida 1972b, p. 44 ff., Engl. p. 40 ff.

other and outside.[49] But the border is also not a non-being, for it first constitutes this 'outside' of what *is* by separating a being from its specific non-being. Its function is that of pure difference: in belonging neither to the inside nor to the outside, it ~~is~~ prior to them both as their condition of possibility. The εἶδος as πέρας precedes the difference between being and non-being; without itself being a being, it determines the Being of being.

The consequences of this situation for the concept—and the specific constitution of the concept—of unity will be clear. It seems immediately plausible that the unity of an object is connected to its border and the separation between the object and what lies outside of it. To the extent that the concept of the εἶδος in its connection with ordinary language and in its opposition to material, ὕλη, presupposes a visible border between an object and its surroundings, an object without an εἶδος cannot be a single object, but must rather be either several objects or a fragment that is constituted only by means of its relationship to the greater whole of which it is a part. The shoe, however, is only *a* shoe if its unity is not only distinct from the non-unity of its mere parts, the fragments of its self, but also from the endless diversity of the world beyond the conditions of its own existence. The shoe is not *a* shoe if the field of its unity is indeterminable because it is not finite, but endless. The determinable finiteness of what is 'one' is thus a central component of this definition of unity. It is this consideration that determines the central categories of unity in the *Poetics*.

There, Aristotle defines tragedy, as remarked above, by means of the notions of wholeness, closure and the magnitude of the action it depicts (*Poet.* 7, 1450 b23–25). The fact that the magnitude is not accidental depends directly on the possibility and presence of a border to an outside: only what has limits has an extension that can be deter-

49 Heidegger 2002, p. 89 recognizes this when he writes on τέλειον in *Metaphysics* Δ 16 (which he understands in the sense of τὸ τελειοῦν): 'Wenn wir zusammenfassen, so ist primär festzuhalten: Τέλος hat die Bestimmung von *Grenze* [...]. Hier müssen wir aber vorsichtig sein. Ein Pfad durch eine Wiese hört auf bei einem Gartenzaun. Der Gartenzaun ist aber nicht τέλειον. Das Pfad-Sein als solches ist nicht bestimmt durch den Gartenzaun. Das, wobei der Pfad aufhört, ist selbst ein Seiendes, das in derselben Weise ist wie das, was bei ihm aufhört. Vermutlich ist τέλειον nicht ein Seiendes, ein Stück des Seienden, dessen Ende es ausmacht, sondern τέλειον ist ein *Sein*, eine *Weise des Seins selbst*. Τέλειον ist Grenze nicht als ein Seiendes zu einem Seienden, dessen Grenze es ist [...]. Das τέλειον ist eine Bestimmung des Seins des Seienden und nicht irgendeine Eigenschaft wie etwa weiß oder schwarz. Das Worüber-hinaus-nichts hat den Charakter der Grenze im Sinne einer Bestimmung des Seins' (his italics, my spacing). *Cf.* Derrida 1978, p. 93: 'Il *y a* du cadre, mais le cadre *n'existe pas*' (his italics).

mined. The demand for *τι μέγεθος* is thus based—as opposed to what, at first glance, appears to be the case—only secondarily on the psychological limitations of the audience; rather, it belongs, prior to all contingent performance-conditions, to the ontological definition of a mimetic text. But the two concepts of *τὸ ὅλον* and *τὸ τέλειον* are also constitutively dependent on the *πέρας*. In *Metaphysics* Δ 26, Aristotle offers two definitions for *τὸ ὅλον*: it is either something that does not lack any part belonging to it by nature—here, the natural composition of a thing is understood as a determinable or limitable field of pertinence—or something that comprises its content in such a way that it becomes one—here, the determinacy of the inside becomes the condition of totality.[50] Aristotle repeats the first definition, although without recourse to the notion of *φύσις*, in his definition of the relationship between the part and the whole at the end of *Poetics* 8 (1451 a32–35): 'The several incidents of the actions (*sc.* must be) so closely connected that the transposition or withdrawal of any one of them will disjoin and dislocate the whole. For that which makes no perceptible difference by its presence or absence is no real part of the whole.'[51] Here, it is even truer that the whole is essentially constituted by means of its border: 'Now a whole', we read immediately after the definition of tragedy at the beginning of the seventh chapter (1450 b26 f.), 'has a beginning, a middle and end.'[52]

In the *Poetics*, the concepts of *τὸ ὅλον* and *τὸ τέλειον* are not easily separated.[53] Both terms imply each other and share their determinacy by means of the border. The same connection becomes explicit in the *Metaphysics* when Aristotle defines *τὸ τέλειον* in Δ 16, for here he must again have recourse to the categories of inside and outside and to the border between the two of them (1021 b12–17):

> *τέλειον λέγεται ἓν μὲν οὗ μὴ ἔστιν ἔξω τι λαβεῖν μηδὲ ἓν μορίον (οἷον χρόνος τέλειος ἑκάστου οὗτος οὗ μὴ ἔστιν ἔξω λαβεῖν χρόνον τινὰ ὃς τούτου μέρος ἐστὶ τοῦ χρόνου) καὶ τὸ κατ' ἀρετὴν καὶ τὸ εὖ μὴ ἔχον ὑπερβολὴν πρὸς τὸ γένος, οἷον τέλειος ἰατρὸς καὶ τέλειος αὐλητὴς ὅταν κατὰ τὸ εἶδος τῆς οἰκείας ἀρετῆς μηθὲν ἐλλείπωσιν.*

50 *Cf. Met.* Δ 26, 1023 b26–36.

51 *τὰ μέρη* (*sc. χρὴ*) *συνεστάναι τῶν πραγμάτων οὕτως ὥστε μετατιθεμένου τινὸς μέρους ἢ ἀφαιρομένου διαφέρεσθαι καὶ κινεῖσθαι τὸ ὅλον· ὃ γὰρ προσὸν ἢ μὴ προσὸν μηδὲν ποιεῖ ἐπίδηλον, οὐδὲν μόριον τοῦ ὅλου ἐστίν*, tr. Bywater in Barnes 1984, p. 2322 modified.

52 *ὅλον δέ ἐστιν τὸ ἔχον ἀρχὴν καὶ μέσον καὶ τελευτήν*, tr. *id. ibid.*

53 Of the four passages in which we encounter *τέλειος* in the *Poetics*, it appears in two of them together with *ὅλος* (1450 b24, 1459 a19); in the other two, it is not clear that *ὅλος* could not easily be substituted for it (1449 b25, 1452 a2).

> We call 'complete', in one sense, that outside which not even one portion is to be found (as for instance the complete time of each thing is that outside which there is no time to be found which is part of that time); also, that which in respect of excellence and goodness cannot be surpassed relative to its genus, as for instance a doctor is complete and a flautist is complete when they are without deficiency in respect of the form of their own proper excellence.[54]

The closure of the represented action can only be determined if we already know what belongs to the inside of the object, that is, where the border lies. (That is true not only for its extension in time and space, but also for ἀρετή, since here too it must be clear from the very beginning what belongs to the specific virtue of a person by nature—οἰκείας fulfils the same function in this definition as φύσει in the definition of τὸ ὅλον in Δ 26, 1023 b35.) The transference of this condition to the material of literature, as it is undertaken in the *Poetics*, thus demonstrates the necessity of drawing borders. A tragedy only fulfils the conditions of its essential being if it is one—and that means, according to the ontology of the *Metaphysics*, if it participates in the structures of the material/form-dichotomy that prescribe the border as the *condicio sine qua non* of the Being of a specific being.[55] It must therefore be possible to know where the text begins and where it finishes, at what point it separates and distinguishes itself from its other and its outside. In the discourse of the *Poetics*, this distinction is the basis of the aesthetic quality of a mimetic-referential text; in the *Metaphysics*, its existence as a single whole depends on it.[56]

54 Tr. Kirwan ²1993, p. 53, my brackets following Jaeger's edition.

55 Kyriakou 1993, p. 345 n. 5 notes that alongside the typical examples in the *Metaphysics*—stone, wood, *etc.*—a πρᾶξις can also serve in Aristotle as a ὕλη, for example in *EN* V 14, 1137 b13–19, where the πρᾶξις is the ὕλη of a νόμος. On the implications of this passage for the notion of ὕλη, *cf.* Happ 1971, p. 706 f.

56 I give here the third variant named in the summary of *Met.* Δ 1016 b6–11 for the sake of completeness: it is the unity of the λόγος. Aristotle refers here to a definition he has given in 1016 a23–b1: ἔτι δὲ ἓν λέγεται ὅσων ὁ λόγος ὁ τὸ τί ἦν εἶναι λέγων ἀδιαίρετος πρὸς ἄλλον τὸν δηλοῦντα [τί ἦν εἶναι] (*del.* Ross) τὸ πρᾶγμα [...]. οὕτω γὰρ καὶ τὸ ηὐξημένον καὶ φθῖνον ἕν ἐστιν, ὅτι λόγος εἷς, ὥσπερ ἐπὶ τῶν ἐπιπέδων ὁ τοῦ εἴδους. This definition appears to imply a difference analogous to Frege's distinction between *Sinn* and *Bedeutung* (see Frege 1892, p. 26 f.): expressed in the German philosopher's terms, Aristotle is saying that something is 'one' if two λόγοι that each have their own *Sinn*, that is, name a specific and different mode of being, both possess the same *Bedeutung*, that is, refer to the same object such that with respect to this object they cannot be distinguished from each other. On ἀδιαίρετος πρός in this sense, *cf. De anima* Γ 2, 427 a2 and 6 and Ross 1924, vol. I, p. 303 *ad loc.* Aristotle's example in *Met.* Δ is a geometric figure that can be drawn with a larger (ηὐξημένον) or a smaller (φθῖνον) diagram without

On the basis of this discussion, the presuppositions and implications of 'unity' in literary studies become somewhat clearer. Behind the problem of unity is the question of the essence of a text (and thus of interpretation) altogether. Textual unity is only possible if there can be a clear border between a text and its other.[57] Where that is not the case, the logical subject of the thesis of unity loses itself in endlessness: it is only possible to say that something is 'one' if this 'something' can be clearly defined and distinguished from other entities, which thus become the 'outside' of the unity. If this drawing of borders turns out, however, to be impossible, then the question arises as to whether the category 'unified' can be predicated of an existing subject at all.

The transfer of the ὕλη/εἶδος-structure to literature, the adoption of this structure by literary studies has, however, a further implication. Aristotle not only lays with this structure the foundation for an aesthetics whose basic categories are material and form, content and

the unity of the figure which is meant—*τὸ πρᾶγμα*—being destroyed. The unity of the λόγος is thus the unity of identity. What the larger and the smaller triangle *mean* is the triangle *as such*, which is, in both diagrams, the same. In principle, this definition of unity corresponds to Frege's distinction, since here too the two λόγοι are indistinguishable with respect to their referential relationship to *τὸ πρᾶγμα*. In this way, the unity of the λόγος designates the possibility of saying different things but meaning the same thing. It is therefore not surprising when a few pages later Aristotle writes that 'identity', *ταυτότης*, is that kind of unity which is either predicated of more than one subject or of one subject viewed as though it was more than one (*Met.* Δ 9, 1018 a7 ff.). On identity see further *Top.* I 7, 103 a6 ff. (esp. 103 a9–10) and *Met.* I 3, 1054 a20 ff. It is evident that the unity of a literary text can also be thought of as the identity of its object, and is indeed frequently thought of in this way. Every construction of unity in literary studies based on the possibility that the text says the same thing at more than one place relies on this notion of unity. Theories that take this possibility as their point of departure lead to an understanding of the text as the realization of a structure: *τὸ πρᾶγμα*—what it is really all about—is expressed at different places in a different way. The connections made between these passages on the basis of their fundamental identity and the relationships of proximity and distance that they thus enter into give rise to the structure of the text. In Pindaric studies, we could see this working in the theories of Dissen [2]1843, esp. XLV–LXII, Mezger 1880 or even Schadewaldt 1966 on the structure of the epinicians. Bundy's readings of the *First Isthmian* and the *Eleventh Olympian* in the *Studia Pindarica* make use, as we saw above, of the distinction between basic (true) identity and epiphenomenal difference. On Bundy as a structuralist, see above, p. 68 n. 21.

[57] *Cf.* also Friedrich Schlegel's definition of the work of art—'Gebildet ist ein Werk, wenn es überall scharf begrenzt, innerhalb der Grenzen aber grenzenlos und unerschöpflich ist [...]' (*Athenäums-Fragmente* [1798], no. 297; = Schlegel 1958–, vol. II, p. 215)—and Heidegger [8]2003, p. 51 und pp. 69–72. Most's reading of the Simonides-interpretation in Plato's *Protagoras* (Most 1994) emphasizes the systematic meaning of contexts—of what is *outside* the poem—for the interpretations that it is subject to in the course of the dialogue.

expression, or indeed meaning and rhetoric, and which has dominated the theory of art and literature since antiquity. To the extent that the question of the being of the border itself has remained unsolved in metaphysics, the transference of the opposition between content and form and the notion of unity it implies to literature also introduces a theoretical instability into the project of interpretation whose source is the indeterminacy of the being of the border in this opposition. Literary studies cannot 'solve' this problem, because the presuppositions that lead to it are indispensable for its own self-understanding as ἐπιστήμη. At the same time, however, this situation leads us to suspect that here tensions may arise between interpretation and its object, literature. 'Philosophy', writes Paul de Man in a study of Nietzsche's *Ueber Wahrheit und Lüge im aussermoralischen Sinne*, 'turns out to be an endless reflection on its own destruction at the hands of literature.'[58] Will the destruction of philosophy at the hands of literature not take place first and foremost in literary studies?

The parergon, the fold

Pindar, at any rate, seems to understand clearly the importance of the border between the inside of the text and its specific outside, and he formulates this distinction according to all the criteria of definability and indefinability that our reading of Aristotle's *Metaphysics* has led us to expect. The *Second Olympia*, an ode celebrating Theron, the tyrant of Akragas who won a chariot victory in 476, begins with the words:

Ἀναξιφόρμιγγες ὕμνοι,
τίνα θεόν, τίν' ἥρωα, τίνα δ' ἄνδρα κελαδήσομεν;
ἤτοι Πίσα μὲν Διός· Ὀλυμπιάδα δ' ἔστασεν Ἡρακλέης
ἀκρόθινα πολέμου·
Θήρωνα δὲ τετραορίας ἕνεκα νικαφόρου
γεγωνητέον [...]

Hymns that rule the lyre,
what god, what hero, what man shall we celebrate?
Indeed, Pisa belongs to Zeus; and Olympia was founded by Herakles
as the first fruits of war;
but on account of his victorious four-horse chariot, Theron
must be proclaimed [...]

[58] De Man 1979, p. 115.

Following the invocation of the hymns in *general*, an invocation enabled by their existence and presence before and outside of the text which begins here, the singer raises the question of his topic: given the undefined number of possible topics, the one chosen theme will serve to distinguish this song from all others and to realize it as a *specific* text. We are dealing here not primarily with the difference between the genre *ὕνμοι* and the single exemplar, but rather with the relationship between a text and all of its possible alternatives, thus between one unity and other possible unities on the same categorial level. The necessary differentiation of the one song to be sung is carried out by means of the identification of the god (Zeus), the hero (Herakles), and the man (Theron) to be celebrated, and thus takes place in terms of reference: in order to draw a border around the text and its specific other, we must, the ode suggests, establish a clear relationship between it and one or more unambiguously identifiable (since categorially distinguishable) non-linguistic entities outside of it that precede it in time and are therefore potential topics.[59] The possibility of different texts is thus the corollary of the categorial distribution of its possible subjects; the borders of the songs towards each other are crucially conditioned by the borders of the things to which they refer. But this bordering by means of reference is taken back at the end of the ode, when the singer is confronted with the endlessness of what, in principle, could still be said (90–100):

ἐπί τοι
Ἀκράγαντι τανύσαις
αὐδάσομαι ἐνόρκιον λόγον ἀλαθεῖ νόῳ,

[59] *Cf.* the description of the relationship between the daughters of Cadmus and the narrative concerning them as one of anteriority in verse 22 f.: *ἕπεται δὲ λόγος εὐθρόνοις* | *Κάδμοιο κούραις*. On the notion of reference this implies, see Searle 1969, pp. 72–97. Searle argues that whereas successful reference does presuppose the existence of the referential object, it does not require this existence to be temporally prior to the referring signifier. Since one can successfully refer not only to objects that once existed in the past, but also to objects that will exist one day in the future, 'existence', as the condition of reference, must be understood *atemporally* (*ibid.*, p. 77 n. 1). But as his discussion of proper names shows (p. 75 f.), Searle understands the past and the future as past and future *presence*: the past *was* once *there*, just as the future will one day *be there*. This fundamental presence, whose atemporality changes nothing about its ontological priority to the utterance which refers to it, must be given in order for reference—which thus recapitulates in structure the Platonic concept of mimesis: *cf. Philebus* 38 e–39 e—to take place. See further de Man 1979, p. 106 and 121, Derrida 1972a, p. 234 ff., Engl. p. 190 ff., and Schleifer 1985. On Pindar's insistence on reference in this sense, see Most 1985b, p. 156.

τεκεῖν μή τιν' ἑκατόν γε ἐτέων πόλιν φίλοις ἄνδρα μᾶλλον
εὐεργέταν πραπίσιν ἀφθονέστερόν τε χέρα
Θήρωνος. ἀλλ' αἶνον ἐπέβα κόρος
οὐ δίκᾳ συναντόμενος, ἀλλὰ μάργων ὑπ' ἀνδρῶν,
τὸ λαλαγῆσαι θέλων κρυφόν τε θέμεν ἐσλῶν καλοῖς
ἔργοις· ἐπεὶ ψάμμος ἀριθμὸν περιπέφευγεν,
καὶ κεῖνος ὅσα χάρματ' ἄλλοις ἔθηκεν,
τίς ἂν φράσαι δύναιτο;[60]

Yes,
bending the bow at Akragas
I will proclaim a statement on oath with a truthful mind,
that no city within a century has produced a man more beneficent to his friends
in spirit and more generous of hand than
Theron. But enough: upon praise comes tedious excess,
which does not keep to just limits, but at the instigation
of greedy men is eager to prattle on and obscure noble men's good
deeds; for grains of sand escape counting,
and all the joys which that man has wrought for others,
who could declare them?[61]

The immediate end of the song is justified with two arguments. First, the verses 95–98a point to the danger of satiation and the fact that the topic is obscured if singers do not know when to stop praising.[62] The passage that follows is usually read as a conventional rhetorical phrase ('there too many good things to say for someone to be able to say them'). This interpretation can be supported by numerous parallels in the epinicians, for example in the *Sixth Isthmian*, whose myth breaks off with the statement that it would take too long to narrate all the heroic deeds of Herakles and Telamon, or in the *Fourth Nemean*, where the story of Aiakos' son Peleus is cut short with the assertion that there is no way to go through the entire history of the

[60] In verse 97 SM print *θέλον* (following Coppola) and *τιθέμεν* (following Hermann); I read *θέλων* and *τε θέμεν* with the mss. and Race 1997. See on this Wilamowitz 1922, p. 494 f., whose arguments against the article with *λαλαγῆσαι* do not take account of the fact that without it here the syntax is ambiguous, since the infinitive could then be read not only as the object of *θέμεν* but also as the predicate of *θέλων*. A clarification of the passage in the first sense can, as far as I can see, only take place by means of the articular infinitive. The function of the article is then entirely analogous to that attributed by Wilamowitz to *τό* in Soph., *OC* 442 (a verse he explicitly rejects as a parallel).

[61] Tr. Race 1997, vol. 1, p. 73 f.

[62] See Bundy 1986, p. 29 n. 71 and p. 90 n. 123.

sons of Aiakos.[63] The language-philosophical problem at the end of the *Second Olympian* becomes an epistemological one in the closing lines of the *Thirteenth Olympian*: here, the Oligaithid victories are so numerous that they are not merely incommunicable, but as a whole in fact *imperceptible*.[64] At all of these places, the conventional meaning of the figure is apparently obvious: like the sons of Aiakos and the Oligaithidai, Theron too has achieved too many good things for the singer, or indeed anyone, to be in a position to capture the totality of them all in a text.

Now in order to arrive at this immediately plausible result, one has to ignore for a moment the specific grammatical form of *Olymp.* 2. 99 f., a form that links these verses to the opening of the ode and thus the two ends of the text to each other. Like the first verses, the conclusion of the poem asks a question: who, faced with the *endlessness* of Theron's *χάρματα*, could represent their totality in language? We could already observe the theoretical principle at stake here in Aristotle: where there is no border, there can also be no unity. The rhetorical conventionality of the question means that it has no reference to anything in the world that is the case, that its 'reference' is in fact figurative or fictional. But this issue of non-referentiality is precisely what it addresses as a question: under precisely what circumstances can there be a *true* relationship between language and the world, if what is the case is, in its entirety (the condition of truth and of unity), unable to be represented in a text? In other words: we can use the figurality of the final verses of the *Second Olympian* to keep the question that they ask out of the proper meaning of the passage as mere rhetoric, but only on the condition that we are able to maintain the clear and exclusive opposition between 'figurative' language (*i.e.*, a compliment that can-

[63] On *Isthm.* 6. 56: *ἐμοὶ δὲ μακρὸν πάσας <ἀν>αγήσασθ' ἀρετάς*, see Hubbard 1985, p. 28, who sees *Pyth.* 4. 247 f. as a parallel, and Race 1990, p. 51, who compares *Olymp.* 2. 81–85. On *Nem.* 4. 69–72: *Γαδείρων τὸ πρὸς ζόφον οὐ περατόν· ἀπότρεπε | αὖτις Εὐρώπαν ποτὶ χέρσον ἔντεα ναός· | ἄπορα γὰρ λόγον Αἰακοῦ | παίδων τὸν ἅπαντά μοι διελθεῖν*, see Bundy 1986, p. 8 and 58 n. 54 (who notes the similarity of *Nem.* 10. 19 f. [see above, p. 71] and *Isthm.* 1. 60–64), Silk's analysis in Silk 1974, p. 114 n. 12, and Race 1990, p. 43 n. 4, who notes the stylistic use of asyndeton in the break-off formula. See also Gianotti 1975, p. 129 f.

[64] *Olymp.* 13. 112 f.: *καὶ πᾶσαν κάτα | Ἑλλάδ' εὑρήσεις ἐρευνῶν μάσσον' ἢ ὡς ἰδέμεν*, where the impossibility of synopsis, the simultaneous presence to sight of what is found, exacerbates the aporia of verses 44–46 in which the singer expresses his desperation in the face of the many achievements of Xenophanes' family by a comparison with the numberless grains of sand on the seashore: *δηρίομαι πολέσιν | περὶ πλήθει καλῶν· ὡς μὰν σαφές | οὐκ ἂν εἰδείην λέγειν ποντιᾶν ψάφων ἀριθμόν.*

not be a literal question and therefore should not be read referentially) and 'literal' language (the problem of the limits of reference), that enables this exclusion.[65] We were already able to observe in Chapter 3, however, the uncertainty of this distinction in the *First Olympian*. There, the transcendental point of truth, the only place from which the distinction between figurality and literality could be made, turned out to be itself the effect of a rhetorical figure—an anti-*Aufhebung* in which precisely the wrong term, the term standing for materiality and outwardness, returned to encompass itself and its other at the next level of analysis. Here, in the ode for Theron, we are confronted with a situation in which the other, 'non-rhetorical' side of the compliment, the suggestion that the totality is in fact incommunicable, becomes both its alternative and, at the same time, its presupposition.

Nevertheless: the integrity of the *Second Olympian* is not seriously impaired by this curious oscillation. If the specific unity of the song is dependent on the determinacy of its reference, and this reference must be directed towards an outside in order to allow the necessary border between the text and its possible objects of reference to emerge, then in order to identify or assess the unity of the text we will need to know where this border between the text and its other runs, and this is of course exactly what the verses in question signal. The moment the topic of the song threatens to transgress its boundaries and become endless, the text itself ceases: it does not attempt to speak to us from outside itself. The interpretative demand for presence and the Aristotelian requirement of clear definition both seem to be fulfilled.

This simple situation is called radically into question only eight years later in a poem that performs and subverts the ἀρχή (both the origin and the domain of sovereignty) in a particularly subtle fashion. It is the *Sixth Olympian*, composed for Hagesias, a Syracusan with family in Stymphalos, who won the mule race in 468. The poem has been seen for the most part as unproblematic, ever since the late nineteenth century rejected the thesis that the text refers to the victor's immanent migration from Arcadia to Syracuse and that the name 'Aeneas' in verse 88 is that of the Trojan hero, whose legendary journey into the west is to be read as a metaphor for one of Hagesias' own.[66] Studies undertaken in the twentieth century typically stress the

[65] On the problems raised by the interpretation of rhetorical questions, see de Man 1979, pp. 9–12 and above, p. 51 ff.

[66] This was the interpretation put forward in Bornemann 1889; Jurenka refuted it in 1893. On both scholars see Young 1970, pp. 42–45.

lightness of the song, its clarity and simplicity.[67] Accordingly, most analyses identify the three phases of the programme traditional since Schadewaldt: 'praise of the victor' (the verses 1 to 21, the entire first triad), then, after a transition (verses 22 to 28), the 'myth' (verses 29 to 70), and finally the 'second praise of the victor' with the singer-poet's self-apostrophe and prayer for Hagesias' two home towns and the song itself (verses 71 through to the end). The myth itself, the story of Iamos, Hegesias' putative ancestor, appears to be immediately relevant to the occasion, a clear part of the evocation of his inborn or inherited fame or κλέος, possibly with an allusion to the cult of Persephone, particularly important in Sicily.[68] The richly metaphorical proem of the song has tended to play a subordinate role in these interpretations, as befits the relegation of figurative language to the metaphorical margins of the text.[69] It is, since Dornseiff at the latest, an almost classic example of Pindar's allegedly typical 'impressive openings' lacking any organic connection to the rest of the song at all in an almost programmatic fashion:[70]

67 See for example Friis Johansen 1973 ('What we have before us is a poem with a clear and not too subtle unity of subject [...] and which (like some other Pindaric epinicia) should not be taken too seriously', p. 9). Garner 1992 reads the text in the context of the mystery religions. His conclusion: 'As for *Olympia* 6, the poem is unified around a simple message: the victor is blessed in this world, assured immortality in song, and implicated in eternal bliss through a cult of Persephone' (p. 66).

68 On κλέος see Goldhill 1991, p. 157 and Kurke 1991, p. 147 f.; on the cult of Persephone, see Garner 1992, *passim*.

69 Boeckh 1811–1821, vol. II ii, p. 154 offers only a Latin paraphrase ('*Ut aedes magnificae vestibulo columnis ornato augentur, ita carminis exordium splendidum facientes Agesiam Olympicum dicimus victorem* [...]'), Dissen [2]1847, p. 71 f. sees a reference to Hagesias' house ('*Quod per totum hunc librum videbimus, Pindarum comparationes accommodare rebus praesentibus, vel inprimis hic tenendum est, ne aliena inferamus pulcherrimo prooemio* [...]'). For Schadewaldt 1966, p. 271, Pindar declares allegiance in 3 f. to the poetological principle 'daß das reiche Können des Dichters sich nach der Satzung gerade im Prooimion kräftig entfalten sollte'; he is followed by Farnell 1932, p. 40 *ad loc.* An equally poetological interpretation is argued by Bundy 1986, p. 71 n. 91, who, however, on the basis of his different concept of rhetoric (see above, p. 61 ff.), identifies the principle involved differently: 'Here [...] the laudator prefers the virtues of clarity and force to those of allusiveness and insinuation' (and *cf.* Bundy 1986, p. 55 with n. 49).

70 Dornseiff 1921, p. 133 and *cf.* Young 1970, pp. 48–52 and Köhnken 1985, p. 71. Willcock 1995 re-emphasizes this lack of connection with the notion of the 'opening flourish'. See esp. p. 12: 'In content, the odes consist *essentially* of three ingredients [...]' (my italics); further below we find: 'The typical ode is structured in five parts. First comes a striking, attention-demanding opening'. Then *Olymp.* 5 is quoted in order to anchor this division of the text in Pindar's own poetics. In Willcock's individual outlines of the songs, the beginning is then designated as the 'opening flourish' in *Nem.* 4. 1–8

Χρυσέας ὑποστάσαντες εὐτειχεῖ προθύρῳ θαλάμου
κίονας ὡς ὅτε θαητὸν μέγαρον
πάξομεν· ἀρχομένου δ' ἔργου πρόσωπον
χρὴ θέμεν τηλαυγές.

We will build golden columns, setting them up to support the well-walled porch of a chamber,
as if we were to build a palace worth looking at;
for when one begins a work,
one must make its front shine from afar.

There has been a broad consensus about the meaning of this beginning ever since the scholia. 'The poet speaks figuratively', we are told in one ancient or Byzantine commentary, 'like the builder of a magnificent house in having composed the victory ode. He compares the proem to a porch, the hymn to the whole house, and himself to the builder.'[71] Pindar's odes use architectural metaphors for songs at other places, perhaps most impressively at the beginning of the *Sixth Pythian*; it seems by no means far-fetched to adopt such an interpretation here.[72] Nevertheless, questions arise.

The metaphor of the megaron designates the text initially as a space. This space is constituted by having an edge or side, apparently identical to the porch or the columns, that can be seen from far beyond the space.[73] Two areas are thus created by the metaphor: an inside, which stands for the song, and an outside that is defined by the fact

on p. 93; just the 'opening' in *Olymp.* 7. 1–12 at p. 111; and the 'striking opening' in *Olymp.* 2. 1–7 on p. 135.

[71] ἀλληγορεῖ ὁ ποιητὴς ὡς ἐπὶ οἰκίας μεγαλοπρεποῦς κατασκευαστὴς τὸν ἐπίνικον διατεθειμένος. παραβάλλει δὲ προπυλαίῳ μὲν τὸ προοίμιον, τῷ δὲ ὅλῳ οἴκῳ τὸν ὕμνον, ἑαυτὸν δὲ τῷ κατασκευάζοντι. Σ *Olymp.* 6. 1a Dr.

[72] On architectonic metaphors in Pindar in general, see Schadewaldt 1966, p. 217 and *cf. Pyth.* 1. 1–4 κάλλιστον αἱ μεγαλοπόλιες Ἀθᾶναι προοίμιον Ἀλκμανιδᾶν εὐρυσθενεῖ γενεᾷ κρηπῖδ' ἀοιδᾶν ἵπποισι βαλέσθαι. The *Sixth Olympian* will end with a metaphor drawn from the sphere of *natural* growth: ἐμῶν δ' ὕμνων ἄεξ' εὐτερπὲς ἄνθος, 105.

[73] According to Goldhill 1991, p. 147, πρόσωπον is 'a very rare and thus emphatic metaphor', which he interprets as a strongly anthropomorphic transition term from the magnificent megaron to the magnificence of the victor. The word is used similarly in *Pyth.* 6. 14. There has been some debate about whether the term designates the side by which one entered a building or merely the side one saw approaching it from any given direction. Wilamowitz 1922, p. 139 f. cites Eur., *Ion* 188 f. as a parallel: the chorus speaks of 'double *prosopa*' (διδύμων προσώπων) which they see in Delphi before describing the scenes of gods and myths on them. Since however the Gigantomachy to which they explicitly refer was on the north side of the Treasury of Siphnians facing the Sacred Way and not on the entrance side to the west, the πρόσωπον is the side seen by an observer, regardless of what side this then happens to be.

that it stops where the song begins.

Now at the interface of this beginning stand the columns, or rather the porch that they support. They serve to mark the difference between the inside and the outside. But here the question arises: to which of the two categories do they belong? Are the columns a part of the building, that is, a part of the hypothetical megaron? Or are they only a kind of preliminary construction that does not really belong in any integral sense to the actual work, the ἔργον? Wilamowitz's commentary on this passage reflects the problematic status of the metaphor. It is, he writes, the poet's 'confession' (*Eingeständnis*) that the relationship of the proem to the poem is like that of a porch to a house.[74] What that means becomes clear in Dornseiff, who cites Aristotle's *Rhetoric* for the thesis that a poet 'can readily attach [as a proem] whatever happens to occur to him at any given moment'.[75] What Pindar therefore has to 'confess' here is that the identity of the text proper is constituted by factors and traits that are not contained by the opening passage and to which it can demonstrate no substantial or structural connection. The problematic status of the proem with a view to the 'inside' of the ode becomes, for Wilamowitz, readable in the metaphor of the columns: it is not organic, somewhat artificially grafted, even if, as he is concerned to point out, the passage shows 'careful and successful work'.[76] The implicit construction of unity itself leads to the opening of the song being excluded, removed from the 'real' text.

The reservations expressed here by Wilamowitz and Dornseiff are the product of aesthetic theories based on the notion of quasi-organic unity.[77] It is nevertheless worthwhile, before we consign the proem without further ado to the inside of the megaron, to look at the passage a little more closely. For the megaron is not, in fact, built: it is part of a hypothetical comparison contrary to fact and explicitly marked as such

[74] Wilamowitz 1922, p. 310.

[75] 'Das Prooimion ist beim γένος πανηγυρικόν unerläßlich. Es liegt in der Sache begründet, daß man bei so einem delikaten Beginnen wie dem Loben von Personen nicht mit der Tür ins Haus fällt. Aber die Wahl des Eingangs steht vollkommen frei. Aristotl. rhet. III, 14 meint, man könne ohne weiteres anbringen, was einem gerade in den Sinn kommt.' Dornseiff 1921, p. 116, my translation. This passage—*Rhet.* III 14, 1414 b28—is also quoted by Bundy 1986, p. 43 n. 26. Interestingly, Aristotle speaks here of ἐκτοπίζειν, of removing oneself from the place of the real topic. Here too the spatiality of the topic is the prerequisite for the distinction between inside and outside.

[76] *Cf.* Wilamowitz 1922, p. 162 n. 1 on *Nem.* 27 ff.: '[Aias'] Lob wird auf Grund eines Skolion breit ausgeführt, wirklich nur als ein anorganisch aufgesetztes Schmuckstück.'

[77] See above, p. 104 ff.

(ὡς ὅτε, 'as if').[78] The only thing to be built is the porch together with its columns, and this *in the future*: πάξομεν, 'we *will build*'.

Now this at first surprising future belongs to a group of *futura* in the epinicians whose function has repeatedly been the subject of research.[79] This group consists of verbs, mostly *verba dicendi* or verbs which can readily be interpreted as metaphors for *verba dicendi*, at places where one would rather expect a present. One of the most difficult examples is *Pythian* 9. 71–75:

> καί νυν ἐν Πυθῶνί νιν ἀγαθέᾳ Καρνειάδα
> υἱὸς εὐθαλεῖ συνέμειξε τύχᾳ·
> ἔνθα νικάσαις ἀνέφανε Κυράναν, ἅ νιν εὔφρων δέξεται
> καλλιγύναικι πάτρᾳ
> δόξαν ἱμερτὰν ἀγαγόντ᾽ ἀπὸ Δελφῶν.

> And now, in divine Pytho, she has joined Karneiadas' son
> with flourishing good fortune;
> where in the moment of victory he made Kyrana glorious, and she *will welcome* him
> in his fatherland of beautiful women,
> having brought desirable fame from Delphi.

The singer tells us that Kyrana, the eponymous nymph of the victor Telesikrates' city, *will* welcome him after his victory. Normally, however, the victory odes are performed after the athlete's return to his πάτρα. Is Telesikrates' homecoming therefore still in the future? This was Boeckh's conclusion. But since nothing in the text speaks for a performance in Delphi (and the poem's length, amongst other things, speaks against it[80]), he argued that the song must have been written for a performance in Thebes.[81] That was dangerously close to an *argumentum ex silentio*. Apart from this passage, nothing suggests that this song

[78] *Cf. Isthm.* 6. 1. where ὡς ὅτε explicitly signals that the song is not performed at a 'thriving drinking party of men' (*pace* Dissen [in Boeckh 1811–1821, vol. II ii, p. 522] and, for different reasons, Thummer 1968, vol. 2, p. 100 *ad loc.*; the right interpretation is given by Privatera 1982, p. 90). *Cf.* however Hummel 1993, p. 331, § 411, who cites P. Monteil's translation of *Olymp.* 6. 2 as 'assemblons *une sorte de* palais magnifique' (*La phrase relative en grec ancien* [Paris, 1963], p. 277).

[79] Bundy 1986, p. 21 f. (who, however, does not mention this passage); Slater 1969a; Pfeijffer 1999a; see further the brief survey of research in D'Alessio 2004, pp. 272–276.

[80] See Gelzer 1985 for the characteristics of songs that were presumably performed directly after the ἀγῶνες at the festival sites.

[81] Boeckh 1811–1821, vol. II ii, p. 321, followed by Wilamowitz 1922, p. 263 ff. and Lesky ^{3}1971, p. 230.

was sung anywhere other than in Cyrene, and that is where most scholars have assumed it was performed.[82] But why, then, the future? For Bundy, δέξεται refers to nothing beyond the song itself: this and other such *futura* (he counts 18) 'refer without exception to the present, and only by treating a given ode in a philological vacuum can one refer them to a time beyond the occasion of the ode itself.'[83] Bundy is of course arguing here against interpretations such as Boeckh's which would relate the poem to an extra-textual reality and thus open its borders towards the outside (even if, paradoxically, this possibility is designated as a 'philological vacuum'). But if this is the case, why does the poet not write δέκεται?[84]

It is this question, amongst others, that Pfeijffer's *First Person Futures* attempts to answer. The Dutch scholar assigns δέξεται and 15 other *futura* to a group he calls '"fictional" futures announcing the ode as a whole': 'Such futures project the beginning of the performance to a future moment [...]. It is clear that such a presentation is fictional. It creates the illusion that the ode has not started yet.'[85] Pfeijffer understands this fiction as a part of the Pindaric interest in spontaneity, 'a concern that betrays itself [...] notably in the so-called 'break-off' passages, where the poet dramatizes his own role, staging himself as [...] intruding into his poem in order to break off a narrative.' The poet who violates the borders of his own work in order to stop a story imitates extemporary speech with a view to masking 'the formality of the

[82] Carey 1981, p. 65, D'Alessio 1994, p. 131 n. 47 and Gentili *et al.* 1995, pp. 233 and 238 are representative. Krummen 1990, p. 275 leaves the question open but considers a performance in the precincts of Iolaos in Thebes as a possibility. Felson 2004 arrives by means of an analysis of the deictic elements of the song at the conclusion that the text 'neither designate[s] nor contradict[s] the localization of th[e] poetic performance at Cyrene' (p. 367).

[83] Bundy 1986, p. 22.

[84] Carey 1981, p. 86 *ad loc.* explains the future on aesthetic grounds: 'In view of the extreme improbability of any local other than Cyrene for the performance, it is most reasonable to regard δέξεται as a dynamic substitute for the flat δέκεται, or even δέδεκται.'

[85] Pfeijffer 1999a, p. 33 (from which the following quotation is also taken). Into this category fall: *Olymp.* 6. 1–4 *πάξομεν*; *Olymp.* 10. 7–12 *τείσομεν*; *Pyth.* 9. 71–5 δέξεται; *Nem.* 3. 1–13 κοινώσομαι, ἕξει; *Nem.* 9. 1–10 κωμάσομεν, ὄρσομεν, ἐπασκήσω; *Isthm.* 1. 1–6 θήσομαι, ζεύξω; *Isthm.* 6. 74–5 πίσω; *Isthm.* 8. 1–8 δαμωσσόμεθα; *Pae.* 2. 1–4 [δι]ώξω; *Parth.* 2. 11 and 15 ὑμνήσω, μιμήσομ'. Comparable cases are Alcm., *fr.* 28 and 29 Davies and (probably) Theognis 943. On the (questionable) homogeneity of this group, see D'Alessio 2004, p. 275 f., who argues for a distinction between 'cases where the future announcement is compatible with a reference-point *during the performance* and those in which, with the *performance as a whole* set in the future, the temporal zero-point is incompatible with any moment during the performance' (p. 276, his italics).

occasion and the coldness of the contractual relationship' by presenting the praise of the victor in such a way that it appears 'voluntary'.[86] According to this thesis, *Pythian* 9. 71–75 performs a fictional procession or κῶμος from Delphi to Cyrene that is still underway and from whose perspective the reception of the victor in his home city is a prolepsis (more or less in Genette's sense).[87]

Now this highly plausible solution, on which I in no way want to cast doubt at this point,[88] achieves two things: it takes the future seriously whilst at the same time avoiding the otherwise unmotivated hypothesis of a Theban performance. But all this comes at a significant cost to the integrity of the borders of the text, a price that Pfeijffer nowhere explicitly discusses but that reveals itself in his metaphors of betrayal and intrusion. If the break-off formula is a break-in on the part of the speaker into the text, then the 'fictional future' is exactly the opposite: the place from which the speaker of the text says δέξεται must be placed outside of his own text, in a time in which the text as event is not yet taking place. If we now ask: when does the *Ninth Pythian* begin?, it must, on this logic, be possible to answer: before it has begun.[89]

The paradoxical nature of this situation, in which the speaker of the

86 Pfeijffer 1991, p. 33 f. D'Alessio 1994, p. 127 has some judicious remarks on this relationship between friendship and business. On simulated spontaneity in archaic literature in general, see Scodel 1996.

87 Pfeijffer 1999a, p. 41 (and *cf.* Gentili *et al.* 1995, p. 607 *ad loc.*). On prolepsis, see Genette 1972, p. 82 and pp. 105–115.

88 Or only a very little: Pfeijffer's specific hypothesis of a fictional κῶμος is not necessary in order to describe the effect of the passage. Felson 2004, p. 376 f. draws our attention to the fact that the deictic particles in verses 51–58—ἔνθα, 54, νῦν, 55 and ἵνα, 56a—appear in reverse order in the epode of the same triad, verses 67–75: ἵνα, 69, νῦν, 71 and ἔνθα, 73. In the first of the two passages, Chiron prophesies Kyrana's arrival in Libya; in the second, the speaker describes Telesikrates' homecoming. The future in verse 73a thus creates an analogy to the prophetic perspective of the centaur, as whose contemporary counterpart the singer positions himself. The future continues to affect the temporality of the ideal presence of the performance, however, in Felson's interpretation as well.

89 D'Alessio 2004 writes that 'Pindar […] dramatizes the process of [the songs'] creation – their history before their performance – even creating in some cases a *gap* between text and performance' (p. 279, his italics). This gap is what interests us here: it demonstrates the insufficiency of a theory of Pindaric unity that presupposes the identity of the text as the logical subject of unity and the presence of the performance. D'Alessio draws no theoretical consequences from this observation for the question of unity or the ontology of the text; *cf.* however Felson 2004, pp. 365–367, who continues to designate the loss of the original performance as an interpretative problem and the written text as the mere 'remains' (p. 367) of the originary fullness of the real song.

text calls its borders into question, emerges just as clearly in the *Sixth Olympian*. What is Pfeijffer's solution here? 'In [*Olympian* 6. 1–4] the image [...] has reference to the composition of an eye-catching proem, as the following sentence specifies. The future πάξομεν projects this construction of the proem into the future. Thus it is constitutive of the same proemial fiction as we have seen: it projects the beginning of the performance into the future.'[90] But here, as we have seen, the text names or refers to the constitutive function of its boundary at precisely this point. If now the beginning of the song is displaced into the future, this announcement of it is externalised: it no longer belongs to the space of the text, but must instead take place outside of it in order to point towards it from beyond its borders. The rhetorical force of the future complicates the border between text and context immensely; it imports the outside of the text into its inside and removes itself in the very same moment from just this text.[91]

The interpreter is faced with a situation here that reminds us once again of the passage quoted above from the *Kritik der Urteilskraft*.[92] In *La vérité en peinture*, Derrida investigates the status and logic of the 'parerga' listed there.[93] As the French philosopher shows, Kant requires the border between the inside and the outside of aesthetic judgements drawn in § 13 ('The pure judgement of taste is independent of charm and emotion') in order to be able to speak of aesthetic experiences at all. But the examples of *parerga* that follow in § 14 and amongst which we also find 'the colonnades of palaces' break down this distinction in both directions: they belong neither unambiguously to the outside of the work nor to its inside. Their role, like that of Aristotle's εἶδος, is that of pure difference: just as the frame serves to distinguish the picture from the wall on which it hangs—and so, considered from the perspective of the wall, belongs to the picture—so it is also, considered from the perspective of the picture, together with the wall a part of what surrounds it. The *parergon*, writes Derrida,

90 Pfeijffer 1999a, p. 40.

91 D'Alessio 2004, pp. 284–292 offers a survey of comparable passages in Pindar. *Olymp.* 6. 3 does not occur in it, perhaps because D'Alessio views this verse as an announcement of '*the rest of the ode* at the beginning' (p. 275, his italics). But this description would be inaccurate, since the future πάξομεν has as its object not the song, but merely the pillars, *i.e.*, the proem. What is announced here is thus not *the rest of the ode*, but rather only the interface between it and its outside.

92 See above, p. 149 f. We can safely assume that Kant's thought here, if presumably not the passage itself, will have stood at the root of Wilamowitz's pejorative use of the word 'Schmuckstück' (cited above, p. 174 n. 76).

93 Derrida 1978, pp. 44–94; on Kant's example of the pillars, see esp. pp. 67–69.

'stands out [...] against two grounds, but with respect to each of those two grounds, it merges into the other [...]. [I]t is a figure which comes away of its own accord.'[94]

In the light of these considerations, the opening of the *Sixth Olympian* and its role in the academic reception of Pindar take on a particular ambiguity. The self-referential metaphor of the columns reads as a diacritical commentary on its own parergonality; in the history of the interpretation of the ode, this is exactly how it has been read. Unity and identity, to the extent that they are based on the simultaneity of voice and text in the occasional presence of singer and public, are announced by means of a metaphor ('there is an inside and *this* is where it begins: these words already belong to the inside of the text') that subverts its own premises (*'properly speaking*, it *hasn't actually begun yet at all*: these words still belong to the outside of the text').[95] In this way, the speaker is forced to take up a position that is temporally incompatible with the existence of his text: text and voice cannot coincide for the simple reason that on whichever side of this border between inside and outside the singer tries to locate himself (or we try to locate him), he will always turn out to be elsewhere. Here, the text emancipates itself from the moment of orality and becomes *written*, inasmuch as it is the defining trait of writing not to be bound to the presence of a speaker, but rather to presuppose his or her absence.[96] Of course the *Sixth Olympian* can easily be read out or sung, and this will obviously have taken place in Stymphalos in or around the year 468 B.C.; but the voice of the singer can under no circumstances perform the text mimetically, for this would mean speaking without speaking, being present and absent at the same time. The text does not represent a voice, nor does it imitate one; instead, the demand it makes

94 'Le *parergon* se détache à la fois de l'*ergon* (de l'œuvre) et du milieu, il se détache d'abord comme une figure sur un fond. Mais il ne s'en détache pas comme l'œuvre. Elle se détache aussi sur un fond. Le cadre parergonal se détache, lui, sur deux fonds, mais par rapport à chacun de ces deux fonds, il se fond dans l'autre. [...] Du moins est-ce une figure qui s'enlève d'elle-même.' Derrida 1978, pp. 71–73, Engl. p. 61; *cf.* de Man 1989, p. 35.

95 This problem arises, as far as I can see, in principle at least, for all the cases of Pfeijffer's fictional future. Only here, however, is it linked with a metaphor that 'names' its own function as a frame so explicitly.

96 See above, p. 37 ff. Dickson 1990 investigates the strategies by which Pindar binds writing's problematic effects on the categories of meaning to the presence of the voice (see esp. pp. 114–116 and p. 119 on the *Sixth Olympian*). The presence of a phono-(logo)centrism of this kind in the victory odes will surprise no reader of archaic lyric. Our interest here, however, is to make visible a place in the songs that is not subordinated to the intention of such a logocentrism.

on its speaker is always already one step ahead. The voice, capable only of affirming presence, will never be able to (cor)respond to it.[97]

It seems, then, that the beginning of the song is never present, never identical with itself. We therefore cannot in any simple sense say that the metaphor of the columns 'refers' to it as its literal meaning, although at the same time there can be no doubt that *there is* such a beginning.[98] Indubitable closure and indefinite openness at once: it is this maintaining of a distinction and its transgression at the same time to which Derrida refers in 'La double séance' as *le pli*, the 'fold'.[99] 'La double séance' is a reading of Mallarmé's *Mimique*, itself a short meditation on the experience of reading, one evening, the libretto of a mime, 'Pierre Murderer of his Wife', composed by the performer, one Paul Margueritte, after the performance. Mallarmé describes his impressions upon reading the text and then goes on to 'quote' it; it is, he writes,

> a mute soliloquy that the phantom, white as a yet unwritten page, holds [...] at full length to his soul. [...] This—'The scene illustrates but the idea, not any actual action, in a hymen (out of which flows Dream), tainted with vice yet sacred, between (*entre*) desire and fulfillment, perpetration and remembrance; here anticipating, there recalling, in the future, in the past, *under the false appearance of a present* [...].[100]

Derrida analyses the impossible referential structure of this 'mime' at length—whilst preceding its own *livret* and thus imitating nothing, it is nevertheless constrained to write itself according to just this text—and shows that it cannot be accounted for by a Platonic or Idealist theory of mimesis, in which the temporal-ontological priority of (the presence of) what is imitated is necessarily presupposed by the imitation.[101] Noting Mallarmé's designation of its site as a 'hymen', a term

97 To this extent, the phenomenon is also not grasped by a distinction between necessary and fictional mimesis such as that suggested by D'Alessio 2004, p. 269.

98 We should probably on these grounds even question the status of the passage as a 'metaphor' at all.

99 Derrida 1972a, pp. 215–346, Engl. pp. 173–285. See on this Gasché 1986, pp. 217–223 and Bennington 2000, pp. 47–58.

100 '[...] soliloque muet que, tout du long à son âme tient [...] le fantôme blanc comme une page pas encore écrite. [...] Voici – « La scène n'illustre que l'idée, pas une action effective, dans un hymen (d'où procède le Rêve), vicieux mais sacré, entre le désir et l'accomplissement, la perpétration et son souvenir: ici devançant, là remémorant, au futur, au passé, *sous une apparence fausse de présent* [...].' In Derrida 1972a, p. 217, Engl. p. 175 (Mallarmé's italics). The 'citation' is fictional.

101 See Derrida 1972a, pp. 226–238, Engl. pp. 184–193 on *Philebus* 38e–39e.

which signifies both a barrier and its removal, he comments:

> [We read] that the folding was being marked *in* the hymen, in the angle or cleft, in the *entre* by which, dividing itself, it related back to itself. Yet neither (is it) a fold in the veil or in the pure text but rather in the lining which the hymen, of itself, was. But by the same token *is* not: the fold in a lining by which it is, out of itself, in itself, at once its own outside and its own inside; between the outside and the inside, making the outside enter the inside and turning back the antre or the other upon its surface, the hymen is never pure or proper, has no life of its own, no proper name. [...] Along the undiscoverable line of this fold, the hymen never presents itself. It never is—in the present—; it has no proper, literal meaning; it no longer originates in meaning as such, that is, as the meaning of being. The fold renders (itself) manifold but (is) not (one).[102]

The fold denies the possibility of presence, of unity, of meaning: as a figure of in(de)finite deferral, it has no proper name. It is not without significance that the point at which this effect becomes visible in Mallarmé is the moment of intertextuality. *Mimique*, written (on a previously unwritten page) in response to a soliloquy, refers unquestionably to Margueritte's libretto, and even appears to quote it, although the quote is in fact merely an imitation of quotation, illustrating only an appearing, an εἶδος or 'idea', not a presence or 'any actual action', so that it becomes quite unclear at what point reference and self-reference, 'remembrance' and 'perpetration' are to be distinguished from each other, or whether in fact there is, here, any difference at all. This curious doubling which seems to haunt Mallarmé's essay as a self-referential marking or re-marking of reference has the effect of turning the text constantly back upon itself in the very act of pointing most definitively and explicitly to another text or determinate system beyond itself.[103]

We can observe a similar point of referential doubling in the *Sixth*

[102] '[Nous lisons] que la pliure se marquait *dans* l'hymen, dans l'angle ou la fente, l'entre par lequel, se divisant, il se rapportait à lui-même. Pli non plus dans le voile ou dans le texte pur mais dans la doublure que l'hymen, de lui-même, était. Mais aussi bien n'est pas, pli d'une doublure selon laquelle il est, hors de soi, en soi, à la fois son propre dehors et son propre dedans ; entre le dehors et le dedans, faisant entrer le dehors dans le dedans et retournant l'antre ou l'autre en sa surface, l'hymen n'est jamais pur ou propre. [...] Sur la ligne introuvable de ce pli, l'hymen ne se présente jamais, il n'est jamais – au présent –, il n'a pas de sense propre, il ne relève plus de sens comme tel, c'est-à-dire, en dernière instance, comme sense de l'être.' Derrida 1972a, p. 281, Engl. p. 229 (his italics). On the 'hymen', see *ibid.*, p. 258 ff., Engl. p. 209 ff.

[103] *Cf.* Derrida 1972a, p. 249, Engl. p. 202.

Olympian at the moment when Pindar, too, begins to quote another text.[104] After narrowing in on the victor's identity in a series of conditional clauses, each one specifying a defining trait (Olympian victor, seer, member of a Syracusan founding family[105]), the poet announces that 'the son of Sostratos' possesses them all and proceeds (11–21):

> [...] *πολλοὶ δὲ μέμνανται, καλὸν εἴ τι ποναθῇ.*
> *Ἁγησία, τὶν δ' αἶνος ἑτοῖμος, ὃν ἐν δίκᾳ*
> *ἀπὸ γλώσσας Ἄδραστος μάντιν Οἰκλείδαν ποτ' ἐς Ἀμφιάρηον*
> *φθέγξατ', ἐπεὶ κατὰ γαῖ' αὐτόν τέ νιν καὶ φαιδίμας ἵππους ἔμαρψεν.*
> *ἑπτὰ δ' ἔπειτα πυρᾶν νεκρῶν τελεσθέντων Ταλαϊονίδας*
> *εἶπεν ἐν Θήβαισι τοιοῦτόν τι ἔπος· "Ποθέω στρατιᾶς ὀφθαλμὸν ἐμᾶς*
> *ἀμφότερον μάντιν τ' ἀγαθὸν καὶ δουρὶ μάρνασθαι." τὸ καί*
> *ἀνδρὶ κώμου δεσπότᾳ πάρεστι Συρακοσίῳ.*
> *οὔτε δύσηρις ἐὼν οὔτ' ὢν φιλόνικος ἄγαν,*
> *καὶ μέγαν ὅρκον ὀμόσσαις τοῦτό γέ οἱ σαφέως*
> *μαρτυρήσω· μελίφθογγοι δ' ἐπιτρέψοντι Μοῖσαι.*

> [...] but many remember if a noble deed is accomplished with toil.
> Hagesias, the praise stands ready for you
> that Adrastos once justly proclaimed aloud about the seer Amphiaraos, son of Oikles,
> when the earth had swallowed up the man himself and his shining steeds.
> Afterwards, when the corpses of the seven funeral pyres had been consumed, Talaos' son
> spoke a word such as this at Thebes: 'I dearly miss the eye of my army,
> good both as a seer and at fighting with the spear.' This is true as well
> of the man from Syracuse who is master of the revel.
> Though not quarrelsome nor one too fond of victory, yet
> I shall swear a great oath and bear clear witness for him

[104] Garner 1992, p. 48 notes that '*Olympia* 6 is famous for doubling everything: the poem closes with two anchors in a storm, and before this we have had two cities, two gods, two snakes and two gifts.' We could add two hidden pregnancies to this list, and wonder about the logic of some of these doublings, Iamos' 'twofold treasury of prophecy', for example (65 ff.): how will the visible signs of the pyromantic oracle relate to the spoken words of 'the voice that knows no falsehood'? See further below, p. 222.

[105] This list of characteristics, following a general statement about poetry and leading to the identification of the individual victor, exemplifies a not uncommon Pindaric technique for mediating between general categories and specific examples: see Most 1985b, pp. 134–137 with n. 2 for analysis of a related case in *Nem.* 7 and further parallels. We note that the second half of 'La double séance' is a meditation on the logic of examples (Derrida 1972a, pp. 278–346, Engl. pp. 227–285). On *συνοικιστήρ* 6 as a hereditary title, see Σ *Olymp.* 6. 8a Dr.

this at least is so; and the honey-voiced Muses will assist.[106]

The praise that accrues to Hagesias in his double role as seer and warrior/athlete is, it seems, a quotation. The campaign of the Seven against Thebes, mentioned by Pindar at several places, is here the context for a statement on the part of Adrastos who, after the battle, will have been able to find Amphiaraos neither amongst the living nor amongst the dead.[107] The sentence quoted does not merely assert the absence of the Argive seer, but is in fact owed entirely to this absence; Adrastos' recollection of his qualities as *μάντις* and spearman (we recall *μέμανται*, 11) is explicitly connected with his desire for the presence of the vanished warrior (*ποθέω*, 16). But desire and remembrance are, like the wish itself, both forms of representation,[108] and this structure of representation, doubled by Adrastos' exemplarity, is recapitulated on a second level when we note that it is not Amphiaraos himself, but rather Adrastos' laudatory recollection of him that Pindar's singer calls to mind, and which he now intends to transfer to the present victor.

The structure of reference as actualization or *Vergegenwärtigung* in this passage thus seems to be relatively simple: the epinician refers to a mythical figure whose existence—here his familiarity in the tradition—precedes it temporally and ontologically. This structure becomes only slightly more complicated when we take into account that the link between the *Sixth Olympian* and Adrastos' sentence is mediated by the *Thebaid* of the Epic Cycle, as a scholium assures us.[109] In fact, there-

[106] Tr. Race 1997, vol. 1, p. 103 ff.

[107] The story is also alluded to in *Pyth.* 8. 39–56, *Nem.* 8. 51, *Nem.* 9. 11–27, *Nem.* 10. 8 f. and *Isthm.* 7. 10. According to the *Odyssey* (15. 243–255), Amphiaraos died in the battle before the city; against this, Pindar tells how Zeus arranged for him to disappear beneath the earth (*Nem.* 9. 24–27) and assumes his continuing agency as a chthonic *heros* in the Amphiaraion near Thebes (*Pyth.* 8. 58–60, on which see Hubbard 1993). This is the tradition followed by the tragic poets (Soph., *El.* 837–841, Eur., *Suppl.* 925–927), Diod. Sic. IV 65. 8, Strabo IX 2. 10 f., Pausanias I 34. 2, II 23. 2, IX 8. 3 and 19. 4, and Statius, *Theb.* 7. 789–823. Mezger 1888, p. 126 *ad Olymp.* 6. 16 notes that, in the post-Homeric version, Adrastos will have searched in vain for Amphiaraos' corpse upon one of the seven funeral pyres.

[108] According to Freud, remembrance is necessarily implied by the structure of the wish: see *Die Traumdeutung* (= Freud [11]1989, vol. 2), p. 539. If remembrance is representation or *Vergegenwärtigung* in the modus of repetition, the wish as desire in Hegel's sense is *Vergegenwärtigung* in the mode of the negation of negation.

[109] Σ *Olymp.* 6. 26 Dr.: ὁ Ἀσκληπιάδης φησὶ ταῦτα εἰληφέναι ἐκ τῆς κυκλικῆς Θηβαΐδος (= *Thebaid* fr. 10 Bernabé), attached to the lemma *ποθέω*. Note the double structure of this remark on a remark on desire, and that *ταῦτα* leaves the question of citation, para-

fore, the object of the speaker's remembrance is not Adrastos' statement itself, but rather its formulation in the epic poem, and this formulation is not simply repeated or cited in its identity with itself, but rather *imitated* (τοιοῦτόν τι ἔπος, 16).[110] Instead of the representation of representation, therefore, we now have a representation of representation of representation, but structurally, of course, nothing has changed in the relationship of the *Sixth Olympian* to what precedes it. According to the unanimous consensus of research, we are dealing here with an entirely unproblematic case of conventional intertextuality. Pindar refers to the *Thebaid*, he represents or imitates the other, earlier text in order to create a connection between the hero of the mythical campaign against his home city and the present victor. The referential structure of the first part of the *Sixth Olympian* thus fulfils all the essential criteria of the classical theory of intertextual, Platonic or Hegelian mimesis: the priority of the one text to the other remains, as we expect, unquestioned, and the border between imitative victory ode and the imitated epic, which is a consequence of this ontological priority, is kept entirely intact.

Or at least, this is how things seem at first glance. But it soon turns out that the epinician only cites the *Thebaid* (or something like the *Thebaid*, imitates imitating the *Thebaid*) in order to say something about itself. The statement that imitates the passage from the epic poem announces only what will have been said at the end of *this ode here*: τοῦτό γε μαρτυρήσω, 20 f. This future re-marks the quotation and the assertion of its transferability to Hagesias retrospectively as proleptic self-reference: 'Look, I will bear witness to what I have just said.'[111] Certainly, we should not ignore the difference between saying and bearing witness. A witness can only testify to something he or she has *seen*.[112] The witness has recourse to a moment of originary presence, so that his or her speech possesses not merely the status of λέγειν—the repetition of linguistic signs whose anchoring in an origi-

phrase, or mere report entirely open. The fact that the *Sixth Olympian*, the *Thebaid* or both may be imitating more than one other text—*cf. Iliad* 3. 179 and 7. 140, and Hes. fr. 25. 37 MW—only makes the matter more tantalizing.

110 *Cf.* the different reconstructions of the *Thebaid*-passage—a complete hexameter as opposed to Pindar's dactylo-epitrite—in Bernabé.

111 In the further course of the ode, two models of transference are placed over against each other: predication is either genetically inherited (the common, immortal name of Iamos and his descendents in verses 57 and 71, a model that is based on the inclusive figure of the synecdoche) or it is transferred in the sense of the metaphor (Amphiaraos corresponds to Hagesias on the basis of a *tertium comparationis*, as asserted in verse 17).

112 See above, p. 130.

nary intuition the speaker is neither obliged nor able to guarantee—but that of *μαρτυρεῖν*. But what the *Sixth Olympian* is meant to testify to is stated by means of an intertextual allusion in whose double nature as remembrance (representation of the past) and desire (representation of the future) the necessary presence of what is to be witnessed to retreats.

What interests us here, however, is the relationship between self-reference and hetero-reference at this point. We recall: the temporal-ontological outside of the text is meant to be definable in opposition to the text itself; the text must be a unity determinable by means of clear borders between itself and what precedes it. This seemed to be the clear assertion of the *Second Olympian*. But the Adrastos-passage, like the 'metaphor' of the columns before it, does not entirely conform to this model. Pindar refers to the earlier text and refers simultaneously to this reference by making the transferability of the description itself into the object of the statement. The ode comments on itself from the perspective of another text. Is this still self-reference? It is, at the very least, not *simple* self-reference. But at the same time, it is not simply the exo-reference of intertextuality, for the exclusive referent of this quasi-quotation is the *Sixth Olympian* alone.

The aesthetic-hermeneutical postulate of a unity founded in presence and constructed by means of clear borders between the inside and the outside of a text has been the enabling presupposition of the last two hundred years of Pindaric criticism, a presupposition of which Aristotle still provides one of the most rigorous expositions. In this chapter I have been concerned to show that it is subverted at more than one place in the epinicians themselves. It is so difficult to integrate these passages into a conventional reading of the victory odes—as the curious status of the figure of the columns in the *Sixth Olympian* in criticism has shown—because they contradict the first and perhaps most important criterion of meaning, that is, the unity of the field of what is meant. A properly *hermeneutical* interpretation of Pindar, whose legitimacy and necessity within the 'age of metaphysics' is not being denied here, can only marginalise or exorcise these moments from the texts, and thus recapitulate a gesture that the songs themselves (*faisant entrer le dehors dans le dedans et retournant l'antre ou l'autre en sa surface*) already prescribe.

At the same time, the thesis of unity presents itself as a kind of hermeneutical anticipation of the total knowledge of the text, total because its object is constructed as an object capable of totality. The total object that, according to Hegel, can only be known by an absolute epistemological subject—the *absoluter Geist*—after death, finds itself its own symbol in those elements of the text that stand for the latter's orientation towards its own unity. The vanishing point of such, in a certain sense, asymptotic readings is, as a rule, the intention of the speaking subject as wish or desire. It is this intention and the notion of subjectivity it implies to which we now address ourselves.

CHAPTER 5: SUBJECT

Le structuralisme n'est pas du tout une pensée qui supprime le sujet, mais une pensée qui l'émiette et le distribue systématiquement, qui conteste l'identité du sujet, qui le dissipe et le fait passer de place en place, sujet toujours nomade, fait d'individuations, mais impersonnelles, ou de singularités, mais pré-individuelles.
Deleuze, *L'île déserte et autres textes*.

FEW TOPICS IN PINDARIC STUDIES HAVE MADE FEELINGS RUN AS high as the question of the Pindaric ἐγώ. The interest aroused by the ongoing debate, in recent years conducted in terms of deixis and performativity, suggests that more is at stake than merely the semantic content of a pronoun.[1] Instead, closing the gap between the signifier of the first person singular and its signified appears to offer a way, however mediated by the reconstruction of sometimes highly complex performance situations, to reach back behind the text to an authentically historical subjectivity, to make contact with the mind or at least the self-image of Pindar himself in his texts. There is more than one good reason to be interested in the success of such a project. *The literary self as origin* (de Man) seems to promise not only the proof of the poetic quality of the odes according to criteria going all the way back to the Romantic aesthetics of genius.[2] It also appears to guarantee an answer to questions about their meaning and unity: if Pindar's epinicians have a meaning, then this must surely be found—beyond the

[1] See *e.g.* Bonifazi 2004, a discussion of Pindar in terms of subjective intentionality and the desire to communicate, and Kurke 2005 on the ἐγώ of the *Sixth Paean*. Recent theoretical interest in the notion of 'agency' (see Culler 2007, pp. 27–33) is also relevant here.

[2] This—and not primarily the historicist search for 'what really happened'—is the point of assertions such as Boeckh's that the poet can use the song to say 'was [ihm] am Herzen liegt' (Boeckh 1854–1874, vol. VII, p. 385). See further Schmidt 1985, vol. 1, pp. 179–192. The line that Bundy 1986, p. 33 (*cf.* Most 1985, p. 26) sketches from the scholia to the historico-biographical school represented by Wilamowitz disguises the very real differences in the theoretical basis upon which the Alexandrian commentators, the Romantics of the nineteenth century and the positivists of the early twentieth undertook the search for biographical or psychological material in the epinicians.

uncertainty of signs and the fatherlessness of writing—in the orally expressed intention of the poet, either in person or through the medium of a chorus, in a given historical situation. The question 'Who speaks?' becomes in this way a synecdoche for the investigation of the subject's desire to communicate and for the eminent question of the meaning of the texts.

Let us consider some of the stations of this discussion in the twentieth century. Michael Schmid analyses them in terms of a dichotomy between historical and 'radical-formalist' approaches, although in the course of his discussion the notion of formalism is replaced by the term 'rhetorical', a change that is not without its consequences.[3] On the one side of this opposition between history and rhetoric are studies that believe themselves able to discern in Pindar's statements in the first person indications of biographical facts or states of consciousness on the part of the author. Amongst such studies are Wilamowitz's *Pindaros* and Bowra's *Pindar*: both works attempt to discover Pindar's personality or experiences in the texts.[4] One year before Bowra's monograph appeared, however, Lefkowitz published a reading of the epinicians that focused explicitly on the question of the *identity* of the speaker: does the pronoun ἐγώ in the odes refer to the poet or—this an option that had previously been given too little attention—the chorus? Lefkowitz came to the conclusion that 'the chorus speaks only in songs intended for a specific communal purpose, the poet on occasions of international significance.'[5] She assumed, however, that whoever said 'I' had to be the physically present speaker of the respective song: if the persona designated by ἐγώ in a given text could be shown to be that of the poet or composer, on the grounds of the importance of the occasion or otherwise, this meant that Pindar himself had sung.[6] The implications of this approach for the relationship between the category of subjectivity and the text will be clear: the subject is seen as the agency of the present significance of what is said, so that whoever speaks of himself in the first person is called to account for the truthfulness and thus the true meaning of what he says.[7] This constellation

[3] Schmid 1998b, p. 147 ff.

[4] Wilamowitz 1922, Bowra 1964.

[5] Lefkowitz 1991, p. 56 (first published in 1963).

[6] D'Alessio 1994, p. 120 and Schmid 1998b, p. 148, note the potential circularity of this argumentation.

[7] In his letter to d'Alembert from 1758 (Rousseau 1967, p. 187 f.), Rousseau describes the difference between the orator or preacher, who speaks in his own name, and the actor who merely represents a role that may be of no personal importance to him at all

of subject and text structures a whole series of contemporary approaches to the odes: research on orality in Pindar, for example—the notion of 'occasionality' means nothing other than binding the written text back to the truth and originary status of the spoken—is based on this assumption. What an epinician text really means is what an epinician speaker could have said to a given audience at a given time, in a given place, on a given occasion.[8]

But we anticipate. After the publication of Bundy's *Studia Pindarica*, Lefkowitz was forced to revise her thesis.[9] Bundy had shown that the *persona* of the poet in the odes is a role: here, 'I' is not the historical 'Pindar of Thebes' but rather the singer 'privileged to praise the worthiest of men.'[10] Accordingly, the voice of the author is always and in principle hidden behind a mask, for the assertion that one is speaking naturally, without mask or disguise, is a *topos* of epideictic rhetoric in general and of epinician poetry in particular. From this perspective, which saw in Pindar's 'I' a 'rhetorical construct' (Schmid), a much more complex understanding of Pindaric subjectivity in the victory odes became possible which could emphasize the rhetorical nature of the epinician subject on the one hand whilst opening this role for a multiplicity of identities and possible sources on the other. Bremer, for example, finds five subjects in the Pindaric ἐγώ: Pindar's official poetic *persona*; a use of the first person that invites the audience to adopt what is said as their own opinion (the 'first person indefinite'); the chorus; the victor himself; and—seldom and despite Bundy's conclusions—'the individual Pindar of Thebes'.[11] D'Alessio shows that the communicative strategies developed in the poems are more complex but also often less definite than Lefkowitz's thesis of a consistently clear distinction between the *persona* of the chorus and that of the poet in a given text or genre requires; at the same time, however, he notes that where a specific poetic identity *is* constructed in the epinicians, we can often observe how this works as a rhetorical

('Mais un comédien sur la scène, étant d'autres sentiments que les siens, ne disant que ce qu'on lui fait dire, représentant souvent un être chimérique, s'anéantit, pour ainsi dire [...]') in moral terms; see on this Derrida 1967a, p. 428 ff., Engl. p. 302 ff. In Pindaric research, this distinction reappears in statements such as Pfeijffer's (1999a, p. 33) comment on the 'coldness of the contractual relationship' between the commissioning family and the paid singer; see above, p. 177.

[8] *Cf.* in just this sense Pfeijffer 1999b, p. 18 and see above, p. 152.

[9] See Lefkowitz 1991, p. 127. On Bundy see above, p. 61 ff.

[10] Bundy 1986, p. 3 and *cf.* p. 32 ff.

[11] Bremer 1990, p. 45.

strategy for heightening the praise of the victor.[12] On this basis, Schmid's narratological model distinguishes *within* the epinician ἐγώ between the narrator and the focalizer (not least in order to avoid 'confusion between internal and external aspects of the text').[13] The polyvalence of rhetoric emphasized by these scholars might seem more likely to do justice to the phenomena of a changing subjectivity than the historicism of researchers like Lefkowitz.

Do these solutions, however, take the category of the rhetorical seriously? Some doubts may, perhaps, be entertained. For an approach that sees in the speaker the agency of meaning, and which Schmid calls 'historical', does not stand in a simple opposition to rhetoric. The thesis that text and voice are necessarily one—that is, that the meaning of a text is always identical with the intention of a present speaker—has been the most important presupposition of rhetorical theory since Plato. As we saw at the beginning of this study, that Athenian philosopher views language solely as a τέχνη of communication at the disposal of an essentially sovereign subject, so that the speaker who comes to help his λόγος is the decisive authority on the meaning of what is said.[14] Far from being diametrically opposed to historicism, therefore, the modern rediscovery of the rhetoric of the epinicians is its logical continuation. As long as the question of the subject in Pindaric studies is mediated by an understanding of rhetoric according to which the latter consists solely in the implementation of a subjective intention, this question is necessarily connected to the status of the voice and to all of the metaphysical assertions that, in the history of philosophy, have been made in its name. This status itself cannot be questioned from within these approaches, for it is their most essential presupposition.

At this point we may recall de Man's definition of literature: a literary text, wrote the author of *Allegories of Reading*, asserts and denies the mode of its own rhetoricity at the same time.[15] Literariness is that quality of a text that refuses to be appropriated by a 'philosophy of literature'.[16] We saw something of such a refusal in the *Sixth Olympian*:

[12] D'Alessio 1994. *Cf.* Lefkowitz 1963, p. 225 and 1991, p. 56.

[13] Schmid 1998b, p. 154.

[14] See above, p. 27 ff. Schmid himself, who undertakes a narratological reading of the epinicians, is thus prepared to grant that Lefkowitz's and others' concentration on the speaker has a legitimate basis in the oral nature of epinician poetry: see Schmid 1998b, p. 152.

[15] De Man 1979, p. 17; see above, p. 52.

[16] It is—who else?—Derrida who observes that 'la critique littéraire s'est déjà détermi-

it led us to suspect that a theory of Pindaric speech on the basis of the metaphysics of presence will not be able to accommodate certain elements in the texts.

But is there a Pindaric theory of subjectivity that would be in a position to question the philosophical construct of the *subiectum*? Reflections in the epinicians on speech and intention would be the first place to look for such a theory. I will argue in this chapter that, beyond the level of alleged 'assertions' (which are always understood as a kind of communication and for this very reason force their interpreters to efface everything in the texts that does not unambiguously support the model of subjectivity as source), the odes do present an implicit logic of the subject whose contours can be studied on the basis of three major categories: interiority, sovereignty, and materiality.

The pit and the subject

The *interiority* of the literary subject is opposed to the externality of writing or the work; it appears, at first glance, to be a special case of the inwardness of the subject of cognition or action over against the outwardness of the world. In some narratives of the history of philosophy, the discovery or formalization of this interiority is connected with the name of Descartes, in others with developments as early as the third century B.C.[17] In Hellenistic thought, for example, we can discern a move away from notions of the subject based on the relationship between the self and the world, on ἦθος or πρᾶξις, to conceptions that identify the goal of the 'practices of the self' in an inner state, in ἀταραξία or *tranquillitas*. If a central concern of ethical reflection in authors such as Xenophon or Plato is the mastery of the self as a necessary prerequisite of mastery over others—Foucault describes the agonistic structure and teleology of this ἐγκράτεια in *L'Usage des plaisirs*—Epicurus and Stoics such as Seneca seek rather to take pleasure in the inward life of a soul untouched and untroubled by outer turmoil.[18] Here, it would seem, inwardness has been raised to

née [...] comme philosophie de la littérature' ('Force et signification' [= Derrida 1967c, pp. 9–49], p. 47, Engl. p. 28).

[17] See for example Gill 1996, pp. 29–60, who argues that much twentieth century research on archaic or classical notions of subjectivity (in particular the work of Snell and Adkins) is based on a (post-)Cartesian model of the subject that inappropriately privileges the unity and interiority of the self.

[18] Foucault 1984a, pp. 51–85, Engl. pp. 37–68. See Strozier 2002, pp. 139–174 for an study that, whilst extending and refining Foucault's analysis of post-classical ethics in *Le souci de soi* (Foucault 1984b), argues for an 'epistemic shift from exteriority to

the principle of a philosophy that contrasts strongly with the more active or political interests of classical or archaic conceptions of subjectivity, in which the 'divided self' found in Homer and the tragedians serves to model 'outwardness' as the sphere in which such a self must speak and act.[19]

There is much to be said for this analysis. One can nevertheless ask whether the reconstruction of pre-Hellenistic subjectivity it entails does not still privilege a value or an ideal locus of interiority. For it seems clear that the acting or speaking subject is ultimately still an agency that only takes action or speaks when outside and inside have been harmonized—and this *on the inside* of the *φρήν*. This teleology of the inside is the common presupposition of all of these reconstructions of archaic, Homeric or Pindaric subjectivity, regardless of whether they are 'historical' or 'rhetorical' in Schmid's sense. As soon as it speaks, the subject is, as a pure or reconciled interior, the origin or source of its expression, which itself consists solely and entirely of what is meant. This understanding of the relationship between subject and language links modern conceptions of subjectivity to ancient ones; in pointing to changes in late antiquity or the early modern period in the construction of subjectivity in the Western intellectual tradition, the above-mentioned studies nowhere question the model of an ideal, inward desire 'expressed' in the Homeric and Pindaric texts.[20]

interiority as a locus of inquiry [...] locatable in the early Hellenistic period and later in post-Augustan Rome' (p. 139).

[19] Homer has his characters address their *θυμός* directly; Pindar's singer also speaks to his heart; see Pelliccia 1995 for comprehensive documentation. It seems plausible to interpret this 'divided self', which Gill 1996 and others have identified as the *telos* of archaic subjective processuality, as the assessment of one's own speech and actions from the perspective of an 'outside' which is the crucial locus of the constitution of subjectivity altogether.

[20] On the contrary: the objections brought against the theory of an 'identical' subject in the Greek archaic or classical periods are intended, as a rule, to support the (re-)construction of an ancient psychology to which the texts allegedly testify as the external sign of an inward state. On this model, Homer bears witness to the divided subjectivity of 'Homeric man' in such a way that the question of this subjectivity becomes the question of the psychological configuration of an authentic self-consciousness that can be answered according to the criteria of coherence, unity and intention. The paradoxical nature of the hermeneutics on which this kind of psychological archaeology is based lies in the fact that it can and must not take its own heuristic thesis seriously; the attempt to investigate a fragmented subjectivity on the basis of texts that have to be understood as its fundamentally univocal expressions in order to enable this investigation is caught up in a kind of self-contradiction that is resolvable neither by giving up the thesis nor by dispensing with the *telos* of meaning. The literature on the 'archaic self' and its relationship to modern notions of subjectivity is vast. Standard studies are Gill 1996 and 2006;

The strategic value of interiority designates, in Foucauldian theories as in those traditional reconstructions of the ancient self that discuss its division or fragmentation, the place of an immediate knowledge of oneself; it is on this basis that meaning is created.[21] It would be a mistake to seek the ground of this continuity between antiquity and modernity in the area of a common psychology of the ancient or the modern human being; it lies rather in a fundamentally semiotic understanding of language as *expression*. The notion of the subject as a *pit* in which the representations of intelligence are preserved and from which they are extracted in the process of making signs, without in this moment of extraction losing their essential continuity with what they were within, is the logically necessary consequence of an understanding of language as meaning; it is therefore not only Plato's (and, as we will see, partly Pindar's), but also Hegel's and Husserl's.[22] In such conceptions, language is seen merely (but crucially) as the extension of an inner continuity, the merely formal extension of the speaker's *présence à soi* in what Husserl calls 'das einsame Seelenleben', the interior life of the soul.[23]

Pelliccia 1995, pp. 13–114 offers a wide-ranging discussion with respect to Homer; on the role of interiority in later constructions of the self, see Strozier 2002, pp. 175–233 with the literature cited there.

[21] See for example Pelliccia 1995, p. 120 ff. on the opposition between 'inner thought and outer speech'.

[22] See Hegel, *Enzyklopädie der philosophischen Wissenschaften* III, §§ 445–468 (= Hegel 1969–1971, vol. 10, pp. 240–288, Engl. Hegel 2007, pp. 173–206), in particular the discussion of representation and recollection (§§ 452–454) where the philosopher describes the intelligence as 'diesen nächtlichen Schacht, in welchem eine Vielzahl von Bildern und Vorstellung aufbewahrt wären' (§ 453, = *ibid.*, p. 260, Engl. Hegel 2007, p. 187, 'this nocturnal pit'). *Cf.* de Man 1996, p. 100 and Waters 1989, xxxiii. On Hegel's model of the theoretical subject, see further above, p. 81 f. Husserl's conception of the self as an inner space in which the meaning of intention is immediately present for the subject (see Husserl, *Logische Untersuchungen*, Zweiter Band, Erster Teil [= Husserl 1992 (first published in 1901), vol. 3], pp. 30–43 and *cf.* p. 365 f. on 'inner' and 'adequate perception') is the topic of Derrida 1967b.

[23] Husserl's phenomenology can be viewed as the most rigorous version of this tradition. In the *Logische Untersuchungen* from 1901, language can only mean anything—in Husserl's terms, it can only be an *Ausdruck*—by standing in an unbroken relationship to a meaning that in its pure form exists exclusively in the interior solitude of the soul (see Husserl 1992, vol. 2, p. 39 ff.). In the *Ideen zu einer reinen Phänomenologie* published twelve years later, the essential interiority of meaning is retained despite all the revisions to the theory of the 'reines Ich' that have taken place since the *Logische Untersuchungen*. *Ideen* § 124 describes the relationship between the 'pre-expressive' meaning and the 'layer of expression' in the sense that the latter is a fundamentally 'non-productive doubling': 'Ihre Produktivität [...] erschöpft sich im Ausdrücken und der [...] Form des Begrifflichen' (Husserl 1992, vol. 5, p. 287). But the pre-expression has

The seamless transition between inward meaning and outward expression presupposed by these approaches has been challenged for more than one reason in literary theory. The structuralist and psychoanalytic critiques of metaphysics in twentieth century theory are particularly important influences here. For Roland Barthes, who takes up the *déplacement* of the subject in Lacanian psychoanalysis, subjectivity is not the hidden source of a literary text, since the latter is characterized, not by the subject's founding presence, but rather by its radical absence. He writes:

> The subject is not an individual plenitude which one is or is not entitled to pour off into language [...] but on the contrary a void around which the writer weaves a discourse which is infinitely transformed (that is to say inserted in a chain of transformation), so that all writing *which does not lie* designates not the internal attributes of the subject, but its absence. Language is not the predicate of a subject which is inexpressible or which language serves to signify; language is the subject. It seems to me [...] that it is very precisely that which defines literature [...].[24]

These lines from Barthes' *Critique et vérité*, published in 1966, could stand as an apt description of the rediscovery of Pindaric subjectivity in the work of Bundy and those scholars who have adopted his view of the rhetoricity of the odes. Indeed, the French critic's analysis encompasses the entire problematics of this poet's ἐγώ. Pindar

already constituted itself by means of its relationship to a specific outside, an object that establishes the 'new layer' of expressible meaning as soon as it is (predicatively) 'thought'. The interiority from whose perspective the *ob-* of the ob-ject is conceived is indeed not a simple 'inside', as Derrida has noted (Derrida 1967b, p. 22 f. and see also p. 34 f.); nevertheless, Husserl questions its quasi-topological integrity with respect to the intentional structure of subjectivity neither in the *Logische Untersuchungen* nor in the *Ideen*.

[24] '[L]e sujet n'est pas une plénitude individuelle qu'on a le droit ou non d'évacuer dans le langage [...] mais au contraire un vide autour duquel l'écrivain tresse une parole infiniment transformée (insérée dans une chaîne de transformation), en sorte que toute écriture *qui ne ment pas* désigne, non les attributs intérieurs du sujet, mais son absence. Le langage n'est pas le prédicat d'un sujet, inexprimable ou qu'il servirait à exprimer, il est le sujet. Il me semble [...] que c'est cela très précisément qui définit la littérature [...].' Barthes 2002, vol. II, p. 796, his italics; Engl. Barthes 2004, p. 35. Barthes himself notes the proximity of this description of an absence encircled by every truthful writing to Lacan's theories of language and literature; *cf.* 'Fonction et champ du la parole et du langage en psychanalyse' (= Lacan 1999, vol. 1, pp. 235–321), pp. 245–263, Engl. pp. 206–220, on the work of the self (*gen. obj.*) as an other (this formulation—'il [*sc.* le sujet] retrouve l'aliénation fondamentale qui la lui a fait construire *comme une autre*'—p. 248, Engl. p. 208, his italics). The 'writing which does not lie' is very reminiscent of Lacan's 'parole pleine': see *ibid.*, p. 252 ff., Engl. p. 211 ff.

lays claim to his own subjectivity with the greatest possible emphasis, whilst at the same time vanishing entirely within his role as singer. Barthes' *écriture qui ne ment pas* circles the gap that this de-centred subject leaves behind it.

It is this paradox which drives and disquiets research on the Pindaric 'I' and its presence in the poems. The questioning of the interiority of the subject, the space and the borders of its inwardness, must affect the concept of the subject itself. But in the course of this questioning it becomes doubtful whether there can be a phenomenologically rigorous concept of intentional speech, or indeed of intention at all, without a clear separation between outside and inside. Husserl's definition of expression as a meaningful sign, at least, relies crucially on this dichotomy.

In order to examine the structure of Pindaric subjectivity and the role interiority and externality play in it, the common epinician metaphor of the βέλη λόγων, the 'arrows of words', can serve as a point of departure.[25] This starting-point is not arbitrary: the phenomenological notion of the intention of meaning already indicates that, in the metaphor of the projectile, an element of that *intendere* is being addressed from which the philosophical concept takes its name.[26] It is no acci-

[25] The word is a missile: Nünlist 1998, pp. 142–153 offers a survey of this metaphor in Homer and early Greek lyric poetry and notes that the Greek archaic period lacked a clear terminology of literary interpretation: the poets use poetological metaphors because they initially have no terminological alternative for developing a discourse of poetological reflexion (see further Richardson 1986 on the question of how Pindar's poetological terms are taken up by the later literary criticism of Gorgias, Plato and Aristotle). Nünlist discusses sources, conceptions of poetry, the relationship between figurative and non-figurative poetics, poetological images found in individual poets, general tendencies (temporal and generic differences, the position in the course of the text) and the circulation of the songs (the metaphors assume oral circulation; what is seen as problematic is only the possibility of plagiarism [Theognis 19–23]), and comments that 'mit Hilfe der selbstreferentiellen poetologischen Bildersprache [...] der poetische Text [signalisiert], wie er *als poetischer Text* verstanden werden möchte' (p. 363). On the metaphor of the missile in Pindar, see further Dornseiff 1921, p. 58, Simpson 1969 and Pfeijffer 1999b, p. 374 f. *ad Nem.* 3. 65.

[26] The transfer of the Latin *intendere*—in the early period apparently limited to the bow (Ennius, *scen.* 31)—to the soul is classical, already to be found in Cicero as the designation of someone's attention to an object of perception (*Hort.*, fr. 1, *Luc.* 30, *De inv.* II 103 and elsewhere; *cf. intentio animi* at *Tusc.* II 65 *etc.*). The plausible grammatical addition of a target only occurs, however, in later texts: Plin., *Ep.* I 3. 2, then in Christian Latin Tert., *Adv. Marc.* I 12 (both *c. gen.*) and I 20 (with *ad*). In a hermeneutical sense, we first find *intentio* for what a speaker or writer wants to say at Serv., *Praef.* I 2 (*scribentis*) and Donat., *Aen.* I 605, p. 119, 29 (*dicentis*). *Cf.* however Cic., *De orat.* I 90 (as far as rhetoric is concerned, we human beings are created in such a way *ut* [...]

dent that Husserl's entire theory of *cogitatio* and language is constructed from the perspective of *intention*; like the theory of subjectivity in Hegel's *Enzyklopädie*, it too belongs to the history of a metaphysics of the self in which meaning is the bringing forth of something inward, something meant by the subject.[27] In the *Second Olympian*, a song that points to the persuasive power of language as the expression of desire at a crucial point,[28] we find the following passage (83–86):

πολλά μοι ὑπ' ἀγκῶνος ὠκέα βέλη

possemus [...] *id, quod intenderemus, confirmare*) and Pliny's *cum intentionem effectumque muneris nostri vellemus intellegi* (*Ep.* I 8. 13), a usage that comes very close to this meaning and prepares the ground for the Tertullian's later *intentio operis* (*Adv. Marc.* II 29). On the Greek terminological background, in particular the semantic field of τείνειν, see Theiler 1966, pp. 223–225 on the epistemological terminology of Neo-Platonism and Augustine, as well as Engelhardt 1976 and the literature cited there.

[27] See Husserl, *Ideen*, § 37 (= Husserl 1992, vol. 5, pp. 73–75) and *cf.* Brentano 1973, vol. 1 (first published in 1874), p. 124 f.: 'Jedes psychische Phänomen ist durch das charakterisiert, was die Scholastiker des Mittelalters die intentionale (auch wohl mentale) Inexistenz eines Gegenstandes genannt haben, und was wir [...] die Beziehung auf einen Inhalt, die Richtung auf ein Objekt (worunter hier nicht die Realität zu verstehen ist), oder die immanente Gegenständlichkeit nennen würden'; this sentence is cited in the second volume of the *Logische Untersuchungen* (Husserl 1992, vol. 3, p. 380). On Husserl's notion of intention, see further Münch 1993, pp. 179–220. In contrast to his former teacher, Husserl understands intention as an *act*; this leads, in the discussion of linguistic meaning with which the first *Untersuchung* begins, to the assertion that intention refers exclusively to the *will* of the intellectual subject; on the problems this creates, see Derrida 1967b, pp. 34–39. An indication of this notion's influence, which is of course not original to Brentano, on the most elementary levels of the theory of language are the first sentences of KS I (the first edition of which was published in 1879), p. 1: 'Die Syntaxe ist die Lehre vom Satze. Satz ist der *Ausdruck eines Gedankens* in Worten [...]. Gedanke ist der *geistige Akt*, durch den der Mensch zwei Begriffe [...] zu einer Einheit zusammenfaßt [...]' (their spacing, my italics). *Cf.* in a similar sense KG I, p. 1. One sees how the possibility of syntax itself is made to rely crucially on the agency and the authority of the thinking—and that means, here, intending—mind.

[28] *Olymp.* 2. 79–80: as opposed to his father Peleus and to Cadmus, Achilles only reaches the Island of the Blessed because Thetis persuades Zeus by means of prayers (λιταῖς ἔπεισε). As Solmsen 1982 observes, Thetis' ability to persuade Zeus is already a Homeric motif; it is used here, however, to motivate a version of her son's destiny which diverges from the Homeric and Hesiodic tradition (*cf. Od.* 11. 487–491 and, with respect to the heroes in general, Hes., *Op.* 156–173 Solmsen [but *cf.* West 1978, p. 192 *ad* 166]). See further Ibyc. 291 *PMG* = Simon. 558 *PMG*—Achilles lives on the Elysian plain after his death and marries Medea—Newman 1987, p. 92 f., and Nisetich 1988, who sees in 79–80 a transfer of the story of Eos and Memnon in the *Aithiopis* (Argumentum 14 f. Bernabé) to Thetis and Achilles. This rhetoric of persuasion is already present at the beginning of the song in connection with τὸ μέλλον: in verses 12–15, Zeus is to preserve the ancestral land for Theron's family forever because he enjoys (Pindar's?) songs (ἰανθεὶς ἀοιδαῖς, 13).

ἔνδον ἐντὶ φαρέτρας
φωνάεντα συνετοῖσιν· ἐς δὲ τὸ πὰν ἑρμανέων
χατίζει.

I have many swift arrows under my arm
in my quiver
that speak to those who understand; but without exception they
need announcers.

What was particularly controversial about these lines up until only comparatively recently was the interpretation of the second part, ἐς δὲ τὸ πᾶν ἑρμανέων χατίζει.[29] The majority of scholars saw, in these verses, the manifesto of an esoteric poet: Pindar speaks 'darkly', like an oracle or a seer, so that if his words are to be understood by 'the masses' (τὸ πᾶν), they will require 'interpreters' (ἑρμανέων). But in 1986, Most (following Heyne in the eighteenth century and Gundert and Perosa in the twentieth[30]) pointed out (a) that everywhere else we find the expression ἐς τὸ πᾶν in the Greek literature of the fifth century, it is used interchangeably with παντῶς, 'entirely', and (b) that the ἑρμανῆες named here do not have to be 'interpreters' but can just as easily be 'announcers'; the text would then be speaking here of the absolute necessity of retrieving and expressing the thoughts that lie hidden in the inwardness of the subject so that they really do become speech.[31]

[29] The research up to 1964 is summarized by van Leeuwen 1964, pp. 229–232; on the discussion in the 1980s, see Most 1986 and Verdenius 1989. More recent discussions entailing more than a mere report of the suggestions thus far seem to be lacking.

[30] Heyne 1807–1809, vol. i (first published in 1797), p. 32 *ad* 152: 'ἐς δὲ τὸ πὰν, πάντως, ἑρμηνέων χατίζει pro ἑρμηνείας, quae *elocutio* est antiquis; *verbis, carmine, reddenda sunt illa animi cogitata*' (his italics); see further Gundert 1935, pp. 55 and 131 n. 251, and Perosa 1941, p. 51 f.

[31] See Most 1986, esp. p. 307 ('ἐς τὸ πάν [...] functions as an adverb [and] strongly affirms the word it modifies') and p. 311 ('[M]ight we not take the ἑρμανεῖς to be people capable of *expressing* [the themes or ideas which Pindar has available to him], of *speaking them out loud*?' [my italics]). Parallels for ἐς τὸ πᾶν as πάντως are Aesch., *Ag.* 682, *Cho.* 684, *Eum.* 52, 83, 291, 401, 538 and 891, and Eur., *Heracl.* 575. Race 1979 already notes that the expression nowhere means *in vulgus* (this is Boeckh's translation: Boeckh 1811–1821, vol. II ii, p. 32 and 133). For ἑρμηνεύς as 'speaker', Most can cite Eur., fr. 126 Kannicht from the lost *Andromeda*; Philyllios, fr. 11. 2 Kock; Xen., *Mem.* I 2. 52; Thuc. II 60. 5; Pl., *Leg.* XII, 966 b7; and Arist., *Soph. el.* IV, 166 b11. *Cf.* however Verdenius 1989, p. 81, who understands the passage in the sense of the following verses as the assertion that Pindar's words are intuitively and directly comprehensible for the knowledgeable in his audience without the mediation of any discursive-interpretative agency—that is, they *lack* interpreters (this is the meaning of χατίζειν in Hom., *Od.* 16. 35 and Hes., *Op.* 21) because their specific public needs none (with δὲ ἀντὶ τοῦ γάρ in verse 85).

Now this notion of speech as something that flies is of course entirely traditional: the collocation ἔπεα πτερόεντα, 'winged words', occurs in the *Iliad* and the *Odyssey* over 120 times and goes back, it seems, to an Indo-European poetic tradition; words are 'winged', or perhaps 'feathered', because as soon as they are spoken they fly—like a bird or an arrow—as sound from the speaker to his or her addressee.[32] Where a word in Homer is ἄπτερος, 'without feathers', it does not fly, for the simple reason that it is not spoken aloud.[33] In Pindar as in epic, language is rigorously bound to the voice of the speaker: Pindar's 'arrows' are taken from their quiver and fly to 'those who understand'; the distance they cover is that between the speaker and his immediate audience.[34] The metaphor thus describes not only precisely the communicative context that is the presupposition of every historical approach to interpreting the odes and in which they are performed for a public that is present to the speaker and will understand the symbolic system he uses to communicate with it.[35] The arrows also code the claim to a radical identity between what is outside and inside, between intention and its expression, that such

Cf. also Race 1997, vol. 1, p. 72 n. 2, who interprets the reference to the necessity of interpreters as a break-off formula.

[32] The consensus of scholarship is that ἔπεα πτερόεντα always refers to 'speech as *utterance*, as thing *heard* and transmitted' (Martin 1989, p. 30, my italics; see also Pavese 1972, pp. 204–205 n. 1). The question of whether Homeric poetry thought of birds or feathers when it assigned the adjective πτερόεις has been answered by Kirk 1985, p. 75 *ad* Hom., *Il.* 1. 201 in the former sense, and by Latacz 1968, Létoublon 1999 and Latacz *et al.* ²2002, p. 91 *ad* Hom., *Il.* 1. 201 in the latter (see however *LfgrE* III *s.v.* πτερόεις). A summary of older literature can be found in Combellack 1950; see also Vivante 1975, D'Avino 1980–1981, Martin 1989, pp. 30–37 and Létoublon 1999, pp. 321–327. Martin suggests a speech-act-theoretical analysis of the expression: speeches described as ἔπεα πτερόεντα take place as a rule (at least in the *Iliad*) between two people in proximity to each other and have the character of directives (on directives as speech-acts, see Searle 1979, pp. 1–29). Martin's own explanation of the metaphor ('the aural quality resulting from the flight of birds', *ibid.*, p. 36) emphasizes the duration and intensity of what is spoken (see *ibid.*, p. 37). *LfgrE* III, col. 1607 cites Hom., *Od.* 7. 36 where νόημα and πτέρον are connected as an illustration of rapidity. On the Indo-European background of the metaphor, see Durante 1968, Dunkel 1979, pp. 258 and 266 n. 2, and West 1997, p. 230 f.

[33] The verse ὣς ἄρ' ἐφώνησεν, τῇ δ' ἄπτερος ἔπλετο μῦθος occurs four times in the *Odyssey* (17. 57 = 19. 29 = 21. 386 = 22. 398; *cf.* also Aesch., *Ag.* 276 ἄπτερος φάτις); see on this Hainsworth 1960 and Latacz 1968.

[34] Dickson 1990 has noted the priority of the audible over the visible in the implicit semiotics of the epinicians; see in particular his interpretation of the snake-scene in *Olymp.* 8. 41–46 (*ibid.*, p. 112 f.).

[35] See above, p. 152.

approaches require in order to argue that this intention is the final authority in matters of interpretation.[36]

In the structure of this metaphor, the subject takes on the role of the origin, the ἀρχή (here both source and authority) not only of poetry as *voice*, but also of poetry as *meaning*. This meaning is initially found in the absolute interiority of subjectivity, which, as verses 86–88 go on to make clear, belongs to the sphere of φύσις/φυά and is opposed to what merely is μαθητόν, that is, what comes from outside: θέσις, νόμος, τέχνη.[37] The arrow that crosses the border between inside and outside is the connecting link between both domains: the speaker expresses something that is originally inside him, something he wants to say. We can thus already make out a first, perhaps even a primary condition of subjectivity in Pindar, which seems to place him just as firmly within the history of metaphysics as the other authors we have mentioned: an authentic subject is the inward origin of an outward speech whose function consists solely in expressing this inwardness as its secondary or derivative sign. Indeed, the metaphoricity of the arrow is dependent upon just this value of subjectivity, for only the latter can guarantee that behind the figurative language of flight a real, intended, literal meaning is to be found—in other words, that it is not in fact a catachresis. Not only subjectivity, but also the recoverability of meaning itself relies on the postulate of an uncontaminated interiority of thought of which speech is only the outward—and thus in principle dispensable—expression.

Now, before we consider the continuation of this metaphor in the following verses of the *Second Olympian*—it is, for reasons which will rapidly become apparent, somewhat unusual—it is worth observing some of the typical variations on this model of language as a movement

[36] Simpson 1969, p. 453 interprets the metaphor of the bow as a comparison between Pindar and the god of poets and archers, Apollo, and thus also as a figure of the speaker's authority and control over the effects of his own language: 'To appear in such a guise [...] insures that the effect sought will be gained.' Similarly Fitzgerald 1983, p. 62 and Lefkowitz 1991, p. 162 f.

[37] On this opposition, see Miller 1982–1983, pp. 209–211, Hubbard 1985, pp. 107–124 and above, p. 69 ff. The motif of the superiority of natural ability—*poeta non fit, sed nascitur*—is used here, entirely in accordance with the elitist ideology it both presupposes and implies (see Rose 1974, p. 151 ff.), as an means of distancing oneself from real or imagined competitors. What is interesting at this point, however, is the role played by the opposition between inside and outside in the formulation of the difference: the naturally gifted speaker of the *Second Olympian* will realize his inward thought as external speech better and more effectively than those individuals who have first had to acquire their skill from a source outside of themselves (so Most 1986, p. 314), not least because he possesses an originary inwardness which is, in a certain sense, *sui generis*.

from inside to outside in the epinicians.[38] The *Second Isthmian*, a relatively short ode from the years after 472 B.C. for Thrasybulus, Theron's nephew, begins with a combination of the metaphor of the bowman with that of the chariot of the Muses (1–4):[39]

> Οἱ μὲν πάλαι, ὦ Θρασύβουλε, φῶτες, οἳ χρυσαμπύκων
> ἐς δίφρον Μοισᾶν ἔβαινον κλυτᾷ φόρμιγγι συναντόμενοι,
> ῥίμφα παιδείους ἐτόξευον μελιγάρυας ὕμνους,
> ὅστις ἐὼν καλὸς [...]
>
> The men of old, Thrasybulus, who
> mounted the chariot of the gold-wreathed Muses taking with them the fame-making phorminx,
> rapidly shot honey-voiced hymns for boys
> at any one who was beautiful [...].

Songs are being shot, and it is clear that the beautiful boys are, to begin with, their addressees: the singer is to woo and win them over by means of his poetry.[40] The topic of this beginning is thus (also) the rhetoric of persuasion, and it too is figured by the arrows.[41] But immediately, by means of this figure, a new, referential aspect enters into the metaphor, since the boys are not merely to be addressed, but are also themselves the topic of the songs. The *παίδειος ὕμνος* is not only a song *for* a boy, but also one *about* one.[42] Apostrophe and signi-

[38] The metaphor occurs in the following passages: *Olymp.* 1. 111 f., *Olymp.* 9. 5–12, *Pyth.* 1. 12, *Nem.* 3. 65, *Nem.* 6. 27 f., *Isthm.* 2. 3 und *Isthm.* 5. 46–48. We will concentrate here initially on the *Olympians* and *Isthmians*.

[39] The combination (if this is one) occurs in Pindar only here: Simpson's (1969, pp. 458–470) parallels—*Isthm.* 5. 42–53, *Nem.* 1. 1–20 und *Olymp.* 1. 108–112—are merely juxtapositions of the two metaphors and are thus not really parallels at all. On the chariot of the Muses, *cf.* further *Pyth.* 10. 65, *Isthm.* 8. 61–63, *Olymp.* 6. 22–28 and *Isthm.* 7. 16–21, further Verdenius 1982, p. 2 *ad* 2 with n. 5. Simpson 1969, pp. 470–473 understands the opening of the *Second Isthmian* in the sense that the arrows are being shot from the chariot during the journey. See on this Asper 1997, p. 28. n. 33 who rightly observes that Pindar is entirely capable of contaminating vehicles with the same tenor without feeling any overwhelming need to harmonize them; this passage is thus not a combination either.

[40] *Cf.* Bacchyl. 10. 42 f.: *ἕτερος δ' (sc. σοφὸς) ἐπὶ παισί | ποικίλον τόξον τιταίνει.* Aeschylus uses the metaphor of the arrow in *Ag.* 239 ff. to describe the emotional effect of the looks Iphigenia directs towards her sacrificers.

[41] Verdenius 1982, p. 5 notes that *μελίγαρυς* is used in *Od.* 12. 187 of the sirens. *Cf.* also *Hymn. Hom. Ap.* 519 and Alcm., fr. 26. 1, both descriptions of song.

[42] The designation *παίδειος ὕμνος* (on the accent of *παίδειος/παιδεῖος* see Hdn. I 135 Lentz) is obviously a parallel to expressions such as *Καστόρειος ὕμνος* (*Isthm.* 1. 16), this latter a hymn both for and about Castor (see Most 1985b, pp. 50 and 58).

fying intention are, however, not clearly distinguishable here, since both can easily be the tenor of the metaphor.[43]

The situation is different in the *Fifth Isthmian* for a victor from Aegina: here, the metaphor of the arrows is explicitly used to emphasize the singer's ability to celebrate the achievements of the Aeginetans (46–48):

> πολλὰ μὲν ἀρτιεπής
> γλῶσσά μοι τοξεύματ' ἔχει περὶ κείνων
> κελαδέσαι·
>
> My eloquent tongue
> has many arrows in order to
> sing about them.

The passage begins with the same term for multiplicity that we could observe in *Olymp.* 2. 83, and of course it plays the same role within the conventional rhetoric of the ode: it prepares the listener for the reduction of the theoretically possible diversity of topics (πολλὰ μέν) to the one topic that the singer intends to choose, here the athletic triumphs of Kleonikos' family in verses 53 ff.[44] At this point, however, the interpretation of the metaphor (which returns at the end of the poem: πτερόεντα νέον σύμπεμψον ὕμνον, 63) is explicitly guided by the prepositional phrase περὶ κείνων: the arrows are not there to speak *to* the Aiginetans—although this is precisely what is happening; the ode is being performed in front of an Aiginetan audience—but rather to speak *about* them. The difference between a passage such as this and Homer is obvious: the speaking subject is still the starting-point or ἀρχή of the movement of the song, but this time the journey is towards its topic.[45]

43 What is then the *function* of the metaphor? Martin's speech-act-theoretical interpretation of the figure (see above, n. 32), like speech-act theory in general, presupposes that the linguistic form (and here even the content) of an expression is the epiphenomenon of its function. In this respect, Martin's analysis is structurally very similar to Bundy's: see above, p. 61 ff.

44 See Bundy 1986, p. 73 and (in more detail) Race 1990, p. 53 f., who notes that μέν in verse 46 is first answered by ἀλλ' ὅμως in verse 51.

45 The difference has been noted in the scholarship: see Lefkowitz 1991, 62 f. In tragedy, it is usually unclear whether the metaphor is being used in the 'Homeric' or the 'Pindaric' sense: *cf.* Soph., *OT* 783 f., Eur., *Hec.* 603 (*cf.* Pindar, fr. 213. 4 where the νοῦς is also described as an organ of speech), *Hipp.* 499, *Supp.* 456 (probably 'Pindaric'), fr. 494. 1–2 Kannicht from the *Melanippe Desmotis*, fr. 1044 Kannicht (οὔτ' ἐκ χερὸς μεθέντα καρτερὸν λίθον | ῥᾷον κατασχεῖν οὔτ' ἀπὸ γλώσσης λόγον; Kannicht notes the Homeric

The intentionality of referential speech is also the basis of the metaphor of the arrows at the beginning of the *Ninth Olympian*. This time, we are concerned with a certain Epharmostos from Opous who won the wrestling contest in the mid-460s. 'Right after his victory', the ode begins, 'it was enough to sing, "Long live the victor!" over and over again, in order to celebrate him.' Then (5–14):

ἀλλὰ νῦν ἑκαταβόλων Μοισᾶν *ἀπὸ τόξων*
Δία τε φοινικοστερόπαν σεμνόν τ' ἐπίνειμα
ἀκρωτήριον Ἄλιδος
τοιοῖσδε βέλεσσιν
τὸ δή ποτε Λυδὸς ἥρως Πέλοψ
ἐξάρατο κάλλιστον ἕδνον Ἱπποδαμείας·
πτερόεντα δ' ἵει γλυκύν
Πυθῶνάδ' ὀιστόν· οὔτοι χαμαιπετέων λόγων ἐφάψεαι,
ἀνδρὸς ἀμφὶ παλαίσμασιν φόρμιγγ' ἐλελίζων
κλεινᾶς ἐξ Ὀπόεντος·

But now, from the far-shooting bows of the Muses
shoot a volley of arrows such as these
at Zeus of the red lightning
and at the sacred hilltop of Elis,
which Pelops, the Lydian hero, once won
as the fairest dowry of Hippodameia;
and cast a sweet winged
arrow at Pytho. You will surely take up no words that fall to the ground,
while making the lyre vibrate in honour of the wrestling
of a man from famous Opous.[46]

This call goes out to the *κῶμος*, the procession consisting of young men of Opous invited to celebrate the victor now returned home. Their song is to be fired at Zeus, at Olympia and Delphi, but the two places named are, once again, not the addressees of the ode, at least not in the sense of Homer's winged words, which of course presuppose that the person being spoken is within hearing distance. Instead, the localities of victory are again the specific topics of speech, and this in contrast to the *καλλίνικος*, whose generic applicability to every victory without distinction is the background or foil for the epinician

collocation *καρτερὸν βέλος* [*Il.* 5. 104] and its metaphorical transformation in Pindar, *Olymp.* 1. 112: *ἐμοὶ μὲν ὦν* | Μοῖσα *καρτερώτατον βέλος ἀλκᾷ τρέφει*), and the corrupt fr. *adesp.* 529 Snell-Kannicht. Unambiguously 'Pindaric' are Aesch., *Supp.* 446 and *Ag.* 628, probably also *Eum.* 676. *Cf.* also Pl., *Tht.* 180 a2 ff. and *Leg.* 705 e3 ff.

[46] Tr. Race 1997, vol. 1, pp. 149–151.

which now follows.[47] But when the singer promises that his words will not fall to the ground like misfired arrows instead of reaching their goal, this does not mean that the speaker wants to speak about Olympia *etc.* and denies that he might not be able to do so, but rather that by praising Epharmostos' victory instead of something else, he will be choosing the right subject for his song.[48] The metaphor of the arrows takes on, here, a normative force that structures the poetics of the epinicians. Where the arrow that is shot hits the goal at which it is aimed, where the originary distance between both of them is successfully overcome, that is where the poetological *telos* of the ode is to be found.[49]

Proximity and distance, the creation of the one by overcoming the other, in fact structure all of the central metaphors for thematic propriety in Pindar. One of them is the well-known figure of the path.[50] Its close relationship to the metaphor of the arrows finds expression in several songs. The singer of the *First Olympian*, for example, hopes at the end of his ode that Hieron will soon win an Olympian chariot victory (108–112):

εἰ δὲ μὴ ταχὺ λίποι,
ἔτι γλυκυτέραν κεν ἔλπομαι
σὺν ἅρματι θοῷ κλεΐξειν[51] *ἐπίκουρον εὑρὼν ὁδὸν λόγων*
παρ' εὐδείελον ἐλθὼν Κρόνιον. ἐμοὶ μὲν ὦν
Μοῖσα καρτερώτατον βέλος ἀλκᾷ τρέφει·

If he (*sc.* the god) does not suddenly abandon you,
I hope to celebrate an even more pleasant matter

47 Miller 1993a, p. 123, emphasizes the contrast between the song of Archilochus and Pindar's ode with respect to their thematic specificity: 'Whereas the earlier phase has as its own melic component the *τήνελλα καλλίνικε* attributed to Archilochos, in which temporal and spatial immediacy is offset by a merely generic appropriateness of content, the formal ode produced through the agency of the "far-shooting Muses" combines greater distance (both temporal and spatial) from the occasion of victory with a uniquely specific applicability to the case in hand.' On the *καλλίνικος* see further Kurke 1988, pp. 103–106, Morgan 1993, p. 3 f. and Gerber 2002, p. 21 *ad* 1–4.

48 A slightly different case is *Pyth.* 6. 37, where the concern is with the efficacy of what is spoken as a speech-act, once again a very Homeric use of the metaphor.

49 *Cf.* Aesch., *Supp.* 446 and, in a different sense, Theunissen 2000, p. 816 ff.

50 On the metaphor of the path of song in Pindar see Becker 1937, pp. 50–100, Gianotti 1975, pp. 119–121, and Asper 1997, pp. 26–39. Athanassaki 2004, pp. 323–325 reads the switch between first and second person in this passage as the attempt to bridge the distance between *laudator* and *laudandus.*

51 On the future infinitive with *κεν*/*ἄν* see (in addition to KG I, p. 241, § 389) Kannicht 1969, vol. 2, p. 134 *ad* Eur., *Hel.* 448 and Gerber 1982, p. 166 *ad loc.*

with a quick chariot and to find a helpful path of words,
having come to the sunny hill of Kronos. For me
the Muse nourishes the strongest arrow with valour.

Here, the 'path of words' and the 'strongest arrow' connect subjective *ἀρχή* and thematic *τέλος*, so that the journey of the poet and the implicit shooting of the projectile overcome the distance between them. In particular the chariot is an example of the metaphorisation of an object that—this is the singer's hope—will one day really exist: the *ἅρμα* is simultaneously both the chariot with which Hieron could win an Olympic victory and the 'chariot of the Muses'.[52] In one of the most elaborate variations on this idea, the singer of the *Sixth Olympian* suddenly asks, at the point where the song moves from the explicit praise of the victor to the narration of his family's founding myth, to be driven in a chariot to the *γένος* of Hagesias' ancestors and to Pitana (22–28);[53] in the *Fourth Isthmian*, the journey to a specific place is replaced by the hunt 'on roads in every direction' (19–21), but the intentional structure of the metaphor remains the same. In all of these songs, the description of speech is based on a prior distance whose overcoming by words as arrows or by the singer himself constitutes the act of referential speech. Both poles of this distance, the inner point of departure and the outer place of what is referred to, are basic to the metaphor.

In the continuation of the *Second Olympian*, to which we now return, the congruence between intention and voice is also marked by the metaphor of the bow in the verses 89–95 already quoted above:[54]

ἔπεχε νῦν σκοπῷ τόξον, ἄγε θυμέ· τίνα βάλλομεν[55]
ἐκ μαλθακᾶς αὖτε φρενὸς εὐκλέας ὀιστοὺς ἱέντες; ἐπί τοι
Ἀκράγαντι τανύσαις
αὐδάσομαι ἐνόρκιον λόγον ἀλαθεῖ νόῳ
τεκεῖν μή τιν' ἑκατόν γε ἐτέων πόλιν φίλοις ἄνδρα μᾶλλον
εὐεργέταν πραπίσιν ἀφθονέστερόν τε χέρα
Θήρωνος.

Now aim the bow at the mark, come, my heart. At whom

[52] Farnell 1932, p. 11 and Köhnken 1974, p. 205 refer *σὺν ἅρματι θοῷ* exclusively to the victorious future chariot; Schroeder 1900, p. 89, Becker 1937, p. 78 f. and Gerber 1982, p. 165 *ad loc.* note the possible double reference.

[53] See Asper 1997, pp. 28–30 on this passage.

[54] See above, p. 168.

[55] On the present (not the subjunctive, *pace* van Leeuwen 1964, p. 256 *ad loc.*) see Pfeijffer 1999a, p. 304 n. 120.

do we shoot, and this time launch from a kindly spirit our arrows of fame? Yes,
bending the bow at Akragas,
I will proclaim a statement on oath with a truthful mind,
that no city within a century has produced a man more beneficent to his friends
in spirit and more generous of hand than
Theron.[56]

The speaker's bow is once again explicitly not directed at an audience; the metaphor describes, as we have come to expect, the referential relationship of the assertion to its object. This assertion is made under oath and 'with a truthful mind', both characteristics that imply the exact agreement between the λόγος that represents and the νοῦς that is represented.[57] It is striking, however, that the statement made in this way chiastically reverses the clear delineation of the place of the subject from only a few verses earlier: the thoughts within, the place of their phenomenological object and the area where they take on performative force as communication without. As the son of his city, Theron is beneficial in his πραπίδες and without φθόνος with or in his hand.[58] The opposition χείρ *versus* πραπίδες is, in Pindar as in the rest of archaic Greek literature, a commonplace: the hand, locus of an athlete's or a hero's strength, represents his ἀρετή and the intention located in the interiority of his mind by translating it into outward action.[59]

56 Tr. Race 1997, vol. 1, p. 73.

57 On ἀληθής as 'truthful' in this sense see Cole 1983.

58 The *acc. resp.* χέρα must designate the bodily part in which the lack of φθόνος is immediately realized: *cf. Isthm.* 3/4. 71 μορφὰν βράχυς or 87 f. λευκωθεὶς κάρα | μύρτοις; Hummel 1993, p. 103 f., § 102 gives further examples.

59 In *Isthmian* 5. 61, the singer praises Pytheas for being χερσὶ δεξιόν, νόῳ ἀντίπαλον (with the metaphorical attribution of wrestling to the νοῦς); in *Olympian* 4. 24 f., Erginos says of himself that his χεῖρες δὲ καὶ ἦτορ correspond to his quickness on foot. *Cf.* further the opposition of χείρ and βουλαί in *Pyth.* 4. 72 and *Nem.* 8. 8 and the opposition of χείρ and ψυχή in *Nem.* 9. 39. In *Pyth.* 1. 42, the series καὶ σοφοὶ καὶ χερσὶ βιαταί is to be understood disjunctively (see Hummel 1993, p. 193, § 230), thus here too a division of the μαχαναὶ πᾶσαι in the previous verse. More generally, the body in Pindar frequently has the value of the external sign of an inward quality: the body, its beauty or stature, is the signifier of the athlete's qualities, not itself the signified. In the *Eighth Olympian*, the victor Alkimedon has not shamed his appearance by his deeds: ἦν δ' ἐσορᾶν καλός, ἔργῳ τ' οὐ κατὰ εἶδος ἐλέγχων | ἐξένεπε κρατέων πάλᾳ δολιχήρετμον Αἴγιναν πάτραν (19 f.). Dickson 1988, p. 115 observes how the physical beauty of the athlete here becomes the signifier of the values and abilities that must find expression in his achievements: '[T]he body in its physical appearance (*kalos*), that is, primarily as something seen by others (*esorân*), is made to figure as a sign of something else not otherwise (or through itself) visible.' A similar semiotic interpretation of the body takes

As a consequence, the ἔργον thus performed belongs to the order of the signifier, not the signified.[60] But φθόνος clearly belongs to the latter realm, not the former: it is the inward object of representation, not its outward means.[61] Theron's own interiority is thus described by a term

place in *Olymp.* 9. 94 (ὡραῖος ἐὼν καὶ καλὸς κάλλιστά τε ῥέξαις), *Nem.* 3. 19 (εἰ δ' ἐὼν καλὸς ἔρδων τ' ἐοικότα μορφᾷ; see Pfeijffer 1999b, p. 283 *ad loc.*) and *Isthm.* 7. 21–22b (φέρει γὰρ Ἰσθμοῖ | νίκαν παγκρατίου, σθένει τ' ἔκπαγλος ἰδεῖν τε μορφάεις, ἄγει τ' ἀρετὰν οὐκ αἴσχιον φυᾶς). See also Donlan 1973, esp. 369–372, and Hubbard 1985, p. 111 on *Isthm.* 4. 49–55. What can be seen in the body is thus associated with the visible achievement (ἔργον): both are signifiers of an ἀρετή invisible until its incarnation in athletic deed or physical beauty. On the hand as the *locus* of strength and instrument of the victor's ἔργα, see further *Olymp.* 10. 100, *Pyth.* 1. 41 f. and 2. 8, *Nem.* 1. 45 and 5. 19, and *Isthm.* 2. 20–22 and 8. 71.

[60] In *Olymp.* 10. 63, the victor's ἔγρον is opposed to his δόξα, that is, his hope for an as yet unrealized victory. The compound noun εὐεργέτας is used, at the other four places in which it occurs in Pindar, consistently in connection with actions, not merely with attitudes or character traits. In *Pyth.* 4. 30, Eurypylos begins his speech with the words that εὐεργέται use to offer foreign guests a meal; in *Pyth.* 2. 24, we read Ixion's injunction to repay one's benefactor—the main example of this is Zeus, from whom Ixion received (ἑλών) a pleasant life among the gods; in *Pyth.* 5. 44, Karrhotos is described as Arkesilas' benefactor (the general call to meet a εὐεργέτας with a willing mind only makes sense directly after the description of Karrhotos' victory in Arkesilas' name if it refers to the charioteer and his specific achievement); finally, in *Isthm.* 1. 53 Poseidon is described as the εὐεργέτας ἁρμάτων who thus helps them to victory. The translation of εὐεργεσία at *Isthm.* 6. 70 as 'act of kindness' is uncontroversial. The εὐεργέτας is someone who does good deeds; as a characteristic of mere thoughts or personality, the word is used nowhere in the epinicians—except, it would seem, here.

[61] It is clear that envy is an intentional experience in the phenomenological sense: see Husserl 1992, vol. 3, pp. 402–405. Andrew Millar observes that '[φ]θόνος and its derivatives denote both a *state of feeling* (i.e. the malicious desire to deprive others of what is theirs) and an *action* (i.e. the withholding, refusing, or denying of something expected, requested, or deserved, with no implication that ill-will is the motivation). The latter is the regular meaning in Homer [...] and survives throughout the history of the language in the privative compounds (e.g. ἄφθονος which means both "unstinted" [i.e. "abundant"] and "unstinting" [i.e. "generous"]). In Pindar the noun always and the verb and adjective usually denote the psychological state, but cf. *I.* 5, 24–25 [...] and *I.* 1, 43–45 [...], where the construction with the infinitive (in *I.* 5) and the stress laid on the notion of recompense [in both poems] make clear that the sense of stinting, of active refusal or denial, is to the fore' (Miller 1982–1983, p. 210 n. 33). Only the latter passage contains the adjective, but the collocation ἀφθονεραῖσι [...] γνώμαις in *Isthm.* 1. 44 f. explicitly indicates that the attribute of φθόνος belongs to the psychic part of the human being. Bulman compares *Olymp.* 2. 94 with *Pyth.* 3. 71 in the sense of a fundamental psychological dialectics between good and bad desire in Theron and Hieron. Her conclusion: 'They are not merely generous, but rather remarkably free of the φθόνος that seems to infest others. Even then if ἀ. is translated as "generous", we should not underestimate its ethical complexity' (Bulman 1992, p. 28). The metonymy χέρα, that in the *Second Olympian* creates the contrast with the πραπίδες, finds its counterpart in *Pyth.* 8. 72 ὄπιν ἄφονον. The only other passage in Pindar in which the adjective does not mean 'abun-

designating external efficacy, whilst this efficacy itself or rather the bodily part that implements it is given *ex negativo* the inner capacity for φθόνος. That is all the more problematic when we consider that the claim to truthfulness depends entirely on the connection between the two clearly distinct areas of inner intention and its expression. The chiasm is indeed only possible on the basis of the previous distinction between inside and outside which separates the domains of νοῦς and λόγος so that the one can become the perfect expression of the other; it takes place however at the same time as a reversal of the poles of the dichotomy which makes this representational relationship possible in the first place.[62]

The structure of phenomenological intentionality is metaphorically subverted by the localisation of an intentional attitude in a part of the body whose externality is contrasted more than once in the epinicians with the inwardness of subjectivity as origin.[63] It is not thereby

dant' is *Olymp.* 6. 6 f.: *τίνα κεν φύγοι ὕμνον κεῖνος ἀνήρ, ἐπικύρσαις | ἀφθόνων ἀστῶν ἐν ἱμερταῖς ἀοιδαῖς*; Simon Goldhill remarks on these verses: 'The expression of glory in song [...] is bounded by a condition—that the victor meet with citizens who *feel* [my italics here—G.P.] no *phthonos* with regard to pleasant songs' (Goldhill 1991, p. 147). But if we accept that Pindar's *ἀφθονέστερόν τε χέρα* is metonymic in the context of his own system, we must then ask what the metonymy here does. How does it relate to the thesis of the inner subject and the interiority of intention?

62 It could appear that our reading of this passage as a chiasm assumes that, just as the *ἔργον* implies the hand as its executive agency, so too φθόνος accrues in a literal sense not to the hand but instead to the mind and thus—let us admit it—leaves the door disquietingly open for the value of the 'literal' that, in the classical, metaphysical theory of metaphor, is allegedly hiding behind the figure and whose priority we are here calling into question. This opening, however, would not be the consequence of an alleged 'nature' of language, but rather an effect of the intentional logic that Pindar himself sets up with the metaphor of the *βέλη φωνάεντα* in 83 ff. The *συνετοί* understand *by definition* only what is *meant*. But what does 'meaning' mean, if it cannot be distinguished from what is *said* and what can therefore be *mis*understood—that is, in a way in which it was not meant? In other words: *Olymp.* 2. 83–86 constructs precisely the difference between rhetoric and meaning whose subversion we could already observe in the *First Olympian* (see above, p. 121 ff.). *Within* the logic of this distinction between what is said and what is meant, between the figure and its meaning—whose consequences we have attempted to sketch above—grammar and lexicography retain all of their binding force.

63 Such an interpretation of this motif in the *Second Olympian* is by no means 'decontextualised', as is sometimes said of 'deconstructive' readings. Is it not the very essence of political power to maintain control of the regions of the inside and the outside? The suggestion that it is possible to exchange interiority for exteriority in the person of the sovereign implies the absolute transparency of his acts; the performance of power as the pure externality of an unchanged inwardness grounds every act of sovereignty in a disposition that itself seems to underlie no merely political control, but instead to belong to the unquestionable, tendentially divine realm of nature. Doing and Being are thus

'refuted': nothing speaks here for the assumption that we must read the figure of the 'hand without envy' as more important or more central as the metaphor of the quiver. The question is not: is the subject in the *Second Olympian* 'essentially' inward or outward? Rather, my assertion here is that a presentation of Pindaric constructions of subjectivity must take account not only of terms of interiority and the descriptions of language dependent on them, but also of a second series of figures in which elements that, in the first series, construct Pindaric subjects, are not inward, but rather part of an exteriority that cannot be integrated into a genuinely hermeneutic reading of the texts as the expression of an inward meaning by any sublimation of difference. The referentiality of the speech act was a first such element; a second is the speaker's sovereign mastery of his own speech.

Rhetoric breaks (off)

In the so-called 'break-off formula' (*Abbruchsformel*), the author of the epinicians performs his claim to being responsible for and in control of his own texts or of the meaning of these texts.[64] The gesture is remarkable, not least because, in being made at all, it implies that the language of the victory odes has become, at least for a moment, uncontrollable and denies it, for this moment, the status of a *τέχνη*.[65] Only a non-technical language can withdraw itself from the control of a singer. The statement, made repeatedly in research, that this *retrait* of language is a fiction—simulated spontaneity[66]—does not of itself imply that the author here plays any but the most conventional role, or that the subject does not, in fact, determine the entire meaning of what he says. On the contrary: it is precisely in these break-off formulae that one can recognize the essential significance of presence for the claim of the text to be the expression of a sovereign subject.

Whether about Olympia, the origins of Hagesias' family, or the victory of the Kleonymidai: referential speech is, as we have noted, always carried out over a distance that must be overcome. Where this

exhaustively reducible to each other: it is this disguise of a disguise that we can observe here in Pindar's anything but apolitical poetry.

64 The term seems to have arisen in the 1920s: Dornseiff 1921 does not mention it, but see Schadewaldt 1966 (originally 1928), p. 10 and elsewhere. An excellent discussion of the figure in Pindar in general is Race 1990, pp. 41–57.

65 On the notion of *τέχνη* in Pindar see Dickson 1986.

66 Thus Scodel, who speaks of 'pseudo-spontaneity' and argues that the self-correction characteristic of the break-off formula is an allusion to the performance of the text by a chorus, not by a single singer (Scodel 1996, p. 65).

does not succeed, where the distance between the origin and the end remains or even reasserts itself, either no one speaks, or whoever speaks does so about something else, possibly the wrong thing. Here, the normativity of speaking rightly that we observed above in the *Ninth Olympian* again becomes important. In the *Thirteenth Olympian*, the javelin must not miss its target (93–97):

> *ἐμὲ δ᾽ εὐθὺν ἀκόντων*
> *ἱέντα ῥόμβον παρὰ σκοπὸν οὐ χρή*
> *τὰ πολλὰ βέλεα καρτύνειν χεροῖν.*
> *Μοίσαις γὰρ ἀγλαοθρόνοις ἑκὼν*
> *Ὀλιγαιθίδαισίν τ᾽ ἔβαν ἐπίκουρος.*

> I must, when I throw the javelins'
> whirl on its straight path, not hurl beside the target
> the many missiles from my hands.
> For I am come as a willing helper of the Muses
> on their splendid thrones, and for the Oligaithidai.

This passage marks the break: in the verses immediately before it, the singer has told the myth of Bellerophon and Pegasus and now performs his return to singing about the victor with the metaphor of the javelins.[67] If the help that he owes the Muses consists in his singing well, his obligation to the Oligaithidai is that he praises them appropriately. The *σκοπός* thus marks the point at which the song as a structure of reference meets (once again) its rightful object, in this case the family of the victor.[68]

[67] Hubbard 1986a, p. 42 refers the words *εὐθύς* and *ῥόμβος* to different parts of the poem: 'The mythological sequence which the poet has related is like the whirling wind-up (*ῥόμβον*) which necessarily precedes and gives impetus to the final spear cast (= praise of the victor and his family); the various myths are like a repeated circular motion in their paradigmatic equivalence, as opposed to the singular and linear (*εὐθύν*) praise of the victor to which everything builds up.' This does not seem to be the case: a spear must spin along its major axis in the air in order to fly in a straight line. To the extent that they both belong to the vehicle of the metaphor, *εὐθύς* and *ῥόμβος* are part of the same movement.

[68] Hubbard 1986a expresses the *communis opinio* when he asserts that the *σκοπός* is 'the encomiastic programme' (42) in the sense of a number of specific topics required by the genre, here the praise of the victor and his family, the Oligaithidai. This interpretation implies that if Pindar were to continue to tell the story of Bellerophon, he really would speak 'beside the mark' (since he would be speaking about Bellerophon and not about the Oligaithidai). This thesis is problematic for the following reasons: 1. The thematic chain of metaphors for speaking about a given topic in the epinicians sets up a specific logic within which a reading such as Hubbard's would be curiously anomalous.

This encounter, the centralising effect of the eminent object, is most often localized in the victory odes as a negative object of prohibition (*οὐ χρή*) or as the object of a retrospective assertion. We can already see, on the basis of this tendency alone, how plausible it would be to cast the *σκοπός* of speech in the role of Lacan's *objet du désir*, as an object of striving whose merely being named in the symbolic order of language already effects a distance from it.[69] In a passage such as *Nem.* 6. 26–28, the assertion that the target is or has been hit takes the place of a real bull's-eye as its unavoidable substitute:

[...] *ἔλπομαι*
μέγα εἰπὼν σκοποῦ ἄντα τυχεῖν
ὥτ' ἀπὸ τόξου ἱείς

[...] I think that
in making this great claim, I have hit the mark head on,
shooting, like an archer, from my bow.

The exuberant praise of the victor's family has corresponded entirely to what ought to have been said—that, at least, is what the singer believes or hopes (*ἔλπομαι*, 26). The verb signals here, too, that reality—what is the *case*—is not immediately present to the singer; not the *σκοπός* itself, but merely the assertion that the arrow has not flown *παρὰ σκοπόν* is the intentional object of his statement, and that as a not yet adequate intuition (in Husserl's sense).[70] The teleological structure

A statement such as 'your words will surely not miss the mark when you sing of Epharmostos' wrestling' (*cf. Olymp.* 9. 12), interpreted in Hubbard's sense, would have to mean: 'you will continue correctly with the epinician programme if you now commence with the praise of the victor.' Given that the programme consists primarily in the praise of the victor, this line borders on a for Pindar uncharacteristic tautology. 2. 'Mistaking *the praise of the victor*' would further be, for Pindar, an unusually abstract formulation. On the intentional model discussed in the previous section, we ought to expect 'mistaking the Oligaithidai.' Hubbard's interpretation thus implies a certain recursivity of reference, a reference to reference, which in terms of structure would lead to an infinite regression. It is not clear how one might avoid this implication. (*Cf.* Husserl 1992, vol. 3, p. 366 on an analogous problem in Brentano's theory of intention.)

[69] See Weber 2000, pp. 172–186 for a number of considerations that would be relevant to such a reading.

[70] See Münch 1993, pp. 143–145 and 192. On the retrospectivity of the passage, see Gerber 1999, p. 60 f. *ad loc.*, who however identifies the *σκοπός* with the truth of the utterance. On *ἔλπεσθαι* in Pindar see further Day 1991. Silk 1974, p. 105 notes that the tenor (*εἰπών*) and the vehicle (*ἀπὸ τόξου*) of the metaphor can both be used in non-poetic contexts for the sound of a voice (*cf.* Hdt. IV 135. 5 of donkeys; but see also

of these verses is nevertheless evident: at the centre of the song, there is a point which defines what *ought to be* said and thus provides the criterion for the appropriateness of all the statements in the text controlled by it.[71]

On the other hand, the distance between the subject and what should not or cannot be spoken of must not be bridged; instead, where it is lacking it must be created or re-created. After relating in *Olympian* 1. 46–51 the evil neighbour's tale that Pelops had been eaten by the gods, we find the following (52 f.):

> ἐμοὶ δ' ἄπορα γαστρίμαργον μακάρων τιν' εἰπεῖν· ἀφίσταμαι·
> ἀκέρδεια λέλογχεν θαμινὰ κακαγόρους.
>
> But as for me, there is no way I could call one of the blessed gods a glutton—I stand back:
> impoverishment is often the lot of slanderers.

The rejection of what is not to be said takes place by means of the active removal of the subject from the ideal place of the intentional object.[72] The presence necessary for the phenomenological saturation of the intentional act—here the metadiscursive or diacritical statement about the statement—is thus negated: the λόγος of the cannibalistic feast of the gods must not be present, must not be the reachable destination of a path (ἄπορα).[73] The same strategy of removing an inappropriate λόγος is to be found in the *Ninth Olympian* when the narrator rejects the story of Herakles' fight with the gods and instructs his mouth to repudiate, literally 'throw away', the story itself (35–39).[74]

Hom., *Il.* 3. 221 and Hes., *Theog.* 10).

[71] This is probably as close as one can get to Dissen's notion of the *Grundgedanke* in Pindar's own terminology; *cf.* above, p. 94 ff. A similar passage is *Pyth.* 1. 42–45, ἄνδρα δ' ἐγὼ κεῖνον | αἰνῆσαι μενοινῶν ἔλπομαι | μὴ [...] ἀγῶνος βαλεῖν ἔξω [...], where hope and desire are equally at issue. See Gentili *et al.* 1995, p. 343 *ad loc.*, who explain ἀγῶνος ἔξω as 'fuori dei lati della pista, del settore di lancio stabilito'. *Cf.* also *Nem.* 9. 53–55, εὔχομαι [...] ἀκοντίζων σκοποῖ ἄγχιστα Μοισᾶν and fr. 6a (g) SM δοκή]σεις οὐ πάρ σκοπόν with Σ.

[72] The figure of withdrawal in contexts of rejection may (later?) have belonged to everyday language: see Gerber 1982, p. 89 *ad loc.* who cites Pl., *Euthyd.* 303a and Dem. IX 54.

[73] *Cf.* the moment of cessation in *Nem.* 5. 16: στάσομαι on the way to the bloody end of the story of Phokos.

[74] Pelliccia 1995, p. 295 compares this passage with those places in Homer where a speaker rejects what his θυμός wants. See further Miller 1993a, pp. 128–130, Gerber 2002, pp. 39–41 *ad loc.*, and Theunissen 2000, p. 858 f.

The right thing, ὁ καιρός, has been missed; instead, the speaker has landed somewhere else.

But where? In the *Ninth Olympian*, the singer has told how Herakles fought against three gods; in the thematic topology of the epinicians, we are here obviously far from teleological propriety. In the *Eleventh Pythian*, the speaker was on the straight path towards the *telos*, but then asks—given the fact that he has just described how Orestes murdered his mother, a *sujet* only marginally suited to encomium—whether he has not perhaps lost sight of his topic (38–40):[75]

> *ἦρ’, ὦ φίλοι, κατ’ ἀμευσίπορον τρίοδον ἐδινάθην,*
> *ὀρθὰν κέλευθον ἰὼν τὸ πρίν· ἤ μέ τις ἄνεμος ἔξω πλόου*
> *ἔβαλεν, ὡς ὅτ’ ἄκατον ἐνναλίαν;*

> Can it be, my friends, that I became confused at a fork in the road,
> although before I was following a straight path? Or did some crosswind
> throw me off course like a small boat at sea?

Finally—in more than one sense—the end of the *Third Olympian* (42–45):

> *εἰ δ’ ἀριστεύει μὲν ὕδωρ, κτεάνων δὲ χρυσὸς αἰδοιέστατος,*
> *νῦν δὲ πρὸς ἐσχατιὰν Θήρων ἀρεταῖσιν ἱκάνων ἅπτεται*
> *οἴκοθεν Ἡρακλέος σταλᾶν. τὸ πόρσω δ’ ἐστὶ σοφοῖς ἄβατον*
> *κἀσόφοις. οὔ νιν διώξω· κεινὸς εἴην.*

> If water is best, while gold is the most revered of possessions,
> then truly has Theron now reached the furthest point with his achievements and
> from his home grasps the pillars of Herakles. What lies beyond neither wise men
> nor fools can tread. I will not pursue it; I would be foolish.[76]

Theron has bridged the gap between the starting-point of immediate proximity, οἴκοθεν, and the goal of the furthest imaginable distance, ἡ ἐσχατία, in his own person.[77] The pillars of Herakles are the point at

[75] Most 1985a, pp. 14–20 provides a formal-aesthetic analysis of this passage; Mackie 2003, p. 29 offers a more traditional interpretation in the context of a typology of Pindaric break-off formulae.

[76] Tr. Race 1997, vol. 1, p. 85.

[77] See Hubbard 1985, p. 15 f. Mackie 2003, p. 34 interprets this passage in terms of differences between Herakles and Theron: whereas the former sets up boundaries, the latter merely retraces them.

which the journey can go no further, neither for the victor nor for the poem.[78] The speaker, too, has arrived at the boundary of what can no longer be pursued.[79] Here, no more proximity can be created: beyond the pillars, every distance is absolute. Between the appropriate and the inappropriate, the sayable and the unsayable, τὸ ἔσχατον runs as their common border.

As a consequence, ἀρχή and τέλος become interchangeable. We have already observed how the metaphors of the arrows, the path, the hunt—we could have added the bee in *Pythian* 10. 54 and various other figures—structure the referentiality of Pindaric texts, the relationship between speaking and meaning as a movement between two poles. These poles are occupied by different things—beginning and end, centre and edge, inside and outside, subject and object—or they can remain unoccupied. In the latter case, it can seem in some passages as if the subject as the author of meaning in fact vanishes from the song altogether.[80] But more important for the schema of the subject who means and the object which is meant are the places where the ἀρχή- and τέλος-roles are exchanged. In his discussion of the different meanings of ἀρχή in the fifth book of the *Metaphysics*, Aristotle notes that ἀρχή/τέλος-polarities are fundamentally unstable, their identification always a question of a third point, that of the observer, who lies outside of the line both separating and connecting the two ἔσχατα.[81] Thus, the famous beginning of the *First Olympian* issues in the naming of Olympia (1–7), and just as the heart of the singer is to seek (σκόπει, 5) no heavenly body warmer than the sun, so 'we', the speaking subject of the song, will speak (αὐδάσομεν, 7) of no contest greater than the Olympic games. The 'search' as a mode of reference readily corresponds to the other metaphors which code referentiality in the odes. But in what follows, it is not the subject that moves towards its topic, but rather the song that, coming from Olympia, 'throws itself around the thoughts of the wise': ὁ πολύφατος ὕμνος ἀμφιβάλλεται σοφῶν μητίεσσι (8 f.).[82] In this description of inspiration or the relationship of a topic to a σοφός, it is not that the usual τέλος of flight-metaphors has

[78] *Cf. Nem.* 3. 19–21 (cited below, p. 215) and *Isthm.* 3/4. 29–31.

[79] Hubbard 1985, p. 143 notes the ambiguity of 44 f. where both the victor and the poet could be meant.

[80] See for example *Nem.* 3. 64–66 where only the hymn is named as the subject of the action (ἔβαλον) and the singers' voices are described not as the their own instrument but as the song's.

[81] Aristotle, *Met.* Δ 1, 1012 b34–1013 a1.

[82] *Cf.* also *Olymp.* 3. 9 f.: [Πίσας] ἀπό | θεόμοροι νίσοντ' ἐπ' ἀνθρώπους ἀοιδαί.

become the ἀρχή of poetry, but rather that the relationship between inside and outside has been exchanged. If the song in the *Second Olympian* was still the product of the most secluded subjectivity, contained within the φαρέτρα entirely at the disposal of the sovereign subject (83–85), it now comes from the world of phenomena to the singer. If the space of the subject in its interiority encompassed all of those thoughts that, in order to become speech, had to cross the border between inside and outside, this relationship, too, is reversed in the *First Olympian*: it is now the song that encompasses the thoughts of the wise.[83] But if origin and end, ἀρχή and τέλος can be interchanged, the only constant factor that remains is the irreducible distance *between* them that must, in the event of language, be effaced. However the two poles are occupied, the text moves as a structure of signification from the one to the other.

We have already noted above that where the metaphorical overcoming of an originary distance denotes *rhetorical* language, it has no 'literal' meaning. It is impossible to name a rhetorical figure such as metaphor without self-referentially using a metaphor. Aristotle's ἐπιφορά, Quintilian's *translatio*, the German word 'Übertragung' are all metaphors: they give a thing a name that is itself entirely covered by the designation.[84] Distinctions within metaphorical predication such as Richards' 'tenor' and 'vehicle' are still dependent on an element of

[83] *Cf.* Renehan 1969 who simultaneously divides the adjective πολυ-φατος and πολ-υφατος, the latter from ὑφαίνω, and translates: 'the mantle of poesy is thrown around the minds of the poets' (p. 220; he is followed by Fisker 1990). See the critique of this interpretation in Nisetich 1975, p. 56 f. and Gerber 1982, p. 26 *ad loc.* Hummel 1993, p. 216, § 216 believes that -φατος could come from φαίνω instead of φημί (she cites Bacchyl. 13. 61 δόξαν πολύφαντον). Young 1968, p. 121 follows Gildersleeve in finding here a reference to arrows and connects the metaphor with verse 112, so that the common vehicle connects the beginning with the end of the song. Gerber 1982, p. 26 f. doubts that the expression is a metaphor at all and cites passages from Homer and Sophocles in which a sound 'surrounds' someone. One problem with this objection, however, is that in each of the quoted passages the indirect object of the verb (different *composita* with ἀμφί or περί) is a *concretum*, mostly a personal pronoun. It is more difficult to deny the figurative force of ἀμφιβάλλεται here when we consider that its indirect object must be the μήτιες of the wise: in what *literal* sense can an immaterial object be 'surrounded'? It is nevertheless less than evident exactly what kind of figure this verse is: μήτιες σοφῶν could of course be a synecdoche (*pars pro toto*), μητίεσσι could however also be another kind of dative. Against Renehan's interpretation of ὑφαίνω, Nisetich 1975 reads the expression as a reference to φυλλαβολία: the metaphor is that of a crown (this was already the suggestion of Σ 14e Dr., ἡ μεταφορὰ ἀπὸ τῶν στεφάνων). Ἀμφιβάλλεσθαι can also mean 'to embrace' (see LSJ *s.v.*); see Mezger 1880, p. 89 *ad loc.*: 'Das Lied schlingt sich um den Geist der Sänger' and *cf. Pyth.* 9. 87.

[84] See above, p. 141.

movement.[85] In bridging the originary distance between the donor of a metaphorical term and its recipient—Aristotle does, after all, speak of the transfer of an 'alien name' from one thing to another—we find exactly the structure of the journey from ἀρχή to τέλος that is constituted by the language of the arrow, the javelin, the path and the hunt. Seen in this way, the Pindaric metaphors for language are by no means arbitrary or unnecessary, on the contrary: they mark the non-place of an originary absence on which they themselves are based. To the extent that metaphors for speaking—that is, for giving a thing a name that accrues to it but is not identical with it and which has the function of representing or substituting for it—represent this non-identity itself, they are necessarily self-referential or catachrestic. We could already observe this at the end of the *Third Olympian*: the victor as the thematic object of the text and the speaker as its author both find themselves on the border to impassability, and the relationship between these to marginal journeys is not at all clear. Is the extreme that Theron has now reached and beyond which there is nothing more to achieve the model for the border of impassability at which the text stops and falls silent? Or is this journey, itself metaphorical, the pseudo-referential realization of a necessity of epinician speech? More fundamentally: does the interchangeability between ἀρχή and τέλος, inside and outside, that Pindar seems to suggest in some passages also apply to the poles of metaphorical predication—that is, to predication as such?[86]

A passage from the *Third Nemean* illustrates this uncertainty. At the transition from the first to the second triad, the text narrates first the journey of the victor, then of Herakles to the ends of the earth (19–27):

εἰ δ' ἐὼν καλὸς ἔρδων τ' ἐοικότα μορφᾷ

[85] Richards 1936, p. 96 ff. The role of movement in definitions of metaphor is also emphasized by Ricœur 1975, p. 24 f.

[86] The theoretical context of this question is Derrida's analysis in 'Le retrait de la métaphore' (= Derrida ^{2}1998, pp. 63–93), p. 82 ff. of the inversion of the relationship between tenor and vehicle and its implications for the traditional concept of 'metaphor' in Heidegger's *Brief über den Humanismus* (Heidegger ^{3}1996, pp. 313–364, here p. 358: 'Das Denken baut am Haus des Seins [...]. Die Rede vom Haus des Seins ist keine Übertragung des Bildes vom "Haus" auf das Sein, sondern aus dem sachgemäß gedachten Wesen des Seins werden wir eines Tages eher denken können, was "Haus" und "wohnen" sind'). On this reversal, which in Heidegger is by no means limited to this one passage, see further Clark 1986.

ἀνορέαις ὑπερτάταις ἐπέβα παῖς Ἀριστοφάνεος, οὐκ ἔτι[87] πρόσω
ἀβάταν ἅλα κιόνων ὕπερ Ἡρακλέος περᾶν εὐμαρές,
ἥρως θεὸς ἃς ἔθηκε ναυτιλίας ἐσχάτας
μάρτυρας κλυτάς· δάμασε δὲ θῆρας ἐν πελάγεϊ
ὑπερόχους, ἰδίᾳ τ' ἐρεύνασε τεναγέων
ῥοάς, ὁπᾷ πόμπιμον κατέβαινε νόστου τέλος,
καὶ γᾶν φράδασε. θυμέ, τίνα πρὸς ἀλλοδαπάν
ἄκραν ἐμὸν πλόον παραμείβεαι;
Αἰακῷ σε φαμὶ γένει τε Μοῖσαν φέρειν.

If, being fair and performing deeds to match his form,
the son of Aristophanes has embarked on utmost deeds of manhood, it is no easy task to go yet further
across the untracked sea beyond the pillars of Herakles,
which that hero-god established as famed witnesses
of his furthermost voyage. He subdued monstrous beasts
in the sea, and on his own explored the streams of the shallows,
where he reached the limit that sent him back home,
and he made known the land. My heart, to what alien
headland are you turning aside my ship's course?
To Aiakos and his race I bid you bring the Muse.[88]

The victor Aristokleides' ascent to the highest *ἀνορεαί* is not told as a journey, but simply assumed in the metaphor that follows: it is not easy to travel *further*.[89] At the pillars of Herakles, one has to turn back, and at this point Herakles himself—in imitation of the victor? as his example?—does the same. His *τέλος* falls together with the *ἀρχή* of the voyage from his own personal *ἔσχατα*, beyond which everything is impassable, back towards home. The allusions to the end of the *Third Olympian* are unmistakeable, and here as there, the voice of the text follows as the third of those travellers who must turn back at the border of the traversable, the appropriate, what is *right*.[90] The exact relationship of this third journey to the other two—how should we

[87] I follow here Pfeijffer's (1999b, p. 287) suggestion and write *οὐκ* (with *εὐμαρές*) *ἔτι* (with *πρόσω*) instead of SM's *οὐκέτι*.

[88] Tr. Race 1997, vol. 2, p. 25.

[89] Pfeijffer 1999b, p. 285 *ad loc.* compares the metaphor of an ascent to *ἀνορέα* with Simon., fr. 579 *PMG*: only he who *ἵκῃ τ' ἐς ἄκρον ἀνδρείας* (7) by dint of hard labour may behold Ἀρετή. See however also Hes., *Op.* 289–292. The relatively rare construction of *ἐπιβαίνω c. dat.* here, used in Thuc. VIII 70. 5 for the boarding of a ship, could conceivably be intended to prepare the ground for the following maritime imagery, as Carey 1980, p. 155 implies (*cf.* however Pfeijffer 1999b, p. 286 n. 86).

[90] *Cf.* Pfeijffer 1999b, p. 300: 'The phrase [*sc.* *πόμπιμον νόστου τέλος*] turns out to be applicable to the poet himself as well.' See also Kurke 1991, p. 49 f.

define it? Does the headland 'really mean' the voyage of Herakles? Or is Herakles' voyage to the pillars and back a figure for the thematic movement of the text that really does begin its *νόστος* at this point? Has the journey of the text to the border of what is to be said taken its vehicle from the victor's journey *πρὸς τὸ ἔσχατον*? Or are we also to think of the poles of this relationship the other way around: the journey of the hero as the hypostasis of the movement of the text, with all that such a figure would imply? If it seems impossible to decide, then this is because of an instability that always already inhabits the metaphor of the path as pure difference.

The subject of writing

Even if epistemological conditions of this kind appear to constitute the possibility of literature: they mean that, in this poetry at least, such a thing as subjectivity cannot be understood merely according to the categories of intelligible inwardness, intentionality, literality, or—more generally—meaning. But we have not yet given sufficient thought to the specific exteriority which makes this impossible. What is it that contaminates the inwardness of the subject in Pindar's work with its other? And is it, perhaps, this other where Pindar's 'own' notion of an irreducibly material, ateleological subject with no prospect of a final sublimation into inwardness might be situated?

A song that in recent decades has been read above all with respect to a Pindaric or early Greek understanding of time—the *Tenth Olympian*—can help us here further.[91] Given the foundational role of a relationship to time in many philosophical discussions of subjectivity—we can think of Bergson, Husserl, or Heidegger here—it is obvious why one might expect particularly informative answers to questions about the constitution of Pindaric subjectivity from this poem.[92] One inter-

[91] These interpretations—I am thinking here of Kromer 1976 and particularly of Theunissen 2000, pp. 595–697—seem, in their emphasis on the unity and coherence of the texts in the sense discussed in Chapter 4, and in particular in their common assumption that the songs are exclusively the vehicle of the originary intention of their author (see for example Theunissen's repeated references to the 'consciousness of the poet' [Theunissen 2000, p. 596], his feelings and convictions [*ibid.*, pp. 601, 606, 646 and elsewhere] *etc.*) still to be pursuing the metaphysical or onto-theological rehabilitation of the sovereign author called into question by the literary theory of the later twentieth century. Theunissen, who explicitly states that his book makes no claim to be a contribution to literary studies (*ibid.*, V), indeed nowhere discusses the concept of authorship on which his interpretations are based.

[92] Important references are Bergson 1899, p. 75 and more explicitly 1903, p. 200 f.: 'Il n'y a pas de conscience sans mémoire, pas de continuation d'un état sans l'addition, au

face of this relationship, alongside the notion of 'care' (*Sorge*) to which Heidegger draws attention in *Sein und Zeit*, is memory, which Pindar discusses in the first verses of the poem. We should not underestimate the significance of memory for the poetics of the epinicians: the attempt to create a *κλέος* for the victor that will make his achievement (and thus that of the poet who immortalizes it) live on in the remembrance of singers and audiences—*μέγα τοι κλέος αἰεί*, as *Olymp.* 8. 11 says—is the very centre of this poetry. The relationship between the subject and memory is thus more than simply one topic among others.[93]

Let us briefly recall the circumstances of the song. It is written for a Lokrian by the name of Hagesidamos, also the addressee of the *Eleventh Olympian*. Both poems name a victory in the boxing contest of the *παῖδες* as their occasion; the year of this victory is given in a scholium and in one of the Oxyrhynchos papyri as 476 B.C.[94] The traditional order of the two songs, of which the shorter *Eleventh Olympian* will have been the earlier, is a result of the ancient interpretation of the *τόκος*-motif in *Olymp.* 10. 9, which was understood as the promise of the second, later song.[95] The relationship between the two songs, understood not only as a relationship of reference, but also as one of cause and effect (the *Tenth Olympian* was allegedly the first song, which announced the second and thus made it necessary), of desire and fulfilment, of promise, debt and deferral has always been a concern of research.

The poem begins with the poet's address—here, only the father of the *λόγος*, the origin and guarantor of its existence can be speaking—to the Muse and the Truth (1–6).[96]

sentiment présent du souvenir des moments passés. En cela consiste la durée. La durée intérieure est la vie continue d'une mémoire qui prolonge le passé dans le présent [...]', and Husserl, *Ideen* II, § 29 (= Husserl 1991, pp. 111–119) on 'das reine Ich', esp. p. 112 f.: 'Denn ein "stehendes und bleibendes" Ich könnte sich nicht konstituieren, wenn sich nicht ein stehender und bleibender Erlebnisstrom konstituierte, also wenn nicht die originär konstituierten Erlebniseinheiten wieder aufnehmbar, in Wiedererinnerungen zum Neuauftreten fähige und in Übernahme ihrer Seinsqualitäten (als seiend in der immanenten Zeit) auftretende wären [...]'. For Heidegger's understanding of the relationship between recollection and subjectivity, see Heidegger 1975, p. 12.

93 Mackie 2003, pp. 47–67 offers a stylistic description of Pindar's treatment of memory with particular reference to the Muse.

94 Σ inscr. a and *P. Oxy.* 222, col. I 16 (= *FGrH* 415, 1).

95 See Σ *Olymp.* 11 inscr. a and b Dr. on the ancient order and Gelzer 1985 for the criteria on which it has since been reversed.

96 The question of the addressee has been controversial. According to the scholia, the imperative is directed either at the Muses or at the chorus (Σ 1a; *cf.* the paraphrase in 1d,

τὸν Ὀλυμπιονίκαν ἀνάγνωτέ μοι
Ἀρχεστράτου παῖδα, πόθι φρενός
ἐμᾶς γέγραπται· γλυκὺ γὰρ αὐτῷ μέλος ὀφείλων ἐπιλέλαθ'· ὦ Μοῖσ',
ἀλλὰ σὺ καὶ θυγάτηρ
Ἀλάθεια Διός, ὀρθᾷ χερί
ἐρύκετον ψευδέων
ἐνιπὰν ἀλιτόξενον.

Read me (the name of) the Olympian victor,
the son of Arkhestratos, where it is written
in my mind, for I owe him a sweet song and have forgotten. But you, o
Muse, and Zeus' daughter,
Truth, with a correcting hand
ward off from me the charge of harming a guest friend
with broken promises.

Pindar undertakes here the first attempt in European literature to understand the relationship between writing and subjectivity,[97] and he does so by linking writing with memory in a metaphor that occurs in this poem for the first time.[98] The text connects it with two requests, to read out a name (*ἀνάγνωτέ μοι*, 1) and to find a place (*πόθι*, 2). The question of the whereabouts of writing foregrounds its spatiality; the request for reading out loud implies that mere writing alone does not

ἀναμνήσατέ με, ὦ Μοῦσαι); Burgess 1990, p. 273 understands the chorus, Nassen 1975 (followed by Dickson 1990, p. 122) the Muse and the Truth; Kromer 1976, p. 243 speaks simply of 'someone else'. Hubbard 1985, p. 67 takes the directive to be addressed to the audience; his argument, however, that *ἀλλά* in verse 3 and the dual in verse 5 signal a change of addressee is not cogent: the adversative force of *ἀλλά* can just as easily contrast with *ἐπιλέλαθ'* as with *ἀνάγνωτε* (given that the name *Ἀλάθεια* directly follows), whilst two subjects can take both the dual and the plural in the same sentence without difficulty: *cf.* in Pindar *Olymp.* 9. 45 with Gerber 2002, p. 43 *ad loc.* and *Nem.* 10. 64, further KG I, p. 73, § 368. 3, and Hummel 1993, p. 52, § 34. Verdenius 1988, p. 55 *ad loc.* argues for an 'absolute', 'rhetorical' use of the imperative: it is directed at no one. Theunissen 2000, p. 605, true to his hermeneutical model of interpretation, emphasizes the social, communicative dimension of reading, considers however only the options 'chorus', 'audience', and 'rhetoric' (n. 9). It is indeed difficult to see how an invocation of the Muse could as such be a social act. *Cf.* further the verses 60 ff. where the invocation of the Muse is taken up again with the question *τίς* (*cf. Il.* 1. 8).

[97] A project that links him with Rousseau in the eighteenth century: *cf.* Derrida 1967a, pp. 145–148, Engl. pp. 97–100.

[98] It can be found as early as the 450s in Attic tragedy: *cf.* Aesch., *Cho.* 450, *Eum.* 273–275, *Supp.* 179, *PV* 460 f. and 788 f.; Soph., *Phil.* 1325 and fr. 597 Radt from the *Triptolemos*; Eur., *Tro.* 663 *ἀναπτύξω φρένα* 'I will unroll my mind' (like a papyrus roll); see further Kromer 1976, p. 423 and Pfeiffer [2]1978, p. 44 f. According to LSJ *s.v.* II, this passage in Pindar is the first instance of *ἀναγιγνώσκω* in the sense 'to read'.

suffice to create living remembrance.[99]

The connection between spatiality and memory becomes, in the course of the fifth century, an integral element of the theory of remembering. It enables in particular the notion of mnemonic τόποι and thus mnemotechnical systems based on the spatial arrangement of what is to be recalled.[100] But with this spatiality, an element already finds its way into consciousness that despite all internalisation must remain exterior to it.[101] Writing is by definition spatial; this is the crucial difference between it and the voice, whose extension is merely temporal.[102] As long as they remain written, therefore, linguistic signs cannot be integrated into inwardness; the interiority of memory, as long as it is understood as writing, comes under the influence of an irreducible externality. That this influence is also at work at the beginning of the *Tenth Olympian* is seen by Keith Dickson, who notes that the speaker in verse 1 calls upon *others* to read him the contents of his memory (a circumstance, incidentally, that distinguishes this metaphor in Pindar radically from its use by the tragedians): 'Although written in the poet's heart, it is clear from his inability to retrieve it that the name is still in a sense 'outside' him. [...] Writing may indeed have been interiorized, yet the very same act has also introduced a kind of exteriority into the innermost recess of the heart.'[103] The inwardness of

99 Nagy 1990, pp. 171 and 220 notes that the metaphor of reading out loud can also code not only the notion of public performance as opposed to (presumably) private composition, but also the fixity of the composition itself. In this respect it is especially ironic that the metaphor is used here to assert not the security of having a script written down in the mind in advance, but precisely the unreliability of memory.

100 As in the well-known Simonides-anecdote: see Cic., *De orat.* II 86. 351–353 and Quint., *Inst.* XI 2. 11–16. On the topological systems of mnemotechnics in Greek antiquity, see Arist., *De an.* Γ 3, 427 b19 f. with Ross 1961, p. 285 *ad loc.*

101 This is the reason for Hegel's rejection of such systems: *cf.* Hegel, *Enzyklopädie* III, § 462 *A* (= Hegel 1969–1971, vol. 10, p. 279, Engl. Hegel 2007, p. 199 f.). Kant defines the inner sense as time in contrast to the pure externality of space (*Kritik der reinen Vernunft*, § 6, B 49–53; = Kant 1956–1964, vol. III, pp. 80–83); on this basis, Hegel can define time as the *Aufhebung* and 'truth' of space (*Enzyklopädie* II, §§ 254–260, esp. § 257 *Zusatz*; = Hegel 1969–1971, vol. 9, pp. 41–56, esp. p. 48).

102 The spatial extension of the voice as sound is not constitutive of its nature as language; a voice that does not make a sound, such as Husserl postulates for the inward life of the soul, is still language as long as the sequence of words can be experienced as a sequence. A form of writing, on the other hand, that did not allow for spaces between individual linguistic signs (letters, hieroglyphs, syllabic signs), and could thus in principle be reduced to a mathematical point without spatial extension, could not be recognized as language.

103 Dickson 1990, p. 122, the most important discussion of this passage. *Cf.* Kromer 1976, p. 423.

memory, its purity and seclusion, is contaminated by something external that withdraws itself from the control of the subject. This withdrawal is a direct consequence of the spatiality of writing, for the question *πόθι φρένος γέγραπται;* problematizes an undiscoverability that can only arise on the condition that the elements of language are arranged spatially.[104] The subject's inability to locate or control what has been committed to memory is obviously intended to designate his having forgotten it, and it is this state of having forgotten from which the Muse and Truth are now to release him.

The recovery or remembrance of what has been forgotten takes place, however, not by means of an epideixis directed towards the visibility of the written name, but rather by means of the making-audible of a phonic substance: the name of the victor is to be read aloud, since writing is only a medium of *μνήμη*, not *μνήμη* itself, and like every medium implies not only the presence of what is being mediated, but also a no less originary absence that prevents it from *being* this presence.[105] For this reason, the letters of memory cannot embody the desired presence of what is to be remembered in such a way that the speaker is protected from forgetting the past; they cannot *be* this past, but rather only *mean* it.[106] The written obligation thus only becomes contemporary or genuinely present when writing becomes voice.[107] In the living presence of the voice—and we recall that epic models of memory are consistently constructed by means of the living voice of the Muse—every danger of forgetting is banished.

Now this epistemological or metaphysical difference between the mere visibility of writing and the audibility of the voice is not merely the *topos* of Platonic-Aristotelian philosophy that a reading of the *Phaedrus* or *De interpretatione* readily reveals; it is also assumed or even explicitly discussed at several places in the epinicians themselves. One example of this is the portent of the snakes in the *Eighth Olympian*. The central section of the poem, from roughly the middle of the second triad through to the middle of the third (31–53), narrates the building of the wall around Troy by Apollo, Poseidon and Aiakos. As soon as they are finished, three snakes appear and attempt to storm the

104 *Cf.* Arist., *Mem.* II, 451 b18 ff. on the necessity of *searching* for the content of memory, which according to I, 449 b27–29 and 450 a14–17 consists of graphemes.

105 The same is true, of course, for everything written in the ancient world: reading takes place with the help of the voice. This fact of cultural history is however capable of a semiotic or theoretical interpretation; this is my only concern here.

106 See above, p. 49.

107 See also Dickson 1990, pp. 121–123, and *cf.* *Olymp.* 8. 74 f.

defenses (*ἐσαλλόμενοι*, 38). The first two fail to reach the top, fall from the wall and die; the third, however, succeeds with a cry (*βοάσαις*, 40) in crossing the ramparts and entering the city.[108] Apollo interprets the event as a sign from Zeus (41–46):

> *ἔννεπε δ' ἀντίον ὁρμαίνων τέρας εὐθὺς Ἀπόλλων·*
> *"Πέργαμος ἀμφὶ τεαῖς, ἥρως, χερὸς ἐργασίαις ἁλίσκεται·*
> *ὣς ἐμοὶ φάσμα λέγει Κρονίδα*
> *πεμφθὲν βαρυγδούπου Διός·*
> *οὐκ ἄτερ παίδων σέθεν, ἀλλ' ἅμα πρώτοις ἄρξεται*
> *καὶ τερτάτοις." ὣς ἦρα θεὸς σάφα εἴπαις [...].*

> Apollo considered the unfavorable omen and immediately said:
> 'Pergamos will be captured, hero, at the site of your handiwork—
> thus speaks to me the vision Kronos' son
> has sent, loudly thundering Zeus—
> not without your children; but it will begin with the first ones
> and also with the fourth.' So spoke clearly the god [...].

In his analysis of the semiotics of this passage, Dickson draws attention to the fact that while the snakes themselves at no point speak with a voice that can be understood and are explicitly designated by the god as a visible phenomenon, *φάσμα* (43), Apollo's interpretation is nevertheless of something spoken: the sign 'speaks', *λέγει*, a verb whose subject in Pindar (as also in the greater part of the literature of the fifth century) is always a speaking person or an organ of speech.[109] Whereas, in addition, the merely visible aspect of the sign is not immediately comprehensible, but instead requires the exegesis of the mantic god, his interpretation, given immediately and orally, is 'clear', *σάφα* (46). Things are no different in the *Sixth Olympian*, where a distinction is made between 'hearing the voice that knows no lies' (*φωνὰν ἀκούειν ψευδέων ἄγνωτον*, 66 f.)—this is Iamos' prophetic gift, promised to him by his father Apollo, which will make him a *μάντις ἐπιθόνιος ἔξοχος* (50 f.)[110]—and the pyromantic oracle to be established after Herakles' arrival in Olympia. Iamos' ability to hear the voice of

[108] See on this passage Wilamowitz 1922, p. 404 (with justification of Christ's conjecture *ἐνόρουσε* against the mss.' *ἀν-*, *ἐπ-*, or *ἐσόρουσε*) and Dickson 1990, p. 112 f.

[109] For the latter see *Olymp.* 13. 11 f.: *τόλμα τέ μοι | εὐθεῖα γλῶσσαν ὀρνύει λέγειν*. An expression such as Hdt. I 124. 1 *τὰ δὲ γράμματα ἔλεγε τάδε*, used of Harpalos' letter to Cyrus, occurs nowhere in the epinicians.

[110] *Cf. Pyth.* 9. 42 f. and above, p. 131, further Garner 1992, p. 48 f. who compares the encounter between Apollo and Iamos with that between the poet and the Muses in the prologue to Hesiod's *Theogony*.

his father has already been proven in verses 61 ff. by his journey to Olympia; in contrast to Pelops' encounter with Poseidon in the *First Olympian*, the god of dreams and prophecy does not appear visibly to his suppliant, but instead leads him to the place of his future work by the sound of his voice alone, ὄσσα (62).[111] As Dickson notes, however, Iamos' ability to hear the voice of his father stands for nothing less than 'direct access to truth', whilst the epistemological reliability of pyromancy, based on signs of fire, seems to be subtly relativised at the beginning of the *Eighth Olympian*.[112] Finally, in the *Sixth Isthmian*, Zeus sends as a sign an eagle (αἰετόν, 50) in order to indicate that he has heard Telamon's prayer (αἰτεῖς, 52) for a son. The connection between the bird and the son only becomes explicit, however, when Herakles—he too a son who, in the role of the μάντις (51), has privileged access to the truth of the father—speaks the *name* of the desired progeny, Αἴαντα (53). 'Once again', writes Dickson, 'there is a shift from visual to oral communication.'[113]

Pindar's characterisation of memory as writing in the *Tenth Olympian* has to be seen in this context of the epistemological privileging of the voice over against merely visible signs. Like the portents of the snakes and the eagle, so too the letters of the φρήν can only function as signs when they are translated into the medium of the voice which seems to guarantee the immediacy of what is meant. And whilst the interpretation of the fire-signs is a special art, a τέχνη that has to be learned, the voice of the father offers every son enabled by his descent to hear it that special knowledge of the truth that has always been the mark of the μάντις. The epinician privileging of φυά over against τέχνη is also reflected in the semiotics of the victory songs. Conversely, however, this means that the creation of memory over against the living presence of the immediate moment is analogous to the transformation of the voice into writing. If this process does not already mean forgetting, it nevertheless entails its potential as a constant danger, for the path in our passage from the written signs of

111 *Cf. Olymp.* 1. 73 f.

112 Dickson 1990, p. 115, who also identifies an 'analogy between truth and paternity' at this point. On παραπειράομαι in *Olymp.* 8. 3 as 'in making trial of one (also) mistake his will', *cf.* LSJ *s.v.* παρά G IV 1. What the seers seek is, on the other hand, a λόγος, the self-presence of the divine thought (*cf.* Σ 3e Dr.: εἴ τινα λόγον αὐτῶν ἔχει καὶ [*expl.*] φροντίδα) that would no longer need to be interpreted. See also Aesch., *PV* 948 f. (cited by Dickson 1990, p. 127 n. 24) on the special difficulties and visual basis of pyromantic divination.

113 Dickson 1990, p. 117.

the φρήν back into the living present of remembrance is indeed *possible* for the individual self, but only *guaranteed* by the Muse or the Truth—she too, like Herakles, a child of Zeus.

Now what does memory contain? What is to be read out at the beginning of the *Tenth Olympian* is the name of the victor.[114] This name is not immediately spoken in the text, as if to indicate that the singer himself, for a moment, cannot recover the series of phonemes 'Hagesidamos' from the storage vaults of his mind. Rather, immediate access is available only to the relationships of a παῖς to two other names: the name of a place ('Ολυμπιονίκαν, 1) and the name of a father ('Αρχεστράτου, 2). The meaning or the truth of the lost or forgotten name of the victor consists in these two relationships, in particular (as we will see in a moment) in the second.

Memory, then, is a network or system of names whose written or spatial character must be overcome or sublimated in order for it to become remembrance. Do we do these verses an injustice if we choose to discern in them the genuinely metaphysical interpretation of memory in its chronologically first articulation, an interpretation whose basic lineaments are still to be recognized more than two thousand years later in Hegel's *Enzyklopädie*? A comparison of the two models is instructive. The relationship between the subject of thought and memory belongs in the *Enzyklopädie*, as we recall, to the section on the theoretical mind.[115] Thinking takes place in the repeated production of signs whose externality over against the subject is sublimated or *aufgehoben* by a renewed act of internalisation (*Erinnerung*).[116] The interiority of thought is also the goal of thinking: the subject only possesses knowledge of its own (that is, knowledge at all) when what is produced in the representation of intelligence has returned from the outwardness of the sign to the interior of the mind.[117]

[114] So Nassen 1975, p. 220, Dickson 1990, p. 121 and Race 1997, vol. 1. p. 163. Kromer 1976, p. 422 interprets τὸν 'Ολυμπιονίκαν 'Αρχεστράτου παῖδα as a quotation: these words are themselves written in the speaker's memory and are now to be read aloud. *Cf.* Schmid 1990a, p. 69 n. 43.

[115] See above, p. 80 and n. 59.

[116] By virtue of its character as *Aufhebung*, this recollection or *Erinnerung* is not a simple negation of externality (equivalent to its mere annihilation); instead, it preserves a certain externality in the thought that has been internalized and thus recognized as one's own. *Cf.* Nancy 1991, p. 6 ff. on some implications of this definition of the self in Hegel.

[117] Derrida has shown that this process of thinking as the appropriation of a mediated unity of outside and inside *on the inside* models the structure of Hegelian dialectics in the theoretical activity of the psyche: the theoretical mind *is* the process of dialectical

Hegel's notion of recollection or remembrance (*Erinnerung*) plays a double role in his philosophy of mind: it describes not only the goal of intelligence, the complete realization of presence-to-oneself, but also the process by which, at the beginning of thinking, the individual subject receives something like his or her own identity. 'Intelligence, in first recollecting the intuition,' writes Hegel in § 452 of the *Enzyklopädie* of 1830, 'puts the *content of feeling* in its inwardness, in its *own space* and its *own time*. In this way, the content is (*αα*) an *image* [...].'[118] The image is by no means merely a sign of the intuition, for the relationship between both is not arbitrary, but rather consists in the necessary connection between original and copy; in the terminology of Hegel's semiotics, this relationship is 'symbolic'. As soon as the subject is confronted with the same intuition again, the internalised image is brought out again and the present intuition subsumed under it as its general category ('authentic recollection, as it is called', § 454). Hegel is not simply describing, here, the emergence of categorial thought in the subject; rather, individual identity itself, the inwardness of the subject emerges only from remembrance or *Erinnerung* as the process of internalising intuitions and as its result. We therefore read in the *Zusatz* to § 452: 'Here, in *recollection*, we keep our subjectivity, our *inwardness*, in view [...].'[119]

This connection of remembrance with individual subjectivity also holds, so it initially seems, for the first two forms of memory. Memory (*Gedächtnis*) also consists of what has been internalised, but no longer as intuitions that become images, but rather as linguistic signs or, as Hegel explicitly states, *names*. We know what names mean because we

sublimation or *Aufhebung*. See Derrida, 'Le puits et la pyramide' (= Derrida 1972b, pp. 79–127), pp. 83–93, Engl. pp. 73–81.

118 'Als die Anschauung zunächst erinnernd, setzt die Intelligenz den *Inhalt des Gefühls* in ihre Innerlichkeit, in ihren *eigenen Raum* und ihre *eigene Zeit*. So ist er *αα*) *Bild* [...].' Hegel, *Enzyklopädie* III, § 452 (= Hegel 1969–1971, vol. 10, p. 258), his emphasis; Engl. Hegel 2007, p. 186. *Cf.* Hegel 1817, p. 244.

119 'Hier, in der *Erinnerung*, fassen wir unsere Subjektivität, unsere *Innerlichkeit*, ins Auge [...].' Hegel 1969–1971, vol. 10, p. 259, his emphasis; Engl. Hegel 2007, p. 186. *Cf.* the *Philosophische Enzyklopädie* written in Nuremberg in 1808, § 143 (= Hegel 1969–1971, Bd. 4, p. 45 f.): '3. *Erinnerung*. Die Vorstellung als die *erinnerte* oder *allgemein* gemachte Anschauung verhält sich zur unmittelbaren Anschauung als Bleibendes und Allgemeines zum Einzelnen. Die Erinnerung ist nicht sowohl eine Vergleichung zweier einzelner Anschauungen, als daß die jetzige einzelne Anschauung unter die bereits allgemein gemachte oder die Vorstellung subsumiert wird. Die *Dieselbigkeit*, die ich erkenne, ist einerseits die Identität ihres *Inhalts*, anderseits erkenne ich in der jetzigen Anschauung die Identität *meiner* mit mir selbst oder erinnere *mich* in ihr' (his italics, my spacing).

have internalised the individual links between the names and their meanings ('name-retaining memory', § 461) and because we are able to recreate these links at every new encounter with the name ('reproductive memory', § 462). It is easy to see that this situation corresponds exactly, if inversely, to Pindar's description of forgetting: his poet knows the *meaning* of the name—Ὀλυμπιονίκας Ἀρχεστράτου παῖς—but cannot make the connection to the name itself.

Now at this point there is, in Hegel, a complication which will also play a role in the *Tenth Olympian*. The link between the name and its meaning is, in contrast to recollected images and representations, not the possession of the individual subject: language is fundamentally universal, not particular. 'Now language is the work of thought: and hence all that is expressed in language must be universal. What I only mean or suppose is mine: it belongs to me—this particular individual. But language expresses nothing but universality; and so I cannot say what I merely *mean*.'[120] For this reason, the third form, 'mechanical' memory (§ 463) designates the process by which the words become universal and, at the same time, empty of all sense. The names in mechanical memory are 'senseless' because they are now detached from the intentional meaning or *vouloir-dire* of an individual, merely contingent subjectivity; the meaning they bear is instead the work of free intelligence as universality. It was Paul de Man who observed that this senselessness constitutes the definition of the arbitrary sign, in which intelligence 'wilfully' chooses the material signifier.[121] When we recall, however, that for Hegel the individuality of recollection is the condition for thinking at all, we can understand why de Man considered this fact to be extremely disquieting:

> The synthesis between name and meaning that characterizes memory is an 'empty link [*das leere Band*]' and thus entirely unlike the mutual complementarity and interpenetration of form and content that characterizes symbolic art (*Enz. III*, par. 463, p. 281). [...] In memorization, in thought, and, by extension, in the sensory manifestation of thought as an 'art' of writing, 'we are dealing only with signs [*wir haben es überhaupt nur*

[120] 'Indem die *Sprache* das Werk des Gedankens ist, so kann auch in ihr nichts gesagt werden, was nicht allgemein ist. Was ich nur *meine*, ist mein, gehört mir als diesem besonderen Individuum an; wenn aber die Sprache nur Allgemeines ausdrückt, so kann ich nicht sagen, was ich nur *meine*.' Hegel, *Enzyklopädie* I, § 20 *A* (= Hegel 1969–1971, vol. 8, p. 74), his emphasis; Engl. Hegel 1975b, p. 31.

[121] De Man, 'Sign and symbol in Hegel's *Aesthetics*' (= de Man 1996, pp. 91–104), p. 96. *Cf.* Hegel, *Enzyklopädie* III, § 457 *Zusatz* (= Hegel 1969–1971, vol. 10, p. 269 f., Engl. Hegel 2007, p. 193 f.).

> *mit Zeichen zu tun*].' Memory effaces remembrance (or recollection) just as the I effaces itself. The faculty that enables thought to exist also makes its preservation impossible.[122]

The impossibility of preserving thought thus shows itself to be the impossibility of remembering. What then, however, are we to make of Pindar and the epinician poetics of κλέος? Everything will depend on how the victory odes conceive of the exact relationship between the written names contained in memory and their meanings. In what does the truth of the name, for Pindar, consist?

Three episodes in the epinicians will give us a first indication. Here it becomes clear that the truth of the name is first of all the truth of the non-arbitrary symbol. We have already considered Aias' naming on the basis of the sign that promises his birth in the *Sixth Isthmian*; the phonic substance of the name is not arbitrary, but rather imitates the sound of the αἰετός. The same is true of Iamos in the *Sixth Olympian*, where the future seer is named after the protecting powers of his first days, the violets (ἴα, 55). In the *Ninth Olympian*, the myth of Pyrrha and Deukalion is followed by the derivation of the word for 'people', λαοί, from the word for the 'stones', λᾶες, that the couple throw behind them to create human beings (45 f.).[123] In all of these cases—we can also think of the address to Hieron: σύνες ὅ τοι λέγω, | ζαθέων ἱερῶν ἐπώνυμε (fr. 105. 1 f.) at the beginning of a lost hyperchorema[124] and the comment of the scholium that quotes it as an example of a typically Pindaric practice: τότε γὰρ καταφέρεται εἰς τοῦτο ὁ Πίνδαρος, ὅταν ὑπῇ τις ὁμωνυμία (Σ *Nem.* 7. 1a Dr.)—the similarity of the names is not accidental, but instead the result of a participation of the second, derived name in a real, identifying event or context as whose non-arbitrary symbol it now functions (or, in the case of the hyperchorema with its appeal to Hieron, *should* function). The name, based in this way not on convention but on *genealogy*, recalls the thing it names not by the power of a merely (in Hegel's sense) semiotic connection, but rather because it is, originally, a part of it; its truth is its origin.[125]

122 De Man 1996, p. 102 ('wir haben es überhaupt nur mit Zeichen zu tun': Hegel 1969–1971, vol. 10, p. 271).

123 This etymology is first documented in an epic fragment quoted by a scholium (Σ 70d); see also Hes., fr. 234 MW. Gerber 2002, p. 44 also cites *Il.* 24. 611; he sees here, however, only 'word-play'. *Cf.* in this sense Race 1990, p. 2 (cited above, p. 104).

124 Here we can note again the connection between the audible λέγειν and the συνεῖναι of what is spoken; *cf. Olymp.* 2. 83–85 (above, p. 196 f.).

125 *Cf.* Dickson 1990, p. 119: 'The convergence of word and object, sign and signified, *nomen* and *omen* is not simply a hypothetical stance on language debated in Plato's

This becomes clearer when we look more closely at the meanings the two names that play a role in identifying the victor at the beginning of the *Tenth Olympian*, that is, the names of the place and the father, take on in the course of the poem. Let us start with Olympia (43–47):

ὁ δ᾽ ἄρ᾽ ἐν Πίσᾳ ἔλσαις ὅλον τε στρατόν
λᾴαν τε πᾶσαν Διὸς ἄλκιμος
υἱὸς σταθμᾶτο ζάθεον ἄλσος πατρὶ μεγίστῳ· περὶ δὲ πάξαις Ἄλτιν μὲν ὅγ᾽
ἐν καθαρῷ
διέκρινε, τὸ δὲ κύκλῳ πέδον
ἔθηκε δόρπου λύσιν [...].

Thereupon Zeus' valiant son gathered the entire army
and all the booty at Pisa,
and measured out a sacred precinct for his father most mighty. He
fenced in the Altis and set it apart
in the open, and he made the surrounding plain
a resting place for banqueting [...].[126]

The place of victory is separated and fenced in. It is set apart from other places, so that distance and distances emerge. A secluded space. But at the same time (and only on this basis) a holy space, since the measuring out of the sacred precinct, the preliminary to *διάκρισις*, has an addressee, *πατρὶ μεγίστῳ* (45). A referential relationship is thus established between the place and the god who dwells outside of it based on the spatial division of the land. The latter is no longer merely for itself, but also for Zeus. And whilst it is no accident that the direction or the intentionality of the place depends on the distinction between it and its outside, so it is also scarcely unimportant that a son carries out this division and creates this referentiality.

In the course of this process, a part of the place receives a name (49–51):

καὶ πάγον
Κρόνου προσεφθέγξατο· πρόσθε γάρ
νώνυμνος, ἇς Οἰνόμαος ἆρχε, βρέχετο πολλᾷ νιφάδι.

And he called it 'the hill
of Kronos'; for previously
it had no name, when, during Oinomaos' rule, it was drenched with

Cratylos, but instead part of the habitual texture of ancient thought [...].' See further Quincey 1963, p. 142 f., Kraus 1988, pp. 15–41 and Cassirer 2002, p. 26 ff.

[126] Tr. Race 1997, vol. 1, p. 167.

much snow.

The reference to Oinomaos dates the anonymity of the hill back to the time before the arrival of Pelops, who however apparently made no changes to this situation and beside whose tomb the games are now founded (24 f.). At that time, the hill was nameless and therefore—this is the most probable implication of the verses, as one of the scholia remarks (Σ 62a Dr.)—utterly unknown.[127] Herakles' act of naming takes it out of its namelessness and makes it in this way into a possible object of memory according to the model not only of the opening verses, but also of the victors' catalogue in the verses 64–73.

The name of the hill is, however, not arbitrary; rather, its truth consists at least in part in its etymology: the *πάγος* is the result of the (*περι-*)*παγνύναι* already mentioned in verse 45.[128] And the other part? The fact that the hill receives the name of Kronos has been variously interpreted.[129] But is it unimportant that its namer names it with the name of his father's father, his grandfather, and indeed a Grand Father, a *πατὴρ μέγιστος*, who *is not there*? The story of the origin of the name recreates a context in which a son sets up a reference to a male ancestor, here by naming a place. The chain of such referential structures presented in the *Tenth Olympian* reaches from the opening verses of the song where the Olympic victor Hagesidamos is, in the memory of the poet, merely the 'son of Arkhestratos', through the measuring of Olympian earth for Father Zeus (we could say: in his name)—this, incidentally, after the killing of the Moliones, who act in this story exclusively in the interests of an older male relative—to the extended simile at the beginning of the final triad, where the son is nothing but the recipient of his aged father's wealth, the merely temporal extension of a legitimacy of ownership inherited from the first legitimate owner who will, moreover, soon be dead (86–93):

> *ἀλλ' ὥτε παῖς ἐξ ἀλόχου πατρί*
> *ποθεινὸς ἵκοντι νεότατος τὸ πάλιν ἤδη, μάλα δέ οἱ θερμαίνει φιλότατι*

127 *Cf.* also *Olymp.* 1. 82–84, where namelessness (*ἀνώνυμον γῆρας*) is equated with lack of fame.

128 See Quincey 1963, p. 146.

129 Quincey 1963, p. 146 maintains that Pindar ('outrageously') wanted to suggest an etymological (*ἐτήτυμον*, 54) connection between *Κρόνος* and *Χρόνος* (55), since 'Time alone can put the genuine truth (*sc.* of a name) to the proof.' Theunissen 2000, p. 652 f. rejects this interpretation of the passage, but is open to an etymological connection that in his opinion could have been meant by Pindar here. Verdenius 1988, p. 72 *ad loc.* more plausibly refers to the cult of Kronos mentioned by Paus. VI 20. 1.

νόον·
ἐπεὶ πλοῦτος ὁ λαχὼν ποιμένα
ἐπακτὸν ἀλλότριον
θνᾴσκοντι στυγερώτατος·
καὶ ὅταν καλὰ ἔρξαις ἀοιδᾶς ἄτερ,
Ἁγησίδαμ', εἰς Ἀΐδα σταθμόν
ἀνὴρ ἵκηται, κενεὰ πνεύσαις ἔπορε μόχθῳ βραχύ τι τερπνόν.

But as a son, born from his wife, is longed for
by a father already come close to the opposite of youth and warms his mind with great love
(since wealth that falls to the care
of a stranger from elsewhere
is most hateful to a dying man),
so, when a man who has performed noble deeds,
Hagesidamos, goes without song to Hades'
dwelling, in vain he has striven and gained for his toil but brief delight.[130]

As an aging father desires (*ποθεινός*, 87) a son as heir of his wealth, so too a dead man (= father) who has achieved noble things (= wealth) without a song (= son) has only won brief joy. If this equation is to work, the role of the son can only consist in his reference to the father: he relates to him like the song relates to the victor in the verses 91–93, who is of course the real topic of epinician. The son is not *ἀλλότριος*, he does not come from outside (*ἐπακτός*, 89), but is instead by virtue of a genetic connection a part of the interiority of the family that the father defines and whose principle he designates. Perhaps the son even bears the name of the father, just as the *ἐπωνυμία χάρις* of verse 78 bears the name of the games to which it owes its origin and content.[131] Ἁγησίδαμος, 'leader of the people', is in any case very reminiscent of Ἀρχέστρατος, 'ruler of the host'; the meaning of their names is almost identical.

According to the criteria of a Hegelian semiotics, it seems as if the son in this simile is nothing but a symbol of his father, for all the attributes of interiority and natural reference that characterize the symbol accrue to him. It is further clear that the poet is claiming just this naturalness and symbolic character for his song: the poem can only grant the victor's achievement (and thus metonymically the victor himself) permanence if the song *is part of* this achievement and does

[130] Tr. Race 1997, vol. 1, pp. 171, 173.
[131] That is, Ὀλυμπιονίκης ὕμνος; cf. *Olymp.* 3. 3.

not merely refer to it. Son and song must both, according to the logic of κλέος, *be* their respective referents, not merely *mean* them. But it is not difficult to show—on the contrary, it is obvious—that this relationship, created by the symbol, of totality and the presence of the father and the victor is revealed as illusory the moment the son and the song achieve any kind of autonomy, that is to say the moment they do not serve their referents utterly and completely.

In the *Tenth Olympian*, this moment is the moment of death. Pindar's text refers explicitly both to the death of the father (θνᾴσκοντι, 90) and to the death of the victor (εἰς Ἀΐδα σταθμόν | ἀνὴρ ἵκηται, 92 f.). This death is, on the one hand, the condition on which the son legitimately inherits from the father; on the other, it is the condition on which the true meaning of the song becomes apparent.

In what does this true meaning consist? The song is valuable to the ἀνήρ who has arrived in Hades because it retrospectively reveals the permanent character of his earthly 'delight', his τερπνόν. While he is still alive, this τερπνόν is bound to his own person; it is co-extensive with his own existence, like his voice or—better—his own present recollection. In the moment of his death, however, this presence vanishes: only now can it become clear whether the victory possesses an autonomy by virtue of which it can live on without the victor. Such autonomy does not suddenly become the possession of the victory with death, but rather is only now recognized as something that *has always* characterized it. Conversely: whereas the victory, as long as the victor lived, is a καλόν (91) with or without the song—at no point does Pindar's text make the *aesthetic* quality of the victory dependent on the song—it is revealed in the moment of his death, if the song is lacking, as a κενεόν (93), as something 'empty'.

The son, who bears the name of the father, and the song, which bears the name of the contest, are thus heirs. Only the name can inherit; it takes up its inheritance, however, *de iure* always already its own, only in the moment of the absolute absence or the pastness of its truth, in the moment of death of its first, originary bearer. For this reason, writes Derrida in a study of Nietzsche's *Ecce homo*, the name is always and *a priori* a dead man's name, a name of death.[132] But what the name reveals in this relationship to death is nothing other than the principle of writing and the principle of memory as writing.

Let us reconstruct this moment, which is of the greatest importance

[132] Derrida 1984b, p. 44. On the following *cf. id.*, 'Signature événement contexte' (= Derrida 1972b, pp. 365–393), pp. 374 ff., Engl. p. 314 ff.

for the entire level of discourse in Pindar concerned with remembrance and the construction of subjectivity in the *Tenth Olympian*, particularly carefully. Writing—spatial, external, vulnerable to being obscured and forgotten—must, at the beginning of the song, be transformed by the voice into the presence of recollection. To the extent that this *translatio* by the Muse and Truth does not take place, memory remains ineffective. Nevertheless, the opening verses nowhere suggest that the identity of the victor, that is to say, his constitutive link with the place whose name the song bears and the father, is not really written in the memory of the poet. The reality of this lost writing is nowhere doubted, although the singer neither knows where it is nor is in a position to discover it without help. That means: memory is real even when the person who is meant to remember does not, when his intention and genuine resolve to fulfil his promise are not present to him, but rather absent. The ability of writing to bridge this merely temporary absence of present intention also means, however, that it *as writing* must in principle be able to bridge the indefinite absence of such an intention. Certainly: the poem speaks of a writing of the φρήν which will naturally vanish with the death of the individual subject. But the choice of this metaphor for the structure and nature of the φρήν which, as we have noted, is by no means mandatory for a poet in the 470s on account of an existing tradition or possesses the rhetorical conventionality of a cliché, implies that the survival of what is written beyond the immediate context of its origin is always possible, a survival that is in fact of crucial importance for the use made of the metaphor at the beginning of the ode and is rigorously analogous to the survival of the song after the end of the victory and the victor in the final triad. Here as there, the concern is with an autonomy of language, and in particular of *names*, that enables them to exist in the absence of every presence of an individual intending, promising or remembering subject, and thus without the immediate connection to an origin which would grant them their meaning or their truth. The absence or the death of the subject does not create these attributes, but only reveals them as the 'true' nature of (the) writing(,) of the memory(,) of the name from the very beginning.

If death means the writing of the name as memory, then this is the conclusion to which the *Tenth Olympian* and with it the entire Pindaric poetics of κλέος leads us. The song should inherit, and it must, for otherwise the victory has no meaning. But it is at the same time clear that the meaning of the victory in fact only exists by virtue of the inheritance of the song, and that means, in memory, and not in itself as an event. Everything that is *present* about the victory, the object of an exclusively present experience, is meaningless, since it cannot inherit anything from outside itself. Writing that stands, as we have seen, for externality, forgetting and death, must therefore have replaced the absolute presence of the victory from the very beginning so that the name of the victor and the father will be able to live on. In the terms of the first verse of the poem, however, this means that writing and memory must efface voice and recollection.

The writing down of remembrance means the transformation of the symbol into a sign. Despite the invocations of inwardness and the belonging of the son in the verses 86–90, the *telos* of this development cannot be the genetic relationship that Pindar suggests exists between name and thing, but instead only the arbitrary relationship between letter and sound. The real goal of this argumentation is the separation of subject and predicate that, as de Man points out, is characteristic in Hegel's aesthetics for *allegory*—that figure that 'means exactly the non-existence of what it represents', as Walter Benjamin wrote.[133] The language of subjectivity in the epinicians thus promises anything but the authenticity of an historical origin or the inwardness of a genius-poet. Far from consisting in an originary self-presence of meaning, it speaks instead without ceasing of a negative distance to itself, an irreducible alterity whose catachresis is the writing of memory.

[133] De Man 1996, p. 104; see Hegel 1969–1971, vol. 13, p. 512; Benjamin 1972–1986, vol. I 1, p. 406 (cited more fully above, p. 50 n. 68).

CONCLUSIONS

Für uns gehört die Dichtung seit langem
zur Literatur, ebenso das Denken. Man
findet es in Ordnung, daß die Dichtung
und ihre Geschichte literaturhistorisch
abgehandelt werden. Es wäre töricht, diesen
Zustand, der weit zurückliegende Gründe
hat, zu bemängeln oder gar über Nacht
abändern zu wollen. Gleichwohl – ist
Homer, ist Sappho, ist Pindar, ist
Sophokles Literatur? Nein!
Heidegger, *Was heißt Denken?*

HEIDEGGER, FOR WHOM THE WORD 'LITERATURE' MEANT THE object of a technical, objectivising science, called Pindar's work 'poetry' (*Dichtung*).[1] Its special status consisted for the philosopher from Todtnauberg in having been at work long before the ancient distinctions that enable such things as 'literature' ('nature' *versus* 'culture', for example, or 'art' *versus* 'technology' or even—as we have attempted to show here—'rhetoric' *versus* 'meaning') ever came into play. *Dichtung* calls the authorities and instruments of a form of literary studies based on such distinctions into question; it withdraws itself from the reach of a metaphysical model of understanding by putting its presuppositions at stake. In contrast to Heidegger's use of the word, we have chosen here to identify that which retreats with the 'literariness' of literature. In a certain sense, however, the last two hundred-and-thirty-odd pages can be read as a commentary or even a long footnote to this passage from *Was heißt Denken?*

We have now arrived at the, or at least an, end of our investigations—what has been achieved? We promised three levels of argumentation: literary-interpretative, research-historical and literary-theoretical. We will consider them one by one.

1. *Interpretation.* Pindar's epinicians contain a level of reflexion dealing not only with the relationship between rhetoric and meaning in

[1] Heidegger [5]1997, p. 154, Engl. p. 134. Derrida relates this disqualification of literature to Heidegger's valorization of spoken language; see Derrida 1972b, p. 159 f., n. 20, Engl. p. 132 f., n. 36, and Clark 1992, p. 23.

general, but also with questions of the limitation and delimitation of texts and with the constitution of speech as an expression of subjectivity based on this relationship. The *First Olympian* spoke of the impossibility of excluding the effects of figural displacement from the transcendental place of truth as literal meaning; this impossibility forms the basis of the complications we noted in the construction of the text of the *Second* and *Sixth Olympians* and in the situation of the self endlessly mediated by writing in the *Tenth Olympian*. Pindar's metaphors thus show themselves to be more than the merely affirmative symbols of an archaic system of values in Fränkel's sense or even the subversive codings of social models of behaviour in Kurke's; they can also intervene in the fundamental categories of meaning itself. After half a century of work on theories of metaphor from a structuralist or poststructuralist perspective, this will come as no great surprise to contemporary literary studies; it may however be of greater interest to note that these effects are by no means intrinsically 'modern' or 'post-modern', but are instead just as readily to be found in the lyric poetry of the Greek archaic period as in the writings of authors such as Rousseau or Blanchot. If the subversion of the difference between literal meaning and figural rhetoric in the *First Olympian* is reminiscent of a problem in Yeats made explicit by Paul de Man, the difficulties of determining textual borders that Derrida will ascribe more than two thousand years later in readings of Kant and Mallarmé to the parergon and the fold are already present in songs such as the *Sixth Olympian*. The self-referential metaphoricity of what is called 'intention', the catachresis of the self seem in the victory odes, in particular the *Tenth Olympian*, to anticipate concerns first systematically formulated in twentieth-century theory; this is especially true of the genuinely originary notion of writing in this poem. Across the millennia, ancient and modern literatures are linked by a shared entanglement in language; what distinguishes the work of one author from that of another is the specific articulation of this common complicity in the parerga and folds, marks and traces to be found in his or her texts.

There would therefore be more to think about on this relatively simple level in other texts and other corpora; one could imagine a version of classical literary studies which would draw up maps of such elements, a cartography without simple borders, in which every outside could become, in a moment, an inside and *vice versa*. The contours of a specifically *Pindaric* poetics that might emerge from such a project have admittedly been no more than roughly sketched out here.

Such a poetics would naturally not be identical with a hermeneutics or with the appropriation of what the author wanted to say. Perhaps one would discover that Benjamin's divergence between meaning and saying is so virulent in the victory odes because of the constant epinician attempt to speak of values, to ground the notion of value in a realm of literality beyond figural displacement—an attempt that brings the disseminative effects of rhetoric all the more firmly into view. We are not speaking, of course, of *Pindar's* view. The concern and goal of our reading has been to discover what, in the texts, refuses to submit to the dictates of a will to meaning—or even a will to form, when we consider how the parergon makes even the simple desire for closure utopian. But on the border between what is wanted and what cannot be desired, a discourse seems to reveal itself that makes the epinicians a strategic place for questioning the relationship between meaning and what meaning must exclude in order (really) to be (real) meaning.

2. *History of scholarship.* If the texts generated in the history of research have in some respects more to say about the problems that have concerned us here than their authors can have realized, then this too is an effect of the retreat of rhetoric. In particular those Pindarists who have undertaken to make the premises and implications of their philological procedures explicit—August Boeckh is in this respect exemplary—have not only been able to make the philosophical foundations of traditional literary studies visible, but also to reveal the inadequacies of such studies, the latter of course for the most part involuntarily. But Heidegger is right to warn us here of *complaining* about the complicity between philology and metaphysics. What point could such a criticism have, given that the problem of this connection is obviously not the result of an inadequate implementation or application of the models of the philosophers? The examples of Plato, Aristotle and Hegel show with all desirable clarity that the breaks in the commentaries are already contained in the philosophical tradition to which they owe their theoretical cogency. Instead, it would be wiser to ponder the fact that the methodological assumption that no author ever has full control of his or her own text leads in the case of the secondary literature to almost more interesting, certainly more surprising results than it does in the primary texts, where a certain destabilising of the tradition was to be expected, for theoretical reasons, from the very beginning. The realization that authoritative and central works of Pindaric scholarship such as Bundy's *Studia Pindarica* and Boeckh's *Pindari Opera* and *Encyklopädie* rely crucially on arguments that subvert their own metaphysical premises suggests that

a reading of the history of scholarship oriented exclusively towards the question of 'right' and 'wrong' will fail to take account of much of what is going on in the texts. De Man's dialectics of blindness and insight, the thesis that genuinely insightful criticism is in principle always owed to a necessary blind-spot, enables instead a way of reading the history of scholarship that does not merely question traditional evaluations, but can also offer a more sophisticated alternative to the still widespread practice of neatly dividing research into authorities to be cited and adversaries to be opposed.

3. *Theory.* The freedom or the resistance of literature as constitutively figural-material language over against the categories of its interpretation as meaning has been the main theoretical interest of our study. We were concerned in the course of our readings to demonstrate the specific rationality of this freedom or this resistance: it is readily amenable to analysis with the instruments of literary studies, requires however at the same time relinquishing the *unlimited* validity of categories of understanding that in the language of metaphysics posses the value of transcendental signifieds. These categories—truth, unity, intention as *vouloir-dire*—are Pindar's metaphors. Like all metaphors, they possess the structure of a dialectics incapable of sublimation or *Aufhebung*, whose contours become visible in the interaction of the necessity of meaning and its contingency. The *figurality*, in literature, of what, in interpretation, must be *literal* not merely in order for language, but also for meaning to come into being, reveals the latter's metaphysical instability. It is therefore no surprise that the results of such a dialectics, which could not be further removed from those of a metaphorology, a re-appropriation of the metaphor by the logos, are aporetic in nature.

One specific aporia, which has been something like a *leitmotiv* of our investigations here, follows from the requirement that interpretation be as immanent as possible. The techniques of 'close reading' were always grounded theoretically in the aesthetic-hermeneutical thesis that a text must be comprehensible or able to be experienced *on its own terms*. *Homerum ex Homero*: the thesis and its imperative have been current in classical studies for millennia. But this requirement does not without further ado uncover that simplicity and significance in the texts that its adherents seem to expect. It does this only if it is already contaminated, from the outset, by a hypothesis about the texts, about the kind of language to be found in them and the configuration of the subjectivity that speaks there. We have discussed the philosophical, that is, the *non*-immanent provenience of this hypothesis more than once. (One could still call this a result in the history of scholarship if only the possibility of 'history', that is, the reification of the tradition of scholarship based on these premises, did not depend on precisely this hypothesis.) Beyond a certain point that we have attempted to situate, reflexion on methods and presuppositions leads to an impasse that can, indeed, still be described in the language of metaphysics (and we have no other), but which does not belong to the real domain of this language. For this reason, we have spoken with Benjamin and de Man of *allegories* of interpretation—not in order to call for a rejection of immanent literary studies (quite the opposite, in fact), but in order to make clear what we are doing when we read in this way. If the theoretical project can be seen as the attempt to view viewing, then the moments at which the methodological presuppositions of close reading subvert themselves will be a part of this necessary theoria—an abyss, perhaps, but one from which classical literary studies should no longer draw back.

BIBLIOGRAPHY

Abbreviations of the names of ancient authors and works generally follow Simon Hornblower and Anthony Spawforth (eds., 1996), *The Oxford Classical Dictionary* (London/New York). Other abbreviations are:

AJPh	*American Journal of Philology*
BICS	*Bulletin of the Institute of Classical Studies*
CJ	*Classical Journal*
CPh	*Classical Philology*
CQ	*Classical Quarterly*
CSCA	*California Studies in Classical Antiquity*
DK	*Die Fragmente der Vorsokratiker*, ed. Hermann Diels and Walther Kranz, 3 vols. (Berlin, ^{6}1952).
Dr.	*Scholia vetera in Pindari carmina*, ed. A.B. Drachmann, 3 vols. (Leipzig 1903–1927).
FGrH	*Die Fragmente der griechischen Historiker*, ed. F. Jacoby, 3 vols. (Berlin/Leiden, 1923–1958).
GRBS	*Greek Roman Byzantine Studies*
HSCPh	*Harvard Studies in Classical Philology*
ICS	*Illinois Classical Studies*
JHS	*Journal of Hellenic Studies*
KG	Raphael Kühner and Bernhard Gerth (^{3}1898), *Ausführliche Grammatik der griechischen Sprache*, Zweiter Teil: *Satzlehre*, 2 vols. (Hannover/Leipzig).
KS	Raphael Kühner and Carl Stegmann (^{5}1976), *Ausführliche Grammatik der lateinischen Sprache*, Zweiter Teil: *Satzlehre*, 2 vols. (Hannover).
LfrgE	Bruno Snell *et al.* (eds., 1955–), *Lexikon des frühgriechischen Epos* (Göttingen).
LSJ	H.G. Liddell and R. Scott (^{9}1940), *A Greek-English Lexicon*, revised by Sir H. Stuart Jones (Oxford).
MH	*Museum Helveticum*
MLN	*Modern Language Notes*
MW	*Fragmenta Hesiodea*, eds. R. Merkelbach and M. West (Oxford, ^{3}1990).
PMG	*Poetae Melici Graeci*, ed. Denis Page (Oxford, 1962).
QUCC	*Quaderni urbinati di cultura classica*
RhM	*Rheinisches Museum*
SM	*Pindari Carmina cum Fragmentis*, 2 vols., Pars I: *Epinicia*, ed. Bruno Snell and Herwig Maehler (Leipzig, ^{8}1987), Pars II: *Fragmenta, Indices*, ed. Herwig Maehler (Leipzig, 1989).
TAPhA	*Transactions of the American Philological Association*

Ancient texts are cited according to the following editions:

Aristotelis Ars Rhetorica, ed. W.D. Ross (Oxford, 1959).
Aristotelis De Arte Poetica Liber, ed. Rudolph Kassel (Oxford, 1965).
Aristotelis Metaphysica, ed. Werner Jaeger (Oxford, 1957).
Aristotelis Physica, ed. W.D. Ross (Oxford, 1950).
Bacchylides, ed. H. Maehler (Stuttgart/Leipzig, 1992).
Die Fragmente der Vorsokratiker, ed. Hermann Diels and Walther Kranz, 3 vols. (Berlin, ^{6}1952).
Hesiodi Theogonia. Opera et dies. Scutum, ed. Friedrich Solmsen. *Fragmenta selecta*, ed. R. Merkelbach and Martin L. West (Oxford, ^{3}1990).
Homeri Ilias, ed. Martin L. West, 2 vols. (Stuttgart/Leipzig, 1998–2000).
Homeri Odyssea, ed. Peter von der Muehll (Stuttgart/Leipzig, ^{3}1962).
Iambi et elegi Graeci, ed. Martin L. West, 2 vols. (Oxford, ^{2}1989).
Pindari Carmina cum Fragmentis, 2 vols., Pars I: *Epinicia*, ed. Bruno Snell and Herwig Maehler (Leipzig, ^{8}1987), Pars II: *Fragmenta, Indices*, ed. Herwig Maehler (Leipzig, 1989).
Plato, Gorgias. A Revised Text with Introduction and Commentary, ed. E.R. Dodds (Oxford, 1959).
Platonis opera, ed. J. Burnett, 5 vols. (Oxford, 1901–1913).
Platonis opera, ed. E.A. Duke, W.F. Hicken, W.S.M. Nicoll, D.B. Robinson, J.C.G. Strachan, *tom.* 1 (Oxford, 1995): *Euthyphro, Apologia, Crito, Phaedo, Cratylus, Theaetetus, Sophista, Politicus.*
Poetae epici Graeci, ed. Alberto Bernabé, *Pars* 1 (Stuttgart/Leipzig, ^{2}1996).
Poetae Melici Graeci, ed. Denis Page (Oxford, 1962).
M. Fabi Quintiliani institutionis oratoriae libri duodecim, ed. Michael Winterbottom, 2 vols. (Oxford 1970).
Scholia vetera in Pindari carmina, ed. A.B. Drachmann, 3 vols. (Leipzig 1903–1927).

Secondary literature:

ABRAMS, M.H. (1989), *Doing Things with Texts. Essays in Criticism and Critical Theory* (New York/London).
ARRIGHETTI, Graziano, Giovanna Calvani MARIOTTI, Franco MONTANARI (eds., 1991), *Concordantia et Indices in scholia Pindarica vetera*, 2 vols. (Hildesheim).
ASPER, Markus (1997), Onomata allotria. *Zur Genese, Struktur und Funktion poetologischer Metaphern bei Kallimachos* (Stuttgart; Hermes Einzelschriften 75).
ATHANASSAKI, Lucia (2004), 'Deixis, performance, and poetics in Pindar's *First Olympian Ode*', *Arethusa* 37, pp. 317–341.
BARNES, Jonathan (ed., 1984), *The Complete Works of Aristotle. The Revised Oxford Translation*, 2 vols. (Princeton).
BARTHES, Roland (2002), *Œuvres complètes*, 5 vols. (Paris).
BARTHES, Roland (2004), *Criticism and Truth*, tr. Katrine Pilcher Keuneman (London).

BAUGH, Bruce (1993), 'Hegel in modern French philosophy: the unhappy consciousness', *Laval théologique et philosophique* 49.3, pp. 423–438.

BECKER, O. (1937), *Das Bild des Weges und verwandte Vorstellungen im frühgriechischen Denken* (Berlin; Hermes Einzelschriften 4).

BENDER, John and David E. WELLBERY (1990), 'Rhetoricality: on the modernist return to rhetoric', in *iid.* (eds.), *The Ends of Rhetoric. History, Theory, Practice* (Stanford), pp. 3–39.

BENJAMIN, Andrew (ed., 1988), *Post-structuralist Classics* (London).

BENJAMIN, Walter (1972–1986), *Gesammelte Werke*, eds. Rolf Tiedemann and Hermann Schweppenhäuser, 7 vols. (Frankfurt am Main). Partial English translation as: Walter Benjamin (1996–2003), *Selected Writings*, ed. Michael Jennings *et al.*, 4 vols. (Cambridge, MA).

BENJAMIN, Walter (1977), *The Origin of German Tragic Drama*, tr. John Osborne (London).

BENNINGTON, Geoffrey (1988), 'Deconstruction and the philosophers (the very idea)', *Oxford Literary Review* 10, pp. 73–130.

BENNINGTON, Geoffrey (1999), 'Inter', in McQuillan *et al.* (eds.), pp. 103–119.

BENNINGTON, Geoffrey (2000), *Interrupting Derrida* (London/New York).

BENNINGTON, Geoffrey and Robert YOUNG (1987), 'Introduction: posing the question', in Derek Attridge, Geoffrey Bennington, Robert Young (eds.), *Post-structuralism and the Question of History* (Cambridge), pp. 1–11.

BERGSON, Henri (1889), *Essai sur les données immédiates de la conscience* (Paris).

BERGSON, Henri (1903), *Introduction à la métaphysique* (Paris).

BERNADETE, Seth (1960), 'Plato *Sophist* 223b1–7', *Phronesis* 5, pp. 129–131.

BERNET, Rudolf (1986), 'Differenz und Anwesenheit. Derridas und Husserls Phänomenologie der Sprache, der Zeit, der Geschichte, der wissenschaftlichen Rationalität', in Ernst-Wolfgang Orth (ed.), *Phänomenologische Forschungen* 18: *Studien zur neueren französischen Phänomenologie* (Freiburg), pp. 51–112.

BIESECKER, Barbara (1989), 'Rethinking the rhetorical situation from within the thematic of *différance*', *Rhetoric and Philosophy* 22, pp. 110–130.

BITZER, Lloyd (1969), 'The rhetorical situation', *Philosophy and Rhetoric* 1, pp. 1–14.

BLANCHOT, Maurice (1955), *L'Espace littéraire* (Paris).

BLANCHOT, Maurice (1999), *The Station Hill Blanchot Reader. Fiction and Literary Essays*, ed. George Quasha (New York).

BLOOM, Harold (1981), 'Freud and the poetic sublime: a catastrophe theory of creativity', in Perry Meisel (ed.), *Freud: A Collection of Critical Essays* (Englewood Cliffs, NJ), pp. 211–231.

BOECKH, August (1811–1821), *Pindari opera quae supersunt*, 2 vols. (Leipzig).

BOECKH, August (1858–1874), *Gesammelte kleine Schriften*, eds. F. Ascherson, E. Bratuscheck and P. Eichholtz, 7 vols. (Leipzig).

BOECKH, August (^{2}1886), *Encyklopädie und Methodologie der philologischen Wissenschaften*, ed. Ernst Bratuscheck (Leipzig) (first edition 1877). Partial English translation as: August Boeckh (1968), *On Interpretation and Criticism*, tr. John Paul Pritchard (Norman).

BOILEAU, Nicolas (1966), *Œuvres completes*, ed. F. Escal (Paris).

BONIFAZI, Anna (2004), 'Communication in Pindar's deictic acts', *Arethusa* 37, pp. 391–414.

BORMANN, Karl (1971), *Parmenides. Untersuchungen zu den Fragmenten* (Hamburg).

BORNEMANN, L. (1889), 'Pindars sechste olympische Ode', *Philologus* 47, pp. 589–598.

BOURDIEU, Pierre (²2000), *Esquisse d'une théorie de la pratique* (Paris) (first edition 1972). English: Pierre Bourdieu (1977), *Outline of a Theory of Practice*, tr. Richard Nice (Cambridge/New York).

BOWRA, C. Maurice (1964), *Pindar* (Oxford).

BRASWELL, Bruce Karl (1996), 'Die Anfänge der Pindarstudien in der Renaissance', in Margarethe Billerbeck and Jacques Schamp (eds.), *Kainotomia. Die Erneuerung der griechischen Tradition.* Colloquium Pavlos Tzermias (4. November 1995) (Freiburg, Switzerland), pp. 69–80.

BREMER, J.M. (1990), 'Pindar's paradoxical ἐγώ and a recent controversy about the performance of his epinicia', in S.R. Slings (ed.), *The Poet's I in Archaic Greek Lyric* (Amsterdam), pp. 41–58.

BRENTANO, Franz (1973), *Psychologie vom empirischen Standpunkt*, ed. O. Kraus, 2 vols. (Hamburg) (first published in 1874/1911).

BUBNER, Rüdiger (1989), *Ästhetische Erfahrung* (Frankfurt am Main).

BUCHHEIM, Thomas (1994), *Die Vorsokratiker. Ein philosophisches Porträt* (Munich).

BULMAN, Patricia (1992), *Phthonos in Pindar* (Berkeley).

BUNDY, Elroy Lorraine (1986), *Studia Pindarica* (Berkeley) (first published 1962).

BURGESS, Dana L. (1990), 'Pindar's Olympian 10: praise for the poet, praise for the victor', *Hermes* 118, pp. 273–281.

BURGESS, Dana L. (1993), 'Food, sex, money and poetry in "Olympian" 1', *Hermes* 121, pp. 35–44.

BURKERT, Walter (1969), 'Das Proömium des Parmenides und die Katabasis des Pythagoras', *Phronesis* 14, pp. 1–30.

BURTON, R.W.B. (1962), *Pindar's Pythian Odes, Essays in Interpretation* (Oxford).

CALAME, Claude (2003), *Myth and History in Ancient Greece. The Symbolic Creation of a Colony* (Princeton/Oxford).

CAMPE, Rüdiger (1990), *Affekt und Ausdruck. Zur Umwandlung der literarischen Rede im 17. und 18. Jahrhundert* (Tübingen).

CAREY, Christopher (1980), 'Three myths in Pindar: *N.* 4, *O.* 9, *N.* 3', *Eranos* 78, pp. 143–162.

CAREY, Christopher (1981), *Five Odes of Pindar* (New York).

CAREY, Christopher (1989), 'Two transitions in Pindar', *CQ* 39 (ii), pp. 287–295.

CAREY, Christopher (1994), review of L. Kurke (1991), *The Traffic in Praise* (Ithaca/London), *JHS* 114, p. 184.

CARNES, Jeffrey S. (1995), 'Why should I mention Aiakos? Myth and politics in Pindar's Nemean 8 [Part I]', *QUCC* 51, pp. 7–48.

CARSON, Anne (1982), 'Wedding at noon in Pindar's *Ninth Pythian*', *GRBS* 23, pp. 121–128.

CARUTH, Cathy and Deborah ESCH (eds., 1995), *Critical Encounters. Reference and Responsibility in Deconstructive Writing* (New Brunswick).

CASSIRER, Ernst (2001), *Philosophie der symbolischen Formen*, Erster Teil: *Die Sprache* (Hamburg) (first published in 1923)

CASSIRER, Ernst (2002), *Philosophie der symbolischen Formen*, Zweiter Teil: *Das mythische Denken* (Hamburg) (first published in 1925).

CEBULLA, Michael (1992), *Wahrheit und Authentizität. Zur Entwicklung der Literaturtheorie Paul de Mans* (Stuttgart).

CLARK, Timothy (1986), 'Being in mime: Heidegger and Derrida on the ontology of literary language', *MLN* 101, pp. 1003–1021.

CLARK, Timothy (1992), *Derrida, Heidegger, Blanchot* (Cambridge).

COBB, William S. (1990), *Plato's Sophist* (Savage, Maryland).

COHEN, Barbara and Tom COHEN, J. Hillis MILLER, Andrzej WARMINSKI (eds., 2001), *Material Events. Paul de Man and the Afterlife of Theory* (Minneapolis/London).

COLE, Thomas (1983), 'Archaic truth', *QUCC* 13, pp. 7–28.

COLE, Thomas (1992), *Pindar's Feasts or the Music of Power* (Rome).

COMBELLACK, Frederick (1950), 'Words that die', *CJ* 46, pp. 21–26.

CORNFORD, Francis Macdonald (1935), *Plato's Theory of Knowledge* (London).

CORNFORD, Francis Macdonald (1939), *Plato and Parmenides* (London).

COXON, A.H. (ed., 1986), *The Fragments of Parmenides. A Critical Text with Introduction, Translation, the Ancient Testimonia and a Commentary* (Assen/Wolfeboro).

CROTTY, Kevin (1982), *Song and Action. The Victory Odes of Pindar* (Baltimore/London).

CULLER, Jonathan (1982), *On Deconstruction. Theory and Criticism after Structuralism* (Ithaca/New York).

CULLER, Jonathan (2007), *The Literary in Theory* (Stanford).

CURRIE, Bruno (2005), *Pindar and the Cult of Heroes* (Oxford).

CURTIUS, Ernst Robert (1948), *Europäische Literatur und Lateinisches Mittelalter* (Bern).

D'ALESSIO, Giovan Battista (1994), 'First-person problems in Pindar', *BICS* 39, pp. 117–139.

D'ALESSIO, Giovan Battista (2004), 'Past future and present past: temporal deixis in Greek archaic lyric', *Arethusa* 37, pp. 267–294.

DANZ, Jürgen (1982), 'August Böckh: Die Textinterpretation als Verstehen des subjectiven Objectiven', in Ulrich Nassen (ed.), *Klassiker der Hermemeutik* (Paderborn/Munich/Vienna/Zürich), pp. 131–172.

D'AVINO, R. (1980–81), 'Messaggio verbale e tradizione orale. Hom. ἔπεα πτερόεντα', *Helikon* 20–21, pp. 87–117.

DASENBROCK, Reed Way (ed., 1989), *Redrawing the Lines: Analytical Philosophy, Deconstruction and Literary Theory* (Minneapolis).

DAY, Joseph W. (1991), 'The poet's *elpis* and the opening of *Isthmian* 8', *TAPhA* 121, pp. 47–61.

DE JONG, Irene J.F. (1992), Review of R.P. Martin (1989), *The Language of Heroes* (Ithaca/London), *Mnemosyne*, ser. IV., vol. 45, pp. 392–397.

DE JONG, Irene J.F. and J.P. SULLIVAN (eds., 1994), *Modern Critical Theory and Classical*

Literature (Leiden: Mnemosyne Suppl. 130).
DE MAN, Paul (1966), 'La circularité de l'interprétation dans l'œuvre de Maurice Blanchot', *Critique* 229, pp. 547–560. English: 'Impersonality in the criticism of Maurice Blanchot' in de Man ²1983, pp. 60–78.
DE MAN, Paul (1979), *Allegories of Reading. Figural Language in Rousseau, Nietzsche, Rilke, and Proust* (New Haven/London).
DE MAN, Paul (²1983), *Blindness and Insight. Essays in the Rhetoric of Contemporary Criticism* (Minneapolis) (first edition 1971).
DE MAN, Paul (1984), *The Rhetoric of Romanticism* (New York).
DE MAN, Paul (1986), *The Resistance to Theory* (Minneapolis).
DE MAN, Paul (1989), *Critical Writings, 1953–1978*, ed. Lindsay Waters (Minneapolis).
DE MAN, Paul (1996), *Aesthetic Ideology*, ed. Andrzej Warminski (Minneapolis).
DE RIJK, L.M. (1986), *Plato's Sophist. A Philosophical Commentary* (Amsterdam).
DELEUZE, Gilles (1968), *Différence et répétition* (Paris). English: Gilles Deleuze (1994), *Difference and Repetition*, tr. Paul Patton (London/New York: Continuum).
DELEUZE, Gilles (1969), *Logique du sens* (Paris). English: Gilles Deleuze (1990), *The Logic of Sense*, tr. Mark Lester with Charles Stivale, ed. Constantin V. Boundas (London).
DELEUZE, Gilles (2002), *L'île déserte et autres textes. Textes et entretiens 1953–1974* (Paris). English: Gilles Deleuze (2004), *Desert Islands and Other Texts (1953–1974)*, tr. Mike Taormina (New York).
DENNISTON, J.D. (1950), *The Greek Particles* (Oxford).
DERRIDA, Jacques (1967a), *De la grammatologie* (Paris). English: Jacques Derrida (1976), *Of Grammatology*, tr. Gayatri Chakravorty Spivak (Baltimore/London).
DERRIDA, Jacques (1967b), *La voix et le phénomène* (Paris).
DERRIDA, Jacques (1967c), *L'écriture et la différence* (Paris). English: Jacques Derrida (1978), *Writing and Difference*, tr. Alan Bass (Chicago).
DERRIDA, Jacques (1972a), *La dissémination* (Paris). English: Jacques Derrida (1981), *Dissemination*, tr. Barbara Johnson (London).
DERRIDA, Jacques (1972b), *Marges de la philosophie* (Paris). English: Jacques Derrida (1982), *Margins of Philosophy*, tr. Alan Bass (Chicago).
DERRIDA, Jacques (1972c), *Positions* (Paris). English: Jacques Derrida (1981), *Positions*, tr. Alan Bass (Chicago).
DERRIDA, Jacques (1978), *La vérité en peinture* (Paris). English: Jacques Derrida (1987), *The Truth in Painting*, tr. Geoffrey Bennington and Ian McLeod (Chicago/London).
DERRIDA, Jacques (1980), 'The law of genre', tr. Avital Ronell, *Glyph* 7, pp. 202–229.
DERRIDA, Jacques (1984a), 'Deconstruction and the other', in Richard Kearney (ed.), *Dialogues with Continental Thinkers* (Manchester), pp. 105–126.
DERRIDA, Jacques (1984b), *Otobiographies. L'enseignement de Nietzsche et la politique du nom propre* (Paris).
DERRIDA, Jacques (1989), 'Some statements and truisms about neologisms, newisms, postisms, parasitisms, and other small seisms', in David Carroll (ed.), *The States of 'Theory'. History, Art and Critical Discourse* (New York), pp. 63–94.

DERRIDA, Jacques (1990), *Du droit à la philosophie* (Paris).

DERRIDA, Jacques (²1998), *Psyché. Inventions de l'autre* (Paris). English: Jacques Derrida (2007), *Psyche: Inventions of the Other*, tr. Peggy Kamuf & Elizabeth Rottenberg (Stanford).

DERRIDA, Jacques (²2003), *Parages* (Paris).

DERRIDA, Jacques (2004), *Eyes of the University. Right to Philosophy* 2, tr. Jan Plug *et al.* (Stanford).

DETIENNE, Marcel and Jean-Pierre VERNANT (1978), *Cunning Intelligence in Greek Culture and Society* (Hassocks).

DICKSON, Keith M. (1986), 'Damasiphron khrusos: act, implement and tekhne in Pindar', *Ramus* 15, pp. 122–142.

DICKSON, Keith M. (1988), 'The semiotics of *eidos* in *Olympian* 8', *Helios* 15, pp. 115–126.

DICKSON, Keith M. (1990), 'Voice and sign in Pindar', *Ramus* 19, pp. 109–129.

DILTHEY, Wilhelm (1959–), *Gesammelte Schriften* (Stuttgart/Göttingen).

DISSEN, Georg Ludolph (1839), *Kleine lateinische und deutsche Schriften*, eds. Fr. Tiersch, F.G. Welcker and K.O. Müller (Göttingen).

DISSEN, Georg Ludolph (²1843, ²1847), *Pindari carmina quae supersunt cum deperditorum fragmentis selectis ex recensione Boeckhii*, Sect. I: *Carmina cum annotatione critica*. Sect. II: *Commentarius*. Editio altera auctior et emendatio, curavit F.G. Schneidewin (Gotha/Erfurt) (both volumes first published in 1830).

DODDS, E.R. (ed., 1959), *Plato, Gorgias. A Revised Text with Introduction and Commentary* (Oxford).

DONLAN, Walter (1973), 'The origin of *kaloskagathos*', *AJPh* 94, pp. 365–374.

DORNSEIFF, Franz (1921), *Pindars Stil* (Berlin).

DOUGHERTY, Carol (1993), *The Poetics of Colonization. From City to Text in Archaic Greece* (Oxford).

DOUGHERTY, Carol and Leslie KURKE (eds., 1993), *Cultural Poetics in Archaic Greece. Cult, Performance, Politics* (Cambridge).

DRACHMANN, A.B. (1891), *Moderne Pindarfortolkning* (Copenhagen).

DRACHMANN, A.B. (1929), Review of W. Schadewaldt, *Der Aufbau des pindarischen Epinikion* (Halle), *Deutsche Literatur-Zeitung* 50, pp. 1092–1102.

DUBOIS, Jacques, Francis EDELINE, Jean-Marie KLINKENBERG, Philippe MINGUET, François PIRE, Hadelin TRINON (1970), *Rhétorique générale* (Paris).

DUNKEL, G. (1979), 'Fighting words: Alcman *Partheneion* 63 *μάχονται*', *Journal of Indo-European Studies* 7, pp. 249–272.

DURANTE, Marcello (1966), 'Epea pteroenta. Die Rede als "Weg" in griechischen und vedischen Bildern', in R. Schmitt (ed.), *Indogermanische Dichtersprache* (Darmstadt; WdF 165), pp. 242–160.

DÜRING, Ingemar (²2005), *Aristoteles. Darstellung und Interpretation seines Denkens* (Heidelberg) (first published 1966).

ECO, Umberto (²1967), *Opera aperta* (Mailand).

EGGINTON, William (2007), 'Performance and presence, analysis of a modern aporia', *Journal of Literary Theory* 1, pp. 3–18.

EGGS, Ekkehard (2001), 'Metapher', in Gert Ueding (ed., 1992–), *Historisches Wörterbuch der Rhetorik* (Tübingen), vol. 5, coll. 1100–1183.

ELLRICH, Lutz and Nikolaus WEGMANN (1990), 'Theorie als Verteidigung der Literatur? Eine Fallgeschichte: Paul de Man', *Deutsche Vierteljahresschrift für Literaturwissenschaft und Geistesgeschichte* 64, pp. 467–513.

ENGELHARDT, P. (1976), 'Intentio', in Karlfried Gründer, Joachim Ritter †, Gottfried Gabriel (eds.), *Historisches Wörterbuch der Philosophie* (Basel, 1971–2007), vol. 4, coll. 466–474.

FARENGA, Vincent (1977a), 'Pindaric craft and the writing of *Pythia* IV', *Helios* 5, pp. 3–37.

FARENGA, Vincent (1977b), 'Violent structure: the writing of Pindar's Olympian I', *Arethusa* 10, pp. 197–218.

FARNELL, Lewis Richard (1932), *The Works of Pindar*, Vol. II: *Critical Commentary* (London).

FELSON, Nancy (2004), 'The poetic effects of deixis in Pindar's *Ninth Pythian Ode*', *Arethusa* 37, pp. 365–389.

FISKER, Dorthe (1990), *Pindars erste olympische Ode* (Odense).

FITZGERALD, William (1983), 'Pindar's Second Olympian', *Helios* 10, pp. 49–70.

FOUCAULT, Michel (1970), 'Theatrum philosophicum', *Critique* 282 (novembre 1970), pp. 885–908.

FOUCAULT, Michel (1971), *L'ordre du discours* (Paris). English: Michel Foucault (1981), 'The order of discourse', in Robert Young (ed.), *Untying the Text* (Boston), pp. 48–78.

FOUCAULT, Michel (1984a), *Histoire de la sexualité*, vol. 2: *L'usage des plaisirs* (Paris). English: Michel Foucault (1985), *The Use of Pleasure. Volume 2 of the History of Sexuality*, tr. Robert Hurley (New York).

FOUCAULT, Michel (1984b), *Histoire de la sexualité*, vol. 3: *Le souci de soi* (Paris). English: Michel Foucault (1986), *The Care of the Self. Volume 3 of the History of Sexuality*, tr. Robert Hurley (New York).

FOUCAULT, Michel (1994), *Dits et Écrits* I (Paris).

FOWLER, Don (2000), *Roman Constructions. Readings in Postmodern Latin* (Oxford).

FRÄNKEL, Hermann (²1960), *Wege und Formen des frühgriechischen Denkens* (Munich).

FRÄNKEL, Hermann (⁴1993), *Dichtung und Philosophie des frühen Griechentums* (Munich) (first edition 1951).

FRAZER, James George (ed., 1921), *Apollodorus. The Library*, 2 vols. (Cambridge, MA).

FREGE, Gottlob (1892), 'Über Sinn und Bedeutung', *Zeitschrift für Philosophie und philosophische Kritik*, N.F. 100, pp. 25–50.

FREUD, Sigmund (¹¹1989), *Studienausgabe*, 11 vols. (Frankfurt am Main).

FREY, Hans-Jost (1997), 'Übersetzung und Sprachtheorie bei Humboldt', in Alfred Hirsch (ed.), *Übersetzung und Dekonstruktion* (Frankfurt am Main), pp. 37–63.

FRIEDLÄNDER, Paul (³1964–1975), *Die platonischen Schriften*, 3 vols. (Berlin).

FRIIS JOHANSEN, H. (1973), 'Agesias, Hieron, and Pindar's Sixth Olympian Ode', in *Classica et mediaevalia F. Blatt septuagenario dedicata* (Copenhagen), pp. 1–9.

FUJISAWA, Norio (1974), '"Ἔχειν, μετέχειν, and idioms of "paradeigmatism" in Plato's theory of forms', *Phronesis* 19, pp. 30–58.

GADAMER, Hans-Georg (1960/1990), *Wahrhheit und Methode. Grundzüge einer philosophischen Hermeneutik* (Tübingen; = *Gesammelte Werke*, vol. 1). English: Hans-Georg Gadamer (²1989), *Truth and Method*, tr. Joel Weinsheimer & Donald G. Marshall (New York/London).

GADAMER, Hans-Georg (1986/1993), *Wahrheit und Methode. Ergänzungen, Register* (Tübingen; = *Gesammelte Werke*, vol. 2).

GADAMER, Hans-Georg (1989), 'Text and interpretation', in Diane P. Michelfelder and Richard E. Palmer (eds.), *Dialogue and Deconstruction. The Gadamer-Derrida Encounter* (New York), pp. 21–51.

GALINSKY, Karl (1992), 'Introduction: The interpretation of Roman poetry and the contemporary critical scene', in *id.* (ed.), *The Interpretation of Roman Poetry: Empiricism or Hermeneutics?* (Frankfurt am Main/Bern/New York), pp. 1–40.

GARNER, Richard (1992), 'Mules, mysteries, and song in Pindar's *Olympia 6*', *Classical Antiquity* 11, pp. 45–67.

GASCHÉ, Rodolphe (1986), *The Tain of the Mirror. Derrida and the Philosophy of Reflection* (Cambridge, MA/London).

GASCHÉ, Rodolphe (1998), *The Wild Card of Reading. On Paul de Man* (Cambridge, MA/London).

GELZER, Thomas (1985), 'Μοῦσα αὐθιγενής. Bemerkungen zu einem Typ Pindarischer und Bacchylideischer Epinikien', *MH* 42, pp. 95–120.

GENETTE, Gérard (1972), *Figures III* (Paris).

GENETTE, Gérard (1982), *Figures of Literary Discourse*, tr. Alan Sheridan (New York).

GENTILI, Bruno, Paola Angeli BERNHARDINI, Ettore CINGANO, Pietro GIANNINI (eds., 1995), *Pindaro. Le Pitiche* (Verona).

GERBER, Douglas E. (1982), *Pindar's* Olympian One*: A Commentary* (Toronto).

GERBER, Douglas E. (1999), 'Pindar, *Nemean* Six: A Commentary', *HSCPh* 99, pp. 33–91.

GERBER, Douglas E. (2002), *A Commentary on Pindar Olympian Nine* (Stuttgart; Hermes Einzelschriften 87).

GIANOTTI, Gian Franco (1971), 'Sull'*Olimpica* seconda di Pindaro', *Rivista di Filolgia e d'Istruzione Classica* 99, pp. 26–52.

GIANOTTI, Gian Franco (1975), *Per una poetica pindarica* (Torino).

GILDERSLEEVE, Basil L. (²1890), *Pindar. The Olympian and Pythian Odes* (New York); *Errata* in *American Journal of Philology* 15 (1894), p. 399.

GILL, Christopher (1996), *Personality in Greek Epic, Tragedy, and Philosophy. The Self in Dialogue* (Oxford).

GILL, Christopher (2006), *The Structured Self in Hellenistic and Roman Thought* (Oxford).

GODZICH, Wlad (1994), *The Culture of Literacy* (Cambridge, MA/London).

GODZICH, Wlad and Lindsay Waters (eds., 1989), *Reading de Man Reading* (Minneapolis).

GLOY, Karen (1985), 'Aristoteles' Theorie des Einen auf der Basis des Buches I der Metaphysik', in Karen Gloy and Enno Rudolph (eds.), *Einheit als Grundfrage der Philosophie* (Darmstadt), pp. 73–101.

GOLDHILL, Simon (1990), 'The Great Dionysia and civic ideology', in Winkler und Zeitlin (eds.), pp. 97–129.

GOLDHILL, Simon (1991), *The Poet's Voice. Essays on Poetics and Greek Literature* (Cambridge).

GOLDHILL, Simon (1994), 'The failure of exemplarity', in de Jong und Sullivan (1994), pp. 51–73.

GUNDERT, H. (1935), *Pindar und sein Dichterberuf* (Frankfurt am Main).

HABERMAS, Jürgen ([4]1988), *Der philosophische Diskurs der Moderne* (Frankfurt am Main). English: Jürgen Habermas (1987), *The Philosophical Discourse of Modernity*, tr. Frederik Lauwrence (Cambridge, MA).

HACKEL, Christiane (2006), *Die Bedeutung August Boeckhs für den Geschichtstheoretiker Johann Gustav Droysen* (Würzburg).

HAINSWORTH, J.B. (1960), 'ἄπτερος μῦθος: a concealed false division?' *Glotta* 38, pp. 263–268.

HALLIWELL, Stephen ([2]1998), *Aristotle's Poetics* (London).

HAMACHER, Werner (1988), 'The word *Wolke*—if it is one', in Rainer Nägele (ed.), *Benjamin's Ground. New Readings of Walter Benjamin* (Detroit), pp. 147–176.

HAMACHER, Werner (1998), *Entferntes Verstehen. Studien zu Philosophie und Literatur von Kant bis Celan* (Frankfurt am Main). English: Werner Hamacher (1999), *Premises. Essays on Philosophy and Literatur from Kant to Celan*, tr. Peter Fenves (Stanford).

HAMILTON, John T. (2003), *Soliciting Darkness. Pindar, Obscurity and the Classical Tradition* (Cambridge, Massachusetts).

HAPP, Heinz (1971), *Hyle. Studien zur aristotelischen Materie-Begriff* (Berlin).

HARLOS, Christopher (1986), 'Rhetoric, structuralism, and figurative discourse: Gérard Genette's concept of rhetoric', *Philosophy and Rhetoric* 19.4, pp. 209–223.

HARRISON, Stephen (2001), 'General introduction: working together', in *id.* (ed.), *Texts, Ideas, and Classics. Scholarship, Theory and Classical Literature* (Oxford), pp. 1–18.

HAVERKAMP, Anselm (2002), *Figura cryptica. Theorie der literarischen Latenz* (Frankfurt am Main).

HEATH, Malcolm (1986), 'The origins of Pindaric criticism', *Journal of Hellenic Studies* 106, pp. 85–98.

HEATH, Malcolm (1989), *Unity in Greek Poetics* (Oxford).

HEGEL, Georg Wilhelm Friedrich (1817), *Encyklopädie der philosophischen Wissenschaften im Grundrisse* (Heidelberg); quoted according to the facsimile-edition in G.W.F. Hegel, *Sämtliche Werke*. Jubiläumsausgabe in zwanzig Bänden, ed. Hermann Glockner, vol. 6 (Stuttgart, 1927).

HEGEL, Georg Wilhelm Friedrich (1969–1971), *Werke in 20 Bänden*, eds. Eva Moldenhauer and Karl Markus Michel (Frankfurt am Main).

HEGEL, Georg Wilhelm Friedrich (1975a), *Aesthetics. Lectures on Fine Art*, tr. T.M. Knox, 2 vols. (Oxford).

HEGEL, Georg Wilhelm Friedrich (1975b), *Logic. Being Part One of the* Encyclopaedia of the Philosophical Sciences *(1830)*, tr. W. Wallace (Oxford).

HEGEL, Georg Wilhelm Friedrich (1977), *Phenomenology of Spirit*, tr. A.V. Miller (Oxford).

HEGEL, Georg Wilhelm Friedrich (2003), *Vorlesungen über die Philosophie der Kunst* [1823]. Mitschrift Heinrich Gustav Hotho, ed. Annemarie Gethmann-Siefert (Hamburg).

HEGEL, Georg Wilhelm Friedrich (2004a), *Philosophie der Kunst oder Ästhetik. Nach Hegel. Im Sommer 1826.* Mitschrift Friedrich Carl Hermann Viktor von Kehler, eds. Annemarie Gethmann-Siefert and Bernadette Collenberg-Plotnikov (Munich).

HEGEL, Georg Wilhelm Friedrich (2004b), *Philosophie der Kunst. Vorlesung von 1826.* Mitschrift P. von der Pfortdens, eds. Annemarie Gethmann-Siefert, Jeong-Im Kwon and Karsten Berr (Frankfurt am Main).

HEGEL, Georg Wilhelm Friedrich (2007), *Philosophy of Mind*, tr. W. Wallace & A.V. Miller, rev. and comm. M.J. Inwood (Oxford).

HEIDEGGER, Martin (1954), *Vorträge und Aufsätze* (Stuttgart).

HEIDEGGER, Martin (1957), *Identität und Differenz* (Stuttgart).

HEIDEGGER, Martin (1975), *Die Grundprobleme der Phänomenologie* (Frankfurt am Main).

HEIDEGGER, Martin (1992), *Platon: Sophistes* (Frankfurt am Main). English: Martin Heidegger (1997), *Plato's Sophist*, tr. Richard Rojcewicz and Andre Schuwer (Bloomington).

HEIDEGGER, Martin (1993), *Basic Writings*, ed. David Farrell Krell (New York).

HEIDEGGER, Martin ([3]1996), *Wegmarken* (Frankfurt am Main) (first published 1967). English: Martin Heidegger (1998), *Pathmarks*, tr. William McNeill (Cambridge).

HEIDEGGER, Martin ([5]1997), *Was heißt Denken?* (Tübingen) (first published 1954). English: Martin Heidegger (1968), *What is Called Thinking?* tr. J. Glenn Gray (New York).

HEIDEGGER, Martin ([6]1998), *Einführung in die Metaphysik* (Tübingen) (first published 1953). English: Martin Heidegger (2000), *Introduction to Metaphysics*, tr. Gregory Fried and Richard Polt (New Haven/London).

HEIDEGGER, Martin ([4]2000), *Zur Sache des Denkens* (Tübingen) (first published 1967). English: Martin Heidegger (1972), *On Time and Being*, tr. Joan Stambaugh (New York/London).

HEIDEGGER, Martin ([18]2001), *Sein und Zeit* (Tübingen) (first published 1927). English: Martin Heidegger (1962), *Being and Time*, tr. John McQuarrie and Edward Robinson (Oxford).

HEIDEGGER, Martin (2002), *Grundbegriffe der aristotelischen Philosophie* (Frankfurt am Main).

HEIDEGGER, Martin ([8]2003), *Holzwege* (Frankfurt am Main) (first published 1950).

HEIDEGGER, Martin (2003), *The End of Philosophy*, tr. Joan Stambaugh (Chicago: University of Chicago Press).

HEIDEGGER, Martin ([9]2006), *Der Satz vom Grund* (Stuttgart) (first published 1957). English: Martin Heidegger (1996), *The Principle of Reason*, tr. Reginald Lilly (Bloomington/Indianapolis).

HELLWIG, Antje (1973), *Untersuchungen zur Theorie der Rhetorik bei Platon und Aristoteles* (Göttingen; Hypomnemata 38).

HERBART, Johann Friedrich (1897–1912), *Sämtliche Werke*, ed. K. Kerbach, 19 vols. (Langensalza).

HERBART, Johann Friedrich (1993), *Lehrbuch zur Einleitung in die Philosophie*, ed. Wolfhart Henckmann (Hamburg) (= 4th ed. 1837).

HERMANN, Gottfried (1827–1877), *Opuscula*, 8 vols. (Leipzig).

HEXTER, Ralph and Daniel SELDEN (ed., 1992), *Innovations of Antiquity* (New York/London).

HEYNE, Christian Gottlob (1807–1809), *Pindari carmina et fragmenta cum lectionis varietate et annotationibus*, 3 vols. (Oxford).

HORNBLOWER, Simon (2004), *Pindar and Thucydides* (Oxford).

HORSTMANN, Axel (1992), *Antike Theorie und moderne Wissenschaft. August Boeckhs Konzeption der Philologie* (Frankfurt am Main; Philosophie und Geschichte der Wissenschaften: Studien und Quellen, vol. 17).

HOWIE, J. Gordon (1984), 'The revision of myth in Pindar *Olympian* 1. The death and revival of Pelops (25–27; 36–66)', in F. Cairns (ed.), *Papers of the Liverpool Latin Seminar* IV 1983, pp. 277–313.

HUBBARD, Thomas K. (1985), *The Pindaric Mind. A Study of Logical Structure in Early Greek Poetry* (Leiden).

HUBBARD, Thomas K. (1986a), 'Pegasus' bridle and the poetics of Pindar's *Thirteenth Olympian*', *HSCPh* 90, pp. 27–48.

HUBBARD, Thomas K. (1986b), 'The subject/object-relation in Pindar's Second *Pythian* and Seventh *Nemean*', *QUCC* 51, pp. 53–72.

HUBBARD, Thomas K. (1987), 'The cooking of Pelops: Pindar and the process of mythological revisionism', *Helios* 14, pp. 3–21.

HUBBARD, Thomas K. (1992), 'Remaking myth and rewriting history: cult tradition in Pindar's *Ninth Nemean*', *HSCPh* 84, pp. 77–111.

HUBBARD, Thomas K. (1993), 'The Theban Amphiaraion and Pindar's vision on the road to Delphi', *MH* 50, pp. 193–203.

HUMMEL, Pascale (1993), *La syntaxe de Pindare* (Paris).

HUSSERL, Edmund (1965), *Philosophie als strenge Wissenschaft* (Frankfurt am Main) (first publ. 1911).

HUSSERL, Edmund (1970), *Logical Investigations*, tr. J.N. Findlay, 2 vols. (London/New York).

HUSSERL, Edmund (1991), *Ideen zu einer reinen Phänomenologie und phenomenologischen Philosophie* II, ed. Marly Biemal (Dordrecht; Husserliana IV).

HUSSERL, Edmund (1992), *Gesammelte Schriften*, ed. Elisabeth Ströker, 8 vols. (Hamburg).

HYPPOLITE, Jean (1946), *Genèse et structure de la Phénoménologie de l'esprit de Hegel* (Paris). English: Jean Hyppolite (1974), *Genesis and Structure of Hegel's* Phenomenology of Spirit, tr. Samuel Cherniak & John Heckman (Evanston).

IRMSCHER, Johannes (1987), 'August Boeckh als Enzyklopädist der klassischen

Altertumswissenschaft', *Wissenschaftliche Zeitschrift der Humboldt-Universität zu Berlin* 36, pp. 11–14.

JAEGER, Werner (1912), *Studien zur Entstehungsgeschichte der Metaphysik des Aristoteles* (Berlin).

JAKOBSON, Roman (1987), *Language in Literature*, eds. Krystyna Pomorska & Stephen Rudy (Cambridge, MA).

JAKOBSON, Roman and Morris HALLE (1956), *Fundamentals of Language* (Le Hague/Paris).

JURENKA, H. (1893), 'Zur Kritik und Erklärung der sechsten olympischen Ode des Pindar', *Zeitschrift für die Österreichischen Gymnasien* 44, pp. 1057–1066.

KAKRIDIS, Johannes Th. (1970), 'Die Pelopssage bei Pindar', in W.M. Calder & J. Stern (eds.), *Pindaros und Bakchylides* (Darmstadt; WdF 134), pp. 175–190.

KAMBYLIS, Athanasios (1991), *Eustathios über Pindars Epinikiendichtung. Ein Kapitel der klassischen Philologie in Byzanz* (Göttingen; Berichte aus den Sitzungen der Joachim Jungius-Gesellschaft der Wissenschaften 9, 1).

KANNICHT, Richard (ed., 1969), *Euripides, Helena*, 2 vols. (Heidelberg).

KANNICHT, Richard (1988), *The Ancient Quarrel Between Philosophy and Poetry. Aspects of the Greek Conception of Literature.* The Fifth Broadhead Memorial Lecture 1986 (Christchurch).

KANT, Immanuel (1956–1964), *Werke in zwölf Bänden*, ed. W. Weischedel (Frankfurt am Main).

KANT, Immanuel (2000), *The Critique of the Power of Judgment*, tr. Paul Guyer and Eric Matthews (Cambridge).

KERFERD, G.B. (1954), 'Plato's noble art of sophistry (*Sophist* 226a–231b)', *Classical Quarterly* n.s. 4, pp. 84–90.

KIRK, G.S. (1985), *The Iliad: A Commentary*, vol. 1: *Books 1–4* (Cambridge).

KIRKWOOD, Gordon M. (1981), 'Pythian 5.72–76, 9.90–92, and the voice of Pindar', *ICS* 6, pp. 12–23.

KIRKWOOD, Gordon M. (1982), *Selections from Pindar* (Chico).

KLEIN, Jacob (1977), *Plato's Trilogy.* Theaetetus, *the* Sophist *and the* Statesman (Chicago/London).

KNAPE, Joachim (1996), *Allgemeine Rhetorik. Stationen der Theoriegeschichte* (Stuttgart).

KÖHNKEN, Adolf (1971), *Die Funktion des Mythos bei Pindar* (Berlin).

KÖHNKEN, Adolf (1974), 'Pindar as innovator: Poseidon Hippios and the relevance of the Pelops story in Olympian 1', *CQ* n.s. 24, pp. 199–206.

KÖHNKEN, Adolf (1983), 'Time and event in Pindar O. 1.25–53', *Classical Antiquity* 2.1, pp. 66–76.

KÖHNKEN, Adolf (1985), '"Meilichos orga." Liebesthematik und aktueller Sieg in der neunten pythischen Ode Pindars', in *Pindare* (Vandœuvres – Genève; Fondation Hardt, Entretiens sur l'antiquité classique 31), pp. 71–111.

KOJÈVE, Alexandre (1949), *Introduction à la lecture de Hegel, Leçon sur la phénoménologie de l'esprit* (Paris). Partial English translation as: Alexandre Kojève (1980), *Introduction to the Reading of Hegel. Lectures on the Phenomenology of Spirit*, tr. James. H. Nichols, Jr. (Ithaca/London).

KOSCHORKE, Albrecht (1997), 'Platon/Schrift/Derrida', in Gerhard Neumann (ed.), *Poststrukturalismus: Herausforderung an die Literaturwissenschaft* (Stuttgart), pp. 40–58.

KRAUS, Manfred (1988), *Name und Sache. Ein Problem im frühgriechischen Denken* (Amsterdam; Studien zur antiken Philosophie 14)

KRISCHER, Tilman (1965), 'ΕΤΥΜΟΣ und ΑΛΑΘΗΣ', *Philologus* 109, pp. 161–174.

KROMER, Gretchen (1976), 'The value of time in Pindar's Olympian 10', *Hermes* 104, pp. 420–436.

KRUMMEN, Eveline (1990), *Pyrsos Hymnon. Festliche Gegenwart und mythisch-rituelle Tradition bei Pindar* (Berlin; Untersuchungen zur antiken Literatur und Geschichte 35).

KURKE, Leslie (1988), 'The poet's pentathlon: genre in Pindar's First *Isthmian*', *GRBS* 29, pp. 97–113.

KURKE, Leslie (1991), *The Traffic in Praise. Pindar and the Poetics of Social Economy* (Ithaca/London).

KURKE, Leslie (2005), 'Choral lyric as "ritualization": poetic sacrifice and poetic ego in Pindar's Sixth Paian', *Classical Antiquity* 24, pp. 81–130.

KYRIAKOU, Poulheria (1993), 'Aristotle's philosophical *Poetics*', *Mnemosyne* 46, pp. 344–355.

LACAN, Jacques (1999), *Écrits*, 2 vols. (Paris: Éditions du Seuil, Essais) (first published in 1966). English: Jacques Lacan (2006), *Écrits: the first complete translation in English*, tr. Bruce Fink, Héloïse Fink and Russell Grigg (New York/London).

LACAN, Jacques (1973), *Le Séminaire*, livre XI: *Les quatres concepts fondamentaux de la psychoanalyse* (Paris: Éditions du Seuil, Essais).

LATACZ, Joachim (1968), '*ἄπτερος μῦθος – ἄπτερος φάτις*: ungeflügelte Worte?' *Glotta* 46, pp. 27–47.

LATACZ, Joachim, René NÜNLIST, Magdalene STOEVESANDT ([2]2002), *Homers Ilias. Gesamtkommentar*, vol. 1: *Erster Gesang (A)*. Fasc. 2: *Kommentar* (Munich/Leipzig).

LEE, Hugh M. (1978), 'The "historical" Bundy and encomiastic relevance in Pindar', *Classical World* 72, pp. 65–70.

LEFKOWITZ, Mary (1963), 'ΤΩ ΚΑΙ ΕΓΩ: the first person in Pindar', *HSCPh* 67, pp. 177–253.

LEFKOWITZ, Mary (1976), *The Victory Ode* (Park Ridge, NJ).

LEFKOWITZ, Mary (1991), *First-Person Fictions. Pindar's Poetic 'I'* (Oxford).

LEFKOWITZ, Mary (1995), 'The first person in Pindar reconsidered—again', *BICS* 40, pp. 139–150.

LENTRICCHIA, Frank (1980), *After the New Criticism* (Chicago).

LESKY, Albin ([3]1971), *Geschichte der griechischen Literatur* (Bern/Munich).

LÉTOUBLON, Françoise (1999), '*Epea pteroenta* ("winged words")', *Oral Tradition* 14, pp. 321–335.

LÉVI-STRAUSS, Claude (1973), *Anthropologie structurale deux* (Paris).

LIDOV, Joel B. (1993), 'What am I? What am I not? Three recent Pindars', *CJ* 89, pp. 69–79.

LITVAK, Josef (1988), 'Back to the future: a review-article on the New Historicism, deconstruction and nineteenth-century fiction', *Texas Studies in Literature and Language* 30, pp. 120–149.

LIU, Alan (1989), 'The power of formalism: the New Historicism', *English Literary History* 56, pp. 721–771.

LLOYD-JONES, Hugh (1973), 'Modern interpretation of Pindar: the Second Pythian and Seventh Nemean odes', *JHS* 93, pp. 109–137.

LUCAITES, John Louis and Celeste Michelle CONDIT (1999), 'Introduction', in John Louis Lucaites, Celeste Michelle Condit, Sally Caudill (eds.), *Contemporary Rhetorical Theory: A Reader* (New York), pp. 1–18.

MACKIE, Hilary (2003), *Graceful Errors. Pindar and the Performance of Praise* (Ann Arbor).

MAEHLER, Herwig (1963), *Die Auffassung des Dichterberufs im frühen Griechentum bis zur Zeit Pindars* (Göttingen; Hypomnemata 3).

MARSHALL, Donald G. (1983), 'History, theory, and influence: Yale Critics as readers of Maurice Blanchot', in Jonathan Arac, Wlad Godzich, Wallace Martin (eds.), *The Yale Critics: Deconstruction in America* (Minneapolis), pp. 135–155.

MARTIN, Richard P. (1989), *The Language of Heroes. Speech and Performance in the* Iliad (Ithaca/London).

MARX, Karl ([7]1972), *Das Kapital*, vol. 1 (Berlin; Marx Engels Werke, vol. 23) (based on the fourth edition 1890). English: Karl MARX (1976), *Capital*, vol. 1, tr. Ben Fowkes (London).

MCQUILLAN, Martin, Graeme MACDONALD, Robin PURVES, Stephen THOMSON (1999), 'The joy of theory', in McQuillan *et al.* (eds.), pp. ix–xx.

MCQUILLAN, Martin, Graeme MACDONALD, Robin PURVES, Stephen THOMSON (eds., 1999), *Post-Theory: New Directions in Criticism* (Edinburgh).

MEIJERING, Roos (1987), *Literary and Rhetorical Theories in Greek Scholia* (Groningen).

MENKE, Bettina ([2]2001), *Sprachfiguren. Name – Allegorie – Bild bei Walter Benjamin* (Weimar) (first published 1991).

MENNINGHAUS, Winfried (1980), *Walter Benjamin's Theorie der Sprachmagie* (Frankfurt am Main).

MEZGER, Friedrich (1880), *Pindars Siegeslieder* (Leipzig).

MILLER Andrew M. (1982), '*Phthonos* and *parphasis*: the argument of *Nemean* 8.19–34', *GRBS* 23, pp. 111–120.

MILLER Andrew M. (1982–83), '*N.* 4.33–43 and the defense of digressive leisure', *CJ* 78, pp. 202–220.

MILLER, Andrew M. (1993a), '*Inventa componere*: rhetorical process and poetic composition in Pindar's Ninth Olympian Ode', *TAPhA* 123, pp. 109–147.

MILLER, Andrew M. (1993b), 'Pindaric mimesis: the associative mode', *CJ* 89.1, pp. 21–53.

MILLER, Theresa (1997), *Die griechische Kolonisation im Spiegel literarischer Zeugnisse* (Tübingen).

MORGAN, Kathryn A. (1993), 'Pindar the professional and the rhetoric of the κῶμος', *CPh* 88, pp. 1–15.

MORITZ, Karl Philipp (1997), *Werke*, ed. Heide Hollmer and Albert Meier, 2 vols.

(Frankfurt am Main).
MOST, Glenn W. (1985a), 'Des verschieden gesinnten Sinnesverbindung: Zur poetischen Einheit der Alten', in Karen Gloy and Enno Rudolph (eds.), *Einheit als Grundfrage der Philosophie* (Darmstadt), pp. 1–29.
MOST, Glenn W. (1985b), *The Measures of Praise. Structure and Function in Pindar's Second Pythian and Seventh Nemean Odes* (Göttingen; Hypomnemata 83).
MOST, Glenn W. (1986), 'Pindar, O. 2.83–90', *CQ* 36, pp. 304–316.
MOST, Glenn W. (1994), 'Simonides' ode to Scopas in contexts', in de Jong and Sullivan (1994), pp. 127–152.
MÜNCH, Dieter (1993), *Intention und Zeichen. Untersuchungen zu Franz Brentano und zu Edmund Husserls Frühwerk* (Frankfurt am Main).
NAGY, Gregory (1990), *Pindar's Homer. The Lyric Possession of an Epic Past* (Baltimore).
NANCY, Jean-Luc (1991), 'Introduction', in Eduardo Cadava, Peter Connor and Jean-Luc Nancy (eds.), *Who Comes After the Subject?* (New York), pp. 1–8.
NASSEN, Paula J. (1975), 'A literary study of Pindar's *Olympian* 10', *TAPhA* 105, pp. 219–240.
NICHOLSON, Nigel (2007), 'Pindar, history, and historicism', *CPh* 102, pp. 208–227.
NEWMAN, John K. (1987), 'Pindarica', *RhM* 130, pp. 89–93.
NEWMAN, John K. and F.S. NEWMAN (1984), *Pindar's Art: Its Traditions and Aims* (Hildesheim).
NIEHUES-PRÖBSTING, Heinrich (1987), *Überredung zur Einsicht. Der Zusammenhang von Philosophie und Rhetorik bei Platon und in der Phänomenologie* (Frankfurt am Main; Philosophische Abhandlungen, Bd. 54).
NIETZSCHE, Friedrich (1982–1995), *Werke*. Kritische Gesamtausgabe, Abteilung II, 5 vols., eds. F. Bornmann and Mario Capella (Berlin/New York).
NIETZSCHE, Friedrich (1988), *Sämtliche Werke*. Kritische Studienausgabe in 15 Bänden (Berlin).
NIETZSCHE, Friedrich (2003), *Writings from the Late Notebooks*, ed. Rüdiger Bittner, tr. Kate Sturge (Cambridge).
NIETZSCHE, Friedrich (2005), *The Anti-Christ, Ecce Homo, Twilight of the Idols and other writings*, ed. Aaron Ridley, tr. Judith Norman (Cambridge).
NISETICH, Frank J. (1975), '*Olympian* 1,8–11: an epinician metaphor', *HSCPh* 79, pp. 55–68.
NISETICH, Frank J. (1988), 'Immortality in Acragas: poetry and religion in Pindar's second Olympian ode', *CPh* 83, pp. 1–19.
NORRIS, Christopher (1989), 'Philosophy as *not* just a "kind of writing": Derrida and the claim of reason', in Dasenbrock (1989), pp. 189–203.
NORWOOD, Gilbert (1945), *Pindar* (Berkeley/Los Angeles).
NOTOMI, Noburu (1999), *The Unity of Plato's Sophist. Between the Sophist and the Philosopher* (Cambridge).
NÜNLIST, René (1998), *Poetologische Bildersprache in der frühgriechischen Dichtung* (Stuttgart/Leipzig; Beiträge zur Altertumskunde, Bd. 101).
ONG, Walter J. (1958), *Ramus, Method and the Decay of Dialogue. From the Art of Discourse to the Art of Reason* (Cambridge, MA).

PARKE, H.W. (1933), 'The bones of Pelops and the siege of Troy', *Hermathena* 48, pp. 153–162.

PATTON, Paul (1994), 'Anti-Platonism and art', in Constantin V. Boundas and Dorothea Olkowski (eds.), *Gilles Deleuze and the Theater of Philosophy* (New York/London), pp. 141–156.

PAVESE, Carlo Odo (1972), *Tradizioni e Generi Poetici della Grecia Arcaica* (Rome).

PELLICCIA, Hayden (1995), *Mind, Body, and Speech in Homer and Pindar* (Göttingen; Hypomnemata 107).

PERELMAN, Chaim (1979), *The New Rhetoric and the Humanities. Essays on Rhetoric and Its Applications* (Dordrecht/Boston/London).

PERELMAN, Chaim (1984), 'Rhetoric and politics', tr. James Winschester and Molly Black Verene, *Philosophy and Rhetoric* 17.3, pp. 129–134.

PERELMAN, Chaim and Lucie OLBRECHTS-TYTECA (^{2}1970), *Traité de l'Argumentation. La nouvelle rhétorique*, 2 vols. (Brüssel) (first published 1958).

PEROSA, Alessandro (1941), 'La seconda ode olimpica di Pindaro', *Studi Italiani di Filologia Classica*, n.s. 18, pp. 25–53.

PFEIFFER, Rudolph (^{2}1978), *Geschichte der Klassischen Philologie. Von den Anfängen bis zum Ende des Hellenismus*, tr. Marlene Arnold (Munich) (includes Pfeiffer's addenda and corrigenda to the English edition). English: Rudolph Pfeiffer (1968), *History of Classical Scholarship. From the Beginnings to the End of the Hellenistic Age* (Oxford).

PFEIFFER, Rudolph (1982), *Die Klassische Philologie von Petrarca bis Mommsen*, tr. Marlene and Erwin Arnold (Munich) (includes Pfeiffer's addenda and corrigenda to the English edition). English: Rudolph Pfeiffer (1976), *History of Classical Scholarship. From 1300 to 1850* (Oxford).

PFEIJFFER, Ilja Leonard (1999a), *First Person Futures in Pindar* (Stuttgart; Hermes Einzelschriften 81).

PFEIJFFER, Ilja Leonard (1999b), *Three Aeginetan Odes of Pindar: A Commentary on* Nemean *V*, Nemean *III*, *&* Pythian *VIII* (Leiden; Mnemosyne Suppl. 197).

PFLUG, Günther (1975), 'Hermeneutik und Kritik. August Boeckh in der Tradition des Begriffspaars', *Archiv für Begriffsgeschichte* 19, pp. 138–196.

POISS, Thomas (1993), *Momente der Einheit. Interpretationen zu Pindars Epinikion und Hölderlins* Andenken (Wien; Wiener Studien, Beiheft 18).

PRATT, Louise H. (1993), *Lying and Poetry from Homer to Pindar* (Ann Arbor).

PRIVITERA, G. Aurelio (ed., 1982), *Pindaro. Le Istmiche* (Mailand).

PUDELEK, Jan-Peter (2005), Art. 'Werk', in Karlheinz Barck *et al.* (eds., 2000–), *Ästhetische Grundbegriffe* (Stuttgart), vol. 6, pp. 520–588.

QUINCEY, J.H. (1963), 'Etymologica', *RhM* 106, pp. 142–148.

RACE, William H. (1979), 'The end of *Olympia* 2: Pindar and the *vulgus*', *CSCA* 10, pp. 251–267.

RACE, William H. (1987), 'Pindaric encomium and Isokrates' *Evagoras*', *TAPhA* 117, pp. 131–155.

RACE, William H. (1990), *Style and Rhetoric in Pindar's Odes* (Atlanta).

RACE, William H. (ed., 1997), *Pindar*, 2 vols. (Cambridge, MA/London).

RACE, William H. (2002), 'Framing hyperbata in Pindar's *Odes*', *CJ* 98.1, pp. 21–33.
RADKE, Gyburg (2003), *Tragik und Metatragik. Euripides' Bakchen und die moderne Literaturwissenschaft* (Berlin; Untersuchungen zur antiken Literatur und Geschichte 66).
RAPP, Christof (2002), *Aristoteles, Rhetorik*, 2 vols. (Darmstadt).
RAY, William (1984), *Literary Meaning. From Phenomenology to Deconstruction* (Oxford).
REDFIELD, Marc (ed., 2005), *Legacies of Paul de Man* (Romantic Circles Praxis Series: http://www.rc.umd.edu/praxis/deman/index.html, accessed 23 April 2009).
REINHARD, Karl ([3]1977), *Parmenides und die Geschichte der griechischen Philosophie* (Frankfurt am Main) (first published 1959).
RENEHAN, Robert F. (1969), 'Conscious ambiguities in Pindar and Bacchylides', *GRBS* 10, pp. 217–228.
RICE, Philip and Patricia WAUGH (eds., [4]2001), *Modern Literary Theory* (London).
RICHARDS, I.A. (1936), *The Philosophy of Rhetoric* (Oxford).
RICHARDSON, N.J. (1986),'Pindar and later literary criticism in antiquity', *Papers of the Liverpool Latin Seminar, Fifth Volume, 1985* (Liverpool, 1986; ARCA Classical and Medieval Texts, Papers and Monographs 19), pp. 383–401.
RICŒUR, Paul (1975), *La métaphore vive* (Paris).
RILEY, Patrick (1981), 'Introduction to the reading of Alexandre Kojève', *Political Theory* 9.1, pp. 5–48.
RODI, Frithjof (1990), *Erkenntnis des Erkannten. Zur Hermeneutik des 19. und 20. Jahrhunderts* (Frankfurt am Main).
RORTY, Richard (1978), 'Philosophy as a kind of writing: an essay on Derrida', *New Literary History* 10.1, pp. 141–160.
RORTY, Richard (1989), 'Two meanings of "Logocentrism": a reply to Norris', in Dasenbrock (1989), pp. 204–216.
ROSE, Peter W. (1974), 'The myth of Pindar's first Nemean: sportsmen, poetry and paideia', *HSCPh* 78, pp. 145–175.
ROSE, Peter W. (1992), *Sons of the Gods, Children of Earth. Ideology and Literary Form in Ancient Greece* (Ithaca/London).
ROSEN, Stanley (1983), *Plato's* Sophist. *The Drama of Original and Image* (New Haven/London).
ROSIEK, Jan (1992), *Figures of Failure. Paul de Man's Criticism 1953–1970* (Aarhus).
RÖSLER, Wolfgang (1984), 'Die Entdeckung der Fiktionalität', *Poetica* 12, pp. 283–319.
ROSS, W.D. (ed., 1924), *Aristotle, Metaphysics. A Revised Text with Introduction and Commentary*, 2 vols. (Oxford).
ROSS, W.D. (ed., 1961), *Aristotle, De anima, edited with introduction and commentary* (Oxford).
ROTH, Michael S. (1985), 'A problem of recognition: Alexandre Kojève and the end of history', *History and Theory* 24.3, pp. 293–306.
ROUSSEAU, Jean-Jacques (1967), *Lettre à M. d'Alembert sur son Article Genève*, ed. Michel Launay (Paris).
SALLIS, John (1984), 'Heidegger/Derrida – presence', *Journal of Philosophy* 81, pp. 594–

601.

SARTRE, Jean-Paul (1960), *Critique de la raison dialectique* (Paris).

SARTRE, Jean-Paul (1976), *Critique of Dialectical Reason* 1: *Theory of Practical Ensembles*, tr. Alan Sheridan-Smith, ed. Jonathan Rée (London).

SAYRE, Kenneth (1969), *Plato's Analytic Method* (Chicago).

SCALTSAS, Theodore (1992), 'A necessary falsehood in the Third Man Argument', *Phronesis* 37, pp. 216–232.

SCHADEWALDT, Wolfgang (1966), *Der Aufbau des Pindarischen Epinikion* (Darmstadt) (first published 1928).

SCHELLING, Friedrich Wilhelm Joseph (1856–1861), *Sämmtliche Werke*, ed. K.F.A. Schelling, 14 vols. (Stuttgart/Ausgsburg).

SCHELLING, Friedrich Wilhelm Joseph (2000), *System des transzendentalen Idealismus*, eds. Horst D. Brandt and Peter Müller (Hamburg) (first published 1800).

SCHLEGEL, Friedrich (1958–), *Kritische Ausgabe*, ed. Ernst Behler (Paderborn/Munich/Vienna/Zürich).

SCHLEIERMACHER, Friedrich Daniel Ernst (1977), *Hermeneutik und Kritik*, ed. Manfred Frank (Frankfurt am Main) (first published 1838). English: Friedrich Daniel Ernst Schleiermacher (1998), *Hermeneutics and criticism, and other writings*, tr. Andrew Bowie (Cambridge).

SCHLEIERMACHER, Friedrich Daniel Ernst (1981), *Brouillon zur Ethik (1805/06)*, ed. Hans-Joachim Birkner (Hamburg).

SCHLEIERMACHER, Friedrich Daniel Ernst (1984), *Ästhetik (1819/25). Über den Begriff der Kunst (1831/32)*, ed. Thomas Lehnerer (Hamburg).

SCHLEIFER, Ronald (1985), 'The anxiety of allegory: De Man, Greimas, and the problem of referentiality', in Robert Con Davis and Ronald Schleifer (eds.), *Rhetoric and Form: Deconstruction at Yale* (Norman, Oklahoma), pp. 215–237.

SCHMID, Erasmus (1616), Πινδάρου Περίοδος *hoc est Pindari lyricorum principis, plus quam sexcentis in locis emaculati, ut iam legi et intellegi possit,* Ὀλυμπιονῖκαι. Πυθιονῖκαι. Νεμεονῖκαι. Ἰσθμιονῖκαι. *illustrati* (Wittenberg).

SCHMID, Michael J. (1998a), 'Skytála moisân: song and writing in Pindar', *Minerva: revista de filologia clasica* 12, pp. 57–81.

SCHMID, Michael J. (1998b), 'Speaking *personae* in Pindar's epinikia', *Cuardernos de filologia classica. Estudios griegos e indoeuropeos* 8, pp. 147–184.

SCHMIDT, Jochen (1985), *Die Geschichte des Genie-Gedankens in der deutschen Literatur, Philosophie und Politik 1750–1945*, 2 vols. (Darmstadt).

SCHMIDT-HABERKAMP, Barbara (2005), 'Rhetorizität: Moderne und Postmoderne ab 1970', in Gert Ueding (ed.), *Rhetorik: Begriff – Geschichte – Internationalität* (Tübingen), pp. 327–329.

SCHMITZ, Thomas A. (1993), *Pindar in der französischen Renaissance. Studien zu seiner Rezeption in Philologie, Dichtungstheorie und Dichtung* (Göttingen; Hypomnemata 101).

SCHMITZ, Thomas A. (2002), *Moderne Literaturtheorie und antike Texte: Eine Einführung* (Darmstadt). English: Thomas A. Schmitz (2007), *Modern Literary Theory and Ancient Texts. An Introduction* (Malden, MA/Oxford).

SCHOLEM, Gerschom (1983), *Walter Benjamin und sein Engel* (Frankfurt am Main).
SCHROEDER, O. (1900), *Pindari carmina* (Leipzig).
SCODEL, Ruth (1985), Review of *Pindar's 'Olympian One': A Commentary.* By Douglas E. Gerber and *Selections from Pindar.* Edited with an introduction and commentary by Gordon Kirkwood, *CPh* 80, pp. 266–270.
SCODEL, Ruth (1996), 'Self-correction, spontaneity, and orality in archaic poetry', in Ian Worthington (ed.), *Voice into Text. Orality and Literacy in Ancient Greece* (Leiden; Mnemosyne suppl. 157), pp. 59–79.
SCOTT, Mary (1984), 'Charis from Hesiod to Pindar', *Acta Classica* 27, pp. 1–13.
SEARLE, John R. (1969), *Speech Acts. An Essay in the Philosophy of Language* (Cambridge).
SEARLE, John R. (1979), *Expression and Meaning. Studies in the Theory of Speech Acts* (Cambridge).
SILK, Michael (1974), *Interaction in Poetic Imagery with Special Reference to Early Greek Poetry* (Cambridge).
SILK, Michael (1995), 'Language, poetry and enactment', *Dialogos* 2, pp. 109–132.
SILK, Michael (2001), 'Pindar meets Plato: theory, language, value, and the classics', in Stephen Harrison (ed.), *Texts, Ideas, and Classics. Scholarship, Theory and Classical Literature* (Oxford), pp. 26–45.
SIMPSON, Michael (1969), 'The chariot and the bow as metaphors for poetry in Pindar's odes', *TAPhA* 100, pp. 437–473.
SLATER, William J. (1969a), 'Futures in Pindar', *CQ* n.s. 19, pp. 86–94.
SLATER, William J. (1969b), *Lexicon to Pindar* (Berlin).
SLATER, William J. (1976–77), 'Doubts about Pindaric interpretation', *CJ* 72, pp. 193–208.
SLATER, William J. (1979a), 'Pindar and hypothekai', *Teiresias* Suppl. 2: Proceedings of the Second International Conference on Boiotian Antiquities (1979), pp. 79–82.
SLATER, William J. (1979b), 'Pindar's myths: two pragmatic explanations', in *Arktouros: Hellenic Studies presented to B.M.W. Knox* (Berlin/New York), pp. 63–70.
SLATER, William J. (1989), 'Pelops at Olympia', *GRBS* 30, pp. 485–501.
SOLMSEN, Friedrich (1982), 'Achilles on the Islands of the Blessed. Pindar vs. Homer and Hesiod', *AJPh* 103, pp. 19–24.
STARR, David E. (1973–74), 'The sixth sophist: comments on Frederik S. Oscanyan's "On six definitions of the sophist: *Sophist* 221e–231e"', *Philosophical Forum* 5, pp. 486–492.
STEINER, Deborah (1986), *The Crown of Song. Metaphor in Pindar* (New York).
STONEMAN, Richard (1981), 'Ploughing a garland: metaphor and metonymy in Pindar', *Maia* 33, pp. 125–138.
STROH, Wilfried (1976), 'Hesiods lügende Musen', in Herwig Görgemanns and E.A. Schmidt (eds.), *Studien zum antiken Epos* (Meisenheim am Glan), pp. 85–112.
STROZIER, Robert M. (2002), *Foucault, Subjectivity, and Identity. Historical Constructions of Subject and Self* (Detroit).
TAPLIN, Oliver (1998), Letter to Herbert Golder, *Arion*, third series 5.3, pp. 155–158.
TAYLOR, A.E. (^{6}1949), *Plato, the Man and his Work* (London).

THALMANN, William (1984), *Conventions of Form and Thought in Early Greek Epic Poetry* (Baltimore/London).

THEILER, Willy (1966), *Forschungen zum Neuplatonismus* (Berlin).

THEUNISSEN, Michael (2000), *Pindar. Menschenlos und Wende der Zeit* (Munich).

THIERSE, Wolfgang (1990), '"Das Ganze aber ist, was Anfang, Mitte und Ende hat." Problemgeschichtliche Betrachtungen zur Geschichte des Werkbegriffs', in Karlheinz Barck, M. Fontius and Wolfgang Thierse (eds.), *Ästhetische Grundbegriffe. Studien zu einem historischen Wörterbuch* (Berlin), pp. 378–414.

THOUARD, Denis (2002), 'Friedrich Schlegel: de la philologie à la philosophie (1795–1800)', in *Symphilosophie. F. Schlegel à Iéna; avec la traduction de la* Philosophie transcendantale (Paris; Vrin: Bibliothèque des textes philosophiques), pp. 17–66.

THUMMER, Erich (1968–69), *Pindar. Die Isthmischen Gedichte*, 2 vols. (Heidelberg).

TILL, Dietmar (2004), *Transformationen der Rhetorik. Untersuchungen zum Wandel der Rhetoriktheorie im 17. und 18. Jahrhundert* (Tübingen).

TODOROV, Tzvetan (1977), *Théories du symbole* (Paris). Partial English translation as: Tzvetan Todorov (1982), *Theories of the Symbol*, tr. Catherine Porter (Ithaca/New York).

TREVASKIS, John Reginald (1955–56), 'The sophistry of noble lineage (Sophist 230a5–232b9)', *Phronesis* 1, pp. 36–49.

UEDING, Gert (2005), 'II. Aktuelle Bedeutung der Rhetorik in Wissenschaft und Gesellschaft. 1. Offenes System: der Tübinger Wissenschaftsbegriff der Rhetorik', in Gerd Ueding *et al.* (eds., 1992–), *Historisches Wörterbuch der Rhetorik* (Darmstadt), vol. 7, coll. 1429–1439.

VAN LEEUWEN, Johannes (1964), *Pindarus' tweede Olympische Ode* (Assen).

VERDENIUS, W.J. (1942), *Parmenides. Some Comments on his Poem* (Groningen).

VERDENIUS, W.J. (1982), 'Pindar's second Isthmian ode: a commentary', *Mnemosyne* 35, pp. 1–37.

VERDENIUS, W.J. (1988), *Commentaries on Pindar*, Vol. II (Leiden; Mnemosyne Suppl. 101).

VERDENIUS, W.J. (1989), 'Pindar. *O.*2,83–6', *Mnemosyne* 42, pp. 79–82.

VIVANTE, Paolo (1975), 'On Homer's winged words', *CQ* 25, pp. 1–12.

VLASTOS, Gregory (1973), *Platonic Studies* (Princeton).

VLASTOS, Gregory (1991), *Socrates: Ironist and Moral Philosopher* (Cambridge).

VÖHLER, Martin (2005), *Pindarrezeptionen. Sechs Studien zum Wandel des Pindarverständnisses von Erasmus bis Herder* (Heidelberg).

VOGT, Ernst (1979), 'Der Methodenstreit zwischen Hermann und Böckh und seine Bedeutung für die Geschichte der Philologie', in Hellmut Flashar, Karlfried Gründer and Axel Horstmann (eds.), *Philologie und Hermeneutik im 19. Jahrhundert. Zur Geschichte und Methodologie der Geisteswissenschaften* (Göttingen), pp. 103–121.

WALKER, Jeffrey (2000), *Rhetoric and Poetics in Antiquity* (Oxford).

WATERS, Lindsay (1989), 'Introduction. Paul de Man: life and works', in de Man (1989), pp. ix–lxxiv.

WAUGH, Patricia (2006), 'Introduction: criticism, theory, and anti-theory', in *ead.* (ed.), *Literary Theory and Criticism* (Oxford), pp. 1–33.

WEBER, Samuel (1978), 'It', *Glyph* 4, pp. 1–31.
WEBER, Samuel (1986), '"Postmoderne" und "Poststrukturalismus": Versuch eine Umgebung zu benennen', *Aesthetik und Kommunikation* 63.17, pp. 105–111.
WEBER, Samuel (2000), *Rückkehr zur Freud. Jacques Lacans Ent-stellung der Psychoanalyse* (Wien) (first published 1990).
WEISCHE, Alfons (1989), 'Rhetorik und Philosophie in der Antike. *amplificatio – dilatatio* und die stoische Forderung der *brevitas*', in Helmut Schanze and Josef Kopperschmidt (eds.), *Rhetorik und Philosophie* (Munich), pp. 23–33.
WEST, Martin L. (ed., 1978), *Hesiod, Works and Days, ed. with prolegomena and commentary* (Oxford).
WEST, Martin L. (1997), *The East Face of Helicon* (Oxford).
WHEELER, Samuel C. III (1989), 'Metaphor according to Davidson and de Man', in Dasenbrock (1989), pp. 116–139.
WIELAND, Wolfgang (³1992), *Die aristotelische Physik. Untersuchungen über die Grundlegung der Naturwissenschaft und die sprachlichen Bedingungen der Prinzipienforschung bei Aristoteles* (Göttingen) (first published 1962).
WIESNER, Jürgen (1996), *Parmenides. Der Beginn der Aletheia* (Berlin).
WILAMOWITZ-MOELLENDORFF, Ulrich von (1922), *Pindaros* (Berlin).
WILAMOWITZ-MOELLENDORFF, Ulrich von (³1998), *Geschichte der Philologie* (Stuttgart/Leipzig) (first published 1921). English: Ulrich von Wilamowitz-Moellendorff (1982), *History of Classical Scholarship*, tr. Alan Harris, intr. and notes Hugh Lloyd-Jones (Baltimore).
WILLCOCK, M.M. (1995), *Pindar: Victory Odes* (Cambridge).
WOODBURY, Leonard (1972), 'Apollo's first love: Pindar, Pyth. 9.26 ff.', *TAPhA* 103, pp. 561–573.
YOUNG, David C. (1968), *Three Odes of Pindar. A Literary Study of Pythian 11, Pythian 3 and Olympian 7* (Leiden).
YOUNG, David C. (1970), 'Pindaric criticism', in W.M. Calder and J. Stern (eds.), *Pindaros und Bakchylides* (Darmstadt; WdF 134), pp. 1–95.
ZIMA, Peter V. (²1995), *Literarische Ästhetik. Methoden und Modelle der Literaturwissenschaft* (Tübingen/Basel).

INDEX

Greek terms are listed separately at the end of the index.

A

G

H

O

P

Q

R

S

T